GUIDANCE AND COUNSELLING IN INDIA

RAM NATH SHARMA
RACHANA SHARMA

ATLANTIC
PUBLISHERS & DISTRIBUTORS (P) LTD

ATLANTIC
PUBLISHERS & DISTRIBUTORS (P) LTD

7/22, Ansari Road, Darya Ganj, New Delhi
Tel.: +91-11-4077 5252, 2327 3880
E-mail: orders@atlanticbooks.com
Web: www.atlanticbooks.com

Reprint 2007, 2013, 2018, 2020, 2021, 2024, 2026

Published by Atlantic Publishers & Distributors (P) Ltd.

Printed & bound in India by Atlantic Print Services

Preface

Guidance and Counselling is very important part of activity in educational institutions all over the world. But in India literature on this subject is very scanty and hence, there is a great need for an ideal book on the subject in our land. In the present book, *Guidance and Counselling in India*, an attempt has been made to fulfil this need in the wake of changing pattern of socio-economic, socio-educational and socio-cultural systems which are forming complex shape owing to advancement in science and technology and changing nature of human behaviour and a person's adjustment with his family, community and society.

After classifying the Concept of Guidance, the book studies its relationship with Educational specialities, its areas, its types such as self-guidance and guidance to other individuals. It proceeds to discuss Professional Counselling and explains counselling of individuals and in groups. It examines counselling for Vocational Development and leisure time guidance.

The subjects discussed in the book include Guidance Services in India, Student Counselling Group Guidance, Collection, Filing and Dissemination of Occupational Information, Psychological Aspects of Vocation, Vocationalization, Vocational Guidance, The World of Work and Occupation, Institutions of Higher Learning and the World of Work, Job Analysis, Educational Guidance, Pupil Personnel Work in Indian Schools, New Pattern of Education and Guidance Services, Guidance and Counselling in Indian Colleges and Universities, UEIGB and USAB, Individual Testing and Non-Testing Devices in Guidance, Guidance in Adolescence, Guidance of Problem Children, Guidance of Backward Children and Guidance of Gifted Children. The book ends with a look at the future development of Careers Education and Guidance and highlights some useful strategies for change.

Ram Nath Sharma
Rachana Sharma

Contents

1

INTRODUCTION

The term guidance has been used in the above account of the help that psychology can render in the solution of vocational, educational and personal problems. Educational guidance is required in the field of education, vocational guidance in the field of profession and vocation, and personal guidance in the individual's personal life. Before going on to a detailed account of what these three forms entail it would be better to understand what guidance is. Guidance may be defined as the process of helping the individual in selecting, preparing, entering and progressing in the behavioural patterns which comprise human activities in the educational, vocational, recreational field as well as in connection with community service group. This help takes the form of personal help on the psychologist's part. It is, again, in the form of advice. This does not solve problems but only helps the individual in solving his problems. Husband, in his book entitled *Applied Psychology*, has defined the term thus, "Guidance may be defined as assisting the individual to prepare for his future life, to fit him for his place in society."[1] In this way, guidance prepares the individual for his life. It informs the individual of the kind of education that he requires, the subjects that he would be advised to choose in his study, the vocation of which he should apply himself when old enough, as well as the means he should employ when faced with problems that he must solve. In society every individual has a specific status and certain roles that are concomitant with it. For example, a male member is head of his family, and from this position is derived his responsibility of providing for the needs of the family and keeping in mind the proper development of every member. But an individual does not maintain the same status throughout his life. At one and the same or different times he passes through stages where he occupies the status of son, father, husband, teacher or advocate, a citizen of the nation etc. In each of these different statuses he has distinct and definite roles to play. The person who has ability or sense enough to work as befits his status in society is the one who wins the acclaim of society and its approval as well. It is in the performance of these various roles and duties, which conform to his differing statuses, that he needs guidance.

1. Husband, *Applied Psychology*, p. 15.

In this way, the psychologist's guidance helps the individual fit into his role and status in society. Every individual is not fit to take up any and every position in society. Teaching, doctoring, advocacy and a variety of other professions are not jobs that require the same individual qualities from the person occupied in doing them. Introducing fitness in an individual to occupy some position is a matter that has two aspects. The first is that his ability should be commensurate with the requirements of the job and the second that he should try to become qualified to occupy that position. The second of these aspects has some limitations. Whatever the effort expended every person cannot become an artist or author, because every individual does not have the ability or quality to adopt any and every profession. Even every individual cannot become a successful trader as that requires a definite shrewd and calculating mentality that is not possessed by everyone. Hence, in order to prove able for some particular position a person should choose the position that concurs with his capabilities and qualities. Educational psychology helps the individual in his choice. In this way, guidance helps the individual to settle down into positions that are, or are, not of his own choosing. As has been said in the preceding definition guidance helps to prepare the individual for this future life. Preparation for the future life implies creating ability in the individual to bear responsibilities that fall to his lot. These future responsibilities can take a variety of forms. Normally, for example, every boy and girl gets married when he and she grows up, creates a family and indulges in prolific procreation. In this manner, every individual is to face in the future responsibilities concerning his children, responsibilities concerning the partner he has chosen for life as well as further responsibilities of the family in general. And in the normal circumstances, again, most young men and some young women have also to adopt some or the other profession, whether to their liking or not. A child grown up to be not only a man but also a citizen of his country and in this position certain rights devolve upon him that bring with them some additional responsibilities. Consequently, when we talk of preparing an individual for the future we mean to prepare him for bearing his responsibilities ably and sufficiently whether he be called upon to do so in the field of family relations, the economic sphere, the political field or any other situation in life. For this every individual boy and girl should turn to a profession that conforms to the education they have had so that they may be in positions for which they have been prepared and act with skill and confidence. They should decide upon the profession that they would like to adopt. They should have the capacity to face and solve their own problems as well as the problems that are likely to arise in their relation with others. Guidance helps the individual in all these kinds of efforts.

It should be quite apparent from the above detailed discussion on the meaning of the term that guidance helps in determining the objective of life, in establishing a synthesis in life and in solving various kinds of problems. In the words of Jones, "Guidance is the personal help that is given by one person to another in developing life goals, in making adjustment and in solving problems that confront him in the attainment of goals."[2] In this manner guidance is personal assistance. Although guidance is sometimes offered at the group level, yet even in these matters every member of the group is also individually given advice. Applied psychology is based on the conception of individual differences. General experience and scientific research have both established that every single individual has certain abilities, problems and difficulties that are distinctly his own, as distinct from those of others. Evidently, if any advice or guidance is to be rendered, it must be rendered individually and personally. This personal help is forthcoming from one individual to another. One of these two individuals is a psychologist, or one who knows psychology and the other a person who is in need of psychological guidance. Guidance, then, is the help rendered to an individual by the psychologist. In its more extensive sense the term may be taken to comprehend the advice rendered by any individual who is in the know concerning psychology to another who is in need of it. For example, if a father guides his son in the solving a problem, this, too, amounts to guidance, irrespective of the fact that it may or may not be based on the most correct notion of psychological principles. But this extensive meaning of the term is its general meaning and implication. In a scientific analysis it is not taken in its general meaning but reduced to more definite and precise terms whereby its meaning becomes limited. That is why it is first defined. Guidance in psychology, means a particular thing. It is the personal advice or service rendered by a psychologist, and not by any Tom, Dick and Harry, to another person. This guidance takes the form of advice which helps the guided individual to adjust to various conditions and circumstances.

DEFINITIONS OF GUIDANCE

1. Jones. "Guidance involves personal help given by someone; it is designed to assist a person in deciding where he wants to go, what he wants to do, or how he can best accomplish his purposes; it assists him in solving problems that arise in his life. It does not solve problems for the individual, but helps him to solve them. The focus of guidance is the individual, not the problem, its purpose is to promote the growth of the individual in self-direction."

2. J.A. Humphreys and A.E.Traxler. "At any level, guidance implies that the individual attains self-direction just at fast and as far as mental, social and emotional abilities permit. Guidance of the younger or less mature individual, of course, calls for closer direction than does guidance

---

2. Jones, A.J., *Principles of Guidance,* McGraw-Hill Book Co., New York (1951), p. 85.

of the older or more mature individual. The term guidance, moreover, aptly applies to working with an individual all along the lines from early childhood into adulthood."

3. Knapp. "Learning about the individual student, helping him to understand himself, effecting changes in him and in his environment which will help him to grow and develop as much as possible — these are the elements of guidance."

4. Ruth Strong. "Guidance is a process of helping every individual, through his own efforts, to discover and develop his potentialities for his personal happiness and social usefulness."

5. Chisholm. "Guidance seeks to help the individual discover his own talents in comparison to the opportunities of the world and help him prepare himself so that he can find or develop a place in which he can live a well balanced life and contribute his part to the welfare of his fellow man."

6. Brewer. "The word guidance should be used whenever an important activity is to be learnt and assistance is needed by the individual to learn that activity and adjust himself, whether that activity is the choice of leisure time activity or habit of eating or behaviour towards the opposite sex."

7. Ruch and Segel. "On the elementary school level, guidance is predominantly educational guidance, broadly viewed as encompassing the objectives of physical and mental health, well-rounded social development, proper use of leisure time and mastery of the fundamental school processes."

"To these objectives, on the secondary level is added the guidance that facilitates the choice of an occupation, or way of making a living, whether it be one of the semi-skilled, skilled, technical or professional occupations."

8. The Secondary Education Commission. "Guidance involves the difficult art of helping boys and girls to plan their own future wisely in the full light of all the factors that can be mastered about themselves and about the world in which they are to live and work. Naturally, therefore, it is not the work of a few specialists, but rather a service in which the entire school staff must cooperate under the guidance of some persons with special knowledge and skill in this particular field. Guidance in this sense is not confined to the vocational field only. It covers the whole gamut of youth problems and should be provided in an appropriate form at all stages of education through the cooperative endeavour of understanding parents, teachers, headmasters, principals and guidance officers."

9. Mathewson. "Guidance is a continuous and pervasive process as a favourable directional influence upon appropriate social behaviour, personal effectiveness in every-day affairs, academic competence and progress and assimilation of right values and attitudes." "Guidance cannot remain solely remedial or even orientational, it must also be developmental."

10. V. Koos and Kefauver. Guidance has two main phases : (1) The distributive phase whereby youths are distributed to educational and vocational opportunities as effectively as possible; (2) The adjustive phase whereby the individual is assisted to make the optimum adjustment to the opportunities he gets.

11. Kitson. "Guidance is 'individualised education.' Each student is to be helped to develop himself to the maximum possible degree in all respects."

12. Proctor. "Guidance is a process through which an individual or groups of individuals are helped to make necessary adjustment to the environment-inside or outside the school."

13. K.G. Rama Rao. "Guidance is essentially an educative process the outcomes of which are mental and educational preparedness for courses of action centred round the basic functions of men, especially those pertaining to vocational, recreational and community service field."

14. The United States Office of Education. "Guidance is the process of acquainting the individual with the various ways including special training in which he may discover his natural endowments so that he makes a living to his own best advantage and that of society."

15. Hamrin and Erickson. "Guidance is that aspect of educational programme which is concerned especially with helping the pupil to become adjusted to his personal situation and to plan his future in line with his interests, abilities and social needs."

16. Lefever. "Guidance is that systematic, organised phase of the educational process which helps youth in his power to give point and direction to his own life, to the end that he may gain richer personal experiences while making his own unique contribution to our democratic society."

17. Crow and Crow. "Guidance is assistance made available by personally qualified and adequately trained men or women to an individual of any age to help him manage his own life activities, develop his own points of view, make his own decisions and carry his own burdens."

18. Mathewson. "Guidance is the systematic professional process of helping the individual through education and interpretative procedures to gain a better understanding of his own characteristics and potentialities and, to relate himself more satisfactorily to social requirements and opportunities in accord with social and moral values."

19. Dan-Smoor and Miller. "Guidance is a means of helping individuals to understand and use wisely the educational, vocational and personal opportunities they have or can develop and as a form of systematic assistance whereby students are aided in achieving satisfactory adjustment to school and life."

20. Q. Welly Lefever. "Guidance is that systematic, organised phase of the educational process which helps youth grow in his power to give point and direction to his own life, to the end that he may gain richer personal experiences while making his own contribution to our democratic society."

CHARACTERISTICS OF GUIDANCE

1. It is promotion of the growth of the individual in self-direction.
2. It is the process of helping the individual in affecting changes in him.
3. It helps the individual himself through his own efforts.
4. It assists an individual to find his place.
5. It is helping the individual to establish harmonious relationships.
6. It is assisting the individual adjusts himself.
7. It is helping the individual to make appropriate educational, vocational and personal choices.
8. Its programme is organised.
9. Its programme has a structure, system and personnel.
10. It consists of specialised services — testing counselling, educational and vocational information placement and follow up.
11. Its programme is an integral part of the school system.
12. It is helping an individual to identify and develop his potentialities and talents.
13. It is a point of view that includes a positive attitude towards children.

VIEWS ABOUT KINDS OF GUIDANCE

1. Proctor's View

(i) Educational guidance.
(ii) Vocational guidance.
(iii) Guidance in social and civic activities.
(iv) Guidance in health and physical activities.
(v) Guidance in the worthy use of leisure time.
(vi) Guidance in character building activities.

2. Classification by Jones

(i) Course, curriculum and school guidance — "educational guidance".

(ii) Vocational guidance.
(iii) Leisure-time guidance.
(iv) Leadership guidance.

3. Classification by Koos and Kefauver

(i) Educational guidance.
(ii) Vocational guidance.
(iii) Recreational guidance,
(iv) Health guidance.
(v) Civic-social-moral guidance.

4. Classification by Brewer

(i) Educational guidance.
(ii) Vocational guidance.
(iii) Religious guidance.
(iv) Guidance "for home relationships".
(v) Guidance "for citizenship".
(vi) Guidance "for leisure and recreation".
(vii) Guidance "in personal well-being".
(viii) Guidance "in right doing".
(ix) Guidance "in thoughtfulness and co-operation".
(x) Guidance "in wholesome and cultural action".

5. Views of Paterson, Schneinler and Williamson

(i) Educational guidance.
(ii) Vocational guidance.
(iii) Personal guidance (including social, emotional, and leisure-time guidance).
(iv) Health guidance.
(v) Economic guidance.

CLASSIFICATION OF GUIDANCE

Classification according to Area

As has been pointed out, an individual has to run to the psychologist, in the latter's role of a specialist, for personal advice when he fails to solve the problems that confront him. This personal advice is guidance. How this guidance can take effect depends on the fact that it be given in the context of some problem the solution of which is being sought. As a matter of fact it is no easy matter to recount all the possible problems that arise in various spheres of human life, but some psychologists have attempted a classification of them. For example, Jones has divided the problems of life into eight spheres on the basis of their nature :

(1) Related to health and psychological development, (2) Related to house and family, (3) Related to time for recreation, (4) Concerned with personality, (5) Religious, (6) Educational, (7) Social, and (8) Vocational or occupational. Having achieved the classification of problems it becomes possible to classify the kinds or forms of guidance that is to be given correspondingly. For example, vocational guidance is required in connection with profession and educational guidance in the field of education. Psychologists have professed many and various kinds of guidance. For example, Myers has mentioned the following eight kinds of guidance :

(1) Vocational Guidance,
(2) Educational Guidance,
(3) Recreational Guidance,
(4) Civic Guidance,
(5) Community Service Guidance,
(6) Social and Moral Guidance,
(7) Health Guidance,
(8) Leadership Guidance.

The Bureau of Psychology, Uttar Pradesh, has put guidance in these three categories, and much the same classification of guidance kinds has been followed in the other Indian states as well. These three kinds are : (1) Educational guidance, (2) Vocational guidance and (3) Personal guidance.

If the matter is looked at closely it will be seen that the above three classes in fact, include all kinds of classification. If child guidance is considered, for example, and this guidance requires the opening of clinics in various places, it will be found that problems concerning the children are either concerned with education or are of a personal nature. Hence, child guidance is jointly comprehended under educational and personal guidance. Similarly, the various forms of guidance, such as health guidance, recreational guidance, civic guidance, social and moral guidance, community service guidance and leadership guidance are all comprehended in personal guidance.

Dividing of the various spheres of guidance does not imply that these spheres are completely separated and uncounted. In fact, guidance is a dynamic and progressive concept in which advice given on every aspect of human life is comprehended, but nevertheless, with a view to convenience in discussion, its aspects and spheres have been differentiated. Educational guidance and vocational guidance are closely related, and both of them are very intimately concerned with personal guidance. The basis of this correlation between the various spheres is that all problems of human beings are connected with each other. For example, when a person experiences difficulty in selecting a particular curriculum or a definite profession, his indecision may stem from certain personal difficulties. It happens quite often that young men become so engrossed in their love affairs that they are not able to devote any serious thought to their careers and future. Death of a close and loved relative may be another reason why he may be at a loss and groping in the dark. The fundamental problem here is of a personal nature, with the result that all educational or vocational guidance to such an individual will be modified by the personal guidance given to him. On the other hand, many personal problems may be the consequence of certain deficiencies of education and the lack of educational guidance. If a child runs away from school and becomes vagrant, finds no interest in study but chooses to pursue a life of crime or one of anti-social conduct, then it is evident that, there is something wrong somewhere and as likely as not it may be that his choice of curriculum may have been undesirable. In much the same manner certain individual and personal problems may be the outcome of an absence of vocational guidance. A young man, for example, in his school days may have been a very fine sportsman, and by to virtue he would naturally not appreciate a job that ties him down, offers no opportunity of leadership, and does not allow the development of any of his sportsman like qualities like motivation, patience, adventure and courage. If he is forced to take on such a job for a variety of reason, it would be natural for him to become irritable and lose his mental balance and calm to some extent. This may lead to further complications in the form of personal problems. Here the personal problems have been caused by lack of proper vocational guidance. Similarly, educational, vocational and personal guidance are naturally related.

Classification according to Mode of Guidance

The above classification that we have been viewing is made on the basis of problems for which such guidance is required. If the mode of guidance is taken into consideration guidance can be classified in the following manner :

(1) Individual Guidance,

(2) Group Guidance.

Before going on to a detailed description of educational, vocational and personal guidance, it would be advisable to comprehend this classification of guidance made on the basis of its modes :

1. Individual guidance method. In the individual guidance method the person to be guided and his guide, the psychologist, are in direct and personal contact with each other. He invades the ill person's house and makes study of his family conditions, and for this purpose he interviews the various members of the individual's household. Besides the family background, the individual's social, financial and cultural background is also investigated so that no possible source of information is left untapped. And for this it becomes essential to study his neighbourhood and to collect as many facts of his life as are possible so as to build up fairly complete case history. The schools and colleges that he has attended are contacted in order to gain information concerning his behaviour and scholastic attainments there. His teachers, too are consulted on the matter.

Study of this type and the collection of all possible information concerning the individual is followed by testing of the individual himself. He is made to take tests of intelligence, specific mental abilities, interests, attitudes and personality. Interview is another weapon that is used to uncover much information and, incidentally, to learn the patient's opinion of himself. Accordingly, then in individual guidance the following information concerning the individual is gathered :

(1) Information concerning his intelligence, mental abilities, interests, attitudes and personality.

(2) Information concerning family conditions.

(3) Information concerning the social, financial and cultural background.

(4) Other relevant information.

Having gathered all this information it is subjected to close and intelligent scrutiny, and then curative measures are introduced to remove the problems which have made this guidance necessary. Among these efforts are logical arguments, suggestions, psycho-analysis.

The individual guidance method has the following qualities :

(1) It renders almost complete information concerning the individual. Hence a proper cure can be effected.

(2) Cures in this method are simpler and more effective.

Despite these advantages, the method suffers from the following drawbacks :

(1) It consumes much time, with the result that a very large number of psychologists are required if there is a big number of patients.

(2) Accordingly, this method is extremely expensive also.

(3) It needs highly trained and specialist psychologists.

2. Group guidance method. The shortcomings of the individual guidance method are not found in group method because in this a number of people are guided simultaneously. Group guidance should not be interpreted to imply that it involves guiding the group. Actually, the guidance is aimed at the individual because it consists of the personal assistance rendered by a psychologist. In the group guidance technique a complete group is guided. But this guidance is intended to help the individual members of the group to solve their own problems, the sole difference being that the group is comprised of individuals facing more or less the same problems. Evidently, then, there is no need to waste money and time in giving individual guidance to individuals who are facing similar problems and the advice given is likely to be similar. Hence, there can be no questioning of the importance of the group guidance technique. It economises upon time and money.

Nevertheless, group guidance technique lacks all the advantage that accrues from an application of the individual guidance method. Due to the smaller degree of personal contact between the psychologist and his subjects, the cures are not quite so effective as in the case of individual guidance. When group guidance is administered it is also not possible to gather the same amount of authentic information concerning the subject as in feasible in the individual guidance method. Hence, it may be tentatively concluded that group guidance method can be of value only in circumstances in which the problems faced are similar to a degree without wide individual differences and are also not particularly complex.

All kinds of guidance are closely linked up. Guidance includes every phase of life *i.e.*, health, home, family, leisure time, personality, religious life, moral and civic, vocational etc. In other words, guidance is a process of assisting the individual discover himself — his natural endowments, potentialities, aptitudes, etc., and then to provide the proper environment. Crow and Crow have observed, "As now interpreted, guidance touches every aspect of an individual's personality — physical, mental, emotional and social. It is concerned with all of an individual's attitudes and behaviour patterns. It seeks to help the individual to integrate all of his activities in terms of his basic potentialities and environmental opportunities."

Meaning of Guidance for Different Persons

1. For parents. (i) In general Guidance means the general influence exerted in the family while fostering the favourable upbringing of the child plus the assistance students receive from the school by way of reproof, praise, admonition and advice when difficult situations arise.

(ii) Parents having children with special defects or disabilities (psychological or otherwise), guidance may mean a rather special diagnostic and remedial process conducted in the child guidance clinics.

(iii) To parents who desire higher education for their children, guidance may mean chiefly a matter of college advisement.

2. For teachers. (i) It is giving continuous consideration to individual needs of children.

(ii) It is attention to individual problem of adjustment or learning when it emerges in the classroom.

(iii) It is the maintenance of a good psychological tone or climate in the classroom at all times.

(iv) It is a special programme of services provided by counsellors to whom academically inapt pupils may be occasionally referred.

3 For pupils. (i) A period every week when matters like study habits are discussed or when their 'future' is explored.

(ii) A chance to talk over a personal problem with someone who listens, understands and helps.

(iii) The opportunity to obtain information about which college to attend.

4. For school administrator. (i) It means all the things mentioned above and more.

(ii) It is an indispensable phase of school curriculum, very closely allied with instruction yet possessing certain special service aspects demanded by the set-up of education in the school.

(iii) It is a policy and programme that he will have to establish, supervise, evaluate-set of activities in the school for which he must be responsible.

5. For National and State Legislators. (i) It is voting for funds to support and extend guidance services in schools.

(ii) It is an instrument by which youths are identified, advised and directed into professional types of training for occupations crucial to the nation's welfare.

6. For Guidance Counsellor. It is a systematic, continuous professional process of assisting pupils with particular needs and problems in the areas of school progress, personal-social relations and educational vocational counselling.

IMPORTANCE OF GUIDANCE

Adjustment is the basic problem of human life. The person who fails to adjust to his circumstances becomes a failure, suffers himself and inflicts it upon others, and is branded an abnormal being. In this way, educational psychology, through its helping the individual in adjusting himself, helps to spread happiness, peace and organisation in society. Problems in human life do not come to an end, because new ones keep on arising. There is no end to trouble. A child, for example, is faced by very new problems, much of his anxiety being centred around the work forced upon him by the teacher, or the means of dealing with the more recalcitrant of his friends and such minor things. He has not to worry about keeping the home fires burning. But these are problems that gradually engulf every individual as he grows older. As a general rule most people marry and have children who must go to school and with equal inevitability fall ill and be treated for it, only go grow up and get married themselves and keep the almost eternal circle moving forward. Thus one trouble grows out of another, and never lets the individual being sit back contented and unharried. Human psychology is much like this. One desire arises and destroys the being's peace till it is satisfied. Hence, he immediately busies himself in searching for the means to satisfy this desire and achieves this after more or less trouble. But the story does not end here, it is followed by the arising of another desire, and the inevitable circle of objective, search for objective, obstacles in search for means of solving the desire, overcoming of the obstacles, possession of the satisfying object, satisfaction of the desire, and the arising of another desire. It is evident that every individual is continually faced with new objective the achievement of which entails the facing of many other difficulties. As Jones has stated in his definition, guidance helps the overcoming of these difficulties that beset the achievement of an objective.

NEED OF GUIDANCE

The emerging issues and problems make it obligatory for educational planners and administrators to build an appropriate guidance and counselling programme for the development of the individual student of higher education into an adult personality, imbued with social and occupational awareness, intellectual and functional proficiency, discipline and confidence. The classroom activities can not accomplish this task.

Needs to be filled

Guidance and counselling programme should be introduced in colleges and universities to meet the following varied needs of the educational system, administration and students :

1. The total development of the student. Intellectual development through the teaching of subjects alone cannot lead to the total development of the students. What is needed is some method of helping students to understand themselves and helping teachers to understand the students. There has to be a basic and fundamental change in the entire system of education, which recognises that a person remains a barbarian unless he knows something about himself no matter how well a human being is educated in chemistry, physics, economics, history or literature. Self-knowledge in depth must become its primary focus. This is done through a programme of guidance and counselling. Total development of the students requires that individual differences among students are accepted and understood, and all types of experiences are so organise in an institution as to contribute to their total development.

2. Proper choice of courses. Everyone knows that our educational system has grown haphazard. While humanities and the liberal arts are subjects most frequently offered and taken, both in the colleges and the universities they were the oldest and relatively inexpensive areas of knowledge, taken because they require no specified intellectual equipment. Hence, thousands of youngmen educated in these liberal are arts without jobs.

In an article on *'Unrest on Campus'*, Piloo Modi, M.P. wrote, "Our student population reaches the university level, having made up their mind broadly about the courses that they may have a decision, which in almost all cases, is taken by unthinking and unsympathetic parents and relatives with an eye on a more lucrative profession. It is a great tragedy when a potential poet becomes a chemical engineer.... Many a mute inglorious Milton is languishing in the dark engineering world." For the best development of individuals and growth of society the process of herding youths into educational disciplines unconnected with their aptitudes must be checked through a scientific process of guidance and counselling.

3. Proper choice of careers. Our's is highly complex and rapidly changing world of work. The changing requirements in industrial jobs, altered market conditions for professional manpower, the development of para-professional occupations and many other labour market trends are making occupational selection more difficult than ever. The young students in colleges and universities must be informed about various available jobs and openings and the requirements, responsibilities and the nature of work involved in them so that they could measure themselves up to them and develop and crystallise their occupational goal. They should be helped in making meaningful occupational selection. They must be prepared for an entry into them to have a fulfilling and rewarding career.

The majority of students in our colleges and universities are the first generation learners. They have no one with an experience of college or university education background in their family to guide them in the choice of a career. With a right to the best education available, and a wide range of jobs open to them, education available, and a wide range of jobs open to them, these students need mature help in making a judicious occupational choice. This shows the need of adequate guidance and counselling arrangement in our colleges and universities.

4. Vocational development. The process of vocational development covers almost the entire span of life of an individual. It begins quite early in one's life and continues till sometimes after retirement. In this process, the individual passes through *growth, exploration, maintenance and decline.* Guidance services are provided at the colleges and universities to help the students in the process of vocational development by making a possible for them to gain knowledge about themselves their abilities, interests and needs and knowledge about the world of work. Their transition from education to work can be facilitated by providing them opportunities for self-exploration as well as exploration of the world of work while they are still in an educational institution.

5. Development of readiness for choices and changes to face new challenges. In a paper entitled *The Need for Counselling in Higher Education,* presented at the Third International Round Table of Educational Counselling and Vocational Guidance, Miss Newsome, Counselling Officer at the University of Keels, North Strafford Shire,

England, writes, "For the students of higher education the demands of life are likely to be great, in a most different way from the exacting demands of education itself. On graduating he will be called upon to make use of the kind of person he has become as much if not more than what he has learnt in his course of study — not only to make an initial choice of what he is to do on graduating but will be called upon to change his occupation several times in a life time. Readiness for these choices and changes is essential, not only to the student himself but to the society as a whole. To the extent to which he is able to capitalise on his experience and face new challenges with a realistic expectation of success, to that extent he will benefit society. If he is unable to meet the changing demands, not only of the working world but also of his other roles of life, to that extent he will be a liability and will fail to fulfil the expectations which society has for its most able people." Guidance services are needed to develop in the students the ability to cope with their new problems and concerns so that they become more competent to meet the demands which will be made upon them in the future.

6. Minimising the mismatching between education and employment and help in the efficient use of manpower. The hiatus between education and employment has rarely been as wide and as disturbing as it is today. Higher academic education is far too general and diffused to be of practical value to the vast majority of youngmen and women. Most of Indian youngmen and women have no clear objectives or career targets. They go through university courses of learning without acquiring much knowledge or preparing themselves for an uncertain future.

Every year, Indian colleges and universities send thousands of hopeful youngsters into the labour market virtually *unemployable* despite their fancy degrees and diplomas. Employers often complain that of the hundreds of applications that come in response to a single vacancy, at least 80 per cent have no relevance to the job specifications. Few students pursue their education with a clear idea as to what they would eventually like to become. People register at the employment exchange with scant idea about the sort of work they would like to take up. Thus, while jobs go a begging the youth go begging for jobs. The employment of workers ill-suited to their jobs leads to a higher rate of labour placement or to the retention of persons who are inefficient. This is a huge wastage of scant resources. Guidance facilities may help in reducing this wastage and thus ensure efficient use of manpower.

7. Motivating the youth for self-employment. Considering the magnitude of educated job-seekers flowing into the job market in India every year, a sizable fraction of enterprising youth should be initiated into careers of self-employment. Some arrangement needs to be instituted in the colleges and universities to identify the deserving cases fit to take up self-employment. They must be educated on how to proceed about the job of setting up a venture. They must be helped through the cooperation of the concerned agencies in this sphere to prepare technically sound and economically viable projects. Agencies must sponsor their cases to the banks for loans assistance and guide them to overcome the teething trouble through effective follow-up after the commencement of the venture. All this requires, guidance.

8. Helping freshers to establish proper identity. In India the young men and women entering colleges and universities are comparatively young in years. They are passing through a stage between childhood and adulthood, between the morality learned as a child and the ethics to be developed by the adult. They find it extremely difficult to establish a satisfactory identity. This failure or delay leads to what has been called "role diffusion". This crisis in role identity is very acute today. The uncertainties of the future, the conflicts in languages, culture, regions, castes, etc., and the erosion of traditional values has made Indian youth rootless.

In a small study done by Fuster (1964) with Bombay college students, both men and women, it was found that the strongest needs, as reported by the students themselves where they were requested to indicate rank orders, were for *achievement in life, self-reliance and as sense of security, success in college and university, to have an understanding friend and (for the males) MONEY.*

Guidance and counselling programme is needed to help students deal effectively with the normal development tasks of adolescence and face life situations boldly.

9. Identifying and motivating the students from weaker sections of society. Students from weaker sections of society have their own problems and needs. They experience difficulty in adjustment with the peers, teachers and the environment. It is a problem for them to communicate, make friends, utilise the time profitably, make the best use of lectures, make an effective use of library and other facilities available. Guidance facilities are needed for such type to students to enable them to adjust and utilise the available facilities.

10. Helping the students in their period of turmoil and confusion. Normally all the students undergo a great deal to turmoil and searching to give meaning to their lives. They have their conflicts and anxieties. They are disillusioned regarding higher education. They find that instead of imparting them education colleges and universities, just enable them to pass examination. They feel lost and bewildered, when this education does not enable them to get immediate employment. They have their personal conflicts and anxieties about their parents and family, their relations to boy and girl friends. They have the problems of adjusting their personality to the world of people, of ethical ideas and of goals and situations. To tackle all these situations successfully, they need someone to sort out the strands. This is done through guidance.

11. Checking wastage and stagnation. In India average pass percentage at the graduate and post-graduate level is about 50 to 60. Besides thousands of Indian students, unfortunately, drop out, get pushed out and fall out of the system. This problem is becoming more and more serious today. Again majority of our students pass in third division, which is a low qualification for the world of work. This poor achievement may be due to lack of proper study skills and effective study habits, lack of the knowledge for making full use of the facilities provided and so on.

Higher education is a very costly enterprise. Much of the money wasted on poor and low achievers could be saved by a policy of prevention. Preventive education is more sound economically than remedial education. There is a clear need for developing better professional services of a counselling kind — to check the huge wastage of student time and money and also huge state expenditure on education. In this connection, Miller has well said, "If one counsellor could prevent the wastage of only four student years each costing £800 to £1200, he would be earning his keep. Similar savings of graduate salaries foregone as a result of failure or delay would benefit student as well as taxpayer."[3]

12. Identifying and helping students in need of special help. Students who are the gifted, the backward, the handicapped need special opportunities and arrangement to be provided in colleges and universities. Guidance helps in identifying them and providing them with help according to their requirements.

13. Ensuring proper utilisation of time spent outside the classrooms. Students in the colleges and universities spend two to three times as many hours outside classrooms as in them. The manner in which students spend their non-class hours clearly affects their success in achieving both academic competence and personal development of all types. It is, therefore, essential that institutions of higher learning provide positive guidance to students by instructing how they can use those non-class hours. The programme of guidance and counselling is requested to meet this need.

14. Tackling problems of student explosion. Today, the increased demand for higher education is outstripping the growth of facilities in the seats of higher learning. Unfortunate qualitative changes in the nature of entire educative experiences are creating innumerable problems. The students population is highly heterogeneous. Students from a variety of sections — highly affluent and extremely poor, educated in convents and ordinary schools and colleges, rural and urban areas,

3. G.W. Miller, 'Planning courses for student counsellors — a role for Psychology,' *Bulletin, British Psychological Society,* 33 (1970).

students from India and those from different foreign countries are attending colleges and universities. Numerous problems crop up when students from a broad range of families and educational and social backgrounds meet in classes for instruction, in hostels for housing, in cafeterias and mess halls for eating. Guidance and counselling facilities should be provided for helping them to tackle these diverse and complex problems.

15. Check on migration. There is unhealthy trend among the Indian youth of migrating from rural to urban areas and from India to foreign countries. If migration is not checked by proper guidance and counselling, cities will swallow the rural talent and foreign countries will take away national talent.

16. Fulfilling the deficiencies of home. A large number of students come to institutions of higher learning from homes which have not taught them how to deal with their life problems. This is due to various factors such as rapid industrialisation, political and social changes in the occupational structure of the country and the growing complexity of life there are greater pressures and strains in the family. Again, there is gap in the range of sympathetic adults who could be turned to in need, which was formerly filled by adult brothers and sisters, friendly aunts and grand parents when communities and families were more intimate.

Most of the homes are not equipped to be the source of information concerning the qualifications required for different kinds of courses or careers. Such information can come only from agencies which make a full time job of supplying adequate and up-to-date materials. Most of the parents are not trained for helping their grown up children to develop sound study techniques, and obtain reliable information in matters of sex, etc. Seth (1962) collected a sample of students at Allahabad University, whose parents were indicated as the most usual source of help. Forty per cent of student respondents said that they could not discuss their problems with their parents. Professional guidance required to sort out all these problems.

17. Checking incidence of indiscipline. Majority of Indian students lack a sense of direction, a sense of purpose and a sense of fulfilment. They indulge in destructive activities leading to social damage and loss. Adequate guidance and counselling facilities are required to help and guide the youth to worthwhile channels and to make them realise the goal of optimum academic, personal and social development.

18. Need in developing economy. *Guidance and counselling have a challenging role to play in every developing economy, much more so if it is labour intensive.* Selection of a job from a multitude of alternatives, is a very important objective of guidance and counselling although it is not the be — all and end — all of guidance and counselling. The core aim of these services is to help the job-seeking youth to form realistic career notions, in conformity with their capacities, aptitudes and social settings, so that in their adult life, they do not end up as career 'failures'. Wrong career decisions make a big drain on the emotional health of the individuals and the productivity of the society. Guidance is needed to help the youth to build up a desirable self-concept to achieve an ever larger measure of self-appraisal and choose a proper career line. Thus, the provision of guidance and counselling service is India's immediate requirement.

19. Qualitative improvement of education. In India there has been a rapid expansion of educational facilities to cater to the needs of increasing number of children. This has resulted in the fall of educational standards. Consequently there is a strong current of thinking among educationists as well as general public that educational planning should emphasise schemes for the qualitative improvement of education. The introduction of guidance services in the country is an important means for effecting improvement in the quality of education.

20. National development. By helping and identifying and developing human potential which is the richest source of a nation, guidance can help to reduce the wastage of educational facilities and abilities so prevalent in India. Guidance may also help to correct the existing imbalances in the employment situation by channelling young people into occupations where there are manpower shortage. It was help in the reducing labour turn-over and its costs. It may increase efficiency and levels of production by enabling a person to be trained properly and placing them accordingly. At a time when India have embarked upon various programmes of economic development, it is urgent and essential to establish a close link between education and the manpower needs of the country. This may be done through guidance.

21. Fulfilment of the extra-instructional needs of pupils. Dr. K.G. Rama Rao has stated, "Classroom instruction by itself has not the full resources which are essential as well as necessary in an impoverished home for helping the pupils to acquire and preserve the background requirements for successful scholastic or polytechnical career. Proper attitudes to persons, things and ideas of certain value and systematised working and living habits are essential to any career. The need to supplement, correct and complement the areas of education is obvious." This statement points to need of guidance.

Thus, there is need for guidance from the point of view of the society as well as of the individual. Society can make progress if its individuals find places in the occupational, civic and social order where they can contribute their best for the welfare of others.

GUIDANCE AND COUNSELLING

According to Crow and Crow "Guidance is not direction. It is not the imposition of one's point of view upon another. It is not making decisions for an individual which he should make for himself. It is not carrying the burden of another's life. Rather, guidance is assistance made available by competent counsellors to an individual of any age to help him direct his own life, develop his own point of view, make his own decisions, carry his own burdens." Hamrin and Erickson define guidance as "that aspect of educational programme which is concerned especially with helping the pupil to become adjusted to his present situation and to plan his future in line with his interests, abilities, and social needs."

Mathewson believes that "guidance is the systematic professional process of helping the individual through education and interpretative procedures to gain a better understanding of his own characteristics and potentialities and to relate himself more satisfactorily to social requirements and opportunities in accord with social and moral values." Traxler considers guidance as a help which enables "each individual to understand his abilities and interests, to develop them as well as possible and to relate them to life-goals, and finally to reach a state of complete and mature self-guidance as a desirable member of the social order."

According to Jones, "Guidance involves personal help given by someone; it is designed to assist a person to decide where he wants to go, what he wants to do or how he can best accomplish his purpose; it assists him to solve problems that arise in his life."

CHARACTERISTICS OF GUIDANCE

1. **A process.** It helps every individual to help himself, to recognise and use his inner resources, to set goals, to make plans, to work out his own problems of development.

2. **A continuous process.** It is needed right from early childhood, adolescence, adult-hood and even in old age.

3. **Choice and problem points as the distinctive concerns.** Here the individual's unique world of perceptions interacts with the external order of events in his life context.

4. **Assistance to the individual in the process of development rather than a direction of that development.** The aim is to develop the capacity for self-direction, self-guidance and self-improvement through an increased understanding of his problems and his resources as well as limitations to solve the problem.

5. **A service meant for all.** It is a regular service which is required at every stage for every student, not only for awkward situations and abnormal students. It is a positive programme geared to meet the needs of all students.

6. **Both generalised and a specialised service.** It is a generalised service because everyone — teachers, tutors, advisers, deans, parents — play a part in the programme. It is a specialised service because

specially qualified personnel as counsellors, psychiatrists, psychologists join hands to help the individual to get out of his problem.

Guidance and Counselling

The terms 'guidance' and 'counselling' have been loosely or interchangeabley used. According to Tolbert, "Guidance...is the total programme or all the activities and services engaged in by an educational institution that are primarily aimed at assisting an individual to make and carry out adequate plans and to achieve satisfactory adjustment in all aspects of his daily life. Guidance is not teaching but it may be done by teachers. It is not separate from education but is an essential part of the total educational programme. Guidance is a term which is broader than counselling and which includes counselling as one of its services." Butler makes a logical separation of the counselling process discerned as having two phases called 'adjustive' and 'distributive'. In the *adjustive* phase, the emphasis is on the *social, personal* and *emotional* problems of the individual; in the *distributive* phase the focus is upon his *educational, vocational* and *occupational* problems.

According to Arbuckle, Butler's *distributive phase* can be most aptly described as 'guidance' whilst the *adjustive phase* can be considered as the description of 'counselling'.

Principles of Guidance Philosophy

According to Hollis and Hollis, there are eight principles of guidance programme which can be modified to fit locally accepted beliefs. These are as follows :

1. The dignity of the individual is supreme.
2. Each individual is different from every other individual.
3. The primary concern of guidance is the individual in his social setting.
4. The attitudes and personal perceptions of the individual are the bases on which he acts.
5. The individual generally acts to enhance his perceived self.
6. The individual has the innate ability to learn and can be helped to make choices that will lead to self-direction consistent with social improvement.
7. The individual needs a continuous guidance process from early childhood through adulthood.
8. Each individual may at times need the information and personalised assistance best given by competent professional personnel.

FUNCTIONS OF GUIDANCE AND COUNSELLING

1. Adjustmental. Guidance and counselling are *adjustmental* in the sense that they help the student in making the best possible adjustment to the current situations in the educational institution and occupational world, in the home and the community. Professional and individualised aid is given in making immediate and suitable adjustment at problem points. At the same time, the adjustive attitude is to be developed in the individuals.

2. Orientational. Guidance and counselling orientate the students in problems of career planning, educational programming and direction towards long-term personal aims and values. Awareness of the need to plan in the context of the complexity of the world of work is an essential prerequisite of going through education and preparation for after-education career.

3. Developmental function. Guidance and counselling try not only to cure when the problems have occurred and done their damage, but begin before the problems arise and maladjustments occur. If unsolved problems are allowed to accumulate, their total effect may lead the student to the point where his capacity for growth is blocked. In such cases, guidance and counselling may be of little or no help. That way guidance and counselling have a very important developmental function for helping the students achieve self-development and self-realisation. Guidance and counselling also have to discharge the important function of furthering the welfare of the society and be important instruments of national development.

SCOPE OF GUIDANCE AND COUNSELLING

The scope of guidance and counselling is comprehensive. As the life is getting complex day by day, the problems for which expert help is required are increasing proportionately. The scope of guidance, per necessity, is extending horizontally to much of the social context, to matters of prestige in occupations, to the broad field of social trends, and economic development. Guidance is assuming more and more responsibility for the individual in every direction — it helps in the selection of educational courses, and profitable occupation, in job placement; placement in the next stage of education and training; occupational surveys; improvement of study skills, maintenance of mental health; counselling regarding personal adjustment problems; identifying the gifted, the backward and help them achieve the maximum. In short, educational, vocational, avocational, social, personal, moral and even marital problems of individual are the concerns of guidance and counselling. Their scope is indeed very vast.

QUESTIONS FOR EXERCISE

1. Define guidance and explain its characteristics.
2. Discuss the scope of guidance.
3. Explain different types of guidance needed for different categories of persons.
4. Write short note on Importance of guidance.

5. Classify and explain guidance according to its mode and procedure.
6. Explain the different meaning of guidance to different persons.
7. 'Guidance is as old as man himself'. Discuss and make out a case for an organised programme of guidance.
8. Discuss the need for guidance services in the context of conditions prevailing in India.
9. Theory of individual differences is basic to the development of guidance. Discuss.
10. Does a person need guidance only during critical periods of life? Explain. Give reasons for your answer.
11. Distinguish between Guidance and Counselling.

2

Guidance, Education and Discipline

Some individuals need guidance throughout their lives; others need help only during their youth. The chief guidance responsibility of society is toward children and youth and those who, do not have equal opportunities for activities that will satisfy their individual and social needs because of congenital defects, disease, accident, or political-social handicaps. Situations that call for guidance are varied and numerous. Guidance functions whenever choices are to be made and where help is needed in making intelligent decisions. Even when there is no choice possible, guidance may help the individual understand and accept the situation. It may enable him to "cooperate with the inevitable." It may also operate when the individual are not know that a choice is possible by pointing out the avenues that are open to him. In still other circumstances the time may not be favourable for making a choice because of fatigue, emotional strain, or influences that will make an intelligent decision unlikely. In such situations the best help may be to suggest that only those decisions be made which are mandatory, leaving open as many as possible until a later, more favourable, time.

DEVELOPMENTAL GUIDANCE

However, guidance is needed not just in crisis situations but also by normal youngsters coping with normal developmental problems. Developmental guidance is based on the premise that the aim of guidance is not merely the amelioration of trauma or the prevention of mistakes but rather the maximum development of the individual.

Choices are often made on the basis of a person's own past experience or that of others. A person may call to mind some choice that he or one of his friends made in a situation that seems similar to the present one. He might choose to make the same choice again if what was done before was satisfactory. If the result was unsatisfactory, he might decide to do something else. Such a decision may result in a good or poor choice. Although similar in some respects the two situations may be very different. The choice may have been a good one once, but with the passage of time and with changed conditions, it may be quite unsatisfactory now. Guidance may help by assisting the individual to examine the two situations carefully to see in what ways they are alike and in what ways they are different and by helping him to get a broader view of the possible choices.

It is often possible to get some preliminary experience in an occupation that is being considered. Jobs held after school, on Saturdays, holidays, and especially in the long summer vacations, provide helpful experience. These may be available in stores, in offices, on the farm, or elsewhere. The guidance value of such experience varies greatly. It is dependent upon the attitude of the youth, the supervision given, and the physical and social environment of the job.

When youth attempt to use their own experiences as a basis for choice, they are handicapped as their experiences are neither extensive nor of great scope or variety. Choices made on such a basis are not likely to be good ones, but very often they do not see this danger. With youthful enthusiasm and undue confidence in their ability, they often make hasty and unwise decisions. Other avenues of lifework may begin to make a strong appeal to them in later years. They may realise too late that these avenues might well have offered success and satisfaction. The necessary training cannot now be secured without great financial sacrifice that would jeopardise the comfort and welfare of the family. Although they may realise that their early choices were unfortunate, they can do nothing about it now. Wise guidance may be of great value by making them realise that their experience was too limited to give them proper perspective. It will help them review carefully the wide range of occupations within their interest and capabilities.

ADVICE AS GUIDANCE

A very valuable source of help frequently used is the experience of others expressed through advice. Man's superiority over the lower animals is due to his ability to profit not only from his own experience but from that of others; Without this ability there would have been little progress. Such experience may be utilised either directly, through advice given by others, or indirectly, through a knowledge and understanding of history.

Although advice is an old and widely used method of guidance, some guidance authorities maintain that it is harmful. They say that the only time it is safe to give advice to others is when you know they will not use it. This statement grossly exaggerates the dangers of advice. Industrial firms spend millions every year on advice, and it pays. Older men who have had years of experience either in the industry that employs them or in similar industries are used as consultants or advisers. The value of their services is evident in the large salaries given to them. Throughout history sages have been singled out for great honour and reverence. The advice given by a person who has travelled the same way before may be very valuable. Though the old Chinese dynasties stagnated because of the national credo "Walk in the trodden way," but some of the most valuable sources of help are found in the recorded thoughts and experiences of men and women of the past.

All aspects of the past — social, industrial, economic, scientific, artistic, and religious — have much to teach us. Those sources of understanding are too little used in our present programs of guidance. To be of any use the lessons of history must be read and interpreted not only in terms of the past but also in terms of the present. Teachers of English, history, science, art, and music can open up these sources of help and interpret them as well. The lessons of the past that are of the greatest value are those that state fundamental values of life and general principles of conduct. These lessons help in many different situations because they usually do not indicate exactly what one should do but leave it to the individual to determine what definite action will be best. This is in accord with the principle that the purpose of guidance is the development in the individual's ability to solve problems without the help of others. Conditions may have changed so much that the present problem is quite unlike the old one, and what was once a desirable solution may no longer be satisfactory.

Changed conditions are especially likely to appear in affairs involving youth. The changed attitude of parents and teachers toward youth, the greater freedom given to youth, the new emphasis on self-determination, and the relaxing of discipline have profoundly altered the nature of the problems of young people. Today youth are far better informed on scientific, economic, and social conditions and developments than their parents were when they were of the same age. This development greatly increases the complexity and difficulty of the problems of youth and those of their parents who are trying to help them. In boy-girl relations the restrictions that were once thought desirable have in large part been removed, and some conduct which was once frowned upon is now considered acceptable. When the problem relates to the use by teen-agers of our modern high-powered and complex cars, advice based on the days of the horse and buggy is entirely inappropriate. These changed conditions make skillful and well-organised guidance imperative. Guidance now calls for wide experience, deep wisdom, and infinite patience on the part of the one who counsels.

Advice is usually received best and carries more weight when the one who seeks it comes voluntarily to the counsellor because he feels the need for help. Gratuitous advice is usually of little value because most people regard such proffered help as an intrusion on what they consider to be their own affair. It is also often given without knowledge or consideration of the needs of the person advised.

In sum, one's own experience as well as that of others may be very valuable in guidance, but it may not be a safe guide in itself. To be of real value, experience must be interpreted in relation to the particular problem that is at hand. There may be differences, even though slight ones, in the present situation that may be very significant, thus making the solution that was once satisfactory quite unsatisfactory now. For example, action taken fifty years ago based on a certain religious belief may have been useful then, but it may be quite useless or even undesirable now. Even now two persons may have the same beliefs regarding the worth of the individual and his relation to God and yet be on opposite sides of a social problem. The previous family and social experience and the background of each person have a powerful influence on the belief which is held. Guidance must help young people to develop techniques of utilising their own past experience and that of others for the solution of the problems facing them in making their adjustments in life.

GUIDANCE AND EDUCATION

Guidance is the help given by one person to another in making choices and adjustments and in solving problems. It aims at aiding the recipient to grow in his independence and ability to be responsible for himself. It is a service that is universal — not confined to the school or the family. It is found in all phases of life — in the home, in business and industry, in government, in social life, in hospitals, and in prisons; indeed it is present wherever there are people who *need* help and wherever there are people who *can* help.

Very early in the guidance movement Brewer,[1] a consistent advocate of vocational guidance, recognised the close relationship between guidance and education. The nature of this relationship has been a source of much concern and controversy. The different points of view are largely owing to differences in the meaning of the term "education." "Education" may be used to mean (1) the process of changes that take place within the individual, (2) instruction, or (3) the conscious effort of society to guide the individual so that he will be able to live a life that will be socially effective and individually satisfying.

Education is essentially a process; It is something that takes place *in individuals;* It is the process by which changes are made in the individual or, better, by which the individual makes changes in himself. At birth human beings are the most helpless of all animals, absolutely dependent upon others for their very existence. For long years they must be fed, cared for, and protected in order to preserve life and to ensure normal growth and development. By nature man is much less adjusted to his physical environment than any other animal. He must learn to walk, to eat, to make those adjustments that are necessary to cope with physical nature. Habits must be formed, skills developed, and facts learned before it is safe for him to go out into the world alone. Since he is not naturally suited to his physical environment, changes must be made in him before he can be adjusted.

In the present new method, teaching is thought of as helping the child to learn. The child is the active agent in the process. The teacher

1. John M. Brewer, *Education as Guidance,* The Macmillan Company, New York, 1955.

still determines for the most part the ends to be achieved, although even here there may be pupil cooperation; but he also assists the pupil to understand the ends and to accept them as his own. Assistance, so directed, is guidance. If the pupil is able to select his aims. If, after understanding and accepting the ends, the pupil is able to see by himself what he must do to accomplish the ends, the teacher steps aside; no teaching and no guidance are necessary. Whenever, in the learning process, the teacher assists *the learner to choose,* guidance is present.

There is also another way in which guidance enters into the process of education. The teacher, as an agent of society, sets up ends to be accomplished by the pupil, but the method by which different pupils reach the ends may vary. Reaching the ends is important; the method by which the ends are reached is relatively unimportant, except that it should be the method best suited to the individual pupil. Choices in method are often, if not always, possible. The efficient teacher is continually trying to help the pupil find the one that is best suited to him. When the teacher selects the method, there is teaching but no guidance; when he assists the learner to choose a method, guidance is present.

Whenever, in the process of accomplishing the ends, the pupil needs help, it is the teacher's function to give it. This help is usually stimuli in the form of outlines, references, suggestions, leading questions, expressions of approval and disapproval, incentives, and anything else that may help the pupil to learn. This is teaching or instruction; it may or may not be guidance. Teaching conceived of as assisting the learner to *choose* ends or methods is guidance.

Education as Socialisation

Society makes a conscious effort to guide and direct the physical, mental, emotional, and moral growth of the individual so that he may be able to live a life socially effective and individually satisfying. In this broader concept of education, guidance and education are closely related.

The ultraprogressive educator reacts strongly against any form of control of individual development by society and contends that the only object of education is the development of the individual. This development is to be determined not by what society wants but by some inward force or law or principle which, if followed, will result in the maximum or optimum development of each individual. Nor will it satisfy the ultraconservative who emphasises the need for social efficiency as opposed to mere individual development. Each of these elements must be present, but they should be complementary, not antagonistic. This concept of education might seem to make guidance and education synonymous both when we stress the development of the individual for himself as an end and when we emphasise the needs of society, for education is thought of as the conscious effort of society to assist the individual.

However, the important words in this sentence are not "the conscious effort of society," but "assist the individual," and the role of society in the education of individuals may not be "assistance" in the real sense. When society merely determines what shall be taught and does nothing to assist the individual — when the individual is thought of as passive — guidance is not present except in a very indirect and remote way. In a sense the entire conscious effort of society to see that the individual reaches certain goals set up by society is assistance. The physical and social environment which is selected and organised by society for the purpose of making sure that the child will develop properly, the curriculum, the textbooks, library, and laboratories, the organised life of the school, all are instrumental in making sure that the pupil develops in certain ways. The habits and skills developed, the interests and attitudes formed, all are powerful factors. This is, at best, a very mechanical and deterministic kind of assistance. In one sense it is not really assistance at all, for assistance implies more or less independent action on the part of the individual, that is, the enlistment of the individual in the enterprise. In the same sense we could say that we assist the plant to grow by watering it; we assist the post to stand upright by digging a hole and placing the post in it; we assist the boy to be clean by washing his face. This is a misinterpretation of the term "assistance." This mechanical assistance, even though it helps to determine the development of the individual and may materially affect his choices, can hardly be guidance, for it leaves out the all-important part that the individual himself plays in the process.

This broader concept of education includes guidance only when the modern, progressive viewpoint of the place and function of the individual is accepted. When only the goals of society are considered, we may have education but not guidance, for guidance implies assistance in making choices. These choices are individual ones and imply a compromise between, or a synthesis of, the needs of society and the needs of the individual. There are certain situations in education where the element of choice by the individual is prominent, and there are others in which it is not.

There are still a few people who regard education and guidance as separate and distinct, but their number is rapidly diminishing. Such a complete separation is impossible; It violates the essential nature of both elements. The differences of opinion now are chiefly between those who would make guidance and education synonymous terms and those who regard guidance as an aspect and an essential element in education. The reason for this controversy is found partly in the different meanings attached to the term "education" and partly in the failure to distinguish between the parts played by the teacher and by the learner in the process of education. In fact, guidance is found in that area of educational endeavour which involves assistance given by agencies or persons to the individual in making choices and in helping him choose a line of action, a method of procedure, a goal. It is not choosing for him or directing his choice; it is helping him to make the choice.

Education deals with the entire scope of human development. From one standpoint it is the conscious effort of society to change and develop the individual so that he may conform to society, take his place in it, improve it, and in doing this secure his own optimum development. From another standpoint it is the conscious effort of the individual to adjust himself to his physical and social environment, to improve it, and so to secure his own highest development.

The individual and society are two forces working for the same ends. When society merely determines what will be learned and how it will be learned and does nothing to secure the cooperation of the individual in the choice of things to be learned or methods to be used, guidance is not present, for there is no choice by the individual. Society in general and the teacher in particular may need to influence or direct the growth of the individual since wise choices in later life are dependent to a large extent upon habits and attitudes formed in early years. This might be considered good education, but it is not guidance. On the other hand the individual may consciously attempt to establish a goal without help. When he does this, guidance is not present. Although education may, and often does, take place through the effort and initiation of the individual alone, the same thing is true as above : this is education but not guidance. It is only when the cooperation of the individual is secured and assistance given him in choosing his goals or his methods that guidance is present. All guidance is education, but some aspects of education are not guidance; their objectives are the same — the development of the individual — but the methods used in education are by no means the same as those used in guidance.

GUIDANCE AND DISCIPLINE

Considering the relation of guidance to discipline some guidance leaders fear that any contact with discipline will interfere with the success of guidance workers. This fear is quite unwarranted and arises largely from misunderstandings. Guidance functions in all sorts of problem situations, past, present, or future. It is help given or received by all personnel in the school system — superintendent, supervisor, specialist, teacher, custodial worker, student. It is found wherever there are problems to be solved in teaching, in supervision, in discipline. In fact discipline offers one of the most useful and rewarding areas for guidance.

The confusion is best resolved by examining the meanings which may be attached to the term "discipline." Discipline has two different but related meanings. First, discipline is a planned series of activities or exercises considered necessary for the attainment of a certain goal. An example is the training of an athlete for a race or for some other athletic contest. This meaning would include the development of regular exercise, eating, and sleeping habits as well as certain restrictions. Another example of this meaning is the college curriculum leading to a degree. In this first sense discipline also means a set of rules or laws affecting conduct such as the discipline of the church, the law, or medicine. This meaning may be called "positive" discipline.

Second, discipline means punishment for conduct that is considered undesirable. Failure to achieve a required standard in school, for example, may result in punishment, or discipline. The punishment may also be the natural result of undesirable conduct such as the "morning after" a "binge" or failure in a contest because of breaking training. This meaning may be called "negative" discipline. Its purpose is to prevent conduct that is undesirable. It is intended to help the individual understand what is necessary to attain the goal and to motivate him to keep to the exercises and the rules that have been set up.

The two meanings of discipline are closely related. Guidance has a unique function in both of them. It helps set the goal and develop a program of activities leading to it. It also encourages and motivates the individual to keep at the activities and exercises that are essential in attaining the desired end.

GUIDANCE AND PUNISHMENT

When discipline means punishment by some authority for unacceptable behaviour, guidance may help the student to understand why the behaviour is unacceptable. Elementary school is not too early to help students to understand the function of punishment as seen in the history of human society and to comprehend what their community would be without laws leading to the punishment of offenders.

The responsibility for assistance to students in cases of discipline, in both its positive and its negative meanings, may rest upon any school personnel. Teachers have responsibility in this area because they deal directly with that part of the curriculum which is allotted to them. They are responsible for helping the pupils in their classes or subject areas to understand the educational content, to do the exercises required, to attain the desired goals. They must provide the motivation necessary for the attainment of the objectives and administer such punishments as may be necessary for failure to study or to achieve academically. In addition each teacher is responsible for the behaviour of the children in his class and to a large extent for their attendance and health. Without a doubt the chief responsibility for all these guidance services rests upon the teacher.

PREVENTIVE GUIDANCE

By far the most effective discipline is that which operates before the crisis occurs and helps the student to understand and accept the type of behaviour that is demanded by the school. In most cases discipline of this kind helps the student to realise what is required and therefore makes punishment unnecessary. Here the teacher is the most important factor, but the counsellor may also be of real assistance. This type of discipline is not always possible, however, because one cannot always foresee the approaching crisis. Furthermore, not every crisis can be prevented. When a crisis does come, the student is in dire need of help, and the counsellor has a clear responsibility to give him help.

ROLE OF THE COUNSELLOR IN DISCIPLINE

Authorities in the field of guidance agree that the counsellor should not be charged with the responsibility for the administration of punishment because by so doing, he may make it difficult to establish and maintain the rapport that is so essential for counselling and guidance. Experience amply confirms this opinion, but this does not mean that the counsellor never has any responsibility in the field of discipline. In fact, discipline offers one of the richest and most rewarding areas for guidance.

Just as the counsellor should not be involved in the actual punishment of the student, neither should he be the "lawyer for the defense" and seek to free him from punishment. If he has established rapport with the student, however, he may be able to find out why the misdemeanor was committed. He may discover what the student wished to accomplish by the act and help him to understand why his purpose was undesirable and what the effect of such behaviour would be on other students and on the school.

The counsellor can often help the guilty student to realise and frankly confess that his act was undesirable and to accept his punishment as well deserved. Thus it can be seen that the counsellor may have a definite responsibility in cases of discipline and may be able to make a real contribution to the student and to the school by helping the student to understand and modify his antisocial behaviour.

QUESTIONS FOR EXERCISE

1. The National Vocational Guidance Association USA adopted the following statement : "The purpose of vocational guidance is to assist individuals to choose, prepare for, enter upon, and make progress in an occupation." Make a list of ten important problems of youth which are not included in this statement and which you feel should be the responsibility of the guidance department of the secondary school.

2. Find the meanings of the following : to assist, to lead, to advise, to counsel, to guide, to regulate. Compare the definitions of these words and be prepared to discuss the distinctive meaning of guidance.
3. Evaluate the following statements :
   (a) We have no need for a counsellor because in our school every teacher is a guidance worker.
   (b) Our counsellor has absolutely nothing to do with discipline.
   (c) There is nothing new about guidance; after all, guidance is just good teaching.

3

Relation of Guidance to other Educational Specialities

One of the most important developments in the field of education during the past century has been the increased specialisation in educational services. Among the first specialties to emerge were the four large areas of teaching, counselling, administration, and supervision. More recently the specialised services of the physician, the psychologist, the psychiatrist, the dentist, the social worker, and the health educator have been recognised as important to education.

Additionally, we now see the subject-matter supervisor, the curriculum coordinator, and the remedial expert coming into our schools and performing useful functions needed in a complex educational setting. Each speciality has a distinct title and often requires a definite course of training leading to a certificate issued by the state or by some professional organisation of high standing; each one also has a fairly definite core of work and responsibility. Each employs some techniques that are especially characteristic of the specialty. These characteristics and requirements have given a clear and definite professional status to the many educational specialties. Such specialisation has some disadvantages and dangers, but there can be no doubt that it has greatly increased the effectiveness of the entire educational system.

Each of these areas has a definite responsibility for certain services and uses characteristic techniques and thus makes its own contribution to the overall program of education. The lines separating one area of service from another are not clear and distinct. There is considerable overlapping in objectives, in content, and in the techniques used.

The interrelation and overlapping in objectives and techniques may be seen by a brief discussion of the four large areas of service. Teaching is concerned with helping students to learn. Counselling deals with helping students to develop the ability to solve their own problems. Supervision is responsible for providing leadership in improving instruction. Administration is concerned with the control, direction, and management of the school, that is, the provision of conditions favourable for learning.

COMMON OBJECTIVES

The basic services of the school are found in teaching and counselling since both deal directly with the individual student, his problems, and his needs. The function of administration and supervision is to promote the effectiveness of teaching and counselling. All four areas are bound together by the same objectives. Each should supplement, assist, and increase the effectiveness of the other areas in helping students to develop those habits, skills, attitudes, and ideals that will enable them to adjust to modern democratic society and attain a life that will be worthwhile.

COMMON TECHNIQUES

Although there are techniques that are characteristic of each area, they may be used in other areas as well. For example, each of the four areas is concerned with help in learning, and the techniques of teaching are available to all educational specialists and are used by them. Every member of the school staff faces situations that involve face-to-face counselling, and therefore all should use the special techniques of counselling. Many principals and superintendents fail in their dealings with teachers and parents because they do not know the techniques of counselling, and many teachers fail in their relations with students for the same reason.

Some define teaching as helping the child to learn and say that it is fundamentally guidance, since guidance is assistance to individuals in meeting new situations, in solving problems, and in making adjustments. Some of these problems are related to occupations, others to social relations, and still others to the mastery of school subjects. Some of the most important problems of children are connected with learning to read and write, to understand arithmetic skills, to comprehend and appreciate literature. A paraphrase of the standard definition of vocational guidance might be as follows : "Instructional guidance is the assistance given to individuals in understanding and accepting responsibility for the development of skills, in providing situations favourably for learning, in developing the desire to learn, and in making progress in learning."

Some of the best guidance and the most effective counselling is given by skilled teachers to pupils in their classes. At one time or another every teacher has pupils come to him with problems relating to out-of-school, family, or religious difficulties. It is quite natural for students to seek help on such problems; the teacher has, or should have, close contact with students, for he meets them much more frequently than the counsellor. He knows, or should know, about previous difficulties, home conditions, financial problems, and other matters that have troubled them. Whether the teacher is able to give the needed help or not, he cannot refuse to confer with a pupil; if he is a real teacher, he must be interested in him and in his problem.

Every teacher should know what general methods to employ in finding out what the real problem is, and he should make the pupils feel that he cares. He should be able and willing to recognise his own limitations and,, when necessary, to refer the student to the counsellor or someone else who may be better qualified to help him. He should know the best ways of making such referrals because they are among the most important elements in guidance. He should prepare the student for the referral conference by pointing out that the counsellor is able and willing to help him. At the same time he should retain his own interest in the student and make him feel that he will always be ready to confer with him.

Because even the most skilled teacher is not able to give adequate assistance to all pupils for whom he is responsible or to deal successfully with all types of problems, there is now, a definite need for well-trained and competent counsellors in the elementary and secondary schools. These counsellors should be consultants to teachers and parents, helping them to deal with more difficult cases. They should also be resource personnel, assuming responsibility for more difficult problems and for special cases. In the teamwork method the counsellor might well be the chairman or leader of the group.

NECESSARY TEAMWORK

Some authorities seem to believe that such overlapping in objectives and techniques is very undesirable. In their efforts to develop and maintain a special professional status for the counsellor, they contend that counselling is the sole prerogative of the counsellor and that teaching is the prerogative of the teacher. They believe that, when a teacher attempts to counsel a student, he steps out of his role as a teacher and becomes a counsellor and that, when a counsellor teaches, he becomes a teacher and is no longer a counsellor. This idea is the result of the unfortunate confusion in the use of the two terms. The word "counselling" is used both for a technique and for an area of service (that of the counsellor); "teaching" is also used to indicate a technique and a position (that of the teacher). The counsellor often employs the technique of teaching in addition to others, and the teacher uses many techniques, one of which is counselling. But the teacher does not become a counsellor because of this. He does not have the training or the assigned role of a counsellor. When a mother uses first aid for her child, she uses one of the techniques of a physician; but this does not make her one. Neither teaching techniques nor counselling techniques are the sole property of any one area of educational service.

Every service in the school involves the techniques of teaching, counselling, and other educational skills. It should serve to emphasise the pressing need for planned cooperation among all school services. It also means that in the preparation of administrators, supervisors, teachers, and counsellors there should be sufficient emphasis both on teaching techniques, so that all can teach well, and on counselling techniques, so that all can give effective guidance.

GUIDANCE AS AN ORGANISED FUNCTION

It is apparent that guidance is inherent in every part of the school which is concerned with assisting the pupil to make choices, adjustments, and interpretations. Any attempt to confine it to a given area of assistance or to restrict its function to a particular group of the school staff is certain to fail. Such an attempt to simplify the situation by an arbitrary division of the complex whole into separate parts inevitably sacrifices the unity of the process and results in greater confusion. Guidance involves all types of choices and must include within its scope the curriculum, teaching, supervision, and all other activities of the school. The classroom teacher can no more be divorced from guidance than can the counsellor; in many ways he is fundamentally more important. On the other hand, to identify all guidance with the teacher would be equally fatal. Adequate guidance requires the cooperation of the whole school staff — administrators, teachers, personnel workers, and specialists.

Areas of Choice

Must we, then, spread the work of guidance throughout the school with no attempt to coordinate it or to provide specialised services? Is there no place for a department of guidance more or less separate from the work of the classroom teacher and the principal but coordinated with them? To the latter question we must emphatically answer that there is such a place. There are various categories of problems, choices, and adjustments that should be adequately provided for in schools. Some of the most important of these arise at crucial places in the educational progress of the pupil, such as (1) the end of the compulsory attendance age; (2) the completion of elementary school; (3) the beginning of junior high school; (4) the completion of junior high school; (5) the entrance to senior high school; (6) the completion of senior high school; (7) the entrance to college; (8) the leaving of school at any time; (9) the taking up of an occupation.

The choices and adjustments at these times are of extreme importance and call for special forms of assistance. Many facts necessary for an intelligent choice can be provided in the ordinary school; many habits, attitudes, and ideals needed can be taught. In proportion as the school is organised with these needs in view, to that extent will the special work of guidance in providing for information, habits, attitudes, and interests be reduced. If properly planned, any type of organisation should allow ample opportunity to give special attention to ways in which needed information can be made available and assistance given.

Crises requiring Reorganisation of Material

Many choices and problems of adjustment to school and work require a reorganisation of information already obtained from classroom activities as well as a selection from among the facts at hand. Such reorganisation and selection are often very difficult and, without assistance, beyond the power of the individual. They sometimes involve factors other than the individual himself. Difficulties that arise in school or occupation or home are due to clash of personalities or to a complexity of conditions. Adjustment involves not only the individual himself but other people and other factors as well. It is not something that he can work out by himself alone. It can be accomplished only by cooperative effort, and this cannot be left to haphazard activity. Such cooperation must be planned.

Problem Cases

The aim of guidance is to develop individuals so that they will be able to solve their own problems as far as this is possible. But even the best efforts of the school do not result in the entire elimination of problem cases. There are always occasions when every student needs special assistance, and it is probable that some students continually need help. Special facilities must be provided for meeting these needs.

SCOPE OF AN ORGANISED GUIDANCE PROGRAM

Some superintendents and principals believe that no specialised personnel is necessary for guidance. The classroom teacher can provide all the assistance needed. It is the function of the principal to provide for coordination of effort. This attitude is due in part to the very real danger that the provision of a separate guidance department may result in the teachers' feeling that all guidance functions will and should be performed by the counsellors and that they themselves have no guidance responsibilities. In some cases this attitude is due to the failure of the principal or superintendent to understand fully the function of guidance. Some of this confusion could be avoided if we called the specialised department "personnel work" instead of "guidance." Guidance is a function of the entire school. The function of the department of personnel work is to coordinate the guidance activities of the school and to supplement them by specialised work. This department would also have the responsibility of keeping before the rest of the staff the need for assistance in areas that are likely to be neglected and of stimulating all to more effective action. In some schools and colleges this department is called "student services" and is coordinate with administration and instruction. The scope and function of any specially organised department of guidance or pupil personnel in the school system will depend upon the effectiveness with which the system as a whole is organised and administered from the guidance point of view.

We are still in a developmental stage of guidance and do not always know just what problems can be most advantageously handled by specially organised guidance departments. As the curricular and supervisory personnel of the school become conscious of the purpose of guidance and are reorganised in accordance with it, more and more of the actual guidance work may be successfully left to these agencies. We cannot accurately forecast exactly when this will be, nor can we determine completely what activities, if any, should always be performed by the special guidance bureau. It may be found, for example, that much of the work, especially that concerned with securing information and developing the habits, ideals, interests, and techniques necessary to intelligent choice, can be done better if organised as a regular part of classroom procedure and not left to the organised guidance department. On the other hand, it will undoubtedly be found that certain kinds of assistance can be most efficiently and economically given by the department of guidance itself.

At present, organised departments of guidance or pupil personnel are concerned chiefly with certain crises, certain areas of problems, certain very important adjustments that the ordinary work of the school either does not provide for at all or does so very inadequately.

QUESTIONS FOR EXERCISE

1. Show the relationship of guidance to other educational specialities.
2. Explain the scope of organised guidance in school.
3. Is guidance inherent in entire school? Discuss.

4

BASES, OBJECTIVES AND PRINCIPLES

Guidance is based on psychological, philosophical, sociological and pedagogical bases.

1. Psychological bases of guidance. Psychological researches have established that no two individuals are alike. Individuals differ from one another in physical and mental traits. Individual traits have to be analysed for the purposes of education. One should know what types of differences will lead to what result. A scientific basis for the allocation of courses and occupations has to be evolved. For example, secondary school student demands from his educators more than formal instruction and group evaluation, sympathetic understanding and individual attention due to his peculiar traits manifested in his growth. Guidance helps us to apply new psychological insights into the nature of the individual.

2. Philosophical bases of guidance. The Preamble of the Indian Constitution bears testimony to commitment to the individual. Respect and dignity for each individual is exposed in the 'Fundamental Rights'. Constitution provides each individual the freedom to choose and equal opportunity. Freedom involves awareness of the alternatives provided by education which students learn by operating in a truly democratic atmosphere. It requires an inward state of mind, where individuals refuse to act under fear, pressure or any mechanical habit of mind. Schools create an environment and provide facilities to let the individuals blossom out to be creative. The students should pass out of the school with understanding of life, intellectual and spiritual assurances and understanding of themselves. This is possible only through guidance. All guidance is postulated upon freedom of choice. It is intended to enable an individual to help him understand himself.

3. Sociological bases of guidance. Today, industrialisation has changed the entire social pattern. Various kinds of explosion such as population explosion, knowledge explosion, technological explosion and explosion of rising expectations have given rise to unprecedented problems of adjustments which are grave causes of maladjusment among various sections of society. These problems must be solved satisfactorily. Guidance is needed for bringing about proper adjustment.

A home and community are inadequate to meet the challenges of new times, educational institutions must come forward for equipping the youth properly and adequately. All these factors require expert guidance to help young men in the difficult art of social adjustment.

4. **Pedagogical bases of guidance.** As there are intellectually gifted, educationally backward and students of a wide range of varying abilities, a classroom teacher is perplexed over ways and means of providing equality of opportunity of every pupil.

Compulsory education, increasing enrolments, high percentage of dropouts and failures, the problems of wastage and stagnation, different streams require a well-organised programme of guidance in schools which may enter into all phases of student life.

The significance of guidance services in Indian educational institutions must be appreciated in the context of the enormous challenge of development and employment facing the nation during the present century. Guidance and counselling services are required to fulfil contemporary needs, conditions and opportunities. These can help both pupils and educators in making efficient use of India's evolving educational resources.

FUNDAMENTAL OBJECTIVES OF GUIDANCE

Robert Henry Mathewson has given following four main areas of aid to individuals tendered by guidance :

1. **To appraise and interpret personal characteristics.** Self-understanding; the discovery of aptitudes and capacities, attributes of the self, weak points and strong points ability to evaluate the self in relation of personal and several experiences and to use the self more effectively in everyday living is sought by guidance.

2. **To adjust to school, to teachers and pupils.** Guidance aims at satisfactory adjustment to academic work, getting the most out of studies and school activities, diagnosis of severe learning problems and instructional difficulties and their remedy, placement in suitable educational experiences in accord with individual needs and potentialities, etc.

Guidance helps transfer from one course to another or from one programme to another, depending upon need, performance, or other circumstances It provides social adjustment to teachers and other pupils. It develops personal status in school; growth in self-confidence and acceptance of self.

3. **To provide orientation to educational, vocational and avocational opportunities and requirements.** Guidance seeks selection of appropriate courses in line with individuals needs, interests, abilities and circumstances by making choice of various types of experiences in the whole school curriculum including co-curricular activities. Guidance aims at planning a total educational programme, choice of suitable

and feasible types of advanced training programme — college or otherwise — in line with individual needs and social requirements.

Its objective is selection of tentative broad area of preparation of vocational pursuit, information on occupational opportunities and trends. Aid in obtaining work experiences, exploratory try-outs. Assistance in finding suitable employment. Follow-up after leaving school help in early occupational adjustment and interpretation of social and democratic values and relation of individual to these values.

4. To develop personal potentialities. Guidance aims at growth in intellectual and academic capacities, skills and understandings commensurate with personal potentialities. It seeks development of favourable attitudes and habit-disposition. It aims at understanding and assimilation of ideas and of capacity to undertake consistent action in accord with a socially constructive and individually satisfactory philosophy.

1. Objectives and Functions Relating to Curriculum Guidance

(i) Recognition, prevention and remedying to learning difficulties of pupils.
(ii) Orientation and articulation of the students.
(iii) Orientation and articulation of the teachers.
(iv) Orientation and articulation of parents.
(v) Orientation and comprehensive testing programme.
(vi) Providing for test information and interpretation.
(vii) Participating in curriculum development programme.
(viii) Evaluating curriculum outcomes.
(ix) Helping researchers in curriculum development.

2. Objectives and Functions Relating to Personal Development

(i) Identification of learning difficulties of the learners.
(ii) Prevention of learning difficulties of the learners.
(iii) Remedying the learning difficulties of the learners.
(iv) Referring the learners to appropriate experts if found necessary.
(v) Follow up work.

3. Objectives and Functions Relating to Educational and Vocational Guidance

(i) Counselling with learners for helping them to understand their educational and vocational aspirations in relationship to their aptitudes, abilities and achievements.
(ii) Assisting teachers to understand the use of proper methods of assisting students in making educational and vocational decisions.
(iii) Making parents aware of the need for guidance programmes.

4. Objectives of Educational and Vocational Guidance Programme in India

In a UNESCO publication, *The Forms, Methods and Techniques of Vocational and Educational Guidance,* M.D. Bengales lists the following main objectives of educational and vocational guidance :

1. To reveal potentialities and limitations regarding the self-involvement of the individual and increase his self-awareness.

2. To help him to channel his efforts to reach excellence both in education and career and thereby fulfil his aspirations and obtain satisfaction in life.

3. To help him to obtain the maximum advantage of environmental opportunities to develop a fuller and more balanced personality.

4. To acquaint him with the ever-changing world of work by providing two years of special curriculum referred to as the 'Introduction to the World of Work' in the regular school time-table.

5. To infuse in him a forward-looking attitude with a strong motive to pursue his plan of action till success is achieved.

6. To bring in desirable changes in curricular and extra-curricular activities to improve educational standards.

7. To guide the headmaster in promotion and selection of staff members.

The educational and vocational guidance programmes are planned to cover the developmental as well as the adjusting aspects of the individual and to form an integral part of general education.

PRINCIPLES OF GUIDANCE

1. **A slow process.** As it requires a considerable time to make suitable adjustments, the counsellor or the guidance worker needs time to understand the counselee who has a complex personality and who may be confronted with an intense problem.

2. **A continuous process.** Individuals are beset with problems throughout their lives. Guidance is a continuous process. World is changing fast, new and altogether new problems come to the forefront and an individual requires guidance for the solution of these problems. However, as the individual gains maturity, he requires less assistance from his counsellor.

3. **Development of the insight of an individual.** The counsellor should help the individual so that the latter may gains his own insights, accepts responsibility, develops the feeling of self-confidence and ultimately makes his own decisions.

4. **To consider most individuals as average normal persons.** The counsellor is not interested in serving individuals who are normal. The services of the guidance workers are available to all. The counsellor would do well to refer cases of abnormal nature, *i.e.,* extremely slow

learners, emotionally unstable, etc., to child guidance clinics where the services of appropriate specialists are available.

5. Problems of guidance arise out of situations. As the present problems have their roots in the past, the guidance worker is required to go into the past history of an individual who is in need of assistance. The guidance-worker must be aware of the difference between symptoms and causes. For example, if there is a child who is known as a "bully", the symptoms may be summed up as over-aggressiveness, but the underlying cause may be discovered in the fact that child in the past has developed the feeling that he was a rejected child and had no place in the family or school and he wanted recognition and acceptance. Thus, 'why', 'how' and 'when' should be discovered when a problem arises.

6. Guidance problems are interrelated. The personality of an individual is a complex and integrated whole. He is not a disembodied mind, nor is he a body without a mind, he is a psychological organism in constant interaction with a complex array of environmental forces. He responds to his environment as a 'whole being'. Hence, his educational, vocational and personal problems are interrelated.

7. Based on individual differences. As the individuals differ in native capacity, ability and interest, guidance is required for every one separately.

8. Based on planning. Adequate time is required for planning guidance activities during and after school hours.

9. Based on a rigid code of ethics. It needs as that every worker who has access to the confidence of the student should establish and follow a rigid code of ethics.

10. Related to the total development of the student. As guidance is related to the total development, all round harmonious development is the basic aim of guidance.

11. Guidance services must be an integral part of the school organisation. These should not be treated as an isolated work to be left to the counsellor alone. All or most of the members of the staff should take a keen interest and active part in assisting students to solve their problems. Guidance work should be closely integrated with the work done by other agencies engaged in child development work.

12. Guidance and instructional activities are complementary. These activities are interdependent and reciprocal.

13. It is an organised service. Guidance is not an incidental activity of the school. It is a service which is borad-based and has a definite purpose.

14. It is both a specialised and a generalised service. Everyone in the educative process — the teacher, the parent and the counsellor — has an important role to play. For its proper functioning guidance services require the help of a specially trained staff. These specialised personal assisting in student guidance work would include the school counsellor, school psychologist, school social worker, child welfare worker, school physician, school psychiatrist, curriculum expert, placement worker, co-ordinator of school activities.

15. It is meant for all. A guidance programme is not meant only for those who seek it. It must reach the entire student community without their asking for it.

16. It is based on educational objectives. The guidance programme must be based on the educational objectives which in their turn reflect the aim and purpose of a society.

17. Its tools should be as perfect as possible. Proper tools and guidance facilities are essential for proper guidance service.

18. It is a specialised service. A guidance programme needs the services of a qualified and trained counsellor.

19. Flexibility. In terms of educational and community needs a guidance programme is flexible.

20. Its special cases are referred to experts. Assistance and guidance of experts is obtained when there are special cases needing guidance and counselling.

21. In it standards of ethics are observed. Secrecy should be observed in using personal information and records in counselling.

22. Objective data are used in it. Scientific attitude is observed in obtaining and using data.

23. Its work is separated from routine clerical and administrative work. The counsellor should not be given duties of purely clerical and administrative nature of work.

24. Its work is subject to periodicals evaluation. Periodical appraisal is very essential for effective and improved guidance and counselling programme.

Guidance helps us to solve manifold problems concerning :

(i) Physical health, (ii) Home problems, (iii) Problems arising out of leisure, (iv) Personality problems, (v) School or educational problems, (vi) Vocational problems, (vii) Religious and moral problems, (viii) Democratic and political problems, (ix) Marital and sexual problems and (x) Old age problems.

1. Appraisal. It is done by means of
   (i) Tests and rating scales.
   (ii) Parent's ratings.
   (iii) Diagnostic records.
   (iv) Individual inventories.
   (v) Sociometric analyses.
   (vi) Observations.
   (vii) Anecdotes.

- (viii) Educational clinics.
- (ix) Case studies.
- (x) Cumulative records.

2. Adjustment. It is done by means of
    - (i) Change in the environment through
        - (a) Socialised curriculum.
        - (b) Co-curricular activities.
        - (c) Physical surroundings.
        - (d) Community resources.
        - (e) Educational and vocational opportunities.
        - (f) Group contacts.
    - (ii) Changes in the individual through
        - (a) Interviews.
        - (b) Operations.
        - (c) Developmental exercises.
        - (d) Instruction.
        - (e) Guidance.
        - (f) Group process.

According to Crow and Crow, "Guidance is not direction. It is not making decisions for the other individual. It is assistance made available by competent counsellors to an individual of any stage to help him direct his own life, develop his own point of view, make his own decisions and carry his own burdens." The key-note of guidance is to provide opportunity for realisation and self-direction. According to Jones, "The focus of guidance is the individual not his problem, its purpose is to promote the growth of the individual in self-direction."

PERSPECTIVES OF GUIDANCE

1. Narrow perspective. According to a narrow view guidance is a kind of specialised service intended to help an individual is solving problems of crucial nature confronting him in the course of his life. Under narrow concept help is rendered by specialised guidance workers at "problem and choice-points." In the school guidance is the responsibility of the school counsellor, who is concerned with helping the child in choosing a course of study (educational guidance), choosing a career (vocational guidance), and solving certain problems related to personal (emotional) and social adjustment (personal guidance). Counsellors study the characteristics of the child and the characteristics of the job or a course of study in order to match one against the other and they arrive at a decision as to which one to use. Various kinds of tests and inventories are used.

Limitations of Narrow Perspective

(1) It makes guidance as an ancillary service of the school.

(2) Such guidance is restricted to problem students alone.

(3) It puts too much emphasis on the role of the counsellor in the guidance process.

(4) It makes guidance procedures very mechanical.

2. Broader perspective. According to the broader view of guidance, it may be deemed as any kind of assistance rendered to the child which helps him in his best development — educational, vocational personal, social, moral, physical, etc. In this broader view the parent, the teacher, the school counsellor — all become real guidance workers. In this perspective, "Guidance distributes responsibilities among teachers, counsellors, specialists, pupils and parents and which encourages close working relationships among them."

It is an attitude of mind, a philosophy which pervades the whole school system and every activity. Help of guidance in solving problems becomes only one specific activity in the whole process. This basic approach is developmental rather than remedial.

GUIDANCE *vs.* SELECTION

Explaining the relation of vocational guidance and selection Dr. Milton L. Blum and Dr. Benjamin Bolinsky of USA said, "Vocational selection is the process whereby applicants for positions become employees." In such a situation, there is a job available and there are many people seeking it. The number of people who want the job varies with economic conditions and the resulting labour supply. Guidance and selection differ as follows :

1. Frame of reference. The frame of reference in vocational selection is the opposite of that in vocational guidance. In selection these is one job and many people while in guidance there is one individual and many potential jobs.

2. Assumptions. In guidance it is assumed that the client is seeking help. Hence he is likely to be more honest in his statement to a counsellor. In selection the applicant wants and needs the job. He will try to "beat" the personnel department by elaboration.

3. Pressure. In selection the personnel doing the hiring is under pressure to make a choice that would be best for the company. In guidance the counsellor always remembers that he is dealing with the individual.

4. Obligation. In selection it is assumed that when the decision is made not to hire an applicant the company has no further obligation to the individual. In guidance the client's social and economic well-being are in the hands of the counsellor.

5. Tools. The counsellor should understand the theory and application of the counselling interview, psychological tests, occupational information and so on. In selection there are aids, such as interview, the application blank, letters of recommendation, checking claims of the applicant and psychological testing, etc.

6. Area. Guidance and selection operate independently.

Modern Trends in Guidance

1. Art and Science. It is both as an art as well as a science.

2 Worker. The guidance worker is not a mere technician using tests and other tools but is a real guide to the pupils.

3. Nature. The guidance work involves an inter-disciplinary approach. A guidance worker makes use of various disciplines.

4. Area. Guidance services are expanding to reach every pupil. The focus of guidance is being extended to the culturally and economically backward pupils.

5. Scope. The scope of guidance is being extended to cover all the aspects relating to the harmonious development of the pupils.

6. Tools. Guidance worker using a variety of tools in their programmes.

7. Training. Guidance work needs trained counsellors.

8 Recognition. There is a growing recognition of the social implications of guidance programme.

9. Cooperation. Guidance is emerging as a cooperative venture.

QUESTIONS FOR EXERCISE

1. Give psychological and practical justification for the provision of guidance and counselling in schools.
2. Guidance forms an integral part of a Teacher Education Programme. Discuss.
3. Explain the psychological, philosophical, sociological and psychological bases of guidance.
4. Discuss the fundamental purposes and principles of guidance programme.
5. Explain the nature of guidance. Describe the benefits of guidance programme.
6. "Guidance is an attitude of mind and philosophy which pervades the entire school system." Discuss in the light of the relationship of guidance with education.

5

Areas of Guidance

Guidance is the assistance given to individuals in making intelligent choices and adjustments. It is based on the democratic principle that it is the duty and the right of every individual to choose his own way in life insofar as his choice does not interfere with the rights of others. The ability to make such choices is not innate but, like other abilities, must be developed. One of the functions of education is to provide opportunities for the development of such abilities. Guidance is an integral part of education and is centred directly upon this function. Guidance does not make choices for individuals; it helps them make their own choices in such a way as to promote or stimulate the gradual development of the ability to make decisions independently without assistance from others.

In its beginnings guidance was centered on problems related to vocations. It was largely concerned with getting jobs for young people. One of the reasons for this was to reduce juvenile delinquency. Teen-age boys and girls, many of them not in school, had nothing to do; they had time on their hands. Such a situation breeds delinquency.

Even in its beginning, however, the purpose of guidance was more than just finding jobs for youth. Much attention was given to a "wise" choice, that is, one that was suited to the abilities and needs of the individual. Although the vocational aspect has always been stressed, guidance has gone far beyond this; it is now concerned with the entire individual, in all aspects.

GUIDANCE IN EDUCATION

As educational problems head the list of student problems, education is an important guidance area. Guidance in education includes curricula offered by colleges and universities. Vocations in many form. Competitive examinations for entry into institutions and services, etc. Expert help is required by the students in making wise choices to be successful in competitive examinations. Expert assistance is required for enabling the students to make proper adjustment to general academic life at college or university and to realise maximum intellectual, emotional and physical development. Guidance in education may be categorised in the following two classes :

1. *Pre-admission guidance* : It is imparted to help the students make educational plans consistent with their abilities, interests and goals and to select appropriate courses and co-curricular activities to enable them to join careers of their choice.
2. *Post-admission guidance* : (i) It is imparted to enable the students to succeed in their educational plans, for developing good study habits, preparing for examinations properly and facing examinations with confidence.
   (ii) The students must be helped to explore educational possibilities in higher educational institutions in India and abroad. They should be guided in selecting subjects for specialisation and additional course to studies. They should be made familiar with various fellowships, scholarships, competitive examination, etc.
   (iii) Special guidance is needed at crisis points of difficulty in following certain subjects; lacking concentration; getting poor grades; indecisiveness about a change of subject, etc. He has to be guided as to how he could overcome these difficulties and what special efforts he has to make in that direction.
   (iv) The students from backward classes need more guidance so that they progress smoothly. Special efforts are needed to help "first generation learners" whose parents may never have gone to college or university. Because of deficiencies in their own home-background and the inability of their parents to give them much guidance to do well in college and university. These students may have many special academic problems.
   (v) Guidance is required to help the student in rejecting the attitude of blind acceptance of facts; to develop an attitude of interrogation, dependence on evidence, and reasonable explanation of facts. Efforts should be made to ensure that his intellectual pursuits and interests become focalized, few but stable.

GUIDANCE IN VOCATION

1. All persons are not suitable for all vocations. Every vocation requires certain educational and professional background and preparation. In order to guide the students for a right choice of a vocation arrangement has to be made to assist them to have a reasonable estimate of their abilities and limitations, and strike a balance between their aspirations and those of their parents, between their interests and the availability of opportunities. They should be assisted in making decisions and in planning a future and building a career. They should be helped in developing an integrated and adequate picture of themselves and of their role in the world of work.

2. Today, occupational world is changing very fast. New occupational outlets undreamt of before are emerging. It, therefore, should be helped to acquire clearer perspective of the changes that are taking place in the job world.

3. Thus, guidance for vocations needs to be given to the students for efficient use of manpower and greater economy in the execution of work in industry, business and government offices, etc. This guidance should help the students to be able to respond to their changing needs as they grow more mature and as the circumstances and experiences of life pose unpredictable problems, requiring new information, fresh thinking, revised plans, compromise, and for the acceptance of socio-economic conditions and personal limitations that cannot be changed.

Aims and Objectives of Vocational Guidance

As the primary aim of vocational guidance is the promotion of *personal satisfaction with life as a whole,* the objective of vocational guidance consists of the following factors :

1. *Discovery* : Enabling the students to discover about themselves — their abilities, interest, needs, ambitions, limitations and their causes.
2. *Information* : Providing them information about their environment, the advantages and disadvantages of different occupations and educational courses, the qualifications necessary for entry into them, and the range of opportunities available to them.
3. *Frame of Reference* : Providing them with a frame of reference to see themselves in relation to educational and vocational opportunities; to orient them to the helping agencies available to them, and to teach them about future decision-making points in their careers.
4. *Disabuse* : Disabusing the minds of students of any romantic of vague notions about certain jobs.
5. *Counselling* : Providing counselling in order to promote self-understanding and to develop educational and occupational plans.
6. *Placement Service* : Providing placement service to help them to implement those plans.
7. *Follow-up Service* : Providing a follow-up service to help them, if necessary, when faced with future decision-making situations.

GUIDANCE IN AVOCATION

Woodrow Wilson has rightly said, "The real intellectual life of a body of undergraduates, if there be any, manifests itself, not in the classroom, but in what they do and talk of, and set before themselves, as their favourite objects between classes and lectures." Thus, the responsibility of any college or university does not end with covering the syllabus by the teacher's performance. We must remember that the student spends only 5 or 6 hours of a 24 hour day in classes. Besides, class-room teaching ties the area of student services — the intellectual efforts outside of class, physical activities, social interaction, emotional experiences, cultural programmes, etc. Teachers must help the students plan for them and actively participate in them.

Thus, avocational pursuits in which the students engage themselves are no less important in giving a direction to their lives. This is particularly so because college and university students get so many holidays — spring break, autumn break, long summer vacations, and other scheduled and unscheduled holidays. Students in Humanities subjects particularly have much spare time. To use vacant hours profitably, a vocational needs of the students should be met before they grow to troublesome proportion leading to confusion, doubt, anxiety, aimlessness, exploitation by others, indulging in destructive acts or in unwholesome activities. The students should be properly guided for effective participation in varied types of avocational pursuits so that they may shape their interpersonal behaviour in desirable direction and widen their outlook.

In the present day educational institutions hardly 10 per cent students take active part in co-curricular activities at a superficial level. Ninety per cent students are onlookers. The counselling officer can ensure larger participation through sustained encouragement, personnel systematic coaching and training arrangements. There should be guidance and counselling arrangement for guiding the students to take part in team games, intellectual contests, productive hobbies and organisation of small interest groups having healthy aims, etc.

GUIDANCE IN SOCIAL RELATIONSHIPS

Social relationships constitute a problems area for most of the students. They come from a school serving particular linguistic or socio-economic group. Friendships had been formed casually and spontaneously. In a city college/university, student body is heterogeneous drawn from many linguistic and socio-economic group consisting of self-conscious adolescents who tend to formalise their relationship. They are in need of a structured situation within which to socialise, be it the classroom or the college gymkhana, an extra-curricular interest or a class picnic. Even after an entire term at college or university some shy students find themselves friendless. Others do not know where to seek a friend or develop a relationship with persons who have nothing in common. Others who want to be effective as individuals in their groups have to work with people they dislike. Thus, students require guidance to live as socially well-adjusted individuals. They should be helped in making friends, improving their style of conversation and to know how to become leaders in their own groups. They may be guided in developing constructive expression of their emotions and an objective interpretation of situations. They may be taught to diminish their excitability to emotional stimulations and face conflicts. They should be helped in acquiring the feeling of security and being accepted by the group; in developing a social poise; in becoming tolerant towards the behaviour of others; in achieving individuality and freedom from the slavish imitation of the adults or 'heroes'.

GUIDANCE IN PROMOTION OF HEALTH

Society has a special stake in the health and physical well-being of the college and university students in whom it has to invest large resources and to whom it looks for the advancement of national interest. Guidance aims at the total health of the student. Both the preventive and restorative measures are needed to ensure the achievement of this objective.

Health Programme

The basic responsibility for students health programme rests with the Health Officer in-charge of student Health Centre. He should set a climate of acceptance for student problems particularly in the case of early detection of disorders, as students may be afraid to reveal symptoms like those of venereal diseases, tuberculosis, etc.

It is desirable to have a medical check up of all the students in the beginning of the academic session whose reports may be sent to the parents or guardians asking for a written report of the action taken by them.

Measure to promote Preventive and Environmental Health

1. **Supervision.** Supervision of college/university facilities such as hostels and canteens to see that healthful conditions are maintained.

2. **Immunisation.** Specific protection through immunisation against diseases such as smallpox, typhoid, cholera, etc. may be enforced.

3. **Health education.** This is given through formal classes and informal propaganda.

Measures of Diagnosis and Treatment

Following measures may be taken for early diagnosis and treatment of illness :

(i) An adequate physical examination of every student upon entrance to the college or university;

(ii) Follow-up treatment of detected disorders;

(iv) Reference of students to other medical resources when necessary, and

(vii) Maintenance of confidential files and health records to keep track of mind and body's harmonious functioning.

Efforts should be made for rehabilitation of disabled students in collaboration with psychologists, educators and social workers. Remedial measures have to be taken in case of students suffering from speech and hearing defects.

GUIDANCE IN MORAL NEEDS

At home, college/university or in their peer groups students face so many awkward situations. They tell lies; try to dodge and indulge in so many undesirable practices. Guidance about moral needs to be provided to such students to keep them on the track and lead noble lives.

GUIDANCE IN PERSONAL PROBLEMS

Students face many personal problems related to themselves, their parents and family, their friends and teachers, their educational achievement and social adjustment. They often have memories related to home or family creating feelings of disappointment in them. If their parents are expecting too much of them it leaves them with a feeling of incompetence and insecurity as they fail to live up to their expectations. Parents who nag their children create an unfavourable atmosphere for studies at home. At times progress in study is hampered due to strained and unhappy home relationships. Jealousy among siblings, domination of elders, maltreatment of children, lack of a sense of being wanted, lack of a sense of belongingness — all these disturb the mental equilibrium of the young students resulting in low achievement. Expert guidance must be provided to these students to face the situations boldly and with confidence to solve their personal problems.

1. At times students find it difficult to understand the materials of the lectures. They may find the lectures lousy and the educational institution a dump. They may not be liking the teacher and his/her methods of teaching thus landing in poor achievement. Guidance should be provided to such students to enable them to adjust to the situation which they cannot change.

2. Some students are obsessed with such problems as lack of friends; loneliness; sense of inadequacy; inferiority chaos and despair. They need counsel to overcome their difficulties.

3. At times students see a danger to their self-concept. Such students needs to be given guidance to emerge successful out of this crisis of identity, by perceiving their self more accurately with all its assets and liabilities and identification of this self with the more achievable goals.

4. Students at times find it difficult to concentrate learning and recall. They feel tense, anxious and depressed. To get relief from all these, they need guidance.

5. Some students also find it difficult to adjust to heterosexual relations. They are not well-equipped with knowledge about sex. Lack

of proper sex knowledge creates social and emotional conflicts particularly in co-educational college and universities. As most of the students come from unisex schools and colleges, they feel utterly confused in meeting the members of the opposite sex. Much effort is required in making these adolescents understand the normal interaction with the opposite sex and casual acceptance of the sexual growth. These guidance needs to be given to the students in a scientific manner, rather than treat it as a taboo to be secretively learnt from undesirable places. As the students enter colleges and universities at an age when biological sex impulses are new and strong while the consummation of sex has to be delayed. Sex guidance has to be given to the students regarding masturbation, nocturnal emissions, healthy outlets of sex urges, etc.

6. Students who are hard-pressed for finances need guidance regarding the freeship fee concessions, scholarships, stipends, etc. available in the institution or offered by other welfare agencies and how and when to apply. Financial assistance has to be ensured so that no meritorious student is denied education for lack of financial assistance.

7. Some students are harried with the problem of accommodation, particularly in big universities and professional institutions. In most educational institutions, the resident students form only 30 per cent or less of the students body, while 70 per cent of the students are faced with problems of both boarding and lodging. These off-campus-dwellers particularly foreign students should be assisted in obtaining proper accommodation and food services so that the search for these necessities does not interfere with the learning process. The Dean of Students Welfare with his panel of advisers can study the possibilities of securing 'healthy' accommodation with landlords of standing and good reputation in the location around the college or university. Many landlords are willing to accommodate students in spare rooms and guest houses at comparatively cheaper rates provided these students are recommended by the college or university authorities. The landlords may be requested to keep a protective eye on the students staying in the house and to contact the authorities if they need help. Thus, guidance may help the students in avoiding the spending of disproportionate amount of time seeking adequate cheap accommodation.

GUIDANCE IN PROBLEMS OF MARRIAGE

Marital guidance needs to be provided in institutions of higher learning to students for the right choice of life partner or if he/she is married but his/her married life is unhappy.

QUESTIONS FOR EXERCISE

1. Explain various areas of guidance.
2. Describe the area of guidance in education and vocation.

6

Self Guidance

Scientific observation of most forms of life and objects is restricted to the external or objective frame of reference. Because of their ability to report hopes, fears, dreams, and ambitions, only human beings seek to understand the behaviour of the individual from their own point of view. This is the phenomenological approach which stresses that all behaviour, without exception, is completely determined by, and pertinent to, the individual's own field of experience.

A counsellor's concerted attempts to understand the student may be frustrated if his observations are not reconciled with the view that the student holds of himself. Only through drawing out this self-understanding can the power and insight that comes from within the individual be released to mobilise his talents and integrate the assistance which the counsellor may wish to offer.

SYNONYMOUS TERMS

Several terms are virtually synonymous with self-understanding. Among them are "self-image," the "ego," "self-concept," and "phenomenal self." The concept of self-understanding has gained prominence through the theoretical statements and research of Combs and Snygg, Rogers, Jourard, and Super, among others. It is an interesting and stimulating approach to guidance. It provides a dynamic centre around which to group the factors related to one's individual and group behaviour. It involves bringing together into consciousness the characteristics, abilities, aptitudes, potentialities, and ideals of the individual and organises them in such a way that he understands both the ever-changing nature of contemporary society and the personal flexibility he must exhibit if he is to adapt to its demands.

The individual is at the centre of his phenomenological world. We can never completely understand him since we seldom have access to his private world. One's self-concept is the resultant force from the collision of his internal and external worlds. An indication of sound mental health is the ability to value both worlds and not be forced to deny or distort that which is inconsistent with either world. To understand human behaviour we need to assume that all of us have drives to actualise, maintain, and enhance ourselves. Our actions and words, therefore, constitute an attempt to satisfy our needs in the world as we perceive it. Insight into an individual's self-concept frequently is invaluable in understanding his behaviour.

Counsellors quite justifiably direct much attention toward assisting the individual to understand himself. A well-formulated self-concept takes into account the realities of the complex world in which he lives, assists the individual to feel secure within his environment, accurately assesses his areas of personal strength and weakness, and makes logical decisions based upon this assessment. In summary, if the individual is to be assisted in understanding himself, the counsellor must strive to see the world through his eyes.

THE NATURE OF THE SELF

Moustakos suggests fourteen principles which summarise the basic approach and recognition of the self in true experience and the creation of human understanding :

"1. The individual knows himself better than anyone else.
2. Only the individual himself can develop his potentialities.
3. The individual's perception of his own feelings, attitudes, and ideas is more valid than any outside diagnosis can be.
4. Behaviour can best be understood from the individual's own point of view.
5. The individual responds in such ways as to be consistent with himself.
6. The individual's perception of himself determines how he will behave.
7. Objects have no meaning in themselves. Individuals give meanings and reality to them. These meanings reflect the individual's background.
8. Every individual is logical in the context of his own personal experience. His point of view may seem illogical to others when he is not understood.
9. As long as the individual accepts himself, he will continue to grow and develop his potentialities. When he does not accept himself, much of his energies will be used to defend rather than explore and to actualise himself.
10. Every individual wants to grow toward self-fulfillment. These growth strivings are present at all times.
11. An individual learns significantly only those things which *are* involved in the maintenance of *self*. No one can force the individual to permanent or creative learning. He will learn only if he wills to. Any other type of learning is temporary and inconsistent with the self and will disappear as soon as threat is removed.

12. Concepts, ideas, symbols, and events can be denied or distorted, but experience is experienced in the unique reality of the individual person and cannot be untrue to itself. If it threatens the maintenance or enhancement of self, the experience will be of little relevance or consequence to the individual though it may temporarily stifle further growth.
13. We cannot teach another person directly, and we cannot facilitate real learning in the sense of making it easier. We can make learning for another person possible by providing information, the setting, atmosphere, materials, resources, and *by being* there. The learning process itself is a unique individualistic experience. It may be a difficult experience for the individual person even if it has significance for the enhancement of self.
14. Under threat the self is less open to spontaneous expression; that is, is more passive and controlled. When free from threat, the self is more open, that is, free to be and to strive for actualisation."[1]

As described by Moustakos, the self cries for creative expression. Moustakos urges those who would enhance expression of the self in educational settings to maximise the value given individual uniqueness, minimise the threat to the self of the learner, and free him to explore as directed by his own interests and potentialities. This is quite in keeping with the guidance point of view. Because of this, it is especially helpful for those interested in becoming counsellors to be aware of the process by which the image one has of himself is developed and some of the characteristics of the unified self-concept and its component parts.

DEVELOPMENT OF THE SELF-CONCEPT

The ability to understand oneself is an unfolding process that continues throughout life and is influenced greatly by social interaction. Developmental tasks can be noted at each level that assist one in this process. During infancy the child quickly learns to distinguish his mother from other women. In early childhood he becomes aware of some of his physical abilities and limitations which are amplified and strengthened by new learnings. Pre-adolescence is a time when strong sex identity is developed. Family influence weakens at this stage and social acceptability becomes an important and more vital aspect of the self. With added learning the self begins to become more unified, his personal identity is clarified, and his social role begins to take shape. The new identity that emerges during this period is the product of the

1. Clark E. Moustakos, "True Experience and the Self," in Clark E. Moustakos (ed.), *The Self*, Harper & Row Publishers, Incorporated, New York, 1956, pp. 9-11.

conflicting pulls that the cohesive family unit and tangential peer demands produce.

Consciousness of oneself in some cases emerges suddenly, almost without warning. A boy walking to school suddenly realises, "I am myself; I am nobody else." A mother of three children exclaims, "All these years I just did what was expected. I never thought of *me*. At thirty-six I found myself." It is a staggering experience and one that is likely to throw the individual off balance for a time. To some it is electrifying and deeply satisfying; to others it is depressing, for it signifies that a person stands alone in the world.

The greatest single determinant of one's self-concept is his family. Through interaction with this primary reference group the individual develops early experiences of adequacy, acceptance, identification, and expectancies of the society into which he is increasingly moving.

From the first days of life the child begins to develop a sense of whether he is being loved, rejected, or rebuffed. This in turn affects his perception of whether he is an adequate or inadequate individual. The degree to which he feels adequate forms the basis upon which he is able to accept or reject others. Individuals who have no doubt about their adequacy possess the capacity for being quite accepting of others.

Earliest identification of the child is with the family. Progressively, identification moves from the immediate family across the spectrum toward the world of adult life. Relatives, neighbours, and classmates become integrated within the self as the individual develops. The family is reflective of the greater culture of which he is to become a part. It is from the family that the child differentiates goals, values, techniques, and ways of behaving acceptable to society. These, then, lead to the values and directions that he will consider as he makes decisions in the future.

CHARACTERISTICS OF SELF-UNDERSTANDING

An individual has access to much more than can be physically observed. The understanding which he develops of himself is guided by four characteristics :

1. The self-concept is always changing. Admittedly, this means that a student has great difficulty in getting a clear grasp of who he is. It is this fluidity, however, which makes change in behaviour possible. Were an individual's self-concept never to change, he would be unable to adjust to the changing environment that surrounds him. Change may be virtually instantaneous. The older child understands that he is uncertain and relatively incapable of competing with his mother in a household task. When mother leaves and the comparison shifts to younger brother, however, the self takes on a new perspective.

2. The self-concept has a basic stability. Despite the momentary manifestations of change, a deeper understanding of self is carried across events. It is this stability which carries the confident man through defeat after defeat and causes the sudden victor to accept triumph with caution.

3. The self-concept is influenced by the intensity with which one experiences aspects of his environment. That is, one's needs vary from moment to moment. His level of awareness, ranging from very vague to sharp, is dependent upon the particular need which he is currently experiencing. One may enter a room many times throughout the day and night. His level of awareness of lamps within the room will be directly related to the need he experiences for lamps. During daylight hours they may go unnoticed. In darkness they become the object of his immediate search as he enters the room.

4. The self-concept has direction. At any given moment the overt behaviour may seem random, but the self-concept is organised, has purpose, and seeks to satisfy its need in a meaningful fashion. Each of us has experienced the embarrassment of laughing or appearing needlessly gay on the most sombre of occasions. This incongruous behaviour can only be explained by the need within the self to give expression to something other than that toward which primary attention appeared focused.

SELF IMAGE

Thus, so far we have talked of the self-concept as a unified whole. To look at this phenomenon more closely it is useful to think of it as an image rather than a concept. A number of principles have been advanced by Anderson[2] which describe the image's origin, parts, and persistence. These are presented with some interpretive comments for the counsellor :

1. Each person has an image or perception of himself that is unique from the perception he holds of others. Through life's experiences he has developed an identity that is his own. He understands, and usually accepts, differences between himself and others. This perception is developed early in life and maintained vigorously despite environmental influences.

2. This image can be divided into two parts. Each person has a physical image and psychological image. The individual is able to carefully discern the difference between them. He may be the shortest boy in the class, fully realise this, and accept it as nothing more than fact. This shortness, on the other hand, may distress his psychological image of himself. He may ascribe much more than size to the fact that he is the shortest boy.

3. Neither of these images is complete and neither is more than roughly accurate. Each day's experiences in some way shape the self-

2. Camilla M. Anderson, "The Self-image : A Theory of the Dynamics of Behavior," *Mental Hygiene,* Vol. 36, pp. 227-244, 1952.

image of the individual. When events and experiences are unable to change self-perception, the individual forces his environment to adjust to him rather than he to his environment. The data of perception, being based upon experience and impression, is sometimes erroneous. A person's insistence that she is plain and untalented may be grounded in parental comments made when she was young, and no amount of contrary evidence can disabuse her of these beliefs.

4. Both the physical and the psychological image comprise many factors, each of which is subconsciously assigned a value. Just as the heart is more highly prized than the hand, so each factor is given a value which is known only to the self. At times we can observe indications of the value assigned, but the accuracy of our perceptions is not to be trusted. Was "I'd rather be right than President" any indicator of the value assigned? How about, "I may have received a D, but I earned it honestly"?

5. The psychological self-image is formed early in life as a result of a succession of experiences that the child has had with his environment. The adjustments made by the infant to survive the interpersonal experiences he confronts leave him with both an image and a set of defense mechanisms upon which he may call. These mechanisms for the most part remain an integral part of him for the remainder of his life.

6. In the development of the self-image, the first year of life is the most important. Each year thereafter is of less importance until the image is essentially completed before adolescence. The prime reason that the self-image develops so rapidly during this period is that the child's helplessness and dependency are greatest at this time. The greater the sense of helplessness, the more defensive the individual becomes in order to ensure survival.

7. The structure of the self-image determines the day-by-day and the moment-by-moment behaviour of the individual. Decisions and reactions are determined, not by what one is, but by what one believes he is and that which will tend to maintain the image intact. The child whose experience has taught him that he is incompetent will tend to live his life and make his most minute decisions in order to maintain that image. If he has come to believe "I am confident," all energies will be devoted to perpetuate this life pattern.

Then the self-concept can be described as having basic characteristics. Further, it can be seen as having parts which, in turn, are composed of weighted factors. The self-concept is formulated early in life, and its stability, while capable of change, sustains it largely intact.

THE SELF-CONCEPT AND DECISION MAKING

As the individual develops, he faces an increasing array of decisions. One of the purposes of guidance is to make him aware of the decision-making process and how he might use his talents and interests to his best advantage.

Students are frequently unable to tap the sources of self-understanding and do not make appropriate use of that part of them to which they alone have access. Without the employment of this self-understanding, decisions will be based upon external knowledge alone. The self and the individual's uniqueness will be denied consideration.

From the preceding section we learned that the individual knows himself better than anyone else and he alone can develop his potentialities. The counsellor's approach, therefore, is to enlist cooperation and encourage the mobilisation of talents within the student rather than to suggest that he model his decisions after those of his peers or external indicators alone. The counsellor's efforts are directed at facilitating self-awareness and assisting the student to draw fully upon the knowledge and powers to which only he has access. These, then, can be discussed in the light of environmental conditions and influences in order that decisions reflect awareness of self and surroundings.

INFORMATION AND THE INDIVIDUAL

Controversy has surrounded the collection and use of information for decades. The argument is advanced frequently that some forms of standardised test results, when shared openly with the student, may do more to debilitate than motivate him because of misunderstanding that may never be clarified. Intelligence test scores in the hands of the inept might well have this result.

Information collected to assist the student in better self-understanding frequently is misused, also. Although the expressed purpose in soliciting this information is to increase the individual's awareness, the teacher or counsellor may feel unqualified to use it fully, may be threatened by the student's response, or may feel that the student can be helped in other ways and not choose to share an interpretation with the individual. The student's continued willingness to reveal himself is directly dependent upon his having access to the significance of what he reported.

A basic misunderstanding may lie in the way information is used. A literal interpretation is often meaningless to the student. Only when integrated with existing self-understanding will it take on meaning. The counsellor or teacher, then, can suggest a literal meaning and encourage the student to consider its significance for him. As each part is interpreted, discussed, and integrated, the individual gains new insight and extends his self-understanding.

A student who is interested in considering his work future, for example, might take an interest inventory. The results may indicate preference toward work that is mechanical, yet involves meeting people.

A dentist, TV home repairman, and cab driver are possibilities that immediately might occur to the counsellor. But what are the student's interests and ambitions? What can he identify that he would and would not like to do each day? Does he like a regular pattern of living or variety? Would he like to work inside or outside, in one location or travel? The process of pulling out perceptions such as these, examining his values, and assigning priorities to each is a necessary antecedent to considering any specific job alternatives. With increased self-understanding he can then better integrate the specific results of the interest inventory.

MEASUREMENT OF SELF-UNDERSTANDING

Counsellors are concerned with knowing something of the student's level of self-understanding for two reasons. First, as the student allows the counsellor to view the world through his eyes, the counsellor is able to adjust his own perceptions and be better able to assist the individual in changing or learning behaviour. Second, and more important, a knowledge of the student's self-understanding will allow the counsellor to assist the individual in knowing whether his perceptions of how he is viewed by others are accurate.

Teachers also may assist students in gaining self-understanding. Through a number of means students can reveal something of their thoughts, dreams, fears, and desires. A teacher may assist the student to place these in perspective and to learn from the process of revealing himself. Some of the more promising means of assisting students in this process are described briefly :

1. Autobiography. The autobiography has been mentioned previously as a device for developing realistic self-pictures, but it has further usefulness in that it causes one to be introspective and come to better self-understanding through attempts to communicate something of one's experiences and feelings. Through these life stories the student may relate how he sees himself and how the world looks to him. This instrument, which is discussed at greater length in Chapter 5, has great utility because it can be adapted for nearly any grade level and can be as brief or detailed, as general or specific as seems appropriate. It also lends itself readily to the regular work of the classroom. A piece of autobiographical writing can be discussed by the teacher or counsellor with the student. From this material both may assess the extent of the understanding which the student has of himself.

2. Creative writing. A parallel activity is to ask the student to write about a given topic and draw upon his fantasy life. A title or opening paragraph may be used to lend direction, and he is then asked to express himself as openly as he can. "A Dream I Wish Would Come True" might be used. From the writing, teacher and student can have a helpful interchange that may place many of the student's hopes or fears in perspective.

3. Interview. Perhaps the most useful means of assisting the individual to disclose something of himself is through the interview. Through the establishment of a "safe," non-threatening situation, the student can be helped to share some of his innermost thoughts with the counsellor. As these thoughts are sifted and clarified, greater insight frequently takes place on the part of the individual. The counsellor is able to interpret what the student is thinking in terms of normal behaviour. That which seemed so burdensome may appear quite manageable after inspection. Some minor concerns, on the other hand, may seem to need greater attention as the result of meditating upon them.

4. Group interaction. Some people labour under the delusion that they alone are bothered by a particular feeling, guilt, or problem. Persuasion by a counsellor is not sufficient to convince them that others share their dilemma. A frank exploration of these concerns in a group counselling situation, however, might well convince them that others feel exactly as they do. Varying forms of group interaction may be organised by counsellors to meet this purpose. Chapter 10 discusses this possibility in greater detail.

5. Puppet show. Younger students are less able to respond to written material, but may gain considerable insight through use of a puppet show. The show, which can be developed by the teacher, is centered on a theme that uses students, incidents, and concerns that are closely associated with the audience. At critical moments the students are asked by the puppeteer to suggest what will happen next. An ingenious puppeteer can question the basis for the students' suggestions and assist them to understand why they have predicted these happenings.

Another adaptation of the puppet show makes use of a central character such as a ghost or phantom who cannot be harmed. When doors are locked, he slides underneath. When no exit is available, he glides up the chimney. Although students may understand that he cannot be harmed, the puppeteer creates some anxiety-producing predicaments and urges the class to shout words of encouragement to the puppet hero. "Don't be afraid," shouts one. "Don't let them turn the lights out," cries another. The students' close identification with the puppet hero causes them to broadcast their own intense, but ordinarily guarded, feelings. This can lead to a discussion of the fears we have, the purpose they serve, and the way we might best use them.

6. Scales and checklists. Many scales and checklists are available for use with groups of students. Their function is to assist the student in revealing some of his thoughts and feelings. Because they stimulate the student to record his thoughts in a systematic fashion, they are a valuable means of increasing his self-understanding. When the teacher or counsellor chooses not to share the results with the student, their value is greatly diminished.

Teachers may want to construct their own instruments. A frequently constructed one is based on incomplete sentences. The teacher lists a number of beginnings such as : "My happiest moment is when...," "I feel most useful when I...," "If I had my one wish granted it would be...," "The moment I really dread is...." Lists of adjectives can also be developed and the student asked to check those which are most like and most unlike him or the way he is feeling at the moment. As with their published counterparts these instruments are of greatest value when the results are shared meaningfully with the student.

7. Self-reported observation. Students working with counsellors have sometimes been helped through a structured form of recording their behaviour and then discussing its meaning with the counsellor. An uncomplicated example would be that of a student who uses a study schedule that requires him to record any deviations from the established routine. Another student might fill out a rating sheet on how he used an hour of study time. A third, with a history of disruptive classroom behaviour, might be asked to record how he felt prior to each time he was disruptive. In each case the student and counsellor could review the self-reported observations and discuss their significance in an attempt to increase self-awareness.

8. Spontaneous playacting. Most students readily respond to the opportunity to play the part of someone else. Spontaneous playacting is an activity that draws upon both reality and fantasy life. The student, therefore, feels comfortable in acting out or releasing feelings that he would not divulge through other means. These may be concerned, for example, with his ability to get along with others, the image he believes others have of him, or his perception of himself. The teacher or counsellor, after observing this acting, may be able to assist the student to increase his self-awareness.

9. Video playback. Many possibilities exist for the use of video recorders in order that self-understanding might be enhanced. Recorders may be used to capture students in the act of studying, taking a test, listening to a lecture, or casually visiting in the student lounge. As a student views the playback with a counsellor, he may gain genuine

VALUE OF SELF CONCEPT : THE CASE OF LISA

To see the value of the self-concept as an aid in assisting students to understand themselves, let us examine the case of Lisa.

Lisa's Family

Members:	Father :	Robert Becker, *age* 40
	Mother :	Alice Becker, *age* 34
	Children :	Lisa, *age* 10
		Holly, *age* 8
		Amy, *age* 6
		Mark, *age* 4

insight into his manner of behaving that he could not gain through any comments, however perceptive, on the part of the counsellor. We never cease to be amazed at the way we really appear to others. The video recorder gives us access to that view and may increase self-understanding considerably.

Family Background

The family lived in a newly constructed home in a highly desirable residential area of a large Midwestern city. The home was a short distance from the elementary school and a large shopping centre, was nestled beneath towering elm trees, and overlooked a private golf course. The house, outside and inside, reflected upper-middle-class income and good taste, and both furniture and furnishings were recently purchased.

The father, a specialist in internal medicine, was extroverted, extremely intelligent, and made a most favourable personal appearance. He was born and raised on a large wheat farm, which his brothers still operate. The only member of his family to have extensive formal education, he had held a wide variety of jobs as he worked his way through high school, college, and medical school.

Lisa's mother, a product of the same rural environment, had completed two years of college and taught in a one-room rural elementary school to help finance her husband's education. Lack of a teaching certificate prevented her from working near the city in which he received medical training. Despite a facade of social skill, she frequently revealed that she was really a most insecure person and often mentioned that her education was restricted to two years at a small teachers college.

A fat, unkempt child, Lisa always seemed bothered by a cold or adenoid trouble. Her hair was typically disheveled and very oily in appearance. Her clothes were poorly matched and poorly fitted. Frequently she seemed fatigued and lacked interest in her environment. She was withdrawn, did not interact with other children, and spent much of her time daydreaming.

The second oldest child, Holly, was outgoing, self-assured, and well-liked by her peers. She and Lisa shared a room. Some indication of the difference in children was revealed by the room's appearance. Holly's side was neatly arranged, but alive with her art work, pictures of her TV heroes, and an array of colorful pennants. The wall on Lisa's side was bare except for a picture her mother had hung, her bed was unmade, her clothes were scattered across the bed and floor, and several rumpled facial tissues were noticed.

Neither of the two younger children, Amy and Mark, had entered school, and no data were available about them other than that Lisa's teacher had seen them in the home and remarked that both were spirited and outgoing.

School Performance

Lisa began her schooling in the same rural school where her mother had taught and where her grandmother was now teaching. After five years in this setting, she transferred to the newly constructed elementary school near her new home. Standardised tests results indicated that she was of average intelligence for her class, but was achieving within the bottom quarter.

Her family moved from the rural area to the large city during November, and she was assigned to the fifth grade. During the first days that she attended the new school, her teacher attempted to assess her current level of achievement. Reading skills were extremely deficient, and she seemed to have no background to prepare her for the mathematics curriculum which was being used. Her sole interest was creative writing, in which she exhibited superior thought patterns but very limited communication skills. In all subject areas and class activities except creative writing she was extremely unresponsive.

Continual colds plagued her and caused children to avoid her. The ever-running nose and rumpled tissues were constant signals for peers to stay away. The combination of low academic achievement, lack of general interest, and constant illness perpetuated a withdrawal from the class.

Conflicts Affecting Self-Understanding

During this traumatic period, only a month in length but much longer in terms of its impact upon Lisa, the effects of classroom isolation were evident. Lisa felt unwanted and rejected by peers. Her lack of social skills made attempts at friendship futile. Concurrently, her classmates were rebuffed in their attempts to involve her in their activity. Her complete lack of interest, her constant cold symptoms, and her unkempt physical appearance all caused peers to avoid friendship.

Mrs. Becker identified closely with Lisa's problems, she told the teacher, but was unable to assist Lisa because these problems in her own person had never been resolved. This caused Lisa to feel that her mother did not like her, and she was particularly hurt when she heard her mother making unfavorable comparisons between herself and Holly.

Dr. Becker's heavy professional schedule removed him from the home much of the time, and he did not have constant contact with the problem. He showed interest in Lisa, however, by attending a conference at the request of the teacher and revealed to her that he had not observed Lisa in the context of the problem. He grasped the essence of the problem immediately and was most anxious to take corrective steps. Immediate arrangements were made by Dr. Becker for Lisa to have a thorough physical examination, which led to the removal of her tonsils and adenoids. His ability to communicate with Lisa was evident from comments made by both parents. He promised to talk with her and help her to understand some of the problems confronting her.

Holly's facile manner of adapting to her new environment and making new friends tended to increase Lisa's anxiety. She genuinely wanted to assist Lisa and often helped her with homework assignments even though she was two years younger. For this she received praise from the mother, but Lisa was again somewhat hurt by the obvious difference in competency.

Attempts to Help Lisa

In addition to meeting with Lisa's parents, the teacher told the school counsellor of her concern and asked that he assist Lisa in her adjustment after her return from the hospital. Tests were administered by the counsellor to assess Lisa's academic aptitude and achievement. As reported earlier, she was of average aptitude, but was among the lowest in her class in achievement.

The counsellor talked at length with both Lisa and her teacher separately. He learned that there was a considerable discrepancy between what was happening to Lisa and what she thought was happening. Lisa believed that no one was interested in being her friend, that she was unable to do the work assigned and was regarded by peers and her teacher as not being very intelligent. The teacher told why her classmates had been unable to establish friendships with her. She further indicated that Lisa was having difficulty in adjusting to the work of her new school because of deficient basic skills in several areas and not because of any lack of learning ability, much as the test results had indicated.

As he talked with Lisa, the counsellor examined the discrepancy between her perceptions and those of her classmates as reported by the teacher. He helped her to understand the difficulties she still faced and developed with her some procedures that could be used to overcome them. They developed some specific areas on which to work initially. These included attempting to become friends with at least two members of the class during the next two weeks, asking for assistance from the teacher when directions or tasks were not understood rather than daydreaming, and making a concerted effort to improve personal appearance and hygiene habits.

The counsellor talked with the teacher and general office secretary. Arrangements were made for Lisa to engage in a series of errands that would involve meeting people, taking responsibility, and completing tasks promptly. They would reinforce extroverted behaviour, assertiveness, and alertness.

In studying the case of Lisa, one becomes aware of the differences in self-concept that are indicated for Lisa, her sister Holly, her mother, and her father. Consider the impact of the actions of each upon Lisa. Notice how Holly and Dr. Becker, although apparently of somewhat similar personality type, had rather different impacts upon Lisa. Attention is also drawn to the misperceptions Lisa had of herself and others and the insight she gained through increased understanding of herself. Increased self-awareness, as in the case of Lisa, may occur when parents and educators take direct action to assist the individual.

QUESTIONS FOR EXERCISE

1. Ask someone to give ten different answers to the question "Who am I?" Do these answers give you any clues to the way he views himself? What do you see as the values and dangers of such an assignment in helping you to understand a student?
2. In what ways was your self-concept different during your adolescence from what it is now? How do you account for these changes, and what do they suggest regarding the value of the self-concept as an aid in understanding youth?

7

Guidance to other Individuals

Guidance, like teaching, is a service given by one person to another. When we say that the teacher is "teaching a class," what he is really doing is teaching *each one* in the class — helping each pupil to learn. The counsellor often meets pupils in a group, but his purpose is to help each individual in the group. This help cannot be effective unless the teacher or counsellor knows the problems faced by each pupil and his characteristics, his abilities, and his desires. On the other hand, if the help offered is to be accepted by the individual, he must know himself, his limitations, and his strengths. Successful guidance, like successful teaching, is predicated on the student's being understood by the counsellor and by himself.

Frames of Reference

Human behaviour can be observed from two frames of reference:

1. The external or objective frame of reference. It implies that behaviour is examined from an outside observer's point of view. The teacher who observes that Joan is tired, the mother who believes that Rick is carefree, and the counsellor who comments that Melinda lacks purpose have all made their observations based upon their previous work with these and other children. Their observations may or may not be correct.

2. The phenomenological approach. It seeks to understand the behaviour of the individual from *his own* point of view as discussed in the previous chapter.

IMPORTANCE OF UNDERSTANDING OTHERS

It would seem to be self-evident that effective counselling toward specific goals is impossible without a clear understanding of the individual by the counsellor, the teacher, and the parent, and that guidance should not be attempted unless such understanding is present. But life is full of tragedies in home and in school because of the lack of such understanding. Many parents try to determine the future of their children, especially that of their sons. If the family tradition for generations has been that the firstborn son becomes a physician, lawyer, or minister, then an attempt may be made to fit a boy into the tradition regardless of his abilities or interests. There are certain values in such traditions — common memories, common experiences, common friends that bind families together. However, these decisions are based on the desires of the parents and not on the needs of their children. Such family-centered vocational and educational decisions indicate a lack of appreciation of the importance of understanding the individual.

Students in high school tend to prefer occupations that are of a higher social status than that of their parents. This preference is especially marked in children whose fathers are in unskilled or semiskilled occupations. To understand the meaning of such a preference we need to take account of the desires of the parents which may be finding expression through the vocational selections of the children.

Choices of curriculum in high school are too often made on the basis of the "standing" of the curriculum and not on the needs of the student. The high salaries now paid to sub-professional workers have changed to some extent the relative social status of high-school curriculums, but teachers, as well as parents, are still too inclined to influence the better students to take certain courses because of the prestige involved without sufficient consideration or understanding of the needs, abilities, and interests of the student himself.

It is often said that what the student does, what courses he takes in school or college, what occupation he chooses, should be based on the needs that he, himself, feels. There is no doubt that these are important, but the needs that one feels at any given time may not be based on a clear self-understanding. We often feel a variety of needs at any given time, but some are quite superficial and relatively unimportant. We may feel a "need" for a Cadillac, to "keep up with the Joneses," but an understanding of ourselves and our financial status may make us willing to settle for a used Volkswagen. Assistance in making choices should be based on as thorough an understanding as is possible of the individual, of his basic needs, and of the real circumstances surrounding his decisions.

LIFE AREAS REQUIRING UNDERSTANDING

Understanding an individual is dependent upon knowledge of how he acts in different situations. This understanding may come from observations by those who know him in school, at home, or in the community. These observations need to be combined and judgments made regarding the motives and reasons behind the observed acts. This is by no means an easy thing to accomplish. It calls for sympathetic insight into the desires and needs of students and the unusual ability to put aside any preconceived ideas of what the individual may be.

1. The school. Students do not exist in isolation but in institutional contexts. One of the most important of such contexts is that provided by the school. Schools have characteristic "climates" which do much to influence the behaviour of their students. In some schools, academic achievement is highly valued and study and hard work are methods of pleasing not only the teachers but one's peers. In other schools, athletic skills may have a higher priority and there is much pressure on students to excel in sports. Still other schools give much attention to personal popularity, which may be based on such matters as personality, social skills, and clothes. Whatever the prevailing ethos of the school, it will have a marked influence on the behaviour of the student. The peer group is always an important influence on the child, and if we want to understand his behaviour, we need to understand what his peers think is important.

2. The home. A second life area that is important in our attempts to understand an individual is his home. Research on social class has suggested that varying social economic levels may have varying child-rearing practices and inculcate different values. Certainly we should not stereotype the child and say that because he is lower class he will do thus and so, while a child who is middle class will behave differently. The research is not that clear-cut in its findings. But there do seem to be some generalisations which are possible about a home which would relate the student's behaviour to the status of his parents. A principle of child development has long suggested that the child's interaction with his parents is an important determinant of his total behaviour. A teacher or counsellor might want to consider the kinds of activities that the child engages in at home, the emotional climate of the home as characterised by acceptance or rejection, the nature of the association among the children, and the skills taught or ignored in a home all of which may be of importance in the child's total adjustment and particularly influence his behaviour in school.

When the school and the home stand for the same values, the child may learn them readily. When there is a discrepancy between what the home thinks is important and what the school thinks is important we may well expect some conflict in the child. In such a case the counsellor may be an important bridge between the school and the home and thus help both the parent and the teacher to know and understand the student more completely.

3. The community. Community conditions are of great importance in securing an understanding of individual students and in developing effective self-concepts. Such conditions are fully as significant as those in the home or in the school. Differences in the social status of families in a community often are reflected in the attitudes of different groups of high-school students toward one another. Differences in dress, in habits of speech, in social manner, in points of view, and in values are often seen. In some schools, rivalries and clannish customs often appear and cause feelings of hostility between groups. Neighborhood gangs and ethnic subcultures may be important and divisive influences affecting the student's comfort in the school as well as the extent of his learning. In spite of efforts made by the school staff to overcome these unfavorable conditions, they often continue. In the school itself, students in the college preparatory course are likely to look down on those taking other courses. Such differences often show themselves in school elections and in committee selections. Even though the school faculty does not approve of such practices, they cannot ignore them if they wish to understand the students. Unpopular students do not understand why they are not dated or elected to office and are bewildered or deeply hurt. A knowledge of community and home conditions and sensitivity to such rivalries in and out of the school are the keys to a real understanding of the student.

It is important to keep in mind that understanding an individual involves much more than an assembly of facts about him and his behaviour. Facts themselves are often misleading, and they must be interpreted by reference to other facts and to the circumstances in which they are found. Understanding cannot come merely from observation of what a person does, how he acts, and how he seems to feel. It is important to know the influences that were responsible for his behaviour, "how he got that way," what his purpose was in doing what he did. Many times he himself does not understand why he acted as he did.

PSYCHOLOGICAL BARRIERS TO UNDERSTANDING

A meaningful understanding of the individual is not always easy to secure. Certain psychological barriers may impede our progress toward understanding. Young people especially are reluctant to reveal themselves as they really are. Because of the intensely personal nature of our lives, it is difficult — perhaps impossible — to have complete empathy for another person, that is, to feel what it would be like to be in his position. Finally, because individuals change, we can never be sure that our understanding is up to date — the student in May is not the same student that he was in September.

Reluctance to reveal One's Real Self

Young people in particular are very hesitant to reveal their "true self" to others, especially to adults.

Adolescents often go to great lengths to keep another person from knowing what they really are. They are cruel to keep others from knowing that they are really tenderhearted; they pretend to dislike someone in order to conceal their inner feelings of respect and liking. Many persons, old and young, feel that it is indecent to "bare one's soul and dare the day." It is almost as bad as being a nudist! They also feel that "it is none of your business." This attitude, in itself, reveals something about the individual. A wise and sympathetic counsellor or teacher, who has not forgotten his own youth, can look behind this bravado and learn much about the student.

Difficulty in Understanding Another Person

It is difficult for adults to understand the behaviour of adolescents; we so easily forget what we thought and did when we were "young and gay." A common danger is that we may read our own present motives, feelings, and aspirations into the expressions and activities of the student. Another serious difficulty is that, although we can secure some information about the individual, what we get sometimes interferes with our understanding of him. "We cannot see the forest for the trees." The human being is a complex organic unit. He is "more than the sum of all his parts." We can gather together all the facts that can be obtained about him — his background, his surroundings, his experiences, his many characteristics — and still not understand him. There is real danger in half-truths and in unrelated information. No one type of information can stand alone; it must be considered in relation to all the other data. Real understanding of another person involves an unusual ability to put oneself sympathetically and intelligently in his place. At the same time one must stand apart and be impersonal. The privacy of the individual must be respected; we must not delve too deeply nor be in a hurry to see what the student is not ready to disclose.

Individuals Change

One difficulty in dealing with the adolescent is that he is constantly changing, even from day to day. As a consequence, by the time data are obtained and recorded, he has changed, and the data are important only as they show a developmental picture of the student. Such a picture is important, but it does not tell us what he is now. A current picture is very difficult to attain. Cumulative records have great value in showing the development of the individual from year to year — his scholastic record, his changing interests, his attitudes toward teachers and fellow students, the changes in his personality patterns. But more important is a truly understanding teacher or counsellor who can interpret the conflicting behaviour of the developing adolescent. Such understanding is absolutely essential. The past must not be confused with the present. Records tell us what was; only the individual himself can tell us what is. We must take care not to confuse marks, scores, and records of incidents with the living individual we are trying to understand and help.

SOCIAL CHANGES AS BARRIERS TO UNDERSTANDING

Great and rapid changes in our society increase the difficulty of understanding across the generations. Adults and adolescents live in truly different worlds. The meaning of work, the role of the family, religion, and morals, the philosophy of the schools have all undergone considerable transformation during this century. These changes impede the understanding which is so essential for the function of guidance.

1. Change in the meaning of work. The school counsellor or teacher is apt to be someone who is receiving much satisfaction from his work and to whom work is a very central part of his identification. He may sometimes forget then that many people do not get such satisfaction from their work. Such people may work simply because they need to have money in order to live, but may turn elsewhere for their basic pleasures.

With increased urbanisation, industrialisation, and rationalisation of job activities there may be greater alienation between the worker and his job. Few workers now have the total control over their product that the craftsman traditionally did. As a consequence the likelihood of their achieving deep satisfaction through their work is lessened. Some economists even believe that we are approaching a time when work will occupy a less and less important position in the lives of citizens. A guaranteed annual income may be provided for all our citizens apart from whether or not society has a meaningful job for them to do. Such an idea is quite contrary to our traditional "Protestant ethic" with its view that work is good and an end in itself.

The principles to be derived from the changes in our occupational structure are that the meaning of work may be different to the student than it is to the counsellor; second, that basic life satisfactions may in the future be achieved in new ways less related to job activities; and finally, that in doing vocational guidance we need to remember that the work roles available to our students in the future are literally unknown to us; therefore we should not spend our energies helping a child select a specific occupation but rather help him become a flexible adult able to cope with inevitable changes.

2. Change in the family. In any consideration of the present difficulty in the guidance of youth the changes in the home and community should be kept in mind. In most present-day homes there is no longer the same amount of intimate interrelationship that once was present. The increased tempo of life has too often materially reduced or even eliminated the time or the opportunity for such relationships.

(i) *Change in Family life* : It is difficult to determine all the causes for this change which has been both gradual and complicated. It was not caused by increased time on the job since the "workday" of the majority of workers has decreased until the forty-hour week is now the standard and pressure is being exerted to make it even shorter. Nor can it have been caused by the increased time necessary for household duties, because electrical appliances of all kinds — for cooking, dishwashing, laundry work, housekeeping and refrigeration — have materially reduced the time necessary for such responsibilities. There is actually more time available for home life and for closer relationships. In some homes this "free time" is being utilised to enrich home life and has resulted in closer relationships between parents and children, but this is not always the case.

Factors of Change in Family

(a) *Increased participation of fathers and mothers in activities outside the home in social, civic, church, and political affairs* : Such activities, for example, those of the parent-teacher association, are often very useful and desirable, but they reduce materially the time spent in the home — evenings, Saturdays, and Sundays. These activities make it difficult or even impossible to have the unhurried personal contacts with children which are so essential for effective understanding and assistance.

(b) *Increased independence of children which results in a decrease in the felling of need for help or even for association with parents* : The many out-of-class activities in the school — athletic, musical, dramatic, school government, social — provide group satisfactions and reduce both the time and the need for companionship at home. At home the children have the radio, the television, and the record player at their disposal, and they need no assistance from their parents to enjoy these facilities.

These changes have often resulted in doubts on the part of parents that they are capable of setting standards which are valid in a world so different from that of their own childhood.

(ii) *Change in morals and religion* : Another area of great importance in the lives of young people in which there have been far-reaching and significant changes is that of morals and religion. The reasons for these changes are difficult to determine. Developments in our social, economic, and industrial life probably have contributed to the change, as has the interaction of different beliefs, customs, and morals brought to America from all parts of the world. Whatever the cause, we cannot fail to understand the great importance of different moral codes and religious beliefs to the development of young people, even though both these areas are considered to be the private concern of the family, the church, and the individual rather than of the school. But if the school is interested in getting an understanding of the child and in helping him to develop adequate goals, it cannot neglect these areas, for they have a profound and often a determining influence on such goals. An understanding of the changes in these areas is of very great importance both to the home and to the school.

Many people believe that religion has a greater hold on people than it ever has had and point out that the growth in church membership in all denominations has steadily increased and many new churches are being built. Evangelists attract great numbers of people, and hundreds come forward and announce their determination to accept religion. Some believe that the fear of destruction by atomic bombs and the ensuing uncertainties have served to increase the interest in religion.

Others feel that, in spite of the growth in churches' membership, the real hold of religion on people has perceptibly decreased, that it is no longer as important a factor in our lives as it once was. They say that, although the organised church is still very important, it no longer occupies the position of leadership that it once had. It is certain that family prayers have practically disappeared, and even grace at meals is unusual.

Of one thing we are certain : religious customs have changed. The great majority of people are far more liberal in their beliefs and more tolerant of those who do not believe as they do than they once were. Young people are increasingly thinking for themselves and refusing to accept religious dogmas merely because they have been recognised for centuries. In this atmosphere of controversy, of changing beliefs, and of lack of belief, it is small wonder that young people are confused and often unable to adjust properly and to distinguish between transient and permanent values. Wise assistance is needed. Much of this help must be given by the home and the church, but the school also has a responsibility here.

Our situation regarding morals contains so much that is undesirable that we may even wonder whether our moral standards are not weakening. Racketeering, graft, and corruption are everywhere apparent, in politics, business, industry, government, and labour unions. Some men become wealthy and powerful not because of their contribution to society but because of trickery, clever dealing, influence, control of the political machine, or even theft, intimidation, or murder. Our legal system is slow, cumbersome, and too often ineffective. Criminals sometimes escape just punishment because they have money or influence or because of the work of lawyers who specialise in helping criminals evade the consequences set up by the law. The old virtues of industry, thrift, and honesty have, in some cases, been the actual cause of poverty and suffering. Men who have worked long and hard and who have been thrifty have sometimes been cheated by the unscrupulous and lost their money. They have found themselves poor and ruined not because they were dishonest or prodigal but because they were thrifty and honest.

(iii) *Change in standards of good conduct*: Standards of good conduct are continually changing. Some conduct that was once considered acceptable is now unacceptable, and what was unacceptable is now acceptable. No longer do all believe that conscience is an infallible guide in deciding what is right. Right conduct is determined not only by the motives of the actor but also by the consequences of the act. In the complexity of modern life it is often very difficult to determine the real effects of an act, and this makes it hard to make right decisions. We need to know the probable effects of the proposed action on others and on ourselves before we can decide intelligently what is best to be done.

Many youth indicate relatively little concern about problems of morals and religion or of home and family. Two opposite conclusions might be drawn from these findings. We might say that young people are well adjusted in morals and religion and to home and family since they apparently have few problems in these areas. On the other hand, it is possible that young people have little consciousness of morals or moral obligations. It may be that church and religion are not vital forces in their lives and that they have little trouble with parents and home because parents are not important guiding and restraining influences in their lives. In other words, young people may not be conscious of problems in these areas because they have little sense of moral obligation and little restraint imposed on them. The mounting delinquency rate among youth might indicate that the second conclusion is correct.

3. Change in educational philosophy. One of the most important social changes in recent years has been that in our philosophy of education as it concerns the place of the child in the teaching-learning process. This change is so intermingled with the changes in the home and in religion and morals that it is difficult to tell whether the changes in the philosophy of education are responsible for the changes in the home and society or the reverse. Formerly, education was the process of passing on to the young the cultural heritage of the past. It was the process of inculcating in the young those habits, skills, ideas, and knowledges that were necessary to enable them to take their place in adult society. The central figure in this process was the teacher. The student was the recipient and, as far as possible, passive and obedient. He was thought to be too young to have any voice in determining what he had to do or to learn. Discipline was the process of preventing behaviour that would interfere with this attitude of docility. The curriculum was organised by the school, and methods were developed with the purpose of molding the pupil into the kind of individual who would make a good citizen and an exemplary person. This educational philosophy was the prevailing point of view in the schools of all countries until the beginning of this century.

The new educational philosophy places the child at the centre of the educational process and is concerned primarily with his development, that is, with what he is now rather than what he may become or what society may demand of him. His needs for personal development, his own interests and desires, are dominant. His impulses for action are of extreme importance and should not be unduly restricted. He should have a large part in decisions regarding what he should do — even regarding what he should study. The extreme of this position is that he should not be made to do what he does not want to do. Failures are considered undesirable and should be avoided. Because punishments and restraints are negative, they should either not be used at all or at least be minimised. The rule of promotion for all is sometimes adopted.

Even though some of the extreme implications of this philosophy have not been generally accepted, its impact has been very great. Probably its most important implication is the emphasis it places upon the enlarged place of the individual in choosing his own way of life and in selecting his own activities. Even young children are allowed and often encouraged to make important choices for themselves. Many of these choices may be unfortunate; but when the choice seems undesirable, instead of arbitrarily refusing to allow the child to do what he has chosen to do, we try to help him evaluate the wisdom of his choice.

The underlying idea of this educational position emphasises the fundamental purpose of guidance — helping the individual to make wise choices. The necessity for adequate guidance in the very early years of life in order to develop this ability is emphasised. While this emphasis is certainly desirable, the popularity of this new philosophy has also resulted in much confusion, uncertainty, and even bewilderment among teachers and parents. It has been difficult for them to adjust themselves to it, and they are often at a loss to know what to do.

Parents and teachers who grew up when a different educational philosophy was in vogue often cannot understand the young people of today and are puzzled by their actions. This puzzlement makes them uncertain about the best methods of dealing with today's students. The usual result is that little or nothing is done to change the behaviour of the student or to develop his sense of values.

We have as yet failed to solve the problem of dealing with these delinquent youth. We know that the old method of treating them as criminals is not good; we also know that leniency of the courts does not by itself solve the problem. Some more effective guidance is absolutely essential. Many national and local agencies are working hard to solve the problem, and some of the suggested solutions seem to be hopeful. At the root of any successful plan must be some form of intelligent guidance.

Thus, the last few years have seen great changes in our society. Adults trying to understand adolescents must take account of the fact that the world of their own childhood is gone. It is not likely to return. If you wish to understand today's youth, you must first understand his world — however much a stranger you feel in it, however much you may disapprove of some of its elements — for the youth and his world are so much a part of each other that they cannot be known separately.

AIDS IN UNDERSTANDING STUDENTS

Many techniques are needed to help us understand youth. Such an understanding cannot be attained merely by watching what they are doing. We must know the reasons and motives that impel them to act as they do. This level of understanding requires close and sympathetic personal relationship over a reasonably long period of time. The problem is made more difficult because youth may not understand themselves and therefore are unable to give much direct help to adults who are striving to learn more about them.

1. Cumulative records. A cumulative record is a collection of information about a student and constitutes a picture of his development — physically, academically, and socially. In the past such records were made up of collections of material filed in the counsellor's office. Now some schools are putting this material on magnetic tape and storing it in computers. When a counsellor wishes to retrieve the information, the computer prints out for him the material which he wants and needs.

These records, which have great value in showing year-to-year development, include, as we have stated earlier, his scholastic record, his changing interests, his attitudes toward teachers and fellow students, and the changes in his personality patterns. Well-organised anecdotal records — objective statements of significant incidents — may be very helpful if carefully made from time to time. Autobiographies often reveal characteristics and attitudes unsuspected even by the student himself. Valuable as they are, such records are quite inadequate to provide a real understanding of the pupil. What is needed most is a sympathetic and understanding teacher or counsellor who can interpret the conflicting behaviour of the developing adolescent and look behind and beyond the records themselves to see him as he is. This is essential in any attempt to give guidance to the individual.

2. Cooperation in the school. The development of the self, the ego, is a gradual process which may continue throughout life, but for most people the period of childhood and youth is by far the most important time in the formation of the self. Understanding of an individual comes from a knowledge of how he acts in different situations and why. It might be that the person best able to understand the youth would be the one who has the closest relation to him for the longest period. Often this will be a parent, especially the mother. There is no doubt that the mother can be, and often is, a very knowledgeable observer of how her child acts and how he changes in behaviour as he grows, but parental love and pride often interfere with judgment and obscure important elements essential for understanding.

Teachers see children six to eight hours a day, five days in the week, for nine or ten months a year and observe their acts and judge their motives. Teachers, however, see the individual in a more or less restricted situation and are not completely qualified to understand him. Fellow students, on the other hand, observe their classmates in many types of situations which are more varied and lifelike than those seen by parents or teachers. Although the counsellor is the person who is charged with the responsibility for bringing together all the data in the school records, including the observations and opinions of teachers and peers, he may have comparatively little personal contact with individual students. Often, however, he can judge more objectively than parents and teachers, even though he might not be able to develop a completely accurate understanding of the whole personality by himself.

It must be conceded that there is no way by which the real self of an individual can be accurately determined, but it seems clear that the only way in which the school can approximate such an understanding is by the cooperation of all the individuals and agencies who come in contact with the individual. This means that, since all the institutions in the community have a responsibility for the education and training of children and youth, they must also cooperate in developing an understanding of them.

3. Cooperation with the home. The school and the family share the greatest responsibility for understanding. They are so closely related that there is every reason and need for cooperation, but effective methods to bring this about have as yet not been developed. The major responsibility for initiating such cooperation rests upon the school system. During the past ten years a number of systems have been experimenting with different types of cooperation, some of which seem to be very promising. Efforts are made to clarify the particular responsibility of the school, the family, and the community as well as to eliminate misunderstandings that have arisen among them and to emphasise the need for cooperation and point out ways in which it can be accomplished.

Close personal relations are developed among teachers, parents, business and professional people so that they are known to each other as individuals. Through social occasions and professional meetings they come to know one another better and to realise the necessity for cooperation among friends in all areas, not only in the schools.

In many schools lay people have been invited to come to the school for a variety of reasons so that they can know and understand it better. Some schools are providing "parent" rooms where there are easy chairs and books and pamphlets on school matters and where desirable conferences with teachers, counsellors, and administrators can be arranged.

At present the chief means of cooperation with the home is through reports to the parents on the status and progress of the child, but it is difficult to make such reports meaningful to them. The primary meaning is conveyed by the grades received, promotion or non-promotion, and comments on the child's behaviour. At times conferences are arranged between the teacher and the parents to discuss the status of the pupil. Too often, however, this conference is held only when there is something wrong. If the pupil is getting along well in school, no need for a conference is seen. Likewise, when the teacher visits the home, it is usually because of some problem either in the child's work or in his behaviour. The difficulty in providing these conferences is very great; but in the schools where such methods have been adopted, a very definite change has been seen in the relation between teachers and parents not only in their personal contact but also in their friendly cooperation in the solution of problems of pupils and in the improvement of school facilities.

4. Community information. Teachers and counsellors should know their community if they are to be of maximum help to students. The school needs to know about the community activities of the students. Which ones are active in church work? Which ones are leaders in their neighborhood peer groups? Contacts with service clubs such as Rotary, Kiwanis, and Lions have been found to be very useful in revealing sources of assistance and also in securing information about students who are friends or relations of members of these organisations.

Many schools have found it helpful to initiate some type of community survey, which reveals the resources of the community, such as men and women who are leaders in business or industry and who are willing to talk with students about opportunities and qualities essential to success in life. Such contacts will help students to understand social and economic conditions and to realise how they may prepare themselves for lines of work for which they are especially fitted.

With the expansion of poverty programs there is a new area of community information which needs to be understood by the counsellor. Such programs as those undertaken by the Neighborhood Youth Corps, the Job Corps, and VISTA may be important sources of referral and important forces for community change. The counsellor who is unaware of these community activities is unaware of the environment in which his students live. Although the complexity of and the continuing changes in such programs make it difficult to be up to date with regard to them, the counsellor who is going to continue to do an adequate job will in the future be required to spend more time and energy relating what he does to programs that emanate from municipal, state, and federal sources. The rise of such programs, incidentally, reflects a deeper commitment on the part of America to be useful to its young citizens. These may also reflect a skepticism on the part of the larger society with regard to the worthwhileness of the educational and guidance activities that have traditionally characterised our schools.

QUESTIONS FOR EXERCISE

1. Describe instances where the help offered to you by parents, teachers, counsellors, or others was ineffective or even harmful because they did not know enough about you. If you do not recall any such experiences, describe some instances that you have observed in the case of others.

2. Do you feel reluctant to give information about yourself to others? If so, what are the causes of such reluctance? Describe the situation and the conditions in which you would feel free to give information about yourself.
3. Usually there are differences between the picture we have of ourselves (our self-concept) and the way we are seen by others (our public image). Discuss these differences in the case of someone well known to you. What accounts for such differences? Do you see ways to lessen these differences?

8

LEISURE-TIME GUIDANCE

One of the most important problems arising out of our complex social, economic, and industrial conditions is the effective use of leisure time. With increased life expectancy, shorter working hours, and more systematic retirement plans the place of leisure has assumed increasing importance. Many feel that the schools, along with other institutions, need to take greater responsibility for preparing students for leisure and giving them guidance in its satisfactory use.

Others have pointed to the paradox of considering leisure — a subject associated with reward and relaxation — as a "problem," but a problem it is in the affluent society of today. The vast majority of mankind would, of course, welcome such a "problem," but this fact does not lessen the dilemma leisure poses.

PLACE OF LEISURE IN SOCIETY

Meaning of Leisure

Although the concept of leisure has varied in some respects from time to time, it has always carried with it the idea of free time, that is, spare time at one's disposal. It is usually interpreted as time not spent on the activities of making a living, keeping alive, or maintaining one's efficiency — eating, sleeping, and the ordinary care of the body. It is synonymous with idleness or with time spent on avocations, hobbies, or recreations. These are merely ways of employing leisure time. It is often difficult to distinguish between one's vocational and avocational activities, but the distinction can be made with sufficient definiteness to give a fairly clear idea of the meaning of leisure.

SOCIAL AND PERSONAL FUNCTIONS OF LEISURE

The function of leisure is largely determined by the kind and amount of free time available and the ideals of the time. In different societies leisure assumes different functions — in one it provides an opportunity for conspicuous consumption, in another it enables science and literature to prosper. For different individuals leisure performs different functions also — some benefits are socially and personally desirable, some are not.

1. Related to increased production. When leisure time is merely a short breathing space between long periods of sustained labour, its function has been to increase production. This is accomplished by giving the worker a rest from time to time — the "coffee break" — so that he can recover from fatigue and accomplish more. Sometimes the employer helps his employees to get comfortable homes and provides better working conditions, rest rooms, or recreation facilities. This practice helps his business, for it creates good will and increases production. The Roman emperors provided holidays for the populace, great gladiatorial combats, thrilling spectacles, and sports of all kinds. These activities helped the common people to be satisfied with their lot and to produce more.

2. Related to increased consumption. Leisure is also thought of as a means of increasing consumption. The more time an individual has free from work, the greater is his demand for goods that will help him make his leisure more satisfying. This fact is evidenced by the great demand for sporting goods of all kinds. Consumption of this kind also increases production, and so it is good for business. Both these points of view about the function of leisure are founded on a belief in the sacredness of work and the importance of increasing wealth as an end in itself.

3. Related to crime and delinquency. Crime and delinquency flourish when youth and adults have nothing worthwhile to do, when they have "time on their hands." It has been shown in many cities that, whenever interesting sports and other useful activities are provided, delinquency decreases. Productive people are less likely to engage in crime, but few would subscribe to the notion that we should keep people working simply in an attempt to keep them out of mischief.

4. Related to human development. The functions of leisure time just mentioned fail to touch the most fundamental and important need of an individual — the need for his development as a human being.

If Americans are to meet the problem presented by our enforced leisure, if we are to set up the machinery by which to realise the "dream of America," they must put more emphasis upon the development of the individual himself.

Types of Leisure-Time Activities

The choice of a leisure-time activity should be suited to the needs of the individual, and the basis for choice may well vary with the individual. In most cases, however, it should be sufficiently different from the activities in the regular occupation to afford recreation and real enjoyment. The required skills should be within the participant's capabilities. Before taking up a leisure-time activity, one may ask himself some questions : "Do I have time for it? Can I afford it? Will it meet my social needs?"

There is a great variety of leisure-time activities and a great overlapping in meaning and purpose. Each activity has within itself possibilities of different values or objectives. The value of an activity depends largely on the individual who participates in it. For this reason it is impossible to make any completely satisfactory classification of leisure activities.

1. Relaxation. One of the principal meanings of leisure has always been relaxation. The activities engaged in for this purpose are varied and numerous.

Paradoxical as it may seem, there are those who relax in very systematic and even stylised fashions. Some Eastern religions and Western imitations of them make relaxation a very difficult and complex art.

More generally, however, relaxation may take the form of simply doing what comes naturally. To some this will consist of puttering around the house or garden. Others will take walks with no special aim in mind and no special effort involved.

Passive relaxation is probably the most frequent form. The docile television viewer, record or radio listener or sports viewer probably best exemplifies passive relaxation. While it is customary to be scornful of such activity, the fact that it is quite usual in our society suggests that it does, in some way, fulfil a necessary need.

2. Entertainment. As usually understood, recreation, which is the commonest form of entertainment, may include practically all types of leisure-time activities, especially amateur sports and games — anything done just for fun. However, its original meaning has great significance. "Recreation" has the meaning indicated in "*re*-creation." It means to revive, to refresh, to renew. It presupposes that the individual once had something that he valued and has now lost it or is in danger of losing it because of exhaustion, ill health, neglect, or some other cause; through recreation he wants to get it back. "Re-creation" includes the need for rest or for types of exercise which will renew one's strength. It also includes renewal of happiness, faith, courage, trust in people; the meaning of life, of sorrow, of sickness, of death. It thus includes every type of human activity which helps in the renewal of human values :

(i) *Hobby* : A common type of recreation is a hobby. A hobby may be described as a non-vocational activity that involves more than a mere passing interest and one to which the amateur turns persistently when opportunity permits. Hobbies are recognised as being among the most valuable of the leisure time activities. Some authorities say that every person should have some sort of hobby, but this certainly is an exaggeration because not infrequently a number of varied activities is more valuable to a particular individual. Hobbies may have a great prognostic value for the choice of an occupation.

(ii) *Escape activities* : These are those engaged in as a release from the daily round of labour or from situations that are unpleasant or disturbing. They are calculated to make one forget unhappiness, at least temporarily. They must, therefore, be absorbing activities and as different as possible from the experience that caused the unpleasant emotions. A large number of people employ their spare time in activities that are entirely of this kind. They read detective stories, romantic novels, the sports page, the comics. They go to second-rate movies that appeal entirely to the eye and ear or spend their time before the television set where conversation is taboo. They attend football, baseball, and hockey games that grip their attention and stir the emotions to a point of forgetfulness; they play bridge, tennis, golf and play as strenuously as they work. When they travel, in order to get the most for their money they join a planned tour which leaves them no time to themselves. On shipboard the steward thoughtfully plans their every minute in deck sports, dances, special parties, or bridge. At times we all need such forms of relaxation, but far too often they are the only ones in which we engage. Anyone who looks upon the usual vacation activities of the tourist may well say, "At work man is sublime; at leisure he is ridiculous."

(iii) *Competitive activities* : These are those in which one person or group seeks to surpass another person or group in the exercise of certain skills. Indoor and outdoor games and sports of all kinds come under this heading. These activities are among the most popular ways of spending leisure time and may have very great value for the participants. Some critics say, with a fair amount of truth, that with the great popularity of professional sports we are afflicted with "spectatorship" and do not engage enough in sports directly. There are, however, some real recreational values in being a spectator with a large social group witnessing the same exercises and cheering for "our side."

3. Personal Development. Many thousands of youths and adults are using their leisure time to prepare themselves for college, for better positions in business and industry, and for different types of work. Evening schools, correspondence schools, and radio and television courses are utilised for these purposes.

(i) *Preparing for better positions* : These activities broaden our outlook and vision, and increase our appreciation of music, art, literature, and all that is high and noble. They help us keep in touch with the world and maintain and deepen our intellectual, moral, and spiritual nature. They involve cessation of haste and strenuous struggle and require us to take time to stretch, to think, to enjoy, to appreciate. Thoreau had this purpose in mind when he wrote, "I went to the woods because I wished to live deliberately, to front only the essential facts of life, and see if I could not learn what it has to teach, and not, when I came to die, discover that I had not lived."

(ii) *Creative activities* : These also contribute to personal development. These activities are those where one does not sit passively and enjoy the creation of others but participates in the creation. The field of such activities is very wide and offers opportunity for everyone. Under this category would come the composition of music, painting, sculpturing, dressmaking, cooking, working in wood, metal, or other material, writing, and any other activity in which one is not merely a spectator but actually produces something. Such activities give us satisfaction and a feeling of accomplishment.

(iii) *Service activities* : These may play an important part in personal development. These are the activities that are done to help others. They may take the form of a personal service to a member of the family or a friend or services to various groups and clubs. Many service activities may also become creative ones. Women who volunteer to help in hospitals and men who work with youth groups are performing service activities. Leisure time spent in such activities may give the feeling of satisfaction which comes from being engaged in a socially valuable task.

RESPONSIBILITY OF THE SCHOOL

The curriculum of the school consists of those educative experiences which are under school supervision. Such educative experiences may take the form of regularly scheduled classes or may consist of extracurricular activities.

1. Leisure time class instruction. Through the curriculum are developed the fundamental skills in reading, writing, art, music, home economics, and industrial arts which are essential to effective participation in many of the leisure-time activities. We must rely on class instruction to develop an interest in such activities and a desire to participate in them. There needs to be a somewhat radical change in the attitudes of some superintendents, principals, and teachers before the school can become really effective in its contribution to the leisure-time activities of the students. Even more important is the change that needs to take place in the patrons of the school. The taxpaying public and school boards must be persuaded that activities preparing students for the wise use of leisure are not "fads and frills" to be eliminated when the financial situation becomes acute. More time and attention have to be given to the school's responsibility for assisting the students to develop the skills for effective leisure-time activities and for making wise choices among such activities.

The intelligent choice and wise planning of leisure-time activities are dependent upon knowledge of the different types involved, skill in their use, and real interest and desire to participate in them. Since this is the case, the curriculum of the elementary and secondary school has an important function in leisure-time guidance. Courses in civics, history, general science, English, and geography are now being organised in such a way as to help the pupil learn the facts of modern social, civic, and economic life which are important for him and to develop in him interests and attitudes that will function in his life both in the school and outside it in work and in leisure.

2. Leisure time student activities. Although closely related to the organised classes, the various forms of student clubs and activities and the general school life contribute much toward preparing for wise choice of leisure-time activities. Student participation in the government of the school affords splendid opportunity for acquiring facts about forms of government and for developing right attitudes toward service activities, especially those related to citizenship. The best preparation for civic responsibility in later life is participation in the duties connected with the social group with which one is now connected. For the student, the most important group is the school. If students feel that the responsibility for the government of the school rests partly upon them, they will assume a very different attitude toward the life of the school and toward discipline. One of the reasons why so-called "student" government is not more helpful in civic guidance is that it is often student government in name only. Policies are really decided by the principal, and the officers of the organisation are mere puppets moving at his behest. To be effective, real responsibility should be placed upon the officers of the student body. The government of the school should be a cooperative matter, with definite responsibility being delegated to the students for some decisions. Problems that arise in connection with the government of the school afford excellent material for group discussions, assembly talks, homeroom conferences, and individual conferences between students and principal or teacher.

The student activities program and the general school life are important factors in the acquisition of facts, in the development of skills and attitudes that are useful in adjustment to others, and in general social relationships. Such attainments are vital in appreciation and service activities. Most of one's life is concerned directly with other people, and individual success and happiness are dependent in large measure upon the way in which one gets along with others. Individuals differ by nature very greatly in their power to adapt themselves to social situations; for some, it is very easy; for others, it is extremely difficult; for all, it is largely a matter of training. Everyone needs guidance in social adjustments no matter what sort of home he may come from or how well he may be endowed by nature.

3. Leisure time social skills. Manners are of very great importance, and manners can be learned. In our cosmopolitan high schools, students need special help because there are many social customs of which they are entirely ignorant. Since their homes do not give help, someone else must. Help is given in classes set apart for this special purpose, by the definite provision for social occasions in the school, by parliamentary activities in student assemblies, and in club and class meetings and private conferences. Some schools utilise the entire school life for purposes of social guidance. Formal and informal teas are given to accustom students to such occasions and to train them in conduct proper to the occasion. Parents' receptions are organised with the help of students. Formal and informal dances and parties are employed where invitations are issued and letters of acceptance or regret are sent. These activities are all organised and administered with the definite purpose of giving students the most practical help and training in methods of social conduct and forms of social usage. Such matters are often considered in homeroom discussions. Several very helpful manuals on manners have been written and are now being used in the schools.

Student clubs often serve to develop or to deepen interest in desirable activities that develop into hobbies or avocations in later life and function as leisure-time activities, cultural and appreciative, creative, and service.

4. Leisure time sports. The physical education program is directed partly toward the development of skills in certain games, group and individual, and partly toward the development of an interest and desire to continue such participation after one's school life is over. If this work is to become really effective, studies should be conducted which will show the effect that certain forms of recreation have upon the physical and mental life of the participants and the forms that are best suited to meet the needs of different types of people. We need to examine our school program of athletics and student clubs to determine which ones will be helpful in after school life. We already know, for example, that the great majority of people, after they leave school, will not play football, baseball, hockey, or basketball. They are far more likely to play golf, tennis, or volleyball, or to swim, go hiking, or dance. Group play is valuable in many ways and should not be neglected, but directors of physical education are coming to feel that such games should not crowd out forms of recreation in which most people will engage after they leave school. Definite provision should be made in school for the development of an interest in these forms of sport which have carry-over value in later life.

THE COUNSELLOR'S RESPONSIBILITY

Whether working with children or adults, the counsellor will have as his responsibility helping them integrate their leisure life with other aspects of their existence. The student who is getting in trouble because he has too much time on his hands might be guided into activities which will provide him socially desirable entertainment. He might be helped to join a club, go out for athletics, or develop an appropriate hobby. The adult who appears unduly driven or anxiety ridden may be encouraged to find ways to relax. Again, socially appropriate activities might be pointed out to him and he may be helped in getting started with these new behaviours. Either children or adults whose lives seem to lack meaning, who live at a shallow level and seem to be victims of ennui, may be encouraged and guided toward leisure activities resulting in personal development. Joining organisations which perform socially useful functions, taking courses to make them better and more alert citizens, developing deep interests or hobbies may all be ways in which the counsellor can aid the client to develop better use of leisure time.

Tomorrow's counsellor may find that his major problem is not helping people select vocations but is helping them integrate their work life with their leisure time for greater total personal development. Already, for many workers, the line between labour and leisure is thin and permeable. If America is able to make available creative leisure to its citizens, the distinction between work and leisure will continue to lessen. Certainly the counsellor's role will be central in any such undertaking, for it is the counsellor who particularly asks such questions as "How do I want to use my time?" "What activities and experiences will make me most aware of myself and my world?"

QUESTIONS FOR EXERCISE

1. State several types of leisure-time activities that would be useful and desirable to you.
2. Describe the leisure-time activities of prominent persons.
3. What responsibility should the schools assume for guidance and training in leisure-time activities? Describe what one school is doing to prepare its students to use effectively the leisure they will have as adults.

9

GUIDANCE SERVICES IN INDIA

The programmes of organised guidance undertaken in America towards the close of the nineteenth century made James B. Conant remark, "Guidance is the key-stone of the arch of American education." About 80% of the total output of psychological research comes from American psychological laboratories. The city of Boston in U.S.A. is called "the cradle of vocational guidance". Frank Parsons of Boston is known as "the father of the vocational guidance movement", planned and organised the Vocational Bureau of Boston in 1908. His famous book, *Choosing a Vocation* appeared in 1909. Parsons, extensive work in school guidance had been done by Jesse B. Davis from 1898 to 1907. The Truman L. Kelley emphasised the need for educational guidance. He submitted his dissertation for Doctorate in 1914, under the titles 'Educational Guidance'.

Factors influencing guidance programme. According to Traxler following five factors have influenced the guidance programmes :

(i) *Humanitarianism of philanthropy* : "People should be guided when they are young so that these maladjustments will not occur. This is a job for the school."

(ii) *Religion* : The religious men say that, "We must get hold of people when they are very young and train them for the good life. We must build character in our youth." He looks to the educational institutions to assist him in this task.

(iii) *Mental hygiene* : Hental therapy is the sure way of treating maladjustment. According to the mental hygienist people should learn to get a correct perspective abilities in relation to life goals even when they are young and the schools should provide for guidance in mental hygiene.

(iv) *Social change* : The pressure of numbers and the essentially non-academic character of the students have created new problems for the school administrators. Such individuals must be helped to marshal their assets through guidance.

(v) *Measurement movement* : The application of measurement techniques statistical methods have also contributed to the efficiency of the guidance programmes.

World War I gave impetus to the guidance movement by the scientific action and training of men for war purposes, through intelligence tests administered to millions of men. Intelligence tests and achievement tests antedate the beginning of organised guidance in Australia, Canada, France, Germany, Great Britain and Japan and in other parts of the world.

EVOLUTION OF GUIDANCE AND COUNSELLING MOVEMENT IN INDIA

Guidance and counselling have been a vital aspect of higher education. Good teachers have always been interested in providing understanding assistance to students to help hem overcome problems of learning and adjustment so as to ensure optimum achievement and profitable placement. In the ancient Indian Universities like Nalanda and Taxila, the learned monks were sagacious and wise in their handling of students. Right from admission of students to these seats of higher learning they were occupied with the process of guidance and counselling, informal and incidental to seeing them through to enter the world of work and face life. The process was highly successful as the monks knew the students and no undesirable element could enter or stay in the universities. Even the old Gurukula system of India led to harmonious relations between the teacher and the taught because the number of students was small, courses of study were simple, job opportunities were limited and world of work was more or less stable and students had few problems.

1. Calcutta University. The privilege of introducing the guidance-movement in this country goes to Calcutta University which set up the first psychological laboratory in India in the year 1915. A separate section of research in Applied Psychology was opened under the direction of Dr. G.S. Bose, the then Head of the Department in 1936 in order to adopt psychological tests prepared in America to suit the Indian conditions and to evolve procedures to satisfy the vocational needs of Indian students.

2. Bombay University. In 1941, Batliboi Vocational Guidance Bureau was established in Bombay with the efforts of a retired accountant practising in Calcutta and Mukerjee, a psychologist from Calcutta University.

3. Patna University. In it was established a Department of Psychological Services and Research in 1945, offering personal and vocational guidance to students and constituting a number of psychological tests.

4. Parsi Panchayat. The Trustees of the Parsi Panchayat Funds and Properties established the Parsi Panchayat Vocational Guidance Bureau in 1947. Dr. H.P. Mehta, its first Director, for the first time published the journal of Vocational and Educational Guidance.

5. Uttar Pradesh Government. In 1947, the U.P. Government established the Bureau of Psychology at Allahabad on the recommendations of Acharya Narendra Deo Committee.

6. Bombay Government. In 1950, the Bombay Government set up the Vocational Guidance Bureau in Bombay renamed as Institute of Vocational Guidance in 1957. In 1952, the Vocational Guidance Association of Bombay was formed to coordinate the efforts of various individuals and agencies in the field of guidance in Bombay.

7. Workshop and seminar at Delhi. In March 1953, Dr. W.L. Barnette, an American Fullbright Professor, held a workshop of guidance workers in the country at the Central Institute of Education, Delhi. A second seminar was held in November 1954, again at the Central Institute of Education, Delhi. It was decided to form an All India Educational and Vocational Guidance Association and to affiliate it to the International Association for Vocational Guidance.

8. Secondary Education Commission (1952-53). On the recommendations of Secondary Education Commission (1952-53), the old unilateral education system was replaced by a scheme *of diversified* courses. The Commission provided for seven different streams at the Secondary Stage — humanities, science, agriculture, commerce, technical, fine arts, and home science. As the students were supposed to choose the courses at the Delta stage (Class VIII) hence the need of guidance at this stage. The Commission wrote : "The secret of good education consists in enabling the student to realise what are his talents and aptitudes and in what manner and to what extent he can best develop them so as to achieve proper social adjustment and seek right types of employment." The Commission recommended the introduction of guidance services in the following words : "Educational arid vocational guidance is not to be regarded as a mechanical process whereby the advisers and teachers sort out boys and girls as a grading machine sorts out apples! It is not a question of just deciding that one boy should stay in the form, another work in an aeroplane factory, a third become a teacher and a fourth take to the management of garage. Guidance involves the difficult art of helping boys and girls to plan their own future wisely in the full light of all the factors that can be mustered about themselves and about the world in which they are to live and work. Naturally, therefore, it is not the work of a few specialists, but rather a service in which the entire school staff must cooperate under the guidance of some person with special knowledge and skill in this particular field. Guidance, in this sense, is not confined to the vocational field only. It covers the whole gamut of youth problems and should be provided in an appropriate form at all stages of education through the cooperative endeavour of understanding parents, head-masters, principals and guidance officers." Following were the recommendations of the Commission :

(i) Educational guidance should receive greater attention on the part of the educational authorities.

(ii) To broaden the pupil's understanding of the scope, nature and significance of various occupations of industries, films should be prepared to show the nature of the work in various industries and this should be supplemented by actual visits.

(iii) The services of trained Guidance Officers and Career Masters should be made available in an increasing measure to all educational institutions.

(iv) The Centre should take up the responsibility of opening centres of training for Guidance Officers and Career Masters in different regions to which each State may send a number of teachers or other suitable persons for training.

9. Central Bureau of educational and vocational guidance. In 1954, the Ministry of Education, Government of India, set up the Central Bureau of Educational and Vocational Guidance with following specific functions:

(i) Production and distribution of tools and aids serviceable for guidance work in schools.

(ii) Technical assistance in setting up educational and vocational guidance bureaus in the States.

(iii) Training guidance personnel, particularly psychologists and counsellors.

(iv) Coordinating guidance activities throughout the country.

(v) Preparation of manuals dealing with educational and vocational guidance careers and occupations.

(vi) Coordinating with the Occupational Information Unit of the Directorate General of Resettlement and Employment in the preparation of occupational information material and its distribution in schools.

The Central Bureau had been rendering a valuable and useful service in the field of guidance since its establishment.

In July, 1958 it started a ten months' course for training counsellors in the field of student personnel work in the Central Bureau's premises in the Central Institute of Education, Delhi. The course was primarily designed "to meet the requirements of the personnel responsible for planning and operating educational arid vocational guidance services in the secondary school." The course was limited to 15 candidates only. Trained graduate teachers with at least three years' teaching experience were eligible to be admitted in it. It consisted of (a) Theoretical instruction, (b) Practical training and (c) Field work practice. Since then, many courses have been organised.

Earlier a part of the Ministry of Education, the Bureau is now a part of the Department of Psychological Foundations of the National Institute

FUNCTIONS OF THE STATE BUREAU OF EDUCATIONAL AND VOCATIONAL GUIDANCE

1	2	3	4	5	6	7	8	9
Counselling ↓	Group Guidance	↓	Setting ↓	Training ↓	Seminar ↓	Field Services ↓	Research ↓	Publications ↓
Individual Councelling		Maintenance of State-level Educational and Occupational Information Centres	State level Coordination Committee	(i) Career Master/ Mistresses ↓	(i) Orientation Programmes for Headmaster Headmistresses and Principals of High and Higher Secondary Schools ↓	(i) Developing Guidance Service in High and Higher Secondary Schools of the State ↓	(i) Basic Guidance Problem ↓	(i) News letter ↓
				(ii) Teacher Counsellor ↓	(ii) Short-term Training Programme for Teachers and others about their Roles in the Guidance Programme ↓	(ii) Developing Guidance Services for the District Headquarter Officers	(ii) Construction Standarisation and Development of Psychological Tests	(ii) Brochures on Guidance and Counselling ↓
				(iii) Organising One Academic Year Diploma Course in Guidance and Counselling	(iii) Developing Basic Concepts of Guidance Amongst Education Officers	(iii) Supervision of Guidance Services at District and Schools Levels		(iii) Research Reports.

of Education under the National Council of Educational Research and Training.

The Extension Services Department of the Central Institute of Education, Delhi, conducted two long-term courses in Educational and Vocational Guidance during 1957 and 1958 to provide in-service training of teachers so that they should work either as career-masters or as teacher-counsellors.

10. State Bureaus of educational and vocational guidance. These established to perform the following functions :

(i) Organisation of sample group guidance activities for a few schools.

(ii) Collection of occupational information and production of information material.

(iii) Development and adaptation of translation of tests, questionnaires, check lists, etc.

(iv) Training of guidance workers.

(v) Planning, coordination and supervision of guidance service within the State.

(vi) Consultative and field services.

(vii) Research.

ORGANISATION OF GUIDANCE SERVICES IN INDIA

In India Guidance services at the Secondary stage are organised at the following four levels :

1. Central Government.
2. State Government and Union Territory Administration.
3. Private agencies.
4. Schools.

1. Central Government State

(i) Ministry of Education. The Union Ministry of Education and its technical arm, the National Council of Educational Research and Training, are concerned with guidance services in higher secondary schools at the Central Government level. The Ministry has promoted the development of guidance by providing financial assistance as well as professional leadership to States offered through the Central Bureau of Educational and Vocational Guidance established as a part of the Ministry of Education and later the Bureau was made a part of the Central Institute of Education under the Ministry of Education and at last merged with the National Council of Educational Research and Training (N.C.E.R.T.).

(ii) N.C.E.R.T. As a technical wing of the Ministry of Education, it undertakes the following types of activities in the field of guidance and counselling :

(a) *Leadership* : Fostering and giving leadership to a strong guidance movement in the country.

(b) *Research* : Undertaking research in order to develop a body of knowledge regarding guidance as an aspect of the educational process.

(c) *Training* : Conducting a programme for training specialists in guidance.

(d) *Extension services* : Undertaking extension work in guidance for the in-service training of guidance personnel in different parts of the country.

(e) *Field services* : Offering consultative and field services.

(f) *Publications* : Articles on guidance are published in the two journals of the N.C.E.R.T. *viz.*, Indian Educational Review and the N.I.E. journal.

(iii) National employment service. With its headquarters at the Directorate General of Employment and Training of the Ministry of Labour and Rehabilitation, Government of India, this organisation is primarily concerned with the offering of vocational guidance to school youth and adults through its Vocational Guidance Units. Its Vocational Guidance Officers assist the State and private organisations in conducting training courses for career masters through talks on career and organisation of career conferences. The occupational information literature and posters brought out by the Directorate General of Employment and Training are the mainstay of the occupational information libraries or Corners maintained by the Guidance Bureaus and schools. The Vocational Units of the Employment Exchanges carry out the placement of school leavers in apprenticeship and in vocational training.

2. Guidance services at the state level

State Bureaus of Educational and Vocational Guidance have been set up in almost all the States and Union Territories, some of them administratively a part of the Directorate of Education, others either a part of the State Council of Educational Research and Training as in Andhra Pradesh or of the State Institute of Education as in Kerala and Delhi, or of a training college or separate institutes of guidance which are subordinate offices of the Directorate of Education.

Activities of State Bureaus

(i) Plan coordinating and supervising guidance services within the State.

(ii) Conducting consultative and field services.

(iii) Collecting occupational information and producing informational materials.

(iv) Organising simple group guidance activities.

GUIDANCE AGENCIES AT DIFFERENT LEVELS

(A) National Level

- NCERT Department of Education Psychology Counselling and Guidance → (B) State Level
  - State Guidance Bureau → (C) District Level District Counsellors → (D) School Level School Counsellors Visiting Counsellors Careers Masters
  - Department of Education and Psychology Training Colleges, Universities
  - Private Agencies
- National Employment Services → (B) State Level
  - Directorate of Employment and Training → (C) District Level Employment Exchanges Vocational Guidance Unit → (D) School Level Vocational Guidance Officer
  - University Level → University Employment Information and Guidance Bureau → College Level → Liaison Unit Liaison Officers in Colleges
  - Private Agencies

(v) Carrying out development adaptation and translation of tests, questionnaires, etc.

(vi) Conducting training of guidance workers.

Area of State Directorate of Employment and Training

1. Organisation of occupational information programme.
2. Employment market information programme.
3. Careers study centres.
4. Foreign employment and training information centres.
5. Selection of courses and institutions.
6. Admission matters.
7. Scholarships, fellowships, assistantship and apprenticeships.
8. Information about passport and visa.
9. Employment prospects.
10. Part-time employment.
11. Special units for the handicapped.

3. Training Colleges and University Department of Education and Psychology

These offer one or two courses in guidance in the programme for the degrees of B.Ed. and M.A. in Psychology. Some of these also train career masters through organising short-term courses.

4. Private Guidance Agencies

Some private guidance agencies have been sponsored by charitable trusts, social welfare organisations or educational societies in India.

5. Guidance Services in Secondary Schools

Guidance Services in secondary schools are conducted by the following guidance personnel conducting well-equipped guidance services in schools :

(i) The Principal and his colleagues.

(ii) A guidance counsellor.

(iii) Teacher-counsellor or career masters.

(iv) Specialists in specific areas of service (part-time or full-time), which include the following :

   (a) Social worker.
   (b) Psychologist.
   (c) Doctor, dentist, nurse.
   (d) Parents.
   (e) Community health, welfare and guidance agencies.

Duties of a Career Master/Mistress

(i) To explain guidance point of view to all the members of the school faculty and parents and securing their cooperation.

(ii) To introduce guidance programme in the schools.

(iii) To set up an Educational and Vocational Information Centre/ Corner in the school.

(iv) To collect classify and file educational and occupational information.

(v) To disseminate educational and occupational information through :

(a) Career talks.

(b) Group talks.

(c) Bulletin board display.

(d) Film shows.

(e) Career days, career weeks and career conferences.

(f) Tours, etc.

(g) To introduce Cumulative Record Cards.

POPULARISATION AND CO-ORDINATION OF GUIDANCE SERVICES

On June 2 and 3, 1971 an All India Conference on Vocational Guidance and Testing was convened by the N.C.E.R.T. in collaboration with the Director General, Employment and Training, Delhi and New Delhi. It was attended by the Directors of Public Instructions or their representatives from Chandigarh, Delhi, Himachal Pradesh and Mysore, nine State Directors of Employment or their representatives, fourteen Heads of State Bureaus of Educational and Vocational Guidance or their representatives, seven State Vocational Guidance Officers or their representatives, ten officers from the Directorate General of Employment and Training, Ministry of Labour, Employment and Rehabilitation, New Delhi, and eight officers from the Department of Educational Psychology and Foundations of Education, National Institute of Education, N.C.E.R.T., New Delhi.

RECOMMENDATIONS OF THE CONFERENCE

1. Collaboration of Various Agencies

(i) Training. As there is a great scope for collaboration in the training of guidance workers at various levels, *viz.*, career masters, counsellors and vocational guidance officers, the N.C.E.R.T. and the Central Institute for Research and Training in Employment Service should collaborate in the training of counsellors and vocational guidance officers.

(ii) Occupational information. The responsibility for bringing out occupational information literature should be shared by the various agencies, including the career study centres of National Employment Service.

(iii) Guidance tools. These should be prepared by the proper assessment of persons seeking guidance through collaboration among various agencies in the development of aptitude and other tests should be promoted.

(iv) Evaluation and assessment. When school leavers report for registration at employment exchange cumulative records from schools and assessment reports from guidance agencies should be made available to employment exchanges.

(v) Public relations. Following recommendations were made for the success of the vocational guidance programme :

(a) The confidence of the people should be won.

(b) Publicity should be sought for the programme through mass media such as radio, television and the press.

(c) And if testing is done, it should be done properly.

(d) **Role of Industry.** Industries should be involved in the collaborative effort for providing vocational guidance. Employers should bc educated to appreciate the importance of vocational guidance and selection.

2. Organisation of a Minimum Guidance Programme for Schools

(i) Determined efforts should be made to carry out the programme of guidance in schools.

(ii) Principals and Headmasters should be properly oriented towards guidance.

(iii) Emphasis should be laid on the proper maintenance of the cumulative record cards.

(iv) Provision for a case conference should be made in the suggested minimum guidance programme.

(v) More administrative control is needed by the State Guidance Bureau over counsellors and career masters.

(vi) Only trained and qualified persons should be appointed to guidance positions. The posts of the persons in-charge of guidance in each State should be made very senior posts.

3. Pilot Project for Strengthening Guidance and "Career Advisory Services" for Students at School

(i) Meeting for preparation. The District Guidance Officers participating in the project should meet to discuss the programme to be undertaken and make necessary preparations for launching it and evaluating it. The meeting may be convened by some central agency as early as possible.

(ii) Control. The scheme should be put under the control of the State Bureau of Educational and Vocational Guidance for supervision and technical advice.

(iii) Training of career masters. The career masters for the schools covered in the project should be trained for dissemination of occupational and educational information by the SBEVG or extension centre in the training college.

(iv) **Training of teachers.** Teachers should be trained in the administration and scoring of psychological group tests, particularly the intelligence and aptitude tests as career masters are not trained to undertake this responsibility, nor do they have the time.

(v) **Test construction work.** It should be the responsibility of State or Central institutions which have the necessary resources and competency in the area.

(vi) **Prototype material.** NCERT's prototype material may be quite useful for the programme.

(vii) **Audio-visual material.** The free audio-visual material available with the Central Film Library of the Department of Teaching Aids of NCERT, the Ministry of Information and Broadcasting, and the Ministry of Industrial Development may be used for guidance purposes.

(viii) **Employment exchanges.** Career masters may work in employment exchanges for three or four months so that they may get a sufficient background for their work of imparting occupational information.

(ix) **District Guidance Committees.** These should be formed comprising of employers, teachers, parents and V.G.O's.

(x) **Incentives.** These should be introduced to get good work from guidance personnel. The career masters must get some allowance.

4. Prototype Literature and Techniques in Development of Self-Understanding and Imparting Information from Planning Careers and Courses for Middle and Higher Secondary Schools.

Prototype material may be published by the NCERT, and may be priced.

5. Collaboration in the Development of the General Aptitude Test Battery

Regarding the adaptation of the General Aptitude Test Battery (GATB) of the U.S. Employment of Service to Indian conditions, the following recommendations were made :

(i) It may be adapted in the first instance in English and Hindi, as pilot projects. Any State which offers to adapt it in regional language with its own resources may be allowed to do so.

(ii) **Study of experimental design.** The Directorate General of Employment and Training may request some top-level experts in psychometrics to have a close look at its experimental design for the adaptation of the GATB, and to advise the DGE and T. A Technical Committee for the adaptation of the GATB may be set up for this purpose.

(iii) Coordination. The Directorate General of Employment and Training may be responsible for coordinating the work involved in the adaptation of both the English and Hindi versions of the battery. NCERT staff should be available for consultation.

(iv) Adaptation in Hindi. As far as adaptation in Hindi is concerned, the following will be the distribution of work :

(a) *Haryana* : The State Bureau of Educational and Vocational Guidance, Haryana, will take up the work of modification of the Arithmetic Reason Test and prepare two parallel forms of the test.

(b) *Madhya Pradesh* : The College of Educational Psychology and Guidance, Madhya Pradesh, will be responsible for the preparation of the Vocabulary Test, two parallel forms.

(c) *Rajasthan* : The State Bureau of Educational and Vocational Guidance, Rajasthan, will be responsible for the preparation of the Name Comparison Test in Hindi (Devanagri script, not in Roman alphabet as proposed in the original scheme), two parallel forms.

(d) *Meetings* : Meetings of Heads of State Bureaus of Educational and Vocational Guidance in the Hindi-speaking region may be organised occasionally by the D.G.E. and T. for scrutinising the items of the tests and for facilitating the co-ordination of the work.

(v) Test-material. The D.G.E. and T. will be responsible for printing the test material and making it available to the State Directors of Employment and the Heads of the State Bureaus of Educational and Vocational Guidance.

(vi) Adaptation of the English version of the GATB. It will be the responsibility of the D.G.E. and T. The work done up to this date may be reviewed and revised before administering the tests to students in English-medium schools.

(vii) Training of personnel. The D.G.E. and T. will train the personnel of the Employment Service in the techniques of administration and scoring of the GATB and in the collection of criterion data. Training would be given by the D.G.E. and T. It will also give much training to the staff of the State Bureaus of Educational and Vocational Guidance whenever there is a need to do so.

(viii) Finance. The D.G.E. and T. will bear the financial responsibility for the following :

(a) The test material, and in fact provide the material;

(b) T.A. and D.A. of the staff of Bureaus of Educational and Vocational Guidance, as well as of D.G.E. and T. the State Employment service and

(c) T.A. and D.A. for members of the Technical Committee set up for the purpose.

Causes of Slow Progress of Guidance in India

1. Meagre financial resources and allocations for guidance.

2. Lack of awareness of the need for guidance among people.

3. Inadequate guidance services provided at various levels to India.

4. Appointment in some cases of persons not trained in guidance at school and college level.

5. Very unfavourable pupil-counsellor ratio in school and college.

6. Lack of guidance tools and equipment in educational institutions.

7. Lack of a clear-cut policy in sanctioning grants to educational institution for guidance services.

8. Little provision in the time-table for guidance programmes at schools and colleges.

9. Counsellors have been entrusted with all sorts of duties which make their job burdensome reducing them for guidance.

10. Lack of suitable administrative machinery.

11. Traditional attitudes of teachers which is not in favour of guidance.

TABLE 9.1

EDUCATIONAL AND VOCATIONAL GUIDANCE BUREAUS IN INDIA

Sl. No.	State/Union Territory	Administrative Set-up	Designation of the Head
1.	Andaman & Nicobar Islands	State Bureaus has not been established	—
2.	Andhra Pradesh	Department of Educational Foundations, SCERT, Hyderabad	—
3.	Arunachal Pradesh	There is no State Bureau	—
4.	Assam	The State Bureau is attached to the office of the DPI	Assistant Director
5.	Delhi	The Bureau is a Unit of the SCERT	Guidance Officer
6.	Gujarat	Institute of Vocational Guidance, Ahmedabad	Vocational Guidance Officer
7.	Haryana	Guidance and Counselling Wing is a part of the SCERT, Haryana	Director SCERT
8.	Himachal Pradesh	State Bureau exists under the Directorate of Education, Himachal Pradesh	Assistant Director of Education (Guidance)

Sl. No.	State/Union Territory	Administrative Set-up	Designation of the Head
9.	Karnataka	S.B.E.V.G. is a part of Department of SCERT under the Directorate of Public Instruction	Senior Assistant, D.P.I.
10.	Kerala	S.B.E.V.G. is a part of the State Institute of Education	Counsellor
11.	Madhya Pradesh	S.B.E.V.G. is a part of the Educational Psychology and Guidance, Jabalpur	Principal and Honorary Director
12.	Maharashtra	Institute of Vocational Guidance and Section with a Sub-Bureau at Pune	Principal
13.	Manipur	S.B.E.V.G. is a part of the office of the Director of Education	Senior Research Officer
14.	Mizoram	E.V.G. Unit is attached to SCERT, Mizoram	Asstt. Vocational Guidance Officer
15.	Orissa	—	—
16.	Pondicherry	—	—
17.	Punjab	S.B.E.V.G. exists separately under the Department of Education	Director, Guidance Bureau
18.	Rajasthan	S.B.E.V.G. is a part of the SCERT	Deputy Director SCERT
19.	Sikkim	—	—
20.	Tamil Nadu	—	—
21.	Tripura	S.B.E.V.G. has been set up independently under the Department of Education	Guidance Officer
22.	Uttar Pradesh	Bureau of Psychology functions under the control of State Director of Education and the Director, SCERT. It functions at the regional and school levels.	Director
23.	West Bengal	—	—
24.	Meghalaya	E.V.G.B. is a part of SCERT	Director
25.	Dadra & Nagar Haveli	S.B.E.V.G. exists under Directorate of Education.	Assistant Director of Education.

TABLE 9.2

COMPARATIVE STATISTICS FOR SCHOOL GUIDANCE SERVICES BETWEEN 1963 AND 1985

Kinds of Guidance Programme	Number of Schools 1963	1968	1975	1981	1985	Increase or Decrease during 1981-85
1. Conducted by a full-time counsellor.	40	78	111	180	62	–118
2. Conducted by a part-time (teacher counsellor/visiting counsellor).	356	160	203	702	697	–50
3. Conducted by a career teacher.	564	4,407	7,763	9,093	10,321	+11228
Total No. of schools with any kind of guidance programme	804	4,603	8,077	9,975	10,970	+995

CAREER LITERATURE FOR GUIDANCE CORNER AND LIBRARY IN THE SCHOOL

(A) Publications of Central Institute of Research and Training in Employment Service, Pusa, New Delhi

1. *Economics for a Career*
2. *Learn While You Earn*
3. *Careers in Electric Supply Industry*
4. *Service Occupations as a Career*
5. *UPSC Competitive Examinations*
6. *Admissions to M.B.B.S.*
7. *Careers in Railways*
8. *Art for a Career*
9. *Psychology for a Career*
10. *Careers in Banking Industry*
11. *Careers for Arts and Commerce Graduates*
12. *Admission to Engineering*
13. *Careers in Professional Management*
14. *Biology for a Career*
15. *Careers for Non-Matriculates and School Dropouts*
16. *Careers in Protective Forces*
17. *Careers in Communication*
18. *Careers in Air Transport*

19. *Careers in Teaching*
20. *Advertising as a Career*
21. *Careers in Data Processing*
22. *Careers in Commercial and Secretariat Practices*
23. *Concessions and Priorities Admissible to Ex-Defence Service Personnel*
24. *Careers in Printing*
25. *Careers in Accountancy*
26. *Selling as a Career*
27. *The Physio-Therapist*
28. *Job Seekers' Guides (Craftsman as a Career)*
29. *Careers in Defence Forces*
30. *Facilities for Scheduled Castes and Scheduled Tribes*
31. *History as a Career*
32. *Careers in Agriculture and Allied Fields*
33. *Careers in Marine Transport*
34. *Careers in Road Transport*
35. *Careers in Hoteliering*
36. *You Are 10 +What Do You Like to Be*
37. *Careers for High/Higher Secondary School Leavers*
38. *Careers Through Competitive Examinations*
39. *Careers in Medicine and Allied Fields.*

(B) Publications of University Employment Information and Guidance Bureau, Banaras Hindu University

1. *Economics for Your Career*
2. *Law for Your Career*
3. *Career in Journalism*
4. *Careers in Computer Science/Technology*
5. *Careers in Physical Education and Sports*
6. *Facilities for Physically Handicapped*
7. *Educational and Occupational Opportunities in Chemical Engineering*
8. *Careers Orientation Programme*
9. *The Student Counsellor.*

(C) Publications of Institute of Vocational Guidance and Selection, Bombay

1. *Courses in Pharmacy*
2. *Some Courses for B.Sc. (Chemistry) Student*
3. *Nursing as a Career*

4. *Profession of Company Secretary*
5. *Courses in Social Work*

(D) Publications of University Employment Information and Guidance Bureau, Hissar

1. *Home Science as Your Career*
2. *Career for Veterinary Graduates/Post-Graduates*

(E) Other Government Publications

1. *Pocket Book of Labour Statistics* (Simla Labour Bureau)
2. *National Classification of Occupations* (DIS & T)

(F) Publications of Private Publishers

(a) Doaba House Nai Sarak, Delhi
A Book of Careers (1987).

(b) Creative Career Publishers, Bapu Park, Kotla Mubarakpur, New Delhi.

1. *Educational and Training Facilities in Delhi.*
2. *Agricultural Training Facilities in India.*
3. *Management Training Facilities in India.*
4. *Training Facilities in Medical and Para-Medical Fields.*
5. *Scholarships : Inland and Overseas.*
6. *Training Facilities in Engineering and Technology.*
7. *Educational and Vocational Training Facilities.*
8. *Career in Cricket and Other Sports.*
9. *Training Facilities through Distance Education.*
10. *Career Opportunities under the Central Government.*
11. *General Knowledge.*
12. *Bases of Career Planning.*
13. *Career for Women.*

LIST OF AGENCIES PUBLISHING CAREER LITERATURE AND OCCUPATIONAL INFORMATION MATERIAL

1. Association of Indian Universities, 16, Kotla Marg, New Delhi-110 002.

2. Central Institute of Research and Training in Employment Services, Pusa Road, New Delhi.

3. Central Statistical Organisation, Sardar Patel Bhavan, Parliament Street, New Delhi.

4. Council of Scientific and Industrial Research, Rafi Marg, New Delhi-110 001.

5. Director General of Health Services, Nirman Bhavan, Maulana Azad Road, New Delhi-110 011.

6. Indian Council of Agricultural Research, Krishi Bhavan, Rajendra Prasad Road, New Delhi-110 011.

7. Institute of Vocational Guidance and Selection, 3 Mahapalika Marg Bombay.

8. Ministry of Human Resource Development, Department of Education, Government of India, Shastri Bhavan, New Delhi-110 011.

9. National Council of Educational Research and Training, 17 B, Sri Aurobindo Marg, New Delhi-110 016.

10. Staff Selection Commission, Block 12, Central Government Complex, Lodhi Road, New Delhi-110 003.

11. State Guidance Bureaus in the country.

12. Union Public Service Commission, Dholpur House, New Delhi.

13. University Employment Information and Guidance Bureaux of Various Universities.

14. State Public Service Commission.

15. Private Publishers.

GUIDANCE AT N.C.E.R.T.

Establishment

The (NCERT) National Council of Educational Research and Training was established on 1 September 1961, as an autonomous organisation to function as an academic adviser to the Ministry of Human Resource Development, Department of Education, Government of India. The Ministry draws upon the expertise of the NCERT in formulating and implementing its policies and programmes in school education.

Department of Counselling and Guidance

Qualitative improvement of education, through the application of the disciplines of educational psychology and counselling and guidance, particularly at the elementary, secondary and senior secondary levels, is the major concern of the Department of Educational Psychology, Counselling and Guidance of the NCERT. It has been engaged in research, development and training activities related to counselling and guidance, identification and development of talent, behaviour technology and development of syllabi and instructional materials. Its projects/programmes aim at the optimal development and self-actualisation of the learner, in all aspects of his/her potentialities and functioning. It took steps towards implementing the recommendations contained in the National Policy on Education (NPE) and Programme of Action (POA), bearing on educational psychology, counselling and guidance.

Research Studies Undertaken

1. A Study of Psychological Characteristics *vis-a-vis* Educational and Vocational Planning of Scheduled Caste High School Boys.

2. Improving Cognitive Functions and Classroom Behaviour of Elementary Students by Contingency Management.

3. A Study of the Educational and Vocational Planning, Academic Achievement and Selected Psychological and Home.

ALL-INDIA EDUCATIONAL AND VOCATIONAL GUIDANCE ASSOCIATION

Many guidance seminars have been organised on an all India set up in 1956. An All-India Educational and Vocational Guidance Association seeks the following objects laid down in its constitution :

Objectives

(i) To coordinate educational and vocational guidance activities all over India and to maintain standard in the field.

(ii) To promote public consciousness in the matters pertaining to guidance.

(iii) To consolidate and further guidance in general and educational and vocational guidance in particular.

(iv) To bring together periodically workers in the field of guidance in the country and to take necessary steps for the exchange of ideas, information and research work and the like in the field.

(v) To undertake any other activity in furtherance of guidance in India.

Resolutions

At the Third Annual Meeting of the All-India Educational and Vocational Association held at Jabalpur from April 12 to 15, 1958, the following important resolutions were moved :

1. Counsellors in schools. It is desirable to have full-time counsellors in schools. However, until such full-time counsellors can be appointed, part-time counsellors should be appointed, but their work should be properly supervised and they should be adequately remunerated.

2. Training. For full-time counsellors the duration of training should be one year. For part-time counsellors the period of training should be according to the functions they will have to perform after the training is over. In addition, orientation courses in guidance or the guidance courses integrated with teacher education programme may be offered by training colleges, guidance bureaux, etc.

3. U.G.C. aid. The conference recommends to the University Grants Commission to assist Universities and Colleges in India in the urgent task of setting up organisation on the university campuses for Guidance and Student Personnel Work. For this purpose A.I.E.V.G.A. would be willing and ready to give necessary technical assistance.

4. Professional training of staff. All those employed in a professional capacity in guidance bureaux should have adequate professional training in Guidance.

5. Minimum staff. The minimum staff of the State Bureau should consist of a full-time Director, two counsellors and two full-time assistants.

6. Agencies for test-construction. Special agencies should be set up for test construction at the National as well as State levels with the assistance of Faculties of Education and Psychology.

7. Block grant. The Association resolves to request the Ministry of Education to give a block grant to the Association to meet its financial difficulties.

8. Publications. The Association resolves to request the All-India Council for Secondary Education to assist it by publishing the activities of the Association in its journal and by deputing persons in the Extension Department to the annual conference of the Association, and by recommending to Teachers' Colleges and Extension Departments to subscribe to the Journal of the Association.

9. Small grants. The Association resolves to request State Directors of Education to block small grants to the Association to meet in deficit and to bring the Journal to the notice of the institutions under their control.

A Centrally-sponsored Scheme of Guidance

During the Third Plan the development of the guidance was made a Centrally sponsored scheme of the Ministry of Education in order to provide financial assistance and advice to States.

Features of the Scheme

1. The establishment of State bureaux of guidance in the States where they did not already exist.

2. The strengthening of the existing State bureaux.

3. The establishment of guidance services with a full-time counsellor in 170 multi-purpose schools.

4. The establishment of an occupational information programme with a Career Master in-charge (who is a regular teacher of the school), in about 2,500 schools.

THE EDUCATION COMMISSION

Importance of guidance services

"Guidance services have a much wider scope and function than merely that of assisting students in making educational and vocational choices. The aims of guidance are both adjustive and developmental; it helps the student in making the best possible adjustments to the situations in the educational institution and in the home and at the same time, facilitates the development of all aspects of his personality. Guidance, therefore, should be regarded as an integral part of education and not a special psychological or social service which is peripheral to educational purposes. It is meant for all students not just for those

TABLE 9.3

EDUCATION AND VOCATIONAL GUIDANCE BUREAUS EXISTING IN VARIOUS STATES, THEIR MANAGEMENT AND YEAR OF ESTABLISHMENT

States/ Union Territory		Name of the Institution	Location	Management	Year of Establishment
1. Andhra Pradesh	(i)	State Bureau of Education and Vocational Guidance.	Hyderabad	Government	1957
2. Assam	(ii)	Bureau of Educational and Vocational Guidance, Office of the DPI.	Shillong	Government	1957
	(iii)	Educational and Vocational Guidance Unit Social Service League.	Silchar	Private	1959
3. Bihar	(iv)	Bureau of Educational and Vocational Guidance, Kadam Kuan.	Patna	Government	1956
4. Delhi	(v)	Bureau of Educational and Vocational Guidance.	New Delhi	Government	1966
	(vi)	College of Vocational Studies University.	New Delhi	Governemnt	
5. Gujarat	(vii)	Institute of Vocational Guidance, Shantiniketan Society.	Ahmedabad	Government	1956
	(viii)	Psychological Educational and Remedial Services.	Ahmedabad	Private	1960
	(ix)	Student Counselling Centre, M.S. University of Baroda.	Baroda	Private	1960
	(x)	Secondary School Guidance Bureau, M.S. University of Baroda.	Baroda	Private	1959
	(xi)	Student Psychological Centre, B.M. Institute.	Ahmedabad	Private	1956

...Contd.

Table 9.3 *Contd.*

States/ Union Territory		Name of the Institution	Location	Management	Year of Establishment
6. Haryana	(xii)	State Bureau of Educational and Vocational Guidance.	Chandigarh	Government	1957
7. Himachal Pradesh	(xiii)	State Bureau of Educational and Vocational Guidance.	Shimla	Government	1960
8. Jammu & Kashmir	(xiv)	State Bureau of Educational and Vocational Guidance.	Srinagar	Government	1960
9. Kerala	(xv)	Bureau of Educational Research and Service	Trivandrum	Government	1963
	(xvi)	University Bureau of Educational and Vocational Guidance, University of Kerala.	Trivandrum	Private	1963
10. Madhya Pradesh	(xvii)	Bureau of Educational and Vocational Guidance.	Jabalpur	Government	1956
11. Maharashtra	(xviii)	Institute of Vocational Guidance, 3 Cruckashank Road.	Mumbai	Government	1950
	(xix)	Vocational Guidance Department, Gujarat Research Society.	Mumbai	Private	1954
	(xx)	Vocational Guidance Bureau and Child Centre, St. Xavier's Institute of Education.	Mumbai	Private	1960
	(xxi)	Parsi Panchayat Vocational and Educational Guidance Bureau.	Mumbai	Private	1962
12. Manipur	(xxii)	Bureau of Educational and Vocational Guidance.	Imphal	Government	

13.	Karnataka	(xxiii)	Bureau of Educational and Vocational Guidance, No. 27, V Block, Kumra Park, West Extension, Bangalore.	Bangalore	Government	1959
		(xxiv)	Vocational Guidance Centre, Y.M.C.A.	Bangalore	Private	1955
14.	Orissa	(xxv)	State Bureau of Educational and Vocational Guidance, Radha Nath Training College.	Cuttack	Government	1955
15.	Punjab	(xxvi)	State Bureau of Educational and Vocational Guidance, 17 E Sector.	Chandigarh	Government	1962
		(xxvii)	U.C.N.I. Guidance Service.	Jullundur	Private	1957
16.	Rajasthan	(xxviii)	State Bureau of Educational and Vocational Guidance.	Bikaner	Government	1958
17.	Tripura	(xxix)	Bureau of Educational and Vocational Guidance.	Agartala	Government	
18.	Uttar Pradesh	(xxx)	Bureau of Psychology (Manovigyan Shala).	Allahabad	Government	1947
		(xxxi)	Educational and Vocational Guidance Centre, B.B. College of Education.	Agra	Private	1955
		(xxxii)	Educational and Vocational Guidance Centre, Aligarh Muslim University.	Aligarh	Private	1960
		(xxxiii)	Bureau of Educational Research, Ewing Christian College.	Allahabad	Private	1950
19.	West Bengal	(xxxiv)	Bureau Educational and Psychological Research, David Hare Training College, 25-3, Baligunge, Circular Road.	Kolkata	Government	1953
		(xxxv)	Bureau of Educational and Vocational Counselling Vocational Guidance Society.	Kolkata	Private	1956

who deviate from the norm in one direction or the other. It is also a continuous process aimed at assisting the individual to make decisions and adjustments from time to time."

Suggestions for Development of Guidance in India

1. Priority programmes. Guidance programmes should be included among the 'priority programmes' of the educational expansion activities of the Central and State Government.

2. Guidance in schools. A long-range programme may be planned for the introduction of guidance services in each school.

3. State and Regional level. A well-organised organisation may be established at the State and regional level.

4. Guidance as investment. It should be impressed upon the officers dealing with finance that guidance is important as an investment in human resources.

5. DDR Guidancc. A separate officer designated as the Deputy Director of Education may be appointed at the State level. He should be given adequate powers to issue instruction to the Principals of the schools.

6. Publicity. Adequate publicity may be given highlighting the importance of guidance.

7. Course. The training colleges offer a course in guidance at the B.Ed. or M.Ed. level.

8. Minimum qualifications. Minimum educational and professional qualifications may be laid down for the recruitment of various types of guidance personnel.

9. Training. Training programme are also needed for the research workers.

10. Development of Test-Material. Programmes for development of testing material may be undertaken in the light of Indian environment.

11. Short-term programme. A short-term programme may be chalked out keeping in view the availability of manual resources.

12. Counsellor. In the early stages of the guidance service for providing guidance to the students of classes IX, X, XI, and XII, one Counsellor serving two schools may be appointed.

13. Occupational service. All the schools may be provided with an occupational service.

14. Information centre. The information centre maintained in each school may provide information to students on occupational and educational opportunities and demands, scholarships, public examinations, as well as developing in the pupils desirable attitude towards studies and work.

15. Time-table. One period for each section of classes VIII to XII per week may be allotted for this purpose. The discernible ratio should be one counsellor for 300 students.

16. Career masters. These may be given an intensive training for about three weeks to perform work like this.

17. Cumulative records. Every school may be asked to maintain cumulative record cards of the students. Teachers may be trained for this purpose.

18. Evaluation. The existing system of evaluating the students' academic work may be changed.

19. Extra-curricular activities. Schools may be assisted in organising hobbies and recreational activities to provide some meaningful experiences for the students. These will enable them to explore and develop their interests and abilities.

20. Cooperation between school and home. A closer cooperation between the school and the home may be built up to make guidance programme more effective.

QUESTIONS FOR EXERCISE

1. Describe the organisation of guidance set up in India.
2. Suggest measures for the promotion of guidance services in India.
3. Describe the organisation of guidance services in India.
4. Explain the polarisation and co-ordination of the guidance services in India.
5. Write short note on guidance at NCERT.

10

STUDENT COUNSELLING

The main objective of counselling is to bring about a *voluntary* change in the client. For this purpose, the counsellor provides facilities to help achieve the desired change or make the suitable choice. *The client alone is responsible for the decisions or the choices he make, though the counsellor may assist in this process by his warmth and understanding relationship.* Counselling is not giving information though information may be given. It is not giving advice, making suggestions and recommendations. It is not influencing the client's values, attitudes, beliefs, interests, decisions, etc. with or without any threat or admonition.

COUNSELLING AND PSYCHOTHERAPY

Counselling and psychotherapy are different. Although the psychotherapist uses counselling as one of the techniques of treatment, psychotherapy is concerned mostly with individuals whose behaviours are neurotic. It deals with repressed individuals but counselling is concerned mostly with normal anxieties. It operates in a medical setting whereas counselling operates in an educational setting. It uses play therapy, psychodrama, socio-drama, etc. as techniques; in counselling, such techniques are used as can be employed in educational institutions, industrial establishments etc. It is deeper in scope whereas counselling is broader in scope. A counsellor cannot be a psychotherapist, a psychotherapist can be a counsellor, being better and specially qualified.

OBJECTIVES OF STUDENT COUNSELLING

Dunsmoor and Miller believe that the core of student counselling is to help the student to help himself.

From this point of view they describe the following objectives of student counselling :

1. To give the student information on matters important to success.
2. To get information about student which will be of help in solving his problems.
3. To establish a feeling of mutual understanding between student and teacher.
4. To help the student work out a plan for solving his difficulties.

5. To help the student know himself better — his interests, abilities, aptitudes and opportunities.
6. To encourage and develop special abilities and right attitudes.
7. To inspire successful endeavour toward attainment.
8. To assist the student in planning for educational and vocational choices.

Thus, the goal of counselling is problem clarification and self-directed needs. The counselling officer helps the student to understand the problems and helps the student to help himself. The role of the student is objective self-assessment of the situation and the role of counselling officer is to formulate the decision making process and to act as the stimulator of insights and sensitivities of the student.

Counselling does not solve the problems but only helps in solving it. If solution is not possible it helps face challenges and to live with them

This fact has been well brought out in Hannah's Green-book. Here, the girl bitterly accuses her psychiatrist after an unpleasant incident — what good is your reality when justice fails and dishonesty is glossed over and the ones who keep faith suffer...what good is your reality then?

The response is "...I never promised you a rose garden, I never promised you perfect justice...and I never promised you peace or happiness. My help is so that you can be free to fight for all of these things. The only reality I offer is challenge and being well is being free to accept it or not at whatever level you are capable. I never promise lies and the rose garden world of perfection is a lie and a bore too."

SCOPE OF COUNSELLING

Counselling has a vast scope. According to Williamson, "The techniques of counselling individual students may be observed in greatly modified form, in the individualised service; granting loans and scholarships; handling discipline cases; assignment of rooms and selection of room-mates in dormitories; advising on student activities and programmes; helping students choose vocational objectives; selecting optional courses of study; learning to read at college rate and comprehension."

Educational progress, course programme planning, financial and health matters, and problems of family, social and emotional adjustment are commonly expressed in the context of counselling. Very often, many of these are closely intertwined in experience of the same student. In such instances, terms such as 'vocational problem' and 'emotional problem' are nothing more than convenient labels which serve as tentative and approximate methods of classifying counselling cases. It often happens that a problem which is initially expressed by the student as simply one of learning how to study better or of making a suitable vocational choice turns out to be much more complex than that.

LEVELS OF COUNSELLING

Counselling is a term used quite loosely for face-to-face interviews in which the counsellor attempts non-coercively to help the counsellee or client, or a group of clients, to make personal decisions. It may be helpful to differentiate three levels of activity related to training :

1. *Informal counselling* : It is any helping relationship by a responsible person who may have little or no training for the work. For instance, ladies helping patients in hospitals through friendly conversations with them.

2. *Non-specialist counselling by professionals* : It is the help provided by physicians, lawyers, teachers, ministers, and others who do a great deal of face-to-face work with psychological problems in the course of their other work. Sometimes, special titles are used like "religious counselling" or "financial counselling."

3. *Professional counselling* : It is helping another person with decision and life-plans, whether personal or educational-vocational, by a person specially trained for this work. Professional counsellors are usually psychologists, or educational psychologists. 'Professional' means among other things the possession of master's or doctor's degree with at least a year of supervision by a trained professional and the acceptance of a professional code of ethics. Training for psychologists, among other things, emphasises test interpretation, research, the psychology of personality, occupational information and experience with a variety of clients.

CLASSIFICATION OF COUNSELLING

Counselling can be classified according to the *nature of the problem*, the *complexity of treatment*, and the *competence of the counsellor*. Lloyd Jones and Smith describe various levels of counselling with respect to the depth of the problem, length of contact, degree of need, and the skill of the counsellor.

1. Surface level. At the *Surface level* is the counselling offered when the student wishes only some item of information. The counselling given may be casual; it is brief, and it may be superficial in that it is not extensive or intensive. The need for help is important even though slight, and the relationship maintained through the brief contact should not be less than that maintained during the long counselling session.

2. Prolonged counselling. Counselling at the *next level* requires a more prolonged tact because the counsellee needs more and complicated information. He may, for example, wish assistance in planning a programme of study for a two or four year period. As the problems became more complicated and as more intensive study of the case is required, and more specialised help is needed, counselling at deeper levels becomes necessary.

3. Therapeutic counselling. When the student is seriously disturbed, *therapeutic counselling* may be needed. Williamson feels that counselling is needed not only for helping individuals to gain insight into their emotional conflicts but also for helping them with problems stemming from lack of information, such as information about vocational aptitudes and interests or about work opportunities, so that they may conduct their future adjustments in such a way, that a 'minimum of mal-adaptive repressions' occur.

SITUATIONS REQUIRING COUNSELLING

1. When the student needs not only reliable information but an interested interpretation of such information as meets his own personal difficulties.
2. When the student needs a wise, sympathetic listener with broader experience than his own, to whom he can recount his difficulties and from whom he may gain suggestions regarding his own proposed plan of action.
3. When the counsellor has access to facilities for helping in the solution of a student's problem to which the student does not have easy access.
4. When the student is unaware that he has a certain problem but for his best development, must be around to a consciousness of that problem.
5. When the student is aware of a problem and of the strain and difficulty it is causing, but is unable to define and understand it, and is unable to cope with it independently.

Type of students requiring counselling

1. Those who have a consistent record of under-achievement.
2. Those whose scholastic achievement drops suddenly.
3. Those who need financial aid in order to continue their studies.
4. Those who find it difficult to participate in class and extra-class activities.
5. Those who use exhibitionism for gaining recognition or attention in class.
6. Those who find it difficult to adjust to the college/university.
7. Those who suddenly decide to drop out of college/university.
8. Those who display unusual ability in any direction — intellectual, artistic, musical, etc.
9. Those who have behaviour problems such as drug addiction, aggressiveness, bullying, stealing, shyness, timidity, etc.

KINDS OF COUNSELLING TECHNIQUES

Divided on the basis of the nature of the counselling process and the part of the counsellor; three techniques are used for counselling :

1. Directive or Prescriptive or Counsellor-centred counselling.
2. Non-directive or Permissive or Client-centred counselling.
3. Eclectic counselling.

1. Directive or prescriptive or counsellor-centred counselling. E.G. Williamson is the chief exponent of this viewpoint. Such type of counselling involves six essential steps :

(i) *Analysis* : Collecting from a variety of sources the data needed for an adequate understanding of the student.

(ii) *Synthesis* : Summarising and organising the data so that they reveal the students' assets, liabilities, adjustments and maladjustments.

(iii) *Diagnosis* : Formulating conclusions regarding the nature and the cause of the problems exhibited by the student.

(iv) *Prognosis* : Predicting the future development of the students' problems.

(v) *Counselling* : The counsellor's taking steps with the student to bring about adjustment and readjustment for the student.

(vi) *Follow-up* : Helping the student with new problems or with recurrence of the original problem and determining the effectiveness of the counselling provided to him.

Here the counsellor plays the major role; he does all that he can to get the counsellee to make a decision in keeping with his diagnosis. He tries to direct the thinking of the counsellee by informing, explaining, interpreting and advising.

A considerable use of interpretations and direction by the counsellor has led to this type of counselling being described as directive or counsellor-centred or active approach technique.

2. Non-directive or permissive or client-centred counselling. In this type of counselling, we make use of few or no diagnostic instruments, except in typical situations when the individual is handicapped due to certain limitations. In this type of counselling, it is the client — the counsellee — who is the pivot. Carl R. Rogers is the chief exponent of this viewpoint. The client takes an active part in the process of therapy. He gains insight into his problem with the help of the counsellor. It is he who takes decisions as to the action to be taken. The counsellor's role is passive. This type of counselling is a growth experience. The goal is the independence and integration of the client rather than the solution of a particular problem. The principal function of the counsellor is not to cultivate self-understanding in the client but instead, to create an atmosphere in which the client can work out his own understanding. The emotional elements or the feeling aspects are stressed rather than the intellectual aspects and the counselling leads to a voluntary choice of action.

3. Eclectic counselling. Bordin believed that Rogers and Williamson are towards opposite ends of the pole and the counselling methods may be evaluated along a continuum from non-directive to directive. When a counsellor deliberately tries to incorporate in his practice both directive and non-directive techniques, the result is eclecticism. F.C. Thorne, who is the exponent of this view, finds that it is possible for a counsellor to alternate between directive and non-directive methods even in the same interview without disrupting the non-directive permissive relationship with the client.

Here, the counsellor first studies the personality and needs of the individual. He then selects the technique that would be most helpful for the individual. He can start with the directive one but when the situation demands, the counsellor may switch over to the non-directive and *vice-versa*. The attempt is made to adjust the techniques to the requirements of the situation and the individual. Even techniques like reassurance, merely giving information, case history, testing, etc. can be used to achieve the purpose. The counsellor must be competent and proficient in the use of all available methods. The validity of the results is determined by the skill with which any method is used with reference to ethologic diagnosis and the indications of each individual case. The critical factor is not what method is used but rather the skill with which it is used.

The Process of Eclectic Counselling

1. Counselling may be preceded by an intake interview.
2. During the opening phase of counselling, the counsellor tries to establish rapport and may have to do structuring so that the client understands what to expect of counselling.
3. Often a tentative diagnosis is made which may include the collection of a case history and a plan for counselling is formulated.
4. To enhance the client's self-understanding, information, about him and his background may be gathered from various sources. The client needs to be helped to assimilate this information.
5. Educational, occupational and social information, if needed by the client, may be supplied to him.
6. The client achieves emotional release and insights.

QUESTIONS FOR EXERCISE

1. Distinguish between Counselling and Psycho-therapy and describe objectives of student counselling.
2. What is the scope of Counselling? Describe its various levels.
3. Which situations call for Counselling? Which students require it?
4. Explain kinds of counselling techniques.

11

GROUP GUIDANCE

DEFINITION

1. Jones. "Group guidance is any group enterprise or activity in which the primary purpose is to assist each individual in the group to solve his problems and to make his adjustment." He adds, "Group instruction means help given to pupils in a group; it is opposed to individual instruction but it may still be individualised instruction. Group tests are tests of each individual, not of the group — the term 'group guidance' is not only justifiable but has a very important meaning."

2. Crow and Crow. "Guidance in group situations usually is thought of as referring to those guidance services that are made available by school personnel to large or small groups of pupils."

IMPORTANCE OF GROUP GUIDANCE

(i) Robert H. Knapp stressing the importance of group guidance says, "If meaningful growth experiences are to be provided for a large number of children, the children must be grouped in some manner." Information to a large number of students can be conveyed in much less time than if it were given to each student, for instance, in an interview.

(ii) The counsellor may obtain general background information about his students and their problems which contacts with a large number of students.

(iii) It helps to improve students attitude and behaviour.

(iv) It is used to orient newly arrived pupils to the programme of the school. The newly arrived pupils are acquainted with the history of the school, its traditions, its regulations applicable to the academic, social and personal life of the students, co-curricular activities of the school, various curricular, the courses therein, etc.

(v) It is also very helpful in giving students training in different aspects of leadership.

(vi) Some elements of personality of a child can only be observed in a group situation if the teacher or the counsellor observes the child's reactions as a member of the group.

(vii) To provide adequate individual counselling are requires the services of so many qualified counsellors that it becomes essential to resort to group guidance techniques.

(viii) A teacher counsellor saves time by the group approach and is able to pay more attention to more difficult and complex aspects of the situations faced by an individual student.

(ix) It gives an opportunity to the students to express their anxieties and relieve their pent-up feelings. They generalise their individual problems and discuss them freely is group situation.

OBJECTIVES OF GROUP GUIDANCE

Kitch and McCreasy have listed the following objectives of group guidance :

1. To assist in the identification of common problem.

2. To provide information useful in the solution of adjustment problem.

3. To provide opportunities for experiences that promote self-understanding.

4. To lay the foundation of individual counselling.

ADVANTAGES OF GROUP GUIDANCE

1. Efficiency. As it enables the counsellor to convey information to the students in much less time the teacher can utilise his time in finding solutions to more difficult and complex aspects of the situation faced by an individual student.

2. Opportunities to study students in group situations. Through group guidance the counsellor gets opportunities to study the child in group situations and thus acquaints himself with his social attitudes and behaviour.

3. Discussion of common problems of students. In group guidance, the students discuss their common problems with the counsellor and find out ways and means of solving them.

4. Balanced judgements. In group guidance, students usually accept suggestions that have grown out of face exchange of opinions and realistic analysis of attitudes.

5. Enlightenment of the normal student. Through group discussion, the normal student learns to manage his own affairs in better way and thus be more enlightened.

6. Collective judgement on common problems. Group guidance provides outlets for discussion to the problems which the students are unwilling to discuss in private interviews.

7. Individual counselling. Group guidance prepares the way for individual counselling.

8. Contacts with students. The teacher counsellor comes into contact with a large number through group guidance of students than through interviews.

PROBLEMS FOR GROUP GUIDANCE

1. Those relating to educational plans.
2. Those relating to home and school adjustment.
3. Those relating to social situations.
4. Those relating to the use of leisure time.
5. Those relating to job finding.
6. Those relating to personality.
7. Those relating to economic and occupational activities.
8. Those relating to hobbies.

PRINCIPLES OF GROUP GUIDANCE

1. It should be used as a supplement to not as a substitute for counselling.

2. As far as possible the counsellor should encourage members of the group to seek individual counselling help.

3. The nature of the group should be relatively homogeneous in various aspects.

4. A project should be introduced that seems most appropriate to the students.

5. The person responsible for group guidance should be well versed with this guidance technique.

6. The group guidance should be considered as one and not the only means of guidance.

ESSENTIALS OF GROUP GUIDANCE

1. Rapport of the students with the counsellor.
2. Counsellor acceptance of student.
3. Counsellor listening carefully to the group.
4. Counsellor scientific observation of the group.
5. Problem-solving attitude of the counsellor.
6. Effective closing procedure by the counsellor.

TOOLS AND TECHNIQUES OF GROUP GUIDANCE

1. Career conferences.
2. Audio Visual Aids.
3. Visits to work sites.
4. Group Activities.
5. Occupational Information.
6. Group Discussions.
7. Clinical Counselling.

1. CAREER CONFERENCES

Career Conference is a very valuable technique of supplementing the information given to a group by the counsellor or the class teacher. In these conferences, a number of successful persons explain the vocations in which they work and answer questions about their jobs. The duration of the conference may be one day or more. The school counsellor should seek the co-operation of both teachers and the student in planning a conference. The students of the higher secondary classes and their parents should be invited to attend such conferences which should not be treated merely as a show work.

Organisation of Conference

Sufficient care should be taken in the selection of the speakers to explain the problems connected with particular occupations. They should be those who can explain their viewpoints to the students very clearly and who may place occupations in their true perspective. They should be given certain outline which they should keep in view while preparing their talks.

Some occupational or educational films may be shown to the audience in between different speeches. An exhibition may be organised on this occasion containing charts which throw light on careers and courses.

Suggestions for Holding Career Conferences

1. Period. The meeting should last approximately fifty-five minutes. Half of the time should be spent in presenting important facts regarding the field of work and the other half in answering questions.

2. Audience. The audience should consist of students between the ages of thirteen and eighteen.

3. Topics for discussions. Conference discussions should usually cover the following topics :

(i) Importance and history of the work.

(ii) Kinds of tasks involved in the work, tools, materials and processes.

(iii) Personal qualifications; the most essential and also the most desirable ones.

(iv) Special training required, ways of obtaining the training.

(v) Income compensation, pensions and benefits.

(vi) Working conditions, hazards, efforts of work on workers.

(vii) Possibilities of promotion, usual lines of promotion.

(viii) Ways of finding jobs.

(ix) Professional and workers organisations to which the worker belongs.

(x) Sources of further information.

Uses of Career Conferences

(i) The school is brought into directly contact with the community. The community is made aware of the problems of the youth.

(ii) Students get opportunities to hear eminent persons who discuss the actual problems regarding various occupations.

(iii) The parents are made guidance-minded and then think about the occupational future of their children.

(iv) Students are motivated to seek accurate and realistic information about occupational life.

(v) The trade and industry are made aware of their responsibilities in assisting the guidance agencies and the school to provide reliable information about occupations and training facilities for students.

2. AUDIO-VISUAL AIDS

Movie pictures, films strips, photographs, tape recorders and posters are used to present educational and vocational information to the students. A conference on educational and vocational guidance recommends that posters and charts must depict (i) the importance of curricular choice, (ii) the factors to be considered in the curricular choice, (iii) educational and occupational opportunities of each stream of academic study, (iv) indicating surplus and shortage occupations, (v) opportunities under the Five-Year Plans.

Advantages

(i) Audio-visual aids provide a realistic representation of different situations.

(ii) It is easy to show the actual operations and processes involved in an occupation with the help of pictures. Films shown to the students give more intelligent understanding is preceded by introductory remarks and followed by discussions.

(iii) All these methods make learning vivid and attractive.

3. VISITS TO WORK SITES

Group visits to work-sites and educational institutions provided concrete experiences which provide the best bases of every kind of learning. Learning based on actual and direct experience is the most effective one. Previous arrangements with the authorities concerned should be made before any institution or place is to be visited so that they make necessary arrangements to take the visiting party round the institution and sufficient information may be supplied to it. A group conference should be held to discuss that occupation or place immediately after the visit.

4. GROUP ACTIVITIES — VOCATIONAL, RECREATIONAL AND EDUCATIONAL

The Conference on Educational and Vocational Guidance of hobbies and leisure-time activities has given the following illustrative list which can be organised for this purpose :

(i) *Art club* : Drawing, clay modelling; photography, sign painting and decorating.
(ii) *Music group* : Instrumental, dramatics, stage, craft, folk dancing.
(iii) *Wood work* : Carving, picture framing.
(iv) *Textiles* : Weaving, costuming, felt work.
(v) *Trades* : Book-binding, painting, radio, electric wiring.
(vi) *Outdoor sports* : Camping, fishing, scouting, forestry.
(vii) *Personal service* : Laundry, hair-dressing, library.
(viii) *Gardening* : Flower shows, plant study, farming.
(ix) *Cookery* : Candy-making, cooking.
(x) *Animal cure* : Bee keeping, pigeon-raising.
(xi) Scientific Society.
(xii) *Model making* : Aeroplane, etc.
(xiii) School Publications.
(xiv) World Affairs Forum.
(xv) Student Government.

Advantages

(i) By these as a development activities student get opportunities to display their talents in various fields.
(ii) These activities provide occasions for the teachers to study them.

5. OCCUPATIONAL INFORMATION THROUGH SCHOOL SUBJECTS

The simple process of imparting information concerning occupations is that all the teachers teaching various subjects should acquaint the students with the occupational possibilities of their subjects. Occupations are closely related to and to a large extent depend upon the subjects. Teachers of English, History, Economics, Commerce, Physics, Chemistry, Biology, etc., should prepare lists of occupations connected with their subjects. They may also encourage and assist students to prepare such lists through their own efforts. This creates initiative and activity among students.

6. CLINICAL METHOD OF GUIDANCE

Clinical method of guidance and counselling needs more exhaustive data, employs more elaborate techniques and uses psychological tests to play an important role. The opinion of classmates, peers, friends, parents and teachers is also given critical treatment. Data is scrutinised more scientifically to make the diagnosis more complete, meaningful, relevant and valid. More care is exercised in interpreting data. As Bingham said, "When interpreting test results, ingenuity and fertility of insight as well as an understanding of psychological statistics, are indeed to be desired, and richly informed common sense must hold the reins."

Important Steps in Clinical Counselling

1. Analysis of the data. Data is collected regarding individuals's aptitudes, attitudes and personality traits. But only that data analysed which is meaningful and helpful in understanding the problem.

2. Synthesis of the data. The data is organised in such a way so that it gives an easy approach to understand the specific and unique characteristics of the pupil.

3. Diagnosis. The characteristics of the counsellee are found out and put on different profiles. These which are compared with education and vocational ability profiles, help in diagnosing the problems of the individual.

4. Prognosis. Prognosis is intended to formulate an idea about the intensity of the problem and its probable consequences with the technique and possibility of adjustment.

5. Counselling. First of all the individual is motivated to accept the treatment and thereafter he is assisted to modify his behaviour.

6. Follow-up. Follow-up relates to the counselling effects on the counsellee. It seeks to find out whether desired outcomes are visible or not. If not, the counsellor changes his technology of counselling.

7. Evaluation. Follow-up and evaluation are very closely interrelated. Follow-up itself leads to evaluation.

QUESTIONS FOR EXERCISE

1. Discuss the various methods that you would employ in giving guidance to students.
2. What are the advantages of group guidance? Describe techniques of group guidance.

12

Psycho-dynamics of Adjustment

Human situation is a constantly changing one. New conditions and problems are constantly besetting the individual right from his infancy to his death-bed, and he is invariably engaged in trying to find a satisfactory and pleasurable solution to them by employing his intelligence and other gifts of the mind and body. In other words, life is the name of unceasing process, the process of adjustment.

Meaning of Adjustment

What is adjustment? In the words of Laurence F. Shaffer, "Adjustment is the process by which a living organism maintains a balance between its needs and the circumstances that influence the satisfaction of these needs." Accordingly, the process of adjustment has two primary or main elements : one, the needs of the living organism; and two, the conditions of circumstances that influence these needs. These needs can be bio-genic, originating in society, personal or communal, or arising from any other conceivable source. On the other hand, circumstances influencing these needs also can either be inside the individual or outside him. Factors within the individual that influence these needs are his physical and mental states, capacity, attitudes, interests, etc. For example, most weakly constituted individuals cannot fulfil their own psychological motives, and thus their needs are definitely effected by their lack of strength. Factors arising within the environment are usually geographical conditions, social conditions, political and cultural influence. And, these conditions and circumstances can help as well as deter the fulfilment of the individual's requirements. In this manner, the nature influences upon the person's needs can be of two kinds — favourable and unfavourable. Positive or favourable influences help in the fulfilment of needs while unfavourable influences hinder their satisfaction.

Three elements in adjustment

An analysis of the process of adjustment will reveal the presence of three main elements :

1. Motive. The very process of adjustment in the living being is set in motion by the presence within him of some motive or need or requirement.

2. Thwarting conditions. When the environment does not present any features that tend to become obstacles in the fulfilment of these needs, then the adjustment is natural, facile and effortless, and no problem results. But if circumstances create obstacles in the path of such fulfilment, then the process of adjustment progresses further.

3. Varied responses. Once the fulfilment of a need has been obstructed, individual indulges in various actions which are a reaction to the obstacle. Such a reaction can be normal just as much as it can be abnormal.

4. Solution. As a result of these reactions and responses the individual achieves a degree of adjustment with the circumstances. The problem of adjustments is thereby solved.

Example of Adjustment

All these various component element of adjustment can be well understood with the aid of a concrete example. A student is actuated by a strong desirc to stand first in his class, and to do so by scoring very well. He works extremely hard but fails to achieve his objective because he has not the necessary mental equipment. Lack of the requisite intelligence forms an obstacle to the satisfaction of this motive, and hence, as a result, the student condescends to lower his aim somewhat by aiming at securing a second division. In order to accommodate his change of objective the student changes his mode of study. A change of response, suitable modification of the objective, and the means is achieved with satisfaction. The adjustment problem is also solved. Such a process of adjustment is universal phenomenon, and is to be seen at every level of life, at various times and under most conditions.

MOTIVE AND ADJUSTMENT

Generally speaking, the process of adjustment can be set in motion by any motive, for example, our physical needs are constantly being manifested in the form of adjustive behaviour patterns. But from our point of view these needs do not have much importance, for on the one hand, they are easily satisfied, and, on the other, in the event of their dissatisfaction life itself ceases in the organism, thus obviating all further adjustment activity. Hence, social motives and requirements have greater importance for the adjustment process. Social motives are developed within a cultural environment. Individuals of different cultures have different motives, and different cultures do not generate identical motives. For example, our society requires the development and encouragement of such motives as self-respect, self-realisation, acceptance, security, love, sympathy, etc., and these social motives naturally have definite influences upon sex and other biological needs. Just as social motives have greater importance than physiological needs, in the same manner, the process of adjustment place greater emphasis upon motives that are stronger than others. Strong motives, once they have been excited, can only be satisfied. Inability to satisfy them only leads to further dissatisfaction, and this tension is not ended till the objective has been attained.

THWARTING IN ADJUSTMENT

It has been remarked earlier that one important element in the process of adjustment is the presence of conditions that thwart the satisfaction of motives. Many are the forms that this thwarting can take, and is known to take. One form is frustration. If, for example, a person fails to catch a train and reach his destination because his wrist watch is not functioning properly, then he has to face frustration that arises out of the environment. This frustration can also be present in the individual himself. Another form of thwarting or obstacles is conflict. A state of conflict is precipitated when the individual is actuated by more than one motive arising simultaneously. And in the throes of these various motives he cannot decide upon the direction of action that he should adopt. Among the classical example of a state of conflict and indecision is the state of mind of Arjuna, described in the *Gita*, when he is divided between war and peace, between indecision and attachment. If, similarly, a student wants to continue his interest in games while at the same time he does not want to neglect his academic pursuit, then his mind will be battlefield of confrontation between these two desires. This state of conflict and tension will continue till the individual decides upon one particular motive and rejects the other. When conflict extends over a very long period of time, the individual shows signs of mental illness and other abnormalities of behaviour and conduct.

Frustration and conflict, the two forms of thwarting mentioned earlier, are closely related. Normally, when frustration results from some obstruction, the organism involved is seen adopting aggressive and violent behaviour towards the obstacle. Such aggressive behaviour can be direct as well as indirect. In children and unintelligent people it takes a direct form while in the case of most adults and intelligent people it takes a more indirect manifestation. Now, if the child's normal expression of aggression and violence resulting from some form of frustration is curbed and restricted, then it is actually prevented, but at the same time it becomes repressed and gives rise to feelings of fear and insecurity. Thus, some people become violent on being faced with some frustrating feelings of fear and insecurity as a result of the curb on their aggressive behaviour. As to the mode of behaviour that should be adopted in dealing with obstacles that cause frustration, an individual learns through trial and error. Different situations and circumstances find him behaving differently, and the behaviour patterns of adjustment that satisfy him are repeated while the patterns that cause him displeasure are discarded and replaced. And, the various reactions concerning the adjustment to different frustrations gradually take on the form of habits.

Hence, adult individual display permanent individual differences in the patterns of adjustment.

MALADJUSTED REACTIONS

Any state that contradicts that of adjustment is called maladjustment. In this condition contradicting that of adjustment, the individual organism fails to maintain a balance between his needs and the circumstances that influence the satisfaction of them. And, in this condition one observes reactions that are tendentious towards further imbalance. Reactions of this kind included all those behaviour patterns which can be called abnormal. For example, all kinds of mental illness will cited as maladjustment reaction. Maladjustment will be the term to be applied to criminal, delinquent and anti-social behaviour. The maladjusted individual fails to attain to a state of adjustment with his circumstances, and, instead of trying to face up to the situation, tries to run away from it. Abnormal fears and mental formations are to be seen in the individual. Even his mistakes are construed as no mistakes, and he rationalises upon them. Instead of working to achieve something of his own accord, he identifies himself with the achievement of others and thereby satisfies himself. He has very little capacity to cooperate with others, and he finds it difficult to live with them. He prefers solitude and loves to wonder in an imaginary world. Extreme day-dreaming is a maladjusted reaction. Another example of it is the projection of one's faults upon another and holding him responsible for one's own frustrations. Similarly, many apparently adult individuals are seen behaving in a markedly childish manner; this too is a form of maladjusted reaction. Briefly, maladjusted reactions include all such reactions that prove obstacles to adjustment.

CRITERIA OF PERSONALITY ADJUSTMENT

The implication of adjustment is the balance between an individual's needs and the circumstances that satisfy these needs. Hence the evaluation of the adjustment achieved by a person will require the knowledge of two things. The first is the requirement of this person and second the conditions and circumstances that influence the satisfaction of his need. Once these two are known it will be necessary to find the balance that is struck between them. If the balance is good and desirable, then the individual can be said to be properly adjusted, but if the balance is disturbed then the person will be considered maladjusted. Evidently, this adjustment will differ from individual to individual, since, their needs and the conditions that satisfy them need not be common. In this manner, the criterion of personality adjustment is relative to the individual's requirements and the cultural and social complex of circumstances in which he lives. In other words, the criterion changes when these conditions change. For example, in culture that encourages the combative and aggressive spirit men have greater need for this motive in their adjustment. On the other hand, in a culture that places very great stress upon amiability, the adjustment of personality will depend upon this motive, and it will have great influence upon the criterion of adjustment. Adjustment itself is relative to the individual and his circumstances. Thus, the qualitative traits that are required for adjustment of particular society and culture cannot be considered to be efficacious in every society and culture.

Despite the fact that the above limitations are operative everywhere, certain tentative and general criteria of adjustment can be established. Main criteria would be the following :

1. Integration of personality. One criterion of adjustment is the integration of personality. Personality complex of all psycho-physical traits. In this the various mental reactions and processes of intelligence and sentiment, desire and determination, etc., do not subsist in any disorder but rather in a proper organised system of functioning. Conflict is quite absent from them evidently, the proper integration of the personality is an ideal at which one and all should aim. It is only in such a state that persons can have internal peace and total welfare. The integrated personality is flexible, determined and organised. Mcdougall calls it the organisation of character and intelligence. The higher the degree of organisation in an individual's personality the better will be the degree of his adjustment, since in the absence of adjustment the personality cannot be integrated and organised. On the other hand, permanent adjustment is not possible in the absence of personality integration. The individual with an adjusted and organised personality maintains a balanced and practical outlook on life. Failures and frustrations do not disturb him unduly, and he persists in looking calm and master of the situation. His emotions, needs, thinking and other mental activities are adequately balanced and systematic. On the other hand, the personality of a maladjusted person is disintegrated. His life is disturbed, without any peace, and he also tends to disturb the peace of everyone else.

2. Reduction in tension. Another criterion of personality adjustment is the reduction or decrease in tension, a decrease that is consequent upon the fulfilment of his needs, irrespective of whether the fulfilment is achieved through socially acceptable or objectionable modes. It is a psychological fact that whenever someone or the other need of a person remains, dissatisfied it creates a state of tension. And this tension is removed only when the object satisfying that need is obtained. Absence of adjustment results in the increase of tension while its increase helps in reducing tension. In other words, a person's adjustment can be evaluated in terms of tension existing in his mind.

3. Harmony between need and environment. As has been mentioned earlier, the adjusted personality can be recognised from a harmony between his needs and his environment. Greater the degree of such harmony, the better will be adjustment, while on the other hand his personality will be considered less adjusted if this harmony is not of a high order. An adjusted individual has the capacity and energy to accommodate his needs and motives according to his environment, as also to mould this environment to suit his own needs and motives. In this manner, maximum satisfaction and pleasure is to be had in the mutual adjustment and harmony of both environment and requirement. Persons who fail to make an adjustment of their motives and needs to the environment in which they are placed cannot be happy even in the best of circumstances, and are always to be found complaining of the adversity of conditions. Failure of this kind also means that the individual who has not within him the power and capacity to mould conditions according to his own requirements, his usual condition is one of frustration and maladjustment. Problems are a part of everyone's life, but they also add spice to its otherwise dull fare. There is hardly any, if any at all, individual who is never in this life called upon to face a situation that promises conflict, promises him frustration and anger. If such conditions are present then the enterprising individual bends himself to varying and modifying them to suit his own requirements and thus achieves adjustments or otherwise makes changes in his own requirements and needs. For example, it is commonly noticed that some people succeed in making their ends meet very facilely even on a low income, and they give every appearance of being happy and contented. Contrary to such are people who are incessantly complaining of the extremity of their means even when they have a reasonable income. There is a condition of unhappiness, since there is a wide gap between their income and their expenditure, their needs are never even temporarily completely fulfilled. In such a condition the adjustment of personality is liable to be disturbed from two sides, first in case the needs of the person do not conform to the circumstances, and in the second case when the conditions are not propitious to the fulfilment of the needs. Hence, adjustment requires the balance between these two, even if modification and alteration is essential in both.

COMMON MODES OF REACTION TO DIFFICULTIES

Every individual has certain definite needs, and every individual lives in certain specific conditions. It is within these conditions that his needs are fulfilled. When the conditions are favourable no particular difficulty arises in such fulfilment, but for every individual this is not always possible. A condition that is not propitious for the fulfilment of some need is common in the life of every individual, and such circumstances and conditions always prove obstacles in the satisfaction of that need, thus creating problems. Difficulties refer to the conditions that prove obstacles to the satisfactions of a person's needs. As it is, one finds great individual differences in the manner of reacting to these difficulties, but even then there are certain modes of reaction that can be seen in every pattern of reaction behaviour. These methods are roughly the following :

1. Constructive adjustment. One very general form of reaction to difficulties is the mode of constructive adjustments and examples of this mode of behaviour are to be seen everywhere in life. Students in educational institutions are constantly faced with situations that become obstacles to the achievement of their educational and vocational objectives, praise and knowledge of self needs that are basic to them. Most students have recourse to constructive adjustments in order to overcome these situations, such as putting in longer hours of study or consulting numerous books and teachers in order to overcome their academic obstacles. Similarly, when a trader is faced with some problem of his trade, he resorts to some constructive adjustment to solve that problem. If a person is in financial straits then the simplest constructive adjustment would be for him to exercise economy in his expenditure. In constructive adjustment the main feature to be remarked is that it offers a quality of facing the situation rather than running away from it, and making efforts that solve the problem instead of merely postponing it.

2. Substitute adjustments. All individuals do not have the ready wit and wisdom to achieve constructive adjustment and thus retain their mental balance in the face of difficulties. A very large number of individuals have recourse to substitute adjustments when faced with difficult situations. This, also is a common and usual method of reacting of difficulties. For example, in a large number of cases, when students fail to pass at an examination, then, instead of urging them to work harder, they take it upon themselves to blame the teachers in particular and the entire educational system in general, and they daydream themselves into success in future. Some students start avoiding school when they fail while other more enterprising though more censored are the ones who leave home. The question that now arises is whether these reactions are activities of adjustment, since they do not tend to solve the problem inherent in the situation. A close observation will reveal that even through such reactions the individual is trying to satisfy need that in other individuals are solved through constructive and positive adjustment activity. A student failing in an examination is usually defamed and this obstructs his social ambitions and motives. Tensions that are created through this obstruction he tries to end by his activity of running away or transferring the blame on the teachers or by day-dreaming of success. Thus, for this reason are these reactions to difficulties called substitute reactions. Even though no direct satisfaction is forthcoming from such activity, yet the unsatisfied motive is indirectly and momentarily pacified, and in this manner adjustment is improved through decreases in tension. It must be noticed that adjustment is not a question of successful results but one of satisfaction of motives, irrespective of the methods that are adopted, be they normal, originating in disease and mental deficiency. It is often remarked that weak, lean and thin individuals usually walk with a swagger and an imposing style. The psychological reason for this is that in weak and lean individuals the motive of self-respect is suppressed, and in order to overcome this repression, instead of reasoning to some form of constructive adjustment, they walk with a swagger, thus saving their self-respect from injury and their mental balance from collapse. Here, it must be remarked that this should not be interpreted to mean that the satisfaction accorded to a motive by constructive adjustment is equal to the satisfaction caused by a substitute adjustment. The facts of the matter are other than this. Reactions of substitute adjustment usually win scorn and ridicule for the person practising them, from other members of society, and this further causes suppression of the person's desire for social acceptance. A person running to solitude away from this life's ignoble strife can save his desire for competition from being frustrated, but then his motives of security and sociability are frustrated. Hence, it is evident that the substitute adjustment usually results only in more frustration and suppression. On the other hand, these modes of adjustment are also usually harmful for the individual. For example, certain normally ugly individuals are seen trying to attract female attention through undesirable activity since they cannot win it in the normal course, and this usually results in great inconvenience to other more reasonable members of society. One characteristic of proper and constructive adjustment is that not only the individual but entire society benefits from it, besides improving the individual's social relationships.

3. Mental mechanism. Another mode of reacting to difficulties is that of mental mechanisms, main among them being projection, compensation, rationalisation, etc. As a general rule the consequence of these mechanisms is not good either for the individual or for society. Yet, in some degree or other all or some of these mechanisms are to be found in every individual, hence no individual can be declared abnormal on their account. It is only when one of them develops out of proportion that symptoms of abnormality can be discovered. Normally, a tendency to overlook one's owns fault and to blame others for one's failures is only naturally present in men, but if a person is observed in doing this all time and unduly regarding everyone else his enemy, then his conduct will undoubtedly be classed as abnormal. These mechanisms are also called the tools of adjustment, since their objective is the attainment of adjustment through various methods.

SCOPE OF ADJUSTMENT FOR STUDENTS

1. School. Adjustment in school work and to studies and school routines. This includes following adjustments :

(i) Adjustment of academic work, getting most out of specific studies and school activities.

(ii) Adjustment to learning problems and instructional difficulties.

(iii) Adjustment to exploratory experiences.

(iv) Adjustment between class-room objectives and individual outcomes.

(v) Adjustment to appropriate courses in line with individual characteristics.

2. Self. Adjustment to and within the self. This implies the following :

(i) Self-understanding and acceptance.

(ii) Insight into needs, values, attitudes.

(iii) Overcoming of emotional difficulties.

(iv) Maintenance of health and personal hygiene.

3. Society. Adjustment to everyday social requirement and relationships. This means the following :

(i) Adjustment with teachers and pupils.

(ii) Effectively meeting social requirements of living in class-room, school, home, culture and community.

(iii) Understanding of social needs and requirements.

(iv) Understanding group goals.

VIEW OF WILSON AND CHAPMAN

Wilson and Chapman discuss the following problems of adjustment in personal and social sphere :

1. Social Adjustment

(i) How best to get along with a boy or girl friend.

(ii) How to feel socially accepted.

(iii) How best to entertain.

(iv) How best to get information and make decisions about love and marriage.

(v) How to secure facilities for recreation.

(vi) How to acquire social ease.

(vii) How often to have dates, when to get home.

(viii) How best to meet people.

2. Family Relations

(i) Disagreement between child and parents on matters of standards.

(ii) Lack of understanding between the parents and the child.

(iii) Conflicts between brothers and sisters.

(iv) Broken homes.

(v) Too little time with parents.

(vi) Inability to get along with relations.

3. The Use of Time

(i) How to budget time wisely.

(ii) How to study.
(iii) How best to spend leisure time.
(iv) How to deal with time-consuming school subjects.

4. The Future

(i) Decision on vocation.
(ii) Continuing formal education.
(iii) Succeeding academically.
(iv) Succeeding vocationally.

5. Personality

(i) How to develop a good memory.
(ii) How to develop interest.
(iii) How to develop tolerance, tact and broadmindedness.
(iv) How to attract friends.
(v) How to develop physical attractiveness.
(vi) How to develop taste in the selection and wearing of clothes.
(vii) How to overcome bad temper, selfishness and jealousy.
(viii) How to develop character and poise and to overcome self-consciousness and timidity.

6. Part-time Jobs and Money

(i) How to get enough money to do things that have to be done.
(ii) How to get part-time job.
(iii) How to earn money and go to school.
(iv) How to get along on a part-time job.
(v) How to spend money wisely.
(vi) How to save money.
(vii) How to find suitable part-time work.

7. Youth's Health Worries

(i) Sufficient sleep.
(ii) Abnormal weight.
(iii) Teeth, ear, nose, throat trouble, physical fitness.
(iv) Proper diet for good health.
(v) Effects of smoking and drinking upon health, nervousness, nail biting.

Assistance with adjustment problems is given to all persons from birth onwards by parents, relatives, family friends and well-wishers in the community. It is increasingly recognised that professional knowledge and competence are required to deal adequately with many types of personal problems. In the words of Robert Hendry Mathewson, "Guidance and personal service in education, therefore, has come to be defined as the *Systematic professional process* of aiding individuals in making their choice, plans and adjustment in undertaking effective self-direction, and in meeting those problems of personal living that fall within the sphere of educational responsibility."

ROLE OF THE CLASS-ROOM TEACHER IN PUPIL ADJUSTMENT

Describing the role of the class-room teacher in providing a healthy classroom environment that would complement the adjustment process of each pupil, Raymond N. Hatch and Buford Stefflre have enlisted the following activities of the teacher :

1. He provides a class-room climate that permits young people to feel free to express themselves and to put forth their best efforts as individuals and a members of groups.

2. He develops as youngster's self-respect and self-esteem by compliments for work well done, a smile or a word of recognition.

3. He has an appreciation that deviation from acceptable behaviour is caused due to factors that stem from the school, the home and his community.

4. He recognises that a student who "causes no trouble" may be experiencing serious emotional conflicts.

5. He recognises that chronic behaviour cases may be sent to specialists for diagnosis and treatment.

6. He accepts that every pupil is different, and because he is different, he will achieve most if the teacher knows, understands, and plans activities in keeping with his needs.

7. He develops comprehensive records by collecting sociometric information, autobiographies and similar information through class-room setting.

8. He practises good mental health.

9. He participates and contributes to the effectiveness of case conferences.

QUESTIONS FOR EXERCISE

1. Define 'Adjustment'. What factors operate in the school to cause maladjustment in our pupil?
2. Define 'Adjustment'. Discuss some of the common modes of reaction to difficulties.
3. How is information regarding personal adjustment relevant for educational guidance? Give suitable examples in support of your answer. What are some of the useful techniques for personal guidance and counselling?
4. How does the teacher's own personality affect his way of dealing with various attitudes of learners towards him?
5. Explain the various procedures adopted for making adjustment in school work and every-day life?

13

PROFESSIONAL COUNSELLING

Professional counselling is a recent development in colleges and universities, industries and business establishment.

Definition of Counselling

1. **Webster's dictionary.** "Counselling is consultation, mutual interchange of opinions, deliberating together."

2. **Wren** (1962). "Counselling is a dynamic and purposeful relationship between two people who approach a mutually defined problems with mutual consideration of each other to the end that the younger or less mature, or more troubled of the two is aided to a self-determined resolution of his problem."

3. **James Michael Lee and Nathaniel J. Pattan.** "Counselling is the relationship between two persons in which one of them attempts to assist the other in so organising himself as to attain a particular form of happiness, adjustment to a life-situation, or in short, self-actualisation. Counselling always involves a one-to-one relationship, that is one client and one guidance worker in a formal or an informal interview situation."

4. **Merle M. Ohlsen** (1977). "Counselling is an accepting, trusting and safe relationship in which clients learn to discuss openly what worries and upsets them, to define precise behaviour goals, to acquire the essential social skills, and to develop the courage and self-confidence to implement desired new behaviours."

5. **Arbuckle** (1965). "Counselling is helping a person to come to see who he really is, what he has and does not have; what he can do easily, what he can do with difficulty and what he probably cannot do at all.... (It) is a close sharing of a human relationship with one who has for him a high regard; one who can offer him unconditional acceptance, but one who has no guarantees, no answers."

6. **Pepinsky and Pepinsky** (1954). "Counselling relationship refers to the interaction which (i) occurs between two individual called 'counsellor' and 'client', (ii) takes place within a professional setting and (iii) is initiated and maintained as a means of facilitating changes in the behaviour of the client. The Counselling relationship develop

from the interaction between two individuals, one a professionally trained worker and the other a person who seeks his services."

7. Hahn and Maclean (1955). "Counselling as a process which takes place in a one-to-one relationship between an individual beset by problems with which he cannot cope alone and a professional worker whose training and experience have qualified him to help others reach solution to various types of personal difficulties."

8. Blocker (1966). "Counselling as helping an individual become aware of himself and the ways in which he is reaching to behavioural influences of his environment. It further helps him to establish some personal meaning for this behaviour and to develop and clarify a set of goals and values for future behaviour."

9. Harriman. "Counselling is the psychotherapeutic relationship in which an individual (client) receives direct help from adviser (directive counselling) or finds an opportunity to release negative feelings and thus clear the way for positive growth in personality (non-directive counselling)."

10. Humphry and Traxler. "Counselling is the application of the personal recourses of the school or other institutions to the solution of the problems of the individuals."

11. A.J. Jones. "Counselling is a personal and dynamic relationship between two individuals (one of whom is older, or more experienced, wiser than the other), who altogether approaches a more or less well-defined problem of the younger or less experienced or less wise, with mutual consideration for each other to the end that the problem may be clearly defined and that the one who has the problem may be helped to a self-determined solution of it."

12. J.A. Keller. "Counselling is vitally related to learning. As in learning we are concerned with the modification of behaviour, so in counselling. The role of the counsellor is to discover the dissatisfactions (may be called problems) of the counsellor and help him set up some goals and guide him through difficulties and problems."

13. Myers. "Counselling implies a relationship between two individuals in which one gives a certain kind of assistance to the other."

14. Robinson. "The term counselling covers all types of two personal situations in which one person, the client, is helped to adjust more effectively to himself and his environment."

15. Ruth Strong. "Counselling process is a 'joint quest'. The student's responsibility is to try to understand himself and the direction in which he should go and to gain self-confidence in handling problems as they arise. The counsellor's responsibility is to assist in this process whenever the student needs and is ready for help. The counsellor serves as kind of key that unlocks new insights." The same author further observes : "The essence of the counselling process is a relationship in which the individual being counselled feels free to express himself fully and gains clarification of his goals, self-confidence in his ability to realise them, and methods or means of attacking difficulties as they arise. If properly done, counselling increases a student's understanding of himself not for anxieties about himself; helps him to help himself, not depend on the counsellor; prevents trouble rather than merely remedying it after it has gained headway."

16. Shostrom and Brammer. "A self-adjustive process, which helps the client become more self-directive and self-responsible."

17. Willy and Andrew. "Counselling is mental learning process. It involves two individuals — one seeking help and the other a professionally trained person helping the first to orient and direct himself towards a goal which leads to his maximum development and growth in his environment."

18. Williamson. "Counselling is a personalised and individualised process designed to aid the individuals to learn school subject-matter, citizenship tacts and other habits, skills, attitudes and beliefs which go to make up a normally adjusted human being. Counselling aids individuals to eliminate or to modify those disabilities which act as obstacles to learning through the building up of basic skills, including reading and social adjustment."

LEVELS OF COUNSELLING

1. Informal counselling. Informal counselling is done by elders for years without any training.

2. Non-Specialist counselling. It is done a part of the work of the teacher.

3. Professional counselling. It is given by a fully trained professional person, usually known as counsellor.

Situations Calling for Counselling

According to Miss Bragdon, following types of situations call for counselling :

1. A student needs not only reliable information but also an interpretation of such information as meets his own personal difficulties.

2. A student needs a wise listener with a broader experience than his own, to whom he can recount his difficulties and from he may gain suggestions.

3. A student thinks that the counsellor has access to facilities for acting in the solution of his problem and the student has not easy access to those.

4. A student is aware of the problem but is unable to define it.

5. A student is aware of the problem but because of a temporary strain and distraction, he is unable to cope with it intelligently.

Objectives of Counselling

Clarence G. Dunsmoor and Leonard M. Miller state following objectives of counselling :

1. To give the student information on matters important to his success.

2. To get information about the student which will be of help in solving his problems.

3. To establish mutual understanding between students and teachers.

4. To help the student work out a plan for solving his difficulties.

5. To help the student to know his interests, abilities, attitudes, etc.

6. To encourage and develop special abilities and right attitudes.

7. To assist the student in planning educational and vocational choices.

Elements of Counselling

According to Arbucle counselling has following three elements :

1. It involves two persons.

2. Its objective is to assist the counselee solve his problems independently.

3. It is a professional task and must be performed by professionally trained people.

Cattle believes in five elements of counselling :

1. Rapport with the counselee.

2. Communication between the counsellor and the counselee. Tone of voice, I facial expressions, gestures and postures of both the counsellor and the counselee play an important role.

3. Counsellor's through background of the counselling process.

4. Counselee's changes in feelings as counselling proceeds and progresses through various stages.

5. Structured counselling interview.

Characteristics of Counselling

In the words of Williamson, "The history of pedagogy, as well as that of thereby, indicates that some types of direct assistance from outside the individual's human capacities seem to be needed to achieve inner growth." E.W. Failer gives the following characteristics of counselling :

1. It concentrates on the normal individual.

2. It considers breadth rather than depth.

3. It involves a wide range of techniques.

4. It must be a cooperative affair and the counsellor must act as a point of contact.

5. It should not be solely based upon psychology. It must take the help of other branches of study.

6. It should meet all the needs. It should be neither child-centred nor technique centred, nor problem centred and nor counsellor centred alone.

Basic Principles of Counselling

Following are the basic principles of counselling, according to Hann and Maclean :

1. It is strongly dedicated to self-direction and self-realisation of the client or the student.

2. It is the development of the insights and understandings of the relations of self and environment.

3. It is a structured learning situation.

4. Its methods vary with the needs of the client.

5. It is primarily a preventive and remedial process.

6. It is voluntary for the student.

DISTINCTION FROM RELATED CONCEPTS

1. Counselling and guidance. Counselling is a part of guidance, not all of it. It is a specialised or individualised part which deals with the individual at problems points. Thus, all counselling is guidance but all guidance is not counselling.

2. Counselling and interview. While counselling is a part of guidance, interview is only technique used in the process of counselling. Counselling is a wider and comprehensive term.

3. Counselling and advising. Counselling is not synonymous with giving advice. A wise counsellor never gives advice until it is absolutely essential. Counselling is a process in which the counsellor assumes the responsibility for the decisions that are made. In advising, the counsellor accepts the responsibility for the quality of the decisions made. In counselling, the counselee arrives at the decision as a result of process and not because of the advice of the counsellor.

4. Counsellor and teaching. Counselling is not teaching. The following are some of the points of difference between counselling and teaching:

(i) Whereas counselling is one to one relationship, teaching is done in group.

(ii) Whereas counsellor is concerned with social and emotional problems, the teacher is concerned with academic and intellectual problems.

(iii) Counsellor uses many techniques like diagnostic tool, occupational information and several types of tests to understand the psychological make up of the counselee. Teacher uses various techniques like lecturing and audio-visual aids to make the teaching interesting and effective.

(iv) In counselling, the counsellor does not know the subject-matter of the counselling interview. On the other hand, in teaching the teacher knows the subject matter of teaching.

(v) In counselling the most important techniques is interview, but in teaching it is never used as a technique.

(vi) Counsellor increases information about self-occupation training institutions, colleges, apprenticeship programmes, etc. Teacher increases information of instructional activities.

5. Counselling and psychotherapy. Counselling is not psychotherapy although it is used by psychotherapist as one of the techniques of treatment. The following are some of the points of difference between the counselling and psychotherapy :

(i) Counselling is concerned mostly with normal individual having normal anxieties whereas psychotherapy is concerned with individuals whose behaviours are neurotic.

COUNSELLING AND PSYCHOTHERAPY

Psychotherapy	Counselling
1. Operates in a medical setting.	1. Operates in an education setting.
2. Special types of tools and techniques are employed.	2. Uses those tools and techniques that can be used in schools.
3. Deals with individuals having acute problems.	3. Concerned mostly with individuals having normal anxieties.
4. Considers psychology as the only basis for studying individuals.	4. Does not consider psychology as the only basis for studying the individuals.
5. Does not recognise the importance of socio-economic factor for solving the problem.	5. Socio-economic factors are given an important place.
6. Touches a few problems but goes very deep in studying those problems.	6. Touches with problems of the individuals but does not go deeper.
7. Involves one-to-one relationship.	7. Involves one-to-one or one-to-group relationships.
8. Treats each individual as a unique personality and helped accordingly.	8. Teachers usually employ group techniques and individual contacts grow out of the group relationship.
9. The counsellor may not know the subject matter of various subjects.	9. The teacher knows the subject matter.
10. Collects information about occupations, training institutions, college, apprenticeship programmes.	10. Collects information about instructional activities.
11. Makes use of various tools to understand the psychological make-up of the students.	11. Usually depends upon teaching method.
12. Primarily concerned with the problems of social and emotional adjustment.	12. Mainly concerned with the academic attainments and adjustments of the students.

(ii) Counsellor works in educational setting whereas psychotherapist works in medical setting.

(iii) Counsellor uses techniques and tools that can be used in schools whereas psychotherapist uses tools and techniques that are applicable in any situations such as play-therapy, psycho-drama, socio-drama, etc.

(iv) In counselling psychology is not the only basis for studying the individual. In psychotherapy, psychology is the only basis for studying the individual.

(v) Counselling is broader in scope as it touches all the problems of the individual, but does not go deep in them. Psychotherapy is deeper rather than broader in scope. It deals with fewer problems but goes very deep in studying the personality of individual.

Personal problems requiring counselling. G.E. Smith mentions the following needs and problems of adolescents which require counselling :

1. Getting along with one's peers.
2. Making and keeping friends.
3. Getting desirable social experiences.
4. Problems in relations with others.
5. Problems of health.
6. Getting along with teachers.
7. Getting along with parents.
8. Getting along with brothers and sisters.
9. Problems related to personal appearance.
10. Appropriate use of leisure time.
11. Manners and morals.
12. Personal problems connected with planning the future.
13. Problems about money.
14. Understanding sex.
15. Personal behaviour problems.
16. Developing and satisfying philosophy of life.
17. Problems related to school adjustment.
18. Home and environmental problems.
19. Inadequate or excessive participation in school activities.
20. Adjustment needs stemming from feelings of inferiority, inadequate social skill and unfortunate personality traits.
21. Emotional problems resulting from scholastic difficulties.

About the role of counsellor in solving these problems. James Warters observes, "The worker should take care in working with the students to be warm, cordial and friendly, responsive and understanding but at the same time will be impersonal and objective. To be impersonal and objective, however, he need not be or appear to be cold, indifferent of uninterested. Nor shall he be."

FUNCTIONS OF COUNSELLOR

1. Programme of guidance and its organisation. It includes all the services such as vocational information service, self-inventory service, personal date collection, service, counselling service, vocational preparatory service, placement or employment service, follow up or adjustment service and research service.

2. Orientation. A sort of preparation, includes collecting the data about sources and job, disseminating information to pupils and planning the activities.

3. Data collection. About the individual, administering the test and analysing the same.

4. Interview and individual counselling.

5. Outside agencies. Contacting outside agencies like parents, guidance bureaus and employment exchange.

6. Placement and follow-up work.

QUALIFICATIONS OF COUNSELLOR

A. Personality traits. According to Walter B. Jones, the counsellor should have the following five personality traits :

1. *Breadth of interest* : The counsellor should be interested in various types of people, jobs and organisation.

2. *Co-operation* : The counsellor should cooperate with all the staff in a cheerful manner.

3. *Refinement* : The counsellor should not be over-confident but, on the other hand, he should be modest and humble towards the pupils.

4. *Magnetism* : The counsellor would inspire confidence in others and put others at ease.

5. *Considerateness* : The counsellor should appreciate the difficulties of teachers, exhibit human understanding and possess real love for fellowmen.

B. Training and preparation. Myers says that the counsellor must have the following traits :

1. Good liberal education including knowledge of humanities such as sociology, psychology, economics, history, geography, etc.

2. Knowledge of objectives, curriculum and methods of secondary schools.

3. Knowledge of vocational activities.

4. Knowledge of methods of imparting occupational information.

5. Knowledge of principles of guidance.

6. Knowledge of psychological tests in guidance services.

7. Knowledge of organisation of guidance services.

C. Academic qualifications. A seminar of headmasters held in Delhi recommended the following qualifications for counsellor :

1. M.A. in psychology or B.A., B.Ed. (with guidance) or B.A., M.Ed. (with guidance).

2. Diploma course in guidance.

3. Counsellor must have knowledge about personality problem testing, mental hygiene and counselling techniques.

D. Experience. Smith requires the following six types of experiences in counsellor :

1. Competence as a leader in guidance programme.

2. Competence as a counsellor. This includes competence in the following three directions :

(i) Understanding the problems of the child.

(ii) Establishing a rapport with the child.

(iii) Helping the child to solve the problem.

3. Competence in interpreting and using information.

4. Competence in placement and follow-up service.

5. Competence in evaluating the counselling service itself.

TYPES OF COUNSELLING

Counselling theories are of three types : Directive, Non-Directive and Eclectic.

DIRECTIVE COUNSELLING

Assumptions of directive counselling. It is also known as prescriptive or counsellor-centred counselling. It is problem-centred and not paid-centred. In it the counsellor prepares entire plans and sees through the process. According to the leading exponent of his school of thought, E.G. Williamson, following are the assumptions of directive counselling :

1. Efforts should be focused on the problem of the counselee.

2. The counsellor is more competent than the counselee. Therefore, he plays a more active role than the client. He is the pivot, the centre or the leader of the situation.

3. As counselling is primarily an intellectual rather than emotional process. Therefore, the intellectual aspect is given more weightage than emotional aspect.

Steps of directive counselling. According to E.G. Williamson, the following steps are involved in directive counselling :

1. Analysis. Collection of data from a variety of sources by using a variety of tools and techniques. The data is needed for an adequate understanding of the client.

2. Synthesis. Summarising and organising the data so as reveal the client's assets, liabilities, adjustments and maladjustments.

3. Diagnosis. Finding out the root cause of the problem exhibited by the client.

4. Prognosis. Prediction of the future development of the client's problems.

5. Treatment or counselling. This may include some of the following procedures :

(a) Establishing rapport with the student.

(b) Interpreting the collected data to the student.

(c) Advising or planning a programme of action with the student.

(d) Assisting the student in carrying out the plan of action.

(e) Referring to other counsellors for assistance in diagnosing or counselling.

In short, at this stage the counsellor takes steps with the students or client to bring adjustment and readjustment for him.

6. Follow-up. In follow-up the counsellor helps the client with new problems or with recurrences of the original problem. He determines the effectiveness of counselling provided to him.

Advantages of Directive Counselling

1. Counselling is economical in time.

2. It emphasises the problem and not the individual. The counsellor can see the client more objectively than the client himself.

3. Directive counselling lays more emphasis upon the intellectual rather than the emotional aspects of the personality of the individual. The counselee is helped to solve the problem of the intellectual and not at the emotional level.

4. In directive counselling the methods used are direct, persuasive and explanatory.

Limitations of Directive Counselling

1. The client or counselee does not gain any liability of self-analysis or solving new problems of adjustment by counselling.

2. Counselling serves to make the counsellee over-dependent on the counsellor. He never becomes independent of the counsellor. Counselling kills his initiative.

3. Problems regarding emotional maladjustment may be better solved by non-directive counselling and not by directive counselling.

4. Sometimes counselling lacks information regarding the counselee. This lack of information causes wrong counselling.

5. Directive counselling does not guarantee that the counselee will not make mistakes in future.

NON-DIRECTIVE COUNSELLING

Assumptions of non-directive counselling. It is also called Permissive Counselling or Client centred Counselling. The chief exponent of this school of thought is Carl Roger. The client or the counselee is the pivot or the centre in this type of counselling. He plays the primary role. He actively participates in the process, gain insight into his problem with the help of the counsellor and takes decisions as to the action to be taken. The following are the assumptions underlying non-directive counselling :

1. Directive and integration of the client is more important than the client.

2. Emotional aspects are more significant than the intellectual aspects.

3. Creation of an atmosphere in which the client can work out his understanding is more important than cultivating self-understanding in the client.

4. Counselling leads to a voluntary choice of goals and a conscious selection of courses of action.

Steps of non-directive counselling. Rogers suggested the following steps in non-directive counselling :

1. The counselee recognises the need of counselling and comes for help. Thus, help is sought and not given.

2. The counsellor defines the situation and creates congenial atmosphere.

3. The attitude of the counsellor is friendship, sympathy and affection in the counselling. He feels interested in the child and encourages free expression of feeling regarding the problem of individual.

4. The counsellor tries to understand the feeling of the individual.

5. The counsellor accepts and recognises the positive as well as negative feelings.

6. The counsellor pays attention of negative self-feelings of counselee or child. He leads him from negative self-feelings to positive self-feelings, from emotional release to gradual insight.

7. The counsellor helps the counselee to translate his insight into action.

8. Positive steps are taken towards the solution of the problem situation.

9. Gradually, a decreased need for help is felt and the counsellee is the one who decides to end the contact.

Advantages of Non-Directive Counselling

1. It is slow but sure process to make the individual capable of making adjustment.

2. No tests are used in it and thus one avoids all that is laborious and difficult.

3. It removes the emotional block and helps the individual to bring the repressed thoughts on conscious level thereby reducing the tension.

Limitations of Non-Directive Counselling

1. It is a slow and time consuming process. It is not easily possible because a counsellor has to attend many students in school.

2. As the child, the client, the student or the counselee is immature to make the decisions himself, therefore, one cannot rely upon one's resources, judgement and wisdom.

3. The counsellor's passive attitude might irritate the counsellee so much that he may hesitate to express his feelings.

DIRECTIVE *vs.* NON-DIRECTIVE COUNSELLING

The following are the distinctions between directive and non-directive counselling :

1. Different centres of interest. While in directive technique, the problem itself is the centre of interest, in non-directive technique, it is the counselee who is the centre of interest and the problem is incidental. While directive counselling is problem-oriented, counselling-centred active, prescriptive, non-directive techniques is counselee-centred, client-centred or permissive.

2. Different needs for assistance. In directive technique assistance is offered by the counsellor himself as he can see the problem and the solution better than the counselee. In non-directive technique it is assumed that the counselee has within himself the power to solve his own problem, therefore, the counselee may see the problem and the solution better than the counsellor.

3. Different uses of records. In directive technique tests, records and past history are very important in finding the origin of the problem. In non-directive technique, tests, records and past history may be eliminated altogether, as they often interfere with the solution of the problem.

4. Difference in intellectual and emotional aspects. In directive technique the intellectual aspect is given more weightage, on the other hand, in non-directive technique emotional aspect is given more weightage.

5. Difference in type of interview. In directive technique rapport is not essential but in non-directive technique rapport is very essential.

6. Difference in post contact. In directive counselling post contact is counsellor-initiated follow up while in non-directive technique, post contact is on counsellee's initiative.

7. Difference in counsellor's role. While in directive technique counsellor's role is active in non-directive counselling counsellor's role is one of intent listening or passive.

ECLECTIC COUNSELLING

Nature of eclectic counselling. Eclectic counselling is defined as the synthesis and combination of directive and non-directive counselling. It represents a middle class status between the two extremes represented by the non-directive technique on the one hand and the directive technique on the other. In eclectic counselling, the counsellor is neither too active as the directive counselling, nor too passive as in non-directive counselling. He just follows the middle path between these two extremes.

In eclectic counselling the counsellor first takes into consideration the personality and needs of the counsellee. He selects the directive or non-directive technique that seems to serve the purpose best. The counsellor may start with the directive technique. When the situation demands, he may switch over to the non-directive counselling and *vice-versa.* An attempt is made to adjust the techniques to the requirements of the situation and the individual.

Assumptions of Eclectic Counselling

1. In general, passive methods should be used whenever possible.

2. Active methods may be used with specific indication.

3. In the early stages when the client is telling his story passive techniques are usually as the methods of choice. This permits emotional release.

4. Until simpler methods have failed, complicated method should not be attempted.

5. All counselling should be client-centred.

6. Every client should be given an opportunity to resolve his problems non-directly. Inability of the client to progress therapeutically as using passive methods alone, is an indication for utilising more directive methods.

7. Directive methods are usually indicated in situational maladjustment where a solution cannot be achieved without cooperation from other persons.

8. Even in reaching the decision to use passive methods, some degree of directiveness is inevitable in all counselling.

Steps of Eclectic Counselling

1. Diagnosis of the cause.
2. Analysis of the problem.
3. Preparation of a tentative plan for modifying factors.
4. Securing effective conditions for counselling.
5. Interviewing and stimulating the client to develop his own resources and to assume its responsibility for trying new modes of adjustment.
6. Proper handling of any related problems which may contribute to adjustment.

Limitations of Eclectic Counselling

1. Eclecticism is not possible because directive and non-directive concepts cannot merged together.
2. Eclecticism is vague, superficial and opportunistic.

To conclude one may say that in spite of the above mentioned limitations, the eclectic counselling proves to be of much practical value in the methodology of counselling.

Types of Counselling According to Humler of Persons

1. Individual Counselling.
2. Group Counselling.

1. INDIVIDUAL COUNSELLING

1. Interview.
2. Rational Emotive Therapy.
3. Behaviour Counselling.

1. Interview

Interview can be used to get information, to give information and to change behaviour. It involves gathering available pertinent facts, making a diagnosis on the basis of all the evidence and formulating an appropriate plan of action. It may be *introductory, fact finding, informative, evaluative, therapeutic.*

Suggestive List of Problems requiring Interview

1. Change of subjects.
2. Guidance at bifurcating stage.
3. Courses where available.
4. Co-curricular activities.
5. Free studentship, fee concessions, etc.
6. Unfair means case.

7. Difficulties at home.
8. Harassment by other students.
9. Misunderstanding with some teachers.
10. Love affair.
11. Prospects after completion of studies.
12. Living in the hostels.
13. How to study?
14. How to prepare for examinations?

Types of Interviews

1. Introductory interview. It is for the purpose of getting mutually acquainted and building rapport, so that follow-up conference and procedures will be welcomed and appreciated.

The counselling officer should make notes about this introductory interview after the student has left the conference room. As there will usually be little information to justify action. It is not advisable to take or recommend any action on the basis of data obtained in the introductory interview.

2. Fact-finding interview. It may be designed to discover the intensity of a counsellee's attitudes towards persons and situations which he cannot reveal in writing or in response to formalised questions which do not allow for indications of strong feelings. It may reveal interests that had not previously been noted, and it may allow the counsellor to determine their strength and their source. It may be used to obtain information concerning relationships with other persons and about activities that are carried out with them.

3. Informative interviews. In it counsellee is interviewed for the purpose of informing him about data have been obtained from other sources, for providing information to answer questions that he has raised or of passing on some decision that has been made about him by a person in a position of authority. The information provided by interview may be about such matters as his performance in tests and their interpretation, the acceptance or rejection of an application for a position or for permission to a change in courses, the decision of the principal/head of the department concerning his success in an examination.

4. Therapeutic interviews. Interview may be used for therapeutic purposes. It gives a chance to the counsellee to talk about himself, his past, his wishes and fears, his hopes and aspirations. It brings new clarity of thought, relief from over-tension, and a new objectivity. It often happens that *how* a thing is said, seems just as important as *what* is said and it is only in the interview that this aspect of the counsellee revelations can be appraised.

Interview Procedure

1. Preparation. The following hints can prove useful in preparation for interviews :

(i) Decide what is to be accomplished.
(ii) Know the interviewee.
(iii) Make appointment.
(iv) Provide for privacy.
(v) Practice taking the interviewee's point of view.
(vi) Know your own personality.

2. The Process

(i) Establish rapport.
(ii) Help the interviewee feel at ease and ready to talk.
(iii) Help the interviewee obtain and organise into a meaningful pattern the information he needs in his choice-making activity.
(iv) Ask unambiguous questions.
(v) Learn to listen.
(vi) Keep control of the interview.
(vii) At the close of the interview, watch for additional information or new leads in the casual remarks the interviewee.

3. Interpretation. Without interpretation the counsellee may remain on a superficial level of self-understanding. The interpretation to students of the varied aspects of their emotional life is essential and it requires great skill and understanding.

4. Developing insights and putting them to work. The process of clarifying and gaining insight leads to the making of decisions and the planning of courses of action.

5. Termination of the contact. The termination of the contact should be a stage in the process planned, not sudden, clear-cut, not indefinite.

6. Recording. There should be an efficient system of recording and maintaining the interview notes. This may require a tape-recorder in the room. In cases, where good rapport has been established, the necessary notes can be taken without disturbing the subject.

Limitations of Interview

1. Suspect validity. The validity of data obtained from interviews is always suspect because the results are contained in judgments made by one person.

2. Varying validity. The validity and reliability of this technique varies with how well and skilfully and interview has been structured and who is conducting it.

3. Bias. Interviewer's bias is a serious limitation of this technique. The interviews report a particular phenomenon according to their own interpretations, understanding, beliefs and attitudes. When interview predictions have been compared with the actual performance of the person. The validity studies of interviews have revealed very low statistical measures.

2. RATIONAL-EMOTIVE THERAPY

Rational-emotive therapy was developed by Albert Ellis according to whom human being is both rational and irrational. Irrationality is the cause of emotional problems, such as guilt, anxiety, anger and depression. These cannot be separated from ideas. Most people make the mistake of rating themselves against other people and then labelling themselves. This prevents them from accepting their natural fallibility and results in self-contempt or in a defensive pose of superiority.

Ellis identified the following eleven irrational ideas which lead to neurosis :

(i) It is absolutely essential for an individual to be loved or approved by every significant person in his environment.

(ii) It is necessary that each individual be competent, adequate and achieving in areas of interest, if the individual is to be worthwhile.

(iii) Some people are bad, wicked or villainous and these people should be blamed and punished.

(iv) It is terrible and catastrophic when things are not in the way an individual wants them to be.

(v) Unhappiness is a function of events outside the control of the individual.

(vi) If something is dangerous or harmful, an individual should constantly be concerned about it.

(vii) It is easier to run away from difficulties and self-responsibility than it is to brace oneself up to lean on.

(viii) Petty events in an individual's life determine present behaviour and cannot be changed.

(ix) An individual should be very concerned and upset by other individual's problems.

(x) There is always a correct and precise answer to every problem and it is catastrophic if it is not found.

The Goal. The goal of rational emotive thereby is to show the client how his misinterpretation of events are causing him problems and to teach him to see things in a more rational manner and aid him in the process of adjustments.

The Process. The responsibilities of the counsellor and the client are defined in the initial interview. The client is responsible for practising any learning acquired during the counselling sessions.

Techniques used. To correct the illogical and self-defeating goals and beliefs of the client, rational-emotive therapists use a wide variety of techniques including persuasion, confrontation, challenge, command, even theoretical arguments.

3. BEHAVIOURAL COUNSELLING

One of the most modern methods of treating disorders of behaviour is behavioural counselling. Overt symptoms are considered important in it. Symptoms are determined by individual differences. Faulty learning is considered the cause of maladjustment. Cure is achieved by treating symptoms without going into the past.

Behavioural basis. Behavioural counselling is based on conditioning for describing behaviour and specifying the conditions under which it is acquired, maintained and eliminated. Behaviour disorders are not symptoms of hidden emotional conflicts that must be under covered and resolved. Behaviour disorder is the problem, not a symptom of the problem. If a therapist can teach a person to respond more appropriately he has "cured" him.

Postulates and assumptions. Behaviour therapies are based on the assumption that all behaviour, normal and abnormal, is learned. The hypochondriac has learned that he gets attention when he is sick. The catatonic has learned that he is safe when he withdraws entirely. The therapist has to extinguish such inappropriate responses and teach the person more satisfying ways of behaving. He does not need to know how or why the person learned to behave as he does.

Behavioural counselling. The technique of behavioural counselling is based on the principle of learning. The most important contribution to behavioural counselling has been made by Pavlov, Skinner, Wolpe and John D. Kumboltz who believed that neurotic behaviour is acquired and is subject to the established laws of learning. The goal of behavioural counselling is to change particular behaviour efficiently and specifically.

The Counselling process. Blackhom and Silverman have suggested the following steps of behavioural counselling :

1. **Problem definition.** The counsellor should specifically define the problem and identify all the circumstances regarding the inappropriate behaviour.

2. **Development and social history of the problem should be prepared.**

3. **Specification of the counselling goals.** The client and the counsellor should come to an agreement as to what the problem actually is.

4. **Selection of methods.** The techniques used in the counselling need to be selected consistent with the client's goals.

Techniques of Behavioural Counselling

1. **Operant conditioning.** It is based on the idea that new behaviour

is rewarded and the old behaviour is ignored a person will learn to behave in a different way.

2. Aversive conditioning. It is a technique for eliminating specific behaviour patterns in which the therapist teaches the person of associate pain and discomfort with the response he wants to unlearn. This behaviour thereby has been successfully used to treat alcoholism, homosexuality, obesity and smoking. Dent treated alcoholics by giving them a drug that produces extreme nausea when mixed with alcohol in the stomach.

3. Desensitisation. In this technique, for reducing irrational behaviour if a client has described several anxiety producing situations, those are ranked from the lowest to the highest in terms of disturbance. The client is instructed in relaxation technique, after which each anxious situation is presented starting with the one that produces the least anxiety. As the situation is recalled until there is no anxiety. This technique has been to cure phobias about snakes, heights, closed rooms and sex.

4. Reciprocal inhibition. There are individuals who feel anxious and unhappy most of the time. Here the therapist establishes a hierarchy, from the least to the most anxiety provoking situations. Next he teaches the client to clear his mind, release tense muscles and relax. Sometimes he may use drugs or mild hypnosis to produce relaxation. Once the client has mastered the technique of deep relaxation, the therapist asks the person to imagine the least threatening scene and to signal when he begins to feel tense. At the signal, the therapist tells him to forget the scene and concentrate on relaxing. After a short period, he instructs him to return to the scene. This process is repeated until the person feels completely relaxed. Gradually they move up the list until the client is able to imagine the situation he most feared without anxiety.

Reasons of success. The success of behavioural counselling depends upon the following :

1. Establishing a valid hierarchy by the client and the therapist.
2. Discovering an adequate reinforcer (co-operant conditioning) by the therapist.
3. Lack of counter conditioning outside the therapy sessions.

Limitations

1. By concentrating only on behaviour, it presents an over-simplified version of human psychology.
2. An individual's mental behaviour is just as important in therapy as his overt behaviour.
3. The behavioural counselling is symptom-oriented. While effort is made to smoother the neurotic symptoms no effort is made to remove the conflict that caused them.

4. There is always a danger of the relapsing into his original condition.

GROUP COUNSELLING

Group Counselling is a relatively new way of working to help people, sometimes successful even with those students who have not responded well to individual counselling. It is a particularly useful way of helping adolescents for whom peer group values are important. In group counselling the interaction taking place in a counselling group offers the student a means of gaining insight and understanding into his own problems through listening to other students discussing their difficulties. Ideas and values previously found unacceptable may become more understandable and sometimes more acceptable. The counselling group helps the individual student to change, and encourages both his desire and his ability to help others through his relationship in an accepting and meaningful social situation.

Advantages of Group Counselling

1. According to Seeman (1963). "It is a safe environment, it is an understanding environment; it is a caring environment; it is a participating environment; and it is an approving environment."

2. It provides an opportunity to be open, honest and frank or a situation in which it is safe to test ideas and solutions to problems and where frank evaluations of efforts to change can be obtained.

3. The counselling officer can use his knowledge of group behaviour to help teachers develop Seeman's optimal conditions for learning within their classroom.

4. Issues such as study skills, human relations, drug abuse, sex education, etc. can be discussed in a group.

Requirements of Group Counselling

1. Individual interview. After the student has attended group counselling sessions, individual interviews may be scheduled to answer any questions a client may have about group counselling; to help the counsellor get to know the student better in order to determine — how he can best be helped and with whom he would best fit in a counselling group; to give the student a chance to discuss the problems with which he hopes to obtain assistance in the group and to assess the readiness fro group counselling and commitment to change his behaviour. The counsellor often supplements the information obtained in the individual interview with a teacher or parent conference and by carefully examining the students' cumulative record.

2. Proper physical arrangement of the room. The room for group counselling should be warm and inviting with fairly comfortable chairs.

3. Homogeneous composition of the group. A homogeneous group consisting of students of the same age, or sex, or having problems is the most helpful. Other counsellors find that the wider talents of a heterogeneous group make for a better counselling situation.

4. Adequate size. A group of six to eight students is probably the best size for maximum group interaction.

QUESTIONS FOR EXERCISE

1. Define 'Counselling'. Differentiate the following terms :
   (a) Counselling and Guidance.
   (b) Counselling and Interview.
   (c) Counselling and Therapy.
   (d) Counselling and Teaching.
2. "The aim of counselling is self-realisation." Discuss and describe the functions of the counsellor.
3. Describe the important features of directive and non-directive counselling. How do these types of counselling differ?
4. Mention the important characteristics of eclectic counselling.
5. What are the personal problems of students which require counselling? How can a counsellor help them solve their problem?
6. Discuss various types of individual counselling.
7. Write short-note on group counselling.

14

Counselling of Individuals

Guidance is not the concern of the counsellor only. Collective efforts of the administrator, librarian, English teacher, and school nurse, among others, are needed if students are to be provided with a comprehensive, effective guidance program.

Counselling is the component of guidance for which the school counsellor takes primary responsibility. Others assist him in gathering the data that comprise the individual inventory and maintaining community contacts so that a placement service may be effective. The task of assisting students to examine conflicting values that are the root of a personal problem or to weigh information as they make plans about schooling and work requires specific education, supervised practice, and experience. Students may find genuine benefit in talking with friends and teachers. To be beneficial for the student, the conversation should have a number of characteristics, such as the establishment of objectives or goals toward which the conversation might point, the quality of *opening up* the area of concern rather than glossing it over, effective use of the decision process by formulating alternatives and projecting consequences of each, and terminal structure that allows the student to review critically what has taken place and makes provision for future meetings if they are needed. Social conversation may or may not be marked by any of these characteristics, depending upon the people involved and the nature of their relationship. Because of their specialised training, Counsellors can develop relationships with students that contain all of these characteristics. They can use accumulated information, test results, and knowledge of community resources as they help the student to understand himself, his environment, and the process of change.

TWO TRADITIONS IN USA

Two traditions that have their roots in the early years of this century are represented within the field of counselling :

1. The first grew initially out of a need to assist immigrants and those living in slums to become employed. This humanitarian purpose was increasingly supported by tools of assessment that were developed within the growing field of measurement and evaluation.

Frank Parson's founding of the Vocational Bureau in Boston in 1908 is frequently cited as the birth of this tradition. Vocational guidance, with its broad interest in social reform and specific skills to help workers obtain employment, gradually blossomed into counselling psychology, with attention given to the normal individual's development in personal and social, as well as vocational and educational, areas.

2. The second tradition also had its beginnings in 1908 with the publication of Clifford Beers' book, *A Mind That Found Itself.* This led to the establishment of the National Committee for Mental Health in 1909. The National Committee first championed adequate living conditions and humane regard for those who had succumbed to serious mental disorders. Later it turned public attention to those with less severe disorders and persuaded educators to become more cognizant of developmental problems such as self-doubt and alienation tendencies among their students.

Inter-relation

Each tradition has influenced the other during the sixty years since their beginnings in 1908. Vocational guidance early demonstrated tendencies toward orderliness and quantification through development of a scientific approach to extensive occupational classification systems, vocational surveys, research methods, and assessment instruments. Mental health programs placed stress upon assisting the individual to develop, change, and cope.

Gradually, as vocational guidance developed into counselling psychology, it was shaken from its authoritarian approach to individuals and became aware of the person as well as his problem. Stress, as never before, was placed upon counselling processes and techniques. At the same time, greater emphasis upon research and publications caused those within the mental health tradition to become more involved in research of the counselling process and assessment of outcomes.

New Proponents

Each tradition is being now advanced by new proponents. Many of the original distinguishing features have been blurred as each has taken on some characteristics of the other. But differences exist. Current interest in environmental manipulation, computerised counselling, and systems approaches to the process may be traced to vocational guidance origins, while those who focus upon the counselling relationship and the personal qualities of the counsellor more nearly follow the mental-health tradition.

ORIENTATION OF STUDENTS TO COUNSELLING

School counsellors could spend a considerable portion of their available time in orienting students to the counselling processes unless they organised some formal system or plan. To introduce each student to counselling through the experience of the interview alone not only is an inefficient use of the counsellor's time, but also may prevent students who need to see the counsellor from knowing of his availability and cause anxieties on the part of students who do see him and are unfamiliar with the process. The counsellor's attempts to be seen as one who treats students as his equal and is willing to meet with them whenever they have a concern, a doubt, or a decision to consider may be seriously harmed by the paternalistic act of calling in a student at the counsellor's convenience, according to a checklist, and without regard to the need of the student.

The problem, therefore, is one of allowing students to visit the counsellor's office as they desire and yet having them familiar with the counselling service in order that they might avail themselves of it. A number of practices have been developed to make the nature of counselling services known to students, parents, teachers, and administrators. First, the counsellor may present programs at school assemblies, before parent groups, or in faculty meetings. In addition to verbal explanation, slides that indicate the various aspects of the counselling service, role-playing interviews, and the playing of model tapes may be used.

Students, however, need to become acquainted with the person, not a figure standing before them in an auditorium or a sequence of slides that show a smiling face and no action. An interim step is to have teachers send small groups of students to see the counsellor for a "get acquainted" visit of a few minutes' duration. If the counsellor is new to the school, this may be done with all students. The experienced counsellor may use this as an ongoing practice of orientation for the class of students just entering the school each fall and students who transfer from other schools during the academic year.

The counsellor introduces himself to the students, let's each student introduce himself to the group, and makes certain that they understand the purpose of the visit. Conversation is focused upon the purposes of counselling, why students might wish to visit the counsellor, how the counsellor might assist them, and what resources he has at his disposal. Although the interaction is not counselling, the counsellor attempts to enter fully and openly into the discussion. To give them the "feel" of the counselling relationship, he may ask one of them to role-play a student who is concerned about English or wondering about his future. The informal nature of the meeting and the security of having peers at his side helps the student to remain calm until he becomes familiar with the counsellor's manner and the physical surroundings. As a terminal exercise, the counsellor shows students how they may sign up for interviews and asks them to visit him when they feel he may be of assistance.

Most students will be receptive to this introduction and visit the counsellor at a later date. Some, however, may express interest in knowing more about the process. The counsellor may then wish to meet at greater length with the student or provide an audio-tape of an interview that can be played publicly, in order that the student may gain further insight.

THE COUNSELLING PROCESS

Meaning

Counselling, as a process, has been defined variously by authors and professors for nearly fifty years. While no single definition has stood the test of time, most contain some reference to difference in role of the student (who is to be assisted or helped) and the counsellor (who is more experienced, frequently older, and has as his function to help.) Also, mention is generally made of the objective or goal in terms of improved adjustment, higher functioning, and greater happiness. Finally, focus is usually placed upon the process involved, the learning that occurs, and the assistance that is given.

Basic Assumptions

Four basic assumptions must be accepted if counselling is to be successful :

1. It is assumed that the student is willing to participate in the process. He may have a concern, a wonderment about the world around him, or curiosity about what he is experiencing. While the process may be unfamiliar to him and he may display resistance at moments, counselling will not be successful unless he participates fully.

2. The counsellor must possess appropriate training, experience, and personal attitudes to function effectively. He must be able to relate easily with the student, assist him in establishing objectives and goals, and employ any ethical means that will assist the student to change or learn behaviours necessary to cope with his environment and work towards the objectives they mutually have established.

3. An appropriate environment is necessary. Depending upon the nature of the interview, this environment must provide assurance of confidentiality, a mood of contemplation, and/or adequate information resources.

4. As the term is used in school settings, counselling must provide a relationship that allows for meeting both immediate and long-term needs. The counsellor must be available at moments when the student needs him for specific assistance. Also, he must work cooperatively with the student in identifying and altering behaviour to meet long-term goals and maintain contact throughout a year or several years, depending upon the organisational structure of counselling services within the school.

Objectives of Counselling

Like the student, the counsellor also has objectives which are the outgrowth of his professional value system and his assumptions about human behaviour. They do not conflict with student objectives because the counsellor's objectives are concerned with the process of counselling rather than with establishing specific goals to ward which the student might work.[1]

1. Clarifying the helping process. The counsellor, because of his training and experience, is able to do this by providing the student with an overall structure that explains who the counsellor is, what he is able to do, and what he expects of the student. He can assist the student in perceiving what the student believes to be his concern or what he might explore with the counsellor. In order that he may understand the student and his world, the counsellor may focus less upon the cognitive or content aspects and attempt to understand how the student really feels, what he is attempting to say, and what he is unable to verbalise. The counsellor may assist the student in talking at times. Should the student wander in talking and lose focus, the counsellor can intervene and bring focus back into the conversation. One client described the process as follows: "It was kind of like going down the highway on a foggy night. I drove my own car, but the counsellor provided the illuminated white line in the middle of the road for me."[2]

2. Assisting the student to examine the psychological dimensions of what he is thinking and saying. The counsellor's approach in this regard is quite the opposite of that of a person engaged in social conversation. In social situations we react to remarks of self-doubt or anxiety by attempting to "close down" the display of emotion. We may interject mirth, change topics, give words of comfort, or suggest that things really couldn't be as they seemed. Counsellors do quite the opposite. Rather than "close down" the student, the counsellor will focus upon the central concern of the student and help him to *open up*. When a test-anxious student suggests that he will fail, the conversationalist reassures, "I can't imagine you failing. You're always done so well." The counsellor, however, probes, "You're certain you'll fail. Why?" The counsellor must be mindful of limits in time and his ability to assist the student. Assisting the student to *open up* carries with it the obligation, on the part of the counsellor, to have the time and skill to follow through and terminate the interview successfully.

3. The counsellor must work to develop a sound relationship with the student. When the student arrives in the guidance suite, the counsellor may greet him cordially and introduce a topic of common interest and experience during the time that they are walking to the counsellor's

1. Adapted from Leona E. Tyler, *The Work of the Counselor*, Appleton-Century-Crofts, Inc., New York, 1961, pp. 54-55.
2. Lawrence M. Brammer and Everett L. Shostram, *Therapeutic Psychology*, Prentice-Hall, Inc., Englewood Cliffs, N.J., 1960, p.183.

office. A relationship cannot be based upon small talk, however. The student has come to the counsellor because he understands he will receive professional assistance, and the relationship must be based upon mutual understanding and respect. The eager apprentice counsellor may work hard to be ingratiating and feel needed. He vows, "This student will like me before we're through." The experienced counsellor, through his skill in putting strangers at ease and getting the relationship going, will ponder, "I'll like this student if I get to know him and draw upon what the student wants, what he prides himself in, what he considers important and is really concerned about."

The three goals must be used in concert. A counselling relationship cannot be developed without structure and the process of helping the student to *open up*. Similarly, counselling will not be successful if the counsellor concentrates upon developing the relationship and assisting the student to open up, but provides no structure.

Dimensions of Counselling

During the course of practice, counsellors find themselves operating at various points along four dimensions. The nature of the relationship of the student's awareness may determine, in part, the counsellor's behaviour. However, the counsellor's basic philosophy concerning human development and the translation of this philosophy into a theoretical approach to counselling also influences his behaviour. Examination of these dimensions is not made to determine which is appropriate and which is inappropriate; rather, they are stated here to help the counsellor order his thinking and understand the meanings and purposes of the four continua.

1. Diagnostic-developmental. Our problem-solving nature sometimes causes us to attempt to "diagnose" and "prescribe" in the best tradition of the family doctor. The counsellor's insight may prove immediately helpful to the student. He may be able to make a specific observation that causes the student to view himself more clearly. More than one-shot problem solving is involved in counselling, however. Concerns frequently are of a developmental nature. The student may wish to explore subtleties of his environment and culture or learn how to relate effectively with peers. In these instances, he will learn more effectively through experiencing than being told.

2. Cognitive-affective. Both intellectual content and personal feeling are the substance of counselling, and a relationship seldom develops in the absence of either. Again, it is the responsibility of the counsellor to assist the student in focusing upon facts and descriptive content at one moment and their affective meaning to the student at another. The counsellor can sometimes combine both in his response. He may say, "You see that you're not accepted, can understand why, but feel pretty angry about it."

3. Observer-participant. The counsellor must, at all times, view himself as operating in two distinctly different ways. A part of him must remain the detached, scientific observer who takes account of student behaviours, formulates thoughts as to their implications, and subjects these thoughts to tests by questioning the student or observing whether or not behaviour is consistent. However, the counsellor is fully involved in the relationship, must act and react, and cannot remain a stoic observer if the relationship is to be marked by involvement and movement.

4. Ambiguity-structure. Stress has previously been placed upon the need for structure within the interview. That the student may need some assistance in understanding the purpose of counselling and what is expected of him in general terms is not argued. At the same time, he needs freedom to decide what he feels is important and how he wishes to proceed. The counsellor, therefore, may vacillate from stimulating student responses through general, ambiguous leads (such as, "And what did this mean to you?") to providing structure when the student's thoughts have wandered ("I'm not sure how that related to your wanting to work").

THE COUNSELLOR'S ATTITUDES AND SKILLS

One may ask, "What sort of personal characteristics would I need in order to become a counsellor?" Extensive research has sought to determine which characteristics would be appropriate and in what combination. Most personality assessment instruments and many screening techniques have been used in this effort. The results have discouraged continuance of this search for a standard personality pattern and, instead, have caused researchers and counsellor educators to view the attitudes and skills of the counsellor as of importance rather than his personality type. The following represents a description of some of the counsellor's basic attitudes and skills :

1. Ethical behaviour. The most basic of attitudes that a counsellor possesses is his ethical behaviour. Because he is concerned with helping people and often is given information of a highly confidential nature, the counsellor must demonstrate a professional attitude toward his work and be ethical in his every act. Unless the student is convinced that he can completely trust the counsellor, he will be inhibited in talking and not participate fully in the relationship.

2. Flexibility. Because of the fluid nature of the counselling relationship, the counsellor must not be rigid. He must be alert to changes in student attitude and student expectation of him. The student at one time may look to him as a peer; at another, an authority figure. The flexible counsellor will find himself moving back and forth along the four dimensions previously discussed as he adapts himself to these changes.

3. Intellectual competence. The counsellor's skills are built upon a thorough knowledge of human behaviour, perceptive mind, and ability to integrate present events with training and experience. An ability to think in an orderly, logical manner is essential if he is to assist the student in setting objectives, placing events in perspective, considering alternatives, and assessing outcomes.

4. Acceptance. Researchers have rather commonly reported that little is accomplished in counselling through advice, persuasion, or threat. Students come to the counsellor for understanding and help. They bring with them the hopes, fears, doubts, and anxieties with which they are concerned. Brammar and Shostram suggest that the counsellor, if he is to convey acceptance, must have made some basic assumptions about the student with whom he is working. He must : (1) regard the student as a person of infinite worth and dignity, (2) accept his right to make his own decisions, (3) believe that he has the potential to choose wisely, and (4) understand that he is responsible for his own life.[3]

5. Understanding. The counsellor must understand the student on two levels. Observation, conference notes, and test results provide a preliminary understanding. The student, however, will feel that he is understood only when the communication of the counsellor moves to a level of feeling, and he indicates that he understands the world of the student and perceives his doubts or hopes as the student does. He will then be thinking *with* rather than *for* or *about* the student. Communication may be non-verbal as well as verbal. The counsellor who understands will be able to integrate the student's words with his use of nods and gestures. The counsellor's communication skills assist the student in : (1) establishing objectives, (2) freeing up his thinking and exploring aspects of the concern that were previously closed to him, (3) formulating alternatives, (4) changing or learning behaviours and (5) assessing possible consequences.

6. Sensitivity. The counsellor must, above all, be honest and sincere in his attitudes. The student is accustomed to the mild deceit that is so much a part of the social conversation "game." If the counsellor hopes to have the student be "open" and candid, the relationship must be marked by complete honesty on the part of the counsellor. Some discretion is needed, of course. The counsellor who remarks, "I can't stand pink shirts on men," merely because this is one of his biases may find that he has alienated a pink-shirted student rather effectively. The counsellor's attitude can therefore be described as one of *appropriate openness*. That is, he is open in all matters that pertain to the relationship and, as with other attitudes, doesn't project his biases about extra-counselling matters into the interview.

3. *Ibid.*, p. 157.

EVALUATING THE EFFECTIVENESS OF COUNSELLING

The effectiveness of counselling is determined by the evaluation of counsellors, supervisors, and students of the behaviour of the counsellor. Students participating in research projects are sometimes asked, "What did the counsellor do to put you at ease?" or "What characteristics did he have that you liked or didn't like?" If we wished to enlist the aid of students in changing the behaviour of counsellors, as is frequently true during the early phases of training, these would be the type of questions we might ask. However, the questions are not directly related to counsellor effectiveness because our primary purpose in counselling practice is not to produce changes in counsellor behaviour.

Student change or development is the purpose of counselling. This implies that an assessment be made, independent of the interview, as to whether the student has altered his behaviour with regard to the objectives he set for himself in counselling. The effectiveness of counselling with the student who seeks help because he needs to improve his grades could best be determined by looking at the grades he has received since termination of the counselling relationship. He may report that he feels happier, has more friends, or no longer worries about skipping church. These changes cannot be considered as indicative of counsellor effectiveness unless one or more of these were objectives he set for himself in addition to obtaining improved grades.

Helping the student to clarify his objectives and state them in terms which are observable is the first essential for determining effectiveness. Developing a system that produces data concerning the student's development since counselling is a second step. This may entail meeting briefly with the student, monitoring his progress through grades assigned and teacher reports, or observing the student in learning and social situations. Measuring outcomes by determining whether or not the student has changed or learned the behaviours necessary to meet the specific objectives that he set for himself at the outset of counselling provides the counsellor with evidence of his effectiveness. Students and school staff, if told candidly why the monitoring is conducted, will be more receptive to the counsellor's method of evaluation.

Initial Interview Procedures

Most counselling within a school setting is, in a sense, initial interviewing. School counselling is not marked by a long series of weekly or biweekly interviews. The student visits the counsellor, for example, in November for one or two interviews, and they may not have another conference until spring of the following year. Although the counsellor follows the student's progress and may have several brief chats in the corridor or at an athletic event, their next meeting starts the process all over again. Quite likely, the objectives established for the first interview or interviews will bear no relationship to those established at a later date. The school counsellor, therefore, must be particularly skilled at initial interviewing. Basic procedures are presented and commented upon :

1. Preparing for the interview and getting started. Counselling can hardly be expected to be effective unless both counsellor and student are prepared for what is to take place. The counsellor may need to review background data concerning the student or read notes made after the last meetings. He may know of some materials or information sources that he could have readily available. The student, if he is aware of the purposes of counselling, should consider how he can best use the time available. As described earlier in the chapter, the counsellor uses his skill in communication to draw upon what the student wants, what he is attempting to say, and what he considers of current primary importance.

2. Developing opening structure. The student needs to know who the counsellor is, what he is able to do, and what he expects of the student. This should be done briefly and simply. Experienced counsellors know how to communicate quickly and effectively, but the novice might well write out and commit to memory what he wishes to say during the opening moments. Although it may never be used quite as it was prepared, it provides a guide that will be helpful in getting started. For example :

COUNSELLOR : Scott, I'm Mr. Jansen. I've been counsellor here three years. Before that I taught science at South High. Because you've recently moved here, I'd like to get us started by asking about your contact with counsellors at your previous school. Could you tell me what counselling means to you as the result of these experiences?

STUDENT : Well, I met once or twice to talk about schedule changes. That's what the counsellors seemed to do most of the time.

COUNSELLOR : It's good that I asked. Scheduling here is handled by our assistant principal and I spend most of my time in meeting with students about whatever concerns seem most relevant to them. It may be wondering about their development, broken friendships, getting into college, or a host of other areas. What we say will be held in strictest confidence. We'll have about thirty minutes to talk today and I'm wondering if there is a particular place you'd like to start.

Such a statement might be used in most interviews with strangers. However, the counsellor should be sensitive to the needs of the student and not allow the structure to get in the way of the student's expression of concern. If he seems anxious to talk, a more appropriate opening would be, "Hi, Scott, Let me close the door and we'll get started."

3. Establishing the objectives. As a product of his training and experience, the counsellor will be aware of objectives he can set for himself in counselling. These stem from his professional value system and the way he conceptualises human development. They are manifested in the ways that he can effectively behave and communicate with students.

During the opening minutes of the interview, the counsellor and student need to establish objectives or goals toward which they can work in the time available. The objectives are not of a fixed nature and may be revised as the interview develops. An objective must be attainable and realistic in order to be a goal worth pursuing. The student who suggests, "I'd just like to be liked by everyone," will need assistance from the counsellor in making the objective realistic. "I wish I had two friends who cared" would be a goal toward which they might work. Counselling without process objectives on the part of the counsellor and student objectives in terms that are meaningful to him is a futile endeavour.

4. Building the relationship. As the interview progresses, the counsellor must continue to build upon the relationship that has been established. His honesty, expression of interest, humanness, and perceptiveness will allow the student to realise that the counsellor is fully committed to assisting him. At times, however, the novice counsellor needs to remember to let a little of himself out. A warm smile, a touch on the hand, a nod of understanding, any act of caring that is shown will help the student to invest a little more of himself and be more honest in his communication.

5. Helping the student to talk. The counsellor may perceive that the student is reluctant to discuss some concerns or some aspects of concerns even though a sound, trusting relationship has been developed. When this occurs, the counsellor may need to give particular assistance to get communication going. The threatening nature of the concern probably prohibits approaching it frontally. The counsellor must therefore rely upon spontaneity and sensitivity in (a) assisting the student to express his feelings, (b) understanding why the student is experiencing difficulty, and (c) helping the student to recognise feelings of which he is unaware or has difficulty accepting. The counsellor's own relaxed and reassuring manner will convey more than the words he uses.

6. Terminating the interview. The counsellor must use his skill in developing closing, as well as opening, structure. He initiates this phase of the interview by pausing longer between responses, focusing more upon cognitive than affective aspects of the student's concern, and not encouraging further exploration of subtleties or tension-producing areas. His sensitivity assists him in determining when the focus might be changed to the summary and plans for subsequent meetings. This may be initiated by his suggestion that "our time is all but up." The counsellor asks the student to summarise those aspects of the interview that were most meaningful and assists him, as necessary, in reviewing the objective and whether or not it was achieved. Plans for the future must then be made. Will there be another interview? When? Where? Or should there be a referral? Should tests be taken? Information sources tapped? When counsellor and student have reached an understanding concerning how they might handle matters such as these, the counsellor stands up (an excellent way to prevent a reopening of concerns) and sees the client to the outer office.

7. Planning the follow-up. After each interview the counsellor should make some brief notes as a check upon his own faulty memory and in order to keep a running record of what has transpired through the series of interviews. These can be reviewed briefly before the next formal contact with the student. Even though no immediate contact is planned with the student, a note can be made to see the student briefly after a week or a month to learn whether the established objectives have been reached and whether the counsellor can be of future assistance. This informal, individual follow-up can be structured to give the counsellor some evidence of whether or not he was effective. A more comprehensive, mass follow-up is conducted separately as a guidance service to study groups such as all seniors, all recent graduates, or all students now in technical schools.

QUESTIONS FOR EXERCISE

1. Discriminate between counselling and conversation. What are the purposes of each? What specific characteristics does counselling have that conversation does not? What skills does a person use in counselling that are not usually used in conversation?
2. Develop an opening statement that would be useful with most students in your school. Without referring to your developed statement, make a list of specific information items concerning the process of counselling which you should communicate to the student during the opening minutes of the interview.

15

Counselling for Vocational Development : Various Theories

The most important job of the school counsellor, in the eyes of parents and students, is that of helping students to plan for and secure employment satisfying to them and requiring activity which they are able to perform in a satisfactory manner. Such is the meaning of counselling to the lay person, and such the major justification for counselling to those who supply the money and facilities which undergird its practice.

The conceptualisation of how a dependent child becomes an economically independent worker has engaged the attention of many guidance theorists. The school counsellor who helps a student make vocational decisions must work from some theory of how the process occurs if he is to choose those activities which will facilitate good decision making and eschew those activities which will interfere with good decision making. Too often, however, the theory is not explicit, its assumptions are unexamined, and hence its correction or validation unlikely. Only after a clear theory of vocational development has been set forth is it profitable to examine the major questions of vocational guidance. How did it happen that you are working at your present job? How is it that your brother became something else? And the man across the street still a third kind of worker? Answers to these questions depend on clear models of the process of vocational development.

TRAIT AND FACTOR APPROACH

The most common formulation with regard to vocational development is based on the idea that the traits of an individual which have vocational salience are somehow matched with those requirements of the occupation in which he works. Recent statistical techniques have permitted the grouping of traits into basic, relatively independent, factors. This advance has permitted more economical measurement methods and clearer understandings of relationships among traits. Early expression of this formulation is found in the work of Frank Parsons, who in his book *Choosing a Vocation* (Agathon Press, 1967) wrote, "In the wise choice of a vocation there are three broad factors : (1) A clear understanding of yourself, your aptitudes, abilities, interests, ambitions, resources, limitations and their causes; (2) a knowledge of the requirements and conditions of success, advantages and disadvantages, compensation, opportunities and prospects in different lines of work; (3) true reasoning on the relations of these two groups of facts." Such is the approach of most vocational counsellors in schools and elsewhere.

Factors in Counselling

1. To discover the characteristics of the individual. This process usually involves a careful interview designed to reveal the interests, experiences, and wishes of the individual. In schools the cumulative record will usually contain much of the basic information desired. The school counsellor will use this information, supplemented as necessary, to delineate more clearly the work-oriented characteristics of the student. In most cases standardised tests will be used to give more precise estimates of his abilities, achievements, interests, and personality dimensions. After gathering such data, inferences will be made about the nature of the student and predictions assayed about the kind of work in which he might find satisfaction and in which he might perform in a satisfactory manner.

2. Analysing the requirements of various occupations and making judgments about the long-term outlook for employment in these occupations. Sometimes such analysis is based on psychometric data which tells us the ability level and special aptitudes of current workers. More generally the analysis is based on "conventional wisdom" and is not subject to empirical testing. Counsellors frequently, by the use of "common sense" or their professional intuition, make judgments about the necessary characteristics of workers in various occupations. What does an individual need in the way of abilities to be a good truck driver? Department store salesman? Bookkeeper? Certainly, the judgment of experienced professionals is better than that of the lay person, but it should be kept in mind that many of the opinions given by counsellors in the counselling interview are based on nothing more than their own limited experience, or worse, their biases. The task of discovering the necessary characteristics of workers in an occupation entails a difficult research procedure. Which worker characteristics are present but not really necessary? Which "good" traits are not functional for productivity, but are useful for smooth interpersonal relationships among the workers? Which characteristics are simply examples of featherbedding and designed to lower competition rather than increase production? Were the traits observed in adult workers present when they were adolescents? Is technology changing the job so that tomorrow's worker will not need to be so strong, or so bright, or so skilled as was yesterday's? Without answers to these and other questions the counsellor will need to hold very tentatively and gingerly his views regarding the characteristics needed by workers in any occupation.

The possibility of predicting the outlook for various occupations is also a very difficult task. After World War II, it was generally believed that there would be an oversupply of engineers because many veterans were attracted to engineering because of technical work they had done in service. Clients were often told that this would be an overcrowded field and were admonished to seek different forms of work. In fact, of course, there never was such an oversupply, and the predictions proved quite false. Research is not available which shows how accurately long-range occupational predictions can be made. The government, through various publications such as *Occupational Outlook Handbook*, supplies predictions, but the method of validating them has not yet been devised. We know when we give a standardised test to a student the limits of its accuracy, but when we give a student a prediction of the job market of the future, we are not able to tell him with equal certainty the parameters of our judgment.

3. Matching of the characteristics of the client with the requirements of the occupation through "true reasoning." In common parlance, this step consists of "fitting the square pegs into the square holes and the round pegs into the round holes." Such a consummation is devoutly to be wished, but much more difficult to do than it seems at first blush. We do not know the likelihood of our having discovered the crucial characteristics of the individual. Is his low reading level really a fatal flaw in his desire to be a teacher, or can it be outweighed by his personal charm? Is every teacher someone who speaks clearly and correctly, or are there successful teachers who do not have this seemingly essential characteristic? This matching process based on "true reasoning" may have to take account of many irrational motives in the individual and irrational hiring practices in the occupation. How many students are in college because "true reasoning" disclosed the wisdom of higher education and how many because their family and friends expected to find them there? How often is "true reasoning" engulfed by emotion, persistence, and denial of what appears to others to be the "facts of life"? In your own vocational decisions what part was played by "true reasoning" and what part by social pressure? By economic circumstance? By whim and accident?

We no longer think of the process of vocational development as putting together a jigsaw puzzle. We recognise that the pieces change shape and that the design is organic and not fixed.

Assumptions

Following assumptions often not clearly stated underlie the Parsonian (or trait and factor) conception of vocational development :

1. Vocational development is largely a cognitive process in which the individual uses reasoning to arrive at his decision. But thinking is not the only process used by decision makers for it is apparent that many important decisions, including vocational ones, are made on the basis of emotion. An anecdote about Freud says that he handled decision making in two ways. When he had a minor decision to make, he gathered all the facts and came to a logical conclusion. When he had a major decision to make, he simply listened to his unconscious! How many choices of college, major, or occupation are based on what one's friends are doing, family wishes, and minor fortuitous circumstances?

2. Occupational choice is a single event. At some point in life the individual "decides" what he shall do for a living. It seems more likely that vocational choice is a slow process through which an individual moves by imperceptible stages from no notion of what he will do to certainty with regard to what he will do. The Parsonian view stresses development very little and choice very much. A counsellor working from such a position might overvalue the series of interviews that he has with a client at any one time just as he might overvalue the "facts" that are to be discussed as opposed to the emotion surrounding the facts.

3. There is a single right goal for everyone making decisions about work. A parallel might be drawn with sentimental novels that imply that a girl goes through her teens looking for "Mr. Right," because she believes that there is only one man that could make her happy as her husband. Or, another analogy might be that of the salmon leaping upriver to find the single right stream in which to lay its eggs. It is now more generally believed that any worker might fit well into a number of occupations. The final choice of an occupation is often made on the basis of unforeseeable and unpredictable circumstances.

4. A single type of person works in each job. While there may be some minimal truth in the idea that there is a "teacher type," "salesman type," "engineer type," etc., it is evident that many different kinds of people manage to be successful as teachers, salesmen, or engineers. While this idea of a single type for each job is not necessarily inherent in the total theory, many counsellors have been misled into believing it.

5. There is an occupational choice available to each individual. An alternative view is that social and economic forces guide a person's vocational development, and he has little control over it. Given the fact that you were born into a particular family of a particular race, a particular socioeconomic level, a particular religion, at a particular time in our history, how much choice did you really have? Were you equally free to be a fisherman or a psychiatrist, a tenant farmer or a teacher, an artist or an accountant? If we believe that many of the choices that seem to be made during a vocational history are not, in fact, choices at all, then we look at the vocational development process in a new and different way. The naive client's request "I'd like to take a test to find out what I'm best suited for" becomes not only impossible to fulfil, but irrelevant. We recognise that while vocational development may involve the minimal presence of appropriate characteristics on the part of the individual and minimal knowledge of the requirements for a vocation, there is no high correlation between the two necessary for development into a successful worker in the field.

Pros and Cons

The trait and factor theory of vocational development has a long and honourable history and still constitutes the rationale for most vocational counselling in schools. However, counsellors approaching their work from this point of view too rarely examine their assumptions to learn the base on which this approach rests. This theory has given great emphasis to test development so that traits and collections of traits — factors — could be measured. It has also given great emphasis to the analysis of worker characteristics and job requirements. The field of vocational psychology is closely allied with this point of view, as are the scientific aspects of vocational counselling.

DEVELOPMENTAL THEORIES

The publication of *Occupational Choice — An Approach to a General Theory* (Columbia University Press. 1951), by Eli Ginzberg, Sol W. Ginsburg, Sidney Axelrad, and John L. Herma, gave the field of guidance a systematic way of viewing vocational development. On the basis of the research and conceptualisation done by these authors, the counsellor was asked to view vocational development as a long-term process, largely irreversible, and resulting in eventual compromise.

Periods of Vocational Development

1. Fantasy period. The process was seen as starting in early childhood and continuing until the twenties. This period of vocational development is divided into three general stages : the fantasy period, the tentative period and the reality period. In the fantasy period, which continues until about age ten, the child responds to the question "What will you be when you grow up?" with fantasy answers selected from the culture to which he has been exposed. These answers represent only a childhood view of the society in which he lives and not his own capabilities or desires. The little boy may say "I want to be an astronaut," or "fireman," or a "cowboy," and none of these answers tell us much about him or his plans. The little girl may say that she wants to be a movie star, a teacher, or an airline stewardess, but again, her answers tell us something about her culture rather than her as an individual.

2. Tentative period. It is from approximately ages eleven to seventeen. This period is characterised by the expanding recognition of the several dimensions of the problem of deciding on a future occupation. The solution must be sought in terms of probable future satisfactions rather than in terms of current satisfactions. This period is subdivided into four stages. When he is eleven or twelve, the boy's choices and plannings are apt to be made largely on the basis of interest. The boy has learned what he likes to do and may make his tentative choices on the basis of such a subjective factor. The next stage, thirteen and fourteen, is that in which choices are made on the basis of recognised capacity. Here the boy may have learned that he is better in school than most and so may plan on high-level occupations; or he may have learned that he is not good in mathematics and may drop from consideration occupations which he thinks call for this skill. He may have learned that he is good on the playground and may begin to think of himself as a professional athlete. The third stage is characterised as the value stage and is placed at approximately ages fifteen and sixteen. Here the boy begins to delineate what is really important to him. Does he most want money, prestige, a chance to be creative, the opportunity to work in a particular setting, or some other value which is enhanced by his vocation? Considerable research has shown that these value commitments actually occur even earlier than these authors believed, are rather stable, and show some relationship to eventual occupational choice. Whilc it is difficult to accurately measure and define values, evidence suggests that counsellors and teachers should be striving to help the student clarify his values and see the bridge between what he thinks is good and what are the requirements and consequences of various kinds of work. Finally, the last substage in this period is that of transition when reality considerations which were on the periphery of consciousness move into a more central position. This shift reflects the fact that the values which an individual hopes to realise through work are deeply embedded in the social and economic structure to which he must adjust himself and, therefore, which he must understand, test, and know through experience.

3. The reality period. It begins in late adolescence continues until the person has finally settled into an occupation which he will hold for some time. During the first part of this period, he explores various occupations either by direct work experience or vicariously. He does so in an attempt to link his decision making to reality. After sufficient exploration, his choices become crystallised and he moves into the vocation in which he will work. This crystallisation is culminated by the stage of specification in which he selects and enters into a particular job with a long-range commitment to a given type of work, perhaps even in a particular company or geographic area.

These three stages provide a framework useful in thinking about vocational development. To the extent that they are accurate, they enable us to know the kinds of learning experiences which may be useful to vocational decision making at various ages. They also give us a rough index as to whether the individual child is "on schedule" in his vocational development.

The general theory embodied in this book may be stated in this way : First, occupational choice is a *process* which takes place over a minimum of six or seven years and more typically over ten years or more. Second, since each decision during adolescence is related to one's experience up to that point, and in turn has an influence on the future, the process of decision making is basically *irreversible.* Third, since occupational choice involves the balancing of a series of subjective elements with the opportunities and limitations of reality, the crystallisation of occupational choice inevitably has the quality of a compromise.

Basic Unchallenged Theses

Although much criticised for what has been seen as an inadequate research design, this book has had a considerable influence on the field of vocational counselling. It has been relatively unchallenged in its basic theses : (1) that we should consider vocational development, not occupational choice, in striving to be helpful to students; (2) that some kind of synthesis or compromise typically occurs because no one can do all that he would like to do, and no one is without some, though perhaps limited, freedom and (3) that decisions are irreversible in that we cannot step into the same stream twice. The concept of irreversibility, often attacked, is best understood as a belief that every decision we make has an influence on future decisions and that there is no way of going back and expunging or erasing the past. This theory is almost entirely concerned with the vocational development of middle-class males, a limitation it shares with practically all vocational theories. Of girls, it is usually only remarked that "they are different" — a difficult proposition to refute. The vocational dynamics, patterns, and motives of girls have been less studied and are less understood than those of boys. The vocational lives of the lower class and the upper class have attracted less attention from theorists than have those of the middle class. It is moot whether these omissions stem from bias and leave the counsellor without needed formulations for his daily work. Possibly vocational decision making is a more crucial developmental concern for middle-class boys than for others. All in all this developmental framework has been found useful by many counsellors who are trying to understand the process by which children become working adults.

Stages of Vocational Development

Robert Havighurst has also become identified with a conception of stages of vocational development that imply appropriate kinds of development for each age level. These stages might be thought of as an extension and particularisation of his better known "development tasks."

1. Identification. This stage runs roughly from ages five to ten. During this period the boy identifies himself with the worker in the family who is an adult male, that is, in most cases with a father. As he begins to understand that he will grow into an adult male, he realises that this role typically requires going to work regularly and supporting a family. Havighurst points out that in many disadvantaged homes there is not a father who is a regular worker with whom the boy can identify. The absence of such an identification figure may well interfere with the healthy or "normal" vocational development of the boy.

2. Acquiring basic talents of industry. From ages ten to fifteen the boy is in a stage where he is acquiring the basic talents of industry. The child begins to learn responsibility and to organise his life so that it includes the notion of work. Work at this stage may include part-time jobs such as carrying papers, chores around the house, or school homework. To pass through this stage successfully, the boy needs to learn to do some work without being specifically told what to do. He learns to organise his time and energy and to put "work before play." Because many of the rewards for industriousness at this stage are given in the school, the child who is not successful in school may have difficulty acquiring the basic talents of industry. He will not learn that it "pays" to work.

3. Acquiring identity as a worker. The next vocational stage, ages fifteen to twenty-five, is given over to acquiring identity as a worker in the occupational structure of society. At this time the boy selects an occupation and begins to prepare for it. In most cases, he will enter into work during this period. He now sees himself not as a prospective worker but as an actual worker. Again, if there are not jobs for him to pursue, because of his own lack of ability or because of economic problems in society, he may have difficulty moving through this stage.

4. Productive person. From ages twenty-five to forty the individual is a productive person and, in most cases, reaches the peak of his skill. He will move up the vocational ladder and most men at this time find that work has become the dominant force in their life. However, those who have not successfully moved through the prior stages cannot reach this peak of productivity.

The individual maintains his productivity from roughly ages forty to seventy. He may be, at this time, not so much concerned with personal productivity since he is more certain and secure about his vocational status. His attentions are now concentrated on his contribution to society so that the major task of this period is to "maintain a productive society." He takes more active interest in professional organisations, labour unions, service organisations, and general community projects. His concern is with raising his own children, providing a better society for them, and his total role as a citizen.

5. Contemplating a productive life. Finally, the last role is that of contemplating a productive life. If he has been a productive person during the first five stages, he will likely be more contented during this stage.

Advantages

Havighurst's conception of vocational development is particularly valuable in its emphasis on the importance of supplying the boy with a proper figure for identification if he is to learn to be a productive worker. He also emphasises the importance of the school and its influence on the individual's vocational development. A secure and interested teacher or counsellor may contribute a good deal to the boy's vocational development, primarily by demonstrating socially acceptable adult male behaviour and by rewarding industriousness and responsibility.

Havighurst's views have special relevance for society's concern with the disadvantaged. How do we aid the child in overcoming the deprivation of the home which does not provide a stable, working father for his identification? What can schools do to teach the child that industriousness pays off in immediate rewards as well as the greater likelihood of later satisfactions? Is early interference with vocational development irreversible, or can compensatory programs help the late starter catch up with his more favoured peers?

Super's Vocational Development Framework

Still another vocational development framework is that advanced by Donald E. Super, particularly in *The Psychology of Careers* (Harper and Row, 1957). Super's theory involves both structural, and developmental aspects, but only the latter will be considered at this point.

Stages of Vocational Development

Super posits five stages of vocational development : (1) growth (to age fourteen), (2) exploration (fifteen to twenty-four), (3) establishment (twenty-five to forty-four), (4) maintenance (forty-five to sixty-four) and (5) decline (after sixty-four). Super elaborates these stages by suggesting that at least three of them have substages. The (growth) stage is subdivided into : (i) a fantasy stage (ages four to ten), (ii) an interest stage (ages eleven and twelve), and (iii) a capacity stage (ages thirteen to fourteen). The exploration stage is subdivided into : (i) a tentative stage (ages fifteen to seventeen), (ii) a transition stage (ages eighteen to twenty-one) and (iii) a trial stage (ages twenty-two to twenty-four). The establishment stage has two substages : (i) a trial stage from ages twenty-five to thirty and (ii) a stabilization from ages thirty-one to forty-four.

Nature of Vocational Concerns

The names of these stages suggests the nature of vocational concerns. Such concerns start in late childhood with tentative probes and questions, become stronger stirrings in early adolescence as recognition of the importance of vocational decisions grows, and finally lead to educational, and sometimes preliminary vocational, decisions. These decisions in turn are evaluated, either are modified or become crystallised, and lead in the mature stages to elaboration and embellishment of vocational behaviours. Each of these stages has its characteristic behaviour and attitudes, and therefore the vocational maturity of an individual may be estimated by relating his chronological age to his vocational behaviour. For example, during the tentative and transition terms of the exploration stage, the individual is engaged in crystallising his vocational choices. This crystallisation is characterised by an awareness of a need to make decisions, the appropriate use of resources, an awareness of factors that need to be considered along with the contingencies which may affect his goals. During the establishment stage the individual is particularly concerned with stabilisation for the first ten years (twenty-five to thirty-five) and interested in consolidation after that. The stabilisation process is marked by an awareness of a need to stabilise, planning for stabilisation, accepting the inevitability of some instability, and obtaining a stable, regular job. The consolidation period is characterised by an awareness of the need to consolidate and advance, securing information on how to consolidate and advance, planning for consolidation and advancement, and executing consolidation and advancement plans. These illustrative attitudes and behaviours show how Super has been able to make concrete and specific his formulation of vocational development. Such specificity has led others to develop instruments to measure an individual's vocational maturity.

These three formulations by Ginzberg, Havighurst, and Super of vocational development all focus on the developmental process by delineating the stages through which an individual passes. Although ages are associated with these various stages, none of the theorists interpret the age limitations rigidly. There is no thought that a boy is somehow abnormal if he still is fantasising about occupations at age fifteen or that he is greatly precocious if he takes account of his capacities at age ten. The ages given are simply very rough approximations of when certain vocational behaviour typically occurs. These vocational development theories give some basis to the counsellor or teacher upon which to consider the vocational development process and help students understand their present and expected decision-making behaviour. Super's formulations have resulted in more research than has that of the other two, and we may hope for more precise and operational statements of his stages.

STRUCTURAL THEORIES

A number of vocational development theories have been advanced which purport to explain the process of vocational development by specifying that part of the structure of the world of work toward which an individual will gravitate. In the broadest sense these theories attempt to explain why an individual ends up in a particular occupation.

Theory of Anne Roe

Anne Roe believes that every individual has a tendency to expend his energies in a particular way which is dependent upon innate predispositions as they are altered by childhood experiences. The combination of these two factors permits predictions about the kind of work in which the individual will find himself.

She makes particular use of the "need" theory associated with Maslow. Childhood treatment by the parent is the prime determiner of eventual vocational placement, she believes. These childhood experiences largely revolve around the satisfaction of needs. Needs which are routinely satisfied do not become unconscious motivators; higher-order needs will disappear entirely if they are unsatisfied, while lower-order needs will become dominant motivators if they are only rarely satisfied. Finally, needs that are satisfied after unusual delay will become unconscious motivators under certain conditions.

The core of her theory consists of spelling out the kind of childhood treatment which will result in various occupational placements. She first divides early childhood experiences into those which take place in a psychologically warm home as opposed to a cold home. Next a home may be designated as one in which the parents are accepting of the child, are avoiding of the child, or concentrate emotionally on the child. A home in which there is much emotional concentration on the child may in turn be either overprotecting or overdemanding. A home in which the child is accepted may be one in which the relationship is casual or loving. Finally, a home in which the parents are avoiding of the child may be one in which he is neglected or rejected. The child will be motivated to seek occupations in which he works with persons if he comes from a home where the climate is loving, overprotecting, or overdemanding. Examples of such occupations are those in service, general cultural, or arts and entertainment. Conversely, a home in which the attitude toward the child is casual, neglecting, or rejecting will tend to lead him toward occupations which are in the fields of technology, outdoor work, or science.

In summary, her theory says that the development and meeting of needs in the early years of childhood determines the general vocational direction toward working with people or away from working with people. Motivation rests largely on the intensity of needs and is a function of the degree of deprivation of an individual combined with his genetic structure.

The level at which an individual will work will vary from unskilled labour to professional and managerial occupations. This level is determined largely by differences in intelligence and in the socioeconomic status of the child's home.

Theoretically, if we examine the child to learn much about his intelligence and if we examine his relation to his parents, we will be able to make accurate predictions of his eventual vocational status, both in terms of its level and in terms of the kind of work which he will do.

What research has been done as a result of this theory does not tend to support Roes original ideas. She has now begun to revise her theory into a three-dimensional paradigm with the axes being loving versus rejecting, casual versus demanding, and over attention versus neglect. She believes that the casual-demanding axis is probably not important in determining whether an individual will go into an occupation where he works with people. She further has expanded her views; she now states that, generally, satisfactory early experiences with interpersonal relations both with parents and with others should permit individual development, which allows free play to individual aptitudes within a wide range of culturally approved activities. These satisfactory experiences are no longer limited just to those with parents but may be with teachers or peers or other significant people in the environment. A further elaboration of the theory takes account of the fact of differing behaviour of the two parents or inconsistent behaviour by one or both.

Her present position seems to be that differentiations among members of the groups can be shown, but the typical personality pattern is never a universal one for any occupation. Furthermore, personality is only one factor in vocational decisions, and its importance may vary from situation to situation. It now seems more important to her that we take into account sex stereotypes and the possession of appropriate abilities as well as the childhood experiences of the worker. She now is more concerned with the total career of the individual and recognises that a number of choices throughout the years are made which result in the total lifework history of the individual. Her greatest contribution has been in pointing to the importance of the satisfactory interpersonal relations in determining the general direction in which an individual will seek further satisfaction in the vocational realm. She also has contributed greatly to our understanding of the relationship of occupational fields. She believes that these occupational fields can be arranged to show their relationship by conceiving of them as making a wheel in which service occupations are next to business contact occupations followed by organisation occupations, general cultural, arts and entertainment, science, outdoor, and, to complete the wheel, technology occupations, which are also next to service occupations but on the other side from business contact occupations. Research has shown that when people change college majors, they are most apt to either stay within one of these eight occupational areas or move to one of the areas next to it in the above arrangement. These findings suggest that the relationships of occupations posited by Roe mirrors their actual relationships as seen by prospective workers.

Theory of J.L. Holland

John L. Holland in *The Psychology of Vocational Choice* (Blaisdell, 1966) and elsewhere has given us a theory of vocational development, the central concept of which is a typology related to work. Holland believes that we can characterise people by their resemblance to one or more personality types and that the closer a person's resemblance to a particular type, the more likely it is that he will exhibit the traits and behaviours associated with that type. He also believes that the environments in which people live can be characterised by their resemblance to one or more model environments. Finally, he believes that the pairing of persons and environments leads to several outcomes which are predictable from our knowledge of the personality types and the environmental models.

Orientations of People

The six orientations or types into which Holland divides people are the realistic, intellectual, social, conventional, enterprising, and artistic and are explained as follows :

1. The realistic. The realistic type is characterised by aggressive behaviour, capabilities in motor coordination, and masculinity. The realistic person tends to act out his problems and avoid tasks involving interpersonal and verbal skills. He seeks concrete rather than abstract problem situations. Such people tend to be low on social skills and sensitivity.

2. Intellectual. The intellectual person tends to think rather than to act, to understand rather than to persuade, and to avoid close social contacts.

3. The social type. He gravitates towards teaching and other close personal relationships. He avoids occupations requiring intellectual problem-solving or physical skills and seeks out occupations calling for skilful interpersonal relations.

4. The conventional person. He has great concern for rules and regulations, great self-control, and tends to subordinate his personal needs while identifying with power and status. He likes structure and order and seeks out occupations where structure is available.

5. The enterprising person. He is verbally skilful but uses these skills to manipulate and dominate people. He is concerned with power and status, as is the conventional person, but they differ in that the former aspires to power and status while the latter honours others for having it.

6. The artistic type. He has strong needs for self-expression and tends to relate with people indirectly through their artistic expression. He dislikes structure and prefers tasks which permit him to express himself. He tends to be more culturally feminine than masculine, show little self-control, and express emotions more readily than most people do.

Evaluation of Holland's Theory

Holland's theory is not very explicit in explaining how people develop into these various types. The presumption is that some combination of genetic and environmental influences result in a given type, but this matter is not very well explained. He is clear, however, in saying that if one of these orientations is much more highly developed than the others, the individual will tend to seek out an occupation in that orientation. Furthermore, if he goes into a school or job which is characterised by the presence of many people with a given orientation, he will tend to become more like them. That is, the student at a teacher's college will be more apt to go into teaching, the student at a school with many engineering majors to go into engineering, etc.

The environments posited by Holland tend to fall into the same six types as the individuals. These types are identified in educational and other environments largely in terms of the vocational goals or status of the people in that situation.

Although Holland has not classified all the occupations, he has sorted many of those requiring a college education into his six typologies. In the realistic class are found such occupations as engineering, farming, and forestry; in the intellectual class such scientific occupations as biology, chemistry, mathematics, and physics; in the social class counselling and guidance, education, social work, and religion; in the conventional class accounting and finance; in the enterprising class law, business management, and sales; and in the artistic class, art, drama, literature, and music.

It is Holland's thesis that if we know an individual's type, we will be able to predict not only his vocational choice but other things about him. His research has shown that his typology permits predictions about the competencies that individuals have (technical, business, social and educational, artistic, and leadership), their life goals, their self-concepts, and their attitudes.

He also is concerned with the level at which an individual will work and believes that intelligence and self-evaluation are the prime determiners of the individual's occupational level.

While typologies are generally suspect, Holland has provided for degrees of purity in his types by taking account not only of the prime orientation, but in some cases, of the second and third most important orientation. His studies of environments have enabled him to classify colleges in what seems to be reasonable fashions. Most of all, his conceptions must be taken seriously in light of the wealth of research he has done, most of which has resulted in many positive findings.

His views might best be summarised by saying that he believes that his six types somehow develop distinct and different life-styles. These differences in life style result in differences in vocational development and in many other factors which are measurable. When a given type is matched with a sympathetic environment, the result is apt to be satisfaction for the individual and satisfactoriness for his work. When this does not happen, the individual tends to change himself and his goals so that they become more congruent. Again, his research has demonstrated that he can predict the kinds of changes that an individual will make as he moves through college. These changes in major tend to result in his moving into an environment where he is more like the others. This theoretical combination which considers life-style and the influence of reference groups makes Holland's vocational development conceptions plausible to many and useful to the counsellor who is engaged in helping students make vocational plans.

Theory of Donald E. Super

Donald E. Super has not only contributed to the developmental theories of vocational behaviour, but is also regarded as a major figure relating personality to occupational choice.

Drawing from differential psychology, self-concept theory, and career patterns, Super has evolved a statement which in essence says that a person strives to implement his self-concept by choosing to enter the occupation he sees as most likely to permit him self-expression. Although there are obvious reality limitations to an individual's choice, as far as possible he will select that occupational role which permits him to be what he sees himself as being. Vocational development then becomes essentially a process of developing and implementing a self-concept. Super believes that people differ in their abilities, interests, and personalities and are therefore qualified for a number of occupations. Each possible occupation requires a given pattern of characteristics, but with tolerances wide enough to allow some variation for individual differences. Because a person's self-concept changes with time and experience, his preferences for vocations may change, and, therefore, we should study not his occupational choice, but his career development. The stages through which a person moves in implementing his vocational self-concept have been previously discussed, but the nature of his career pattern is a function of his socioeconomic level, mental ability, personal characteristics, opportunities, and most of all, his everchanging self-concept. The school and the counsellor can aid in this vocational development by facilitating the individual's process of maturation and by helping him to test his views about himself against reality. This process of implementing a self-concept by vocational choice is characterised by a synthesis between the individual's characteristics and his opportunities. To the extent that his vocational role playing meets with the approval of superiors, he will be encouraged to continue movement in a given direction. This role playing may be in fantasy, in the counselling interview, or in real-life activities such as courses, part-time work, and trial jobs. Finally, Super believes that work and life satisfactions depend upon the extent to which the individual finds adequate outlet for his characteristics in a work situation, thus, permitting him a way of life in which he can play the kind of role which his growth and exploratory experiences have led him to consider congenial and appropriate.

Super's major research is a longitudinal study of students as they move through school and into work. In this study, he has endeavoured to assess the vocational maturity of his subjects at various ages. The vocationally mature individual will be doing different things at different life stages. For example, the vocationally mature fourteen-year-old will be concerned with evaluating his interests and abilities to help him decide on further educational plans, while the vocationally mature forty-five-year-old man will be attempting to maintain his occupational status.

A major contribution of Super is seen as that of viewing vocational adjustment as a developmental process. He has wedded vocational development to self-concept theory in a way that enables us to see the economy of the translation of self-concept into work behaviour. Finally, by his emphasis on career patterns, he has pointed out that the process of vocational development is life-long. This conclusion means that individuals at all ages may profit from vocational counselling because they need to continually reassess their self-concept and test it against reality.

Super thus becomes one of the few theorists with a reasonable explanation for occupational changes in adults. Why does the teacher decide to become a counsellor? Why does the accountant quit his job and go back to college to qualify as a teacher? In both cases, Super would say that the individual's self-concept has changed and he is attempting to implement this new view of himself.

The counsellor's function thus becomes one of aiding his client to clarify his self-concept. Only after a person knows who he is can he determine what he wants to do vocationally. Counselling is thus focused on self-concept clarification and reality testing. This reality testing might be done through the use and consideration of tests and occupational information or by exploratory courses and trial work situations.

ASSUMPTIONS OF RECENT APPROACHES

The assumptions underlying the more recent theories explicated here are quite different from those upon which the trait and factor position rests.

1. Vocational development is not strictly a cognitive process, but also involves affect. As a consequence, the counsellor is expected not just to provide "facts" but to provide a climate and a series of skills which permit the individual client to explore his emotional world. Only after he can come to terms with what he is and what he wants from life can he make reasonable vocational decisions.

2. Vocational development is a process and not an event. These latter-day theorists concern themselves not so much with occupational choices as with careers. They believe that vocational development is a life-long process and not something which is gotten out of the way once and for all in adolescence.

Stemming from this assumption are the further beliefs that for each individual many possible occupations are available and that in any one occupation there is room for various types of people. Any who have worked can attest to the truth of this last assumption. If you walk down the hall of any school, you will find various kinds of people successfully performing as teachers.

3. Careers are not based solely on the wishes of the individual.

QUESTIONS FOR EXERCISE

1. Write your vocational autobiography. Include answers to such questions as these :

   What was your vocational goal when you were seven years old?

   What was your vocational goal when you were in high school?

   When did you first decide on your present occupation?

   Who influenced your choice?

   What satisfactions and dissatisfactions do you find in your present work?

2. Most of the vocational-development theorists concern themselves only with males. How do you think the vocational development of women would differ from that of men? Why? What are the implications of these differences for the work of the school counsellor?

16

The Guidance and Counselling Services

Concerned with meeting student needs, guidance programme can be structured properly help as a service to the student in the identification of his abilities, aptitudes, interests and attitudes; to understand, accept and utilise his traits; opportunities for learning about areas of educational and occupational endeavours; obtaining experiences assisting him in the making of free and wise choices; developing his potential to the optimum so that he may become a capable individual and to aid him in more and more self-directive. An effective guidance programme will have to be organised in the form of a constellation of services comprising of the following specific services to achieve these manifold objectives :

GUIDANCE AND COUNSELLING SERVICES

1. The Pre-admission Service.
2. The Admission Service.
3. The Orientation Service.
4. The Student Information Service.
5. The Information Service.
6. The Counselling Service.
7. The Placement Service.
8. The Remedial Service.
9. The Follow-up Service.
10. The Research Service.
11. The Evaluation Service.

1. THE PRE-ADMISSION SERVICE

Students aspiring for higher education join colleges or universities after completing higher secondary education.

Aim of Pre-admision service

(i) To see that the occupational aspirations of the students are correlated with their scholastic achievement;

(ii) To see that the occupational aspirations of the students are in consonance with the economic condition of their families;

(iii) To ensure that their social bearings are also in tune with their job aspirations;

(iv) To create a positive relationship between the subjects of education and their job aspiration and

(v) To familiarise the students with the repercussions of choosing a particular course of study.

In order to follow occupations where shortage of manpower exists. The students should be acquainted with the present supply and demand position in various occupational fields, estimation of manpower requirements, and projected picture of employment opportunities, shortages and surpluses of occupations.

Pre-requisite knowledge

The prospective candidates for admission to colleges and universities should be made familiar with the following :

(i) Importance of selecting subjects and combinations of subjects.

(ii) Planning for the future.

(iii) Best possible courses where there is demand of trained personnel.

(iv) Knowing one's own assets and liabilities.

(v) Enhancing the prospects through correspondence and part-time courses.

Collaboration Associations

Pre-admission service may be arranged in collaboration with the Employment Exchanges, University Employment Information and Guidance Bureaus, Student Advisory Bureaux, and local resource persons. Facility should be provided to those students who require further guidance and information before deciding a line of action. Such guidance may be provided in the form of meetings with faculty advisors, employment officers, academic advisors and deputy chiefs of the University Employment Information and Guidance Bureaux.

2. THE ADMISSION SERVICE

Aims and objectives. Admission service is one of the important links in the chain of guidance services. It is needed to fulfil the following ends :

(i) To admit the right persons for the right course for the maximum advantage both to the individual and the society;

(ii) To select those candidates most likely to succeed to keep wastage figures and dropout rate at the minimum level.

Organisation

Admission service, comprises a carefully framed criterion of admission, some entrance test and interview. This triple measure is adopted for admission to the various professional institutions such as National Defence Academy and all the colleges and universities.

Central Testing Service

Inter-University Board had proposed to set up a Central Testing Service, at first on a small-scale and under the auspices of the Board. It was felt that even if the efficiency of selection is increased only 10 per cent over that which can be achieved without selection test, the financial saving from not admitting these potential failures, can be tremendous.

3. THE ORIENTATION SERVICE

Admissions to a college or university by a very heterogeneous population students coming from cities, towns and villages, from happy and unhappy homes, from highly educated parents and totally illiterate parents, from well-established peer groups and isolated individuals, from convent schools and colleges and ordinary schools and colleges. Therefore, adequate arrangements must be made in colleges and universities for raising efficiency of all these students in scholarship citizenship, social skills, vocational skills, sense of responsibility, courage and poise.

Aims and Objectives

(i) To provide for articulation and continuity from one level of education to another; from town and village to city and from individual life to college community.

(ii) To provide the fresher with every type of information about college/university routine, its traditions and rules and regulations, facilities and personnel.

(iii) To help the student to become established in his college/university environment so that he may carry on as smoothly as possible with a minimum of mistakes and worry and a maximum of success and satisfaction.

(iv) To help the student in academic success by offering him help with (a) learning to study efficiently, read faster with good comprehension, develop interest in study, take examinations and notes more efficiently and budget the time effectively, (b) information regarding physical plant-library, hostels, classrooms, laboratories, student centre, playgrounds, swimming pools and other physical facilities, (c) facilities for remedial reading and language programme.

(v) To help in social adjustment and citizenship education by welcoming the new students as members having a specific place, rights and responsibilities and informing them about the facilities available in the form of student services on the campus.

(vi) To communicate to the new student that college/university is a self-directed, intellectually-oriented experience.

(vii) To show to the students that in addition to the procedural and socially pleasant experiences of college/university life, there will be high scholastic achievement standards to meet, greater personal qualities to develop, high moral values as well as ethical standards to attain from a rich college/university experience.

(viii) To provide a mutual process of learning on the part of new students, the faculty, and the student body of an institution, whereby each group becomes better acquainted with the others, and each participates in an ongoing process which will help the new students to become an effectively functioning part of institution and help the institution to become responsive to the needs of a changing student body.

The Printed Material

(i) *Introduction of campus* : A leaflet containing campus map and the names of the Heads of Departments and staff members.

(ii) *Time-Table for the Welcome Day.*

(iii) *Calendar of events for the whole year* : It should include all important dates like the last day of registration, examinations, holidays, etc.

(iv) *Students' handbook* : It should include a welcome letter by the Principal/Vice-Chancellor, summaries of courses, degrees and certificates offered, and qualifications for each academic information such as whom to consult regarding selection of compulsory and optional courses; timings and locations of such consultations; whom to contact for change of a subject; registration — when and how; fees — scholarship and fee concessions; classroom procedures; library and its service; the availability of various student services, how to make optimal use of the same, etc.

Orientation Day

It is a day fixed for giving all types of information to the students regarding the clubs and societies, cultural activities open to freshers, financial counselling, health services, student centre, honorary organisations, athletic teams, recreational facilities, special interest clubs, hobbies, hostel accommodation, student Government, rules of conduct, etc. In big colleges and universities, the orientation day may be celebrated faculty-wise. In small colleges, all the students may be gathered at one place for the orientation day programme which must not be a series to talks but must be punctuated with humour and liveliness.

Campus Tour

Campus tour can prove helpful to orient the new students to the physical aspects of the campus — the general set up, location of various blocks — Arts Block, Science Block, Administrative Block, Student Centre, etc. During the tour, the guide, whether a senior student or a member of the faculty, may give special information concerning services provided by offices in each building, the traditions of the college/ university the illustrious alumni, the reputation to live up to, the loyalty to the institution, etc. Each student should have with him a map of campus during the campus tour.

Welcome Desk at the Entrance

The college and university may have a Welcome Desk at the entrance of the college or university for the first week continually manned by senior students. They should greet every new student with a "Heartiest welcome to the college/university — how may we help you?" They should also give him a folder containing a map and handbook. They may also assign him an advisor, book him up for a campus tour under a senior student or faculty member, help him with luggage and make him feel he has joined a community which welcomes him whole-heartedly and is keen to help him.

Teas, Picnics, Games

To enable the new students allay their fears and worries, they should be given the best of the seats and best of the attention and best of the welcome. Short skits or plays along with an informal tea will introduce an informal atmosphere both for the faculty and the students — new and old.

Social Evening

Social evening may include plays, exhibitions, screening of films and talk by the guest speaker followed by a cup of tea or coffee.

Continuous Orientation

Orientation service has to be a continuous service. During the early days it may be concerned with orienting the students regarding the physical facilities offered by the institution, its rules and regulations, expectations and standards. Later, the emphasis may shift to study habits, library orientation and information regarding new policies and circulars received from different agencies as Director of Public Instruction; Director, Sports; Director, Youth Welfare Services; Director, N.C.C.; Director, Welfare of Scheduled Castes, Research Organisations, University Grants Commission, Ministry of Education and Social Welfare, Ministry of Labour and Employment and offer of help by social agencies as Lions Club, Rotary Club, etc. Every term, semester or year of college/ university has its own peculiar problems and difficulties which need constant help on the part of the faculty and administration. Thus, orientation service should be carried on throughout the year.

Orientation of Foreign Students

Special efforts should be made for orienting the foreign students at two stages :

1. Prior to their arrival. Prior to their arrival they need general information about the country they are about to visit; the city they are going to live in; and the college/university they are about to join.

2. On arrival. On arrival, they used specific information such as local transportation, hostel, the whereabouts of organisations and individuals who are in a position to assist them with special services and opportunities. Foreign students also need to be oriented to the culture and society of the host country. Comprehensive printed information should be sent to them before coming to India while specific and detailed information given to them when they arrive here. They may be advised to study the two booklets published by the Indian Council for Cultural Relations — *Studying in India and Toward Understanding India.* Some universities have a post of Dean, Foreign Students who along with his staff takes up this job.

4. THE STUDENT INFORMATION SERVICE

A proper choice of course and careers can be made only if the student knows the opportunities available, the requirements of particular courses and careers and also what he has to bring to any course or career that he may choose.

Objectives of the student information service

(i) To assist the student to obtain a realistic picture of his abilities, interests, personality characteristics, college/university achievement, level of aspirations, state of health, etc.

(ii) To enable the student to know himself on a socio-comparative basis.

(iii) To provide a record of the student's progress.

(iv) To help guidance workers and others to understand him more adequately.

Activities of Service

(A) Collecting essential data about the students;

(B) Orderly maintenance of records to assist the students as well as their advisers/tutors in making important decisions.

(A) Collecting essential data about the students. It may be collected through (i) psychological tests, and inventories and (ii) non-testing devices including observation, interview, questionnaires, records, case study, case conference, etc.

(i) *Psychological tests and inventories* : Psychological tests include as Intelligence Test, Aptitude Tests, Personality Tests and Inventories, Interest Tests and Inventories, and Preference

Record cards reveal valuable information regarding the different facets of the personality of the student. This information helps the counselling officer to gain a deep insight regarding the student. The tests are so designed as to aid in helping clients gain a better understanding of their personal resources. Tests lead to probable information rather than fixed conclusions. They must be supplemented by non-testing techniques.

(ii) *Non-Testing Techniques* : (a) *Observation* : Combined with a good method of recording, the observation is a good technique of obtaining information about the student. Special stress should laid on an understanding of the dynamics of human behaviour. Every item of information should be interpreted in the light of the total picture presented by the individual data.

(b) *Interview* : It is used to elicit predetermined kinds of information for definite purposes; such of the intensity of an interviewer's attitudes towards persons and situations which he cannot or will not reveal in writing or in response to formalised questions. Interview can also be used to obtain information concerning relationships with other persons and about activities that are carried out with them. It permits flexibility, clarification and explanation of certain points. It provides an opportunity for observation to the sensitive and trained eye of the observer. It helps the observer to collect information to study and to understand the student better.

(c) *Questionnaire* : It may be used to obtain quick meaningful information about the student. It can be of great help in collecting general information about the student, his needs and problems and the adjustment difficulty he may be facing.

(d) *Anecdotal record* : It includes a description of the student's conduct and personality in terms of frequent, brief, concrete observations of the student made and recorded by teachers, counselling officer, administrator, etc. Summarised chronologically these observations present a fair account of the personality of the student. It can reveal valuable information about the students attitude towards work, how serious he is at class-work, how difficult does he find to concentrate, how hard-working he is, how does he adjust with his peers and teachers, what are his reactions to the institution.

(e) *Case-study* : It is a technique of collecting comprehensive information regarding the student, his surroundings and his behaviour, sequence of his development in different areas like emotional, social, intellectual and personal. It brings together the information collected by the other tools and techniques in such a manner that these data can be systematically reviewed and analysed and clinical weightage given to them.

(f) *Case conference* : Organised by the co-operative effort of the psychologist, the counselling officer and the teacher it seeks to help an individual student to realise his full potentiality. It coordinates the psychologist's study of the student, counselling officer's understanding and the teacher's practical experience with his behaviour in the class. Each one of the three types of information acquires a unique new meaning through case conference which helps the individual workers to develop new insights.

(B) Orderly maintenance of records. It includes all sorts of information collected about the student suitably compiled in a cumulative record card which may take any one of a number of forms such as a file folder, loose-leaf note-book or a jacket into which sheets of paper containing the data may be kept. It should be progressively developed and maintained and provide a summarised "growth record indicating the direction and rate of development. It may furnish clubs regarding the causes of behaviour problems and failures of the student; disclose his strengths and weaknesses and prove a valuable guide for the counselling officer.

5. THE INFORMATION SERVICE

Information is essential of every guidance progamme, to assist the student, to make better choice, to help him in better adjustment or optimum development. Therefore, information should be organised and utilised as distinct guidance service :

Objectives of Information Service

(i) To develop in the student a broad and realistic view of life's opportunities and problems at all levels of training.

(ii) To create an awareness of the need and an active desire for accurate and valid occupational, educational and personal-social information.

(iii) To assist in learning the techniques of obtaining and interpreting information for progressive self-directiveness.

(iv) To promote attitudes and habits which all assist in the making of choices and adjustments productive of personal satisfaction and effectiveness.

(v) To provide assistance in narrowing choices progressively to specific activities which are approximate to aptitudes, abilities and interests manifested and to their proximity to defined decisions.

Categories of Information

(i) *Educational Information*

(a) Prospectuses from different colleges, universities, professional colleges, institutes of technology, polytechnics, etc.

(b) Directories of various type of colleges and universities.

(c) Books/brochures containing information on scholarships and loans.

(d) Books, pamphlets, brochures, leaflets on developing study skills.

(e) Illustrative material as films, filmstrips posters, charts, etc. regarding educational facilities and processes.

(ii) *Occupational Information*

(a) Occupational abstracts, briefs, guides, monographs and pamphlets.

(b) Occupational files and dictionaries.

(c) Career information manuals.

(d) Illustrative material as films, film strips, posters, charts, etc, regarding different jobs and job processes.

(iii) *Personal-Social Information*

(a) Booklets for increasing self-understanding.

(b) Mental health material.

(c) Personal hygiene material.

(d) Illustrative material as films, filmstrips, posters, charts, etc. regarding personal-social adjustment.

Dissemination of Information

The information can be disseminated by the counselling officer/ liaison officer, the administrator, the teacher, the warden, the doctor, the librarian, etc. It should be suitably compiled maintained and made readily available.

Media of Implementation

A variety of group guidance activities such as educational and career conferences, work experience seminars, discussion groups and individual interviews constitute the main media for implementing the information service.

Factors determining Role

Factors such as physical facilities, financial resources, the educational philosophy of the institution, the psychological orientation of the guidance worker determine whether the information service has to play a central or peripheral role in the total guidance programme.

6. THE COUNSELLING SERVICE

It is intended to establish a relationship between guidance worker and the student in which the former attempts to assist the latter in achieving optimum educational, vocational and personal-social development and adjustment. It may be performed by the trained counselling officer, liaison officer, teacher, administrator, etc.

Objectives of Counselling

(i) To understand what he *can* do and what he *should* do.

(ii) To understand the choices he faces — the opportunities open to him and the qualifications he possesses for the goal he has chosen.

(iii) To handle his difficulties in a rational way and strengthen his best qualities.

(iv) To make his own decisions and plans on the basis of self-understanding, accept responsibility for the decisions and take action on the plans developed.

Procedure of Counselling

Counselling is given only if the counselling officer has enough information regarding the individual's assets and liabilities and of the possible courses of action open to him. Counselling consists of an interview or a series of interviews between the counselling officer and the counsellee. It may also involve the administration of certain psychological tests.

Importance of Counselling

Counselling is helpful in crystallising the problem and reaching a reasonably good solution. Thus, counselling is one of the most distinctive of all the guidance services.

7. THE PLACEMENT SERVICE

Placement is important service in the guidance programme.

Objectives of Placement

(i) To situate himself in the proper scholastic track in the proper course.

(ii) To find out a proper place in the post-college or university or post-university environment.

(iii) To achieve proper choice of co-curricular activities available in college/university.

(vi) To achieve the choice of job-oriented courses.

(v) To get admission in a college or professional institution or university.

(vi) To get part-time jobs, during working session and whole-time jobs after getting education and training.

Procedure of Placement

Appropriate data from sending schools, colleges and universities should be collected and transmitted to receiving colleges, universities and prospective employers. Essentials to make success of this service are : Close contacts with institutions of higher learning as well as with personnel managers in business and industry, and co-ordination among teachers, guidance workers, etc.

Importance of Placement

The service is useful to all types of students — the normal, the intellectually gifted, the emotionally disturbed, the artistically talented, the mentally retarded, etc., to find their appropriate place in an educational or vocational setting.

8. THE REMEDIAL SERVICE

The defects in speech, hearing, reading and study habits can seriously impede the functioning of many able students and restrict the growth of adequate personalities. Therefore, arrangements for remedial help in these and similar other areas must be made in colleges and universities. Special efforts should be made to identify those whose reading skills and oral speech competence are below average to enable them to overcome these handicaps. Speech articulation at low cost can be arranged with the help of tape recorders particularly needed by pre-university or first year of TDC students who are exposed to lectures in English for the first time. This service is also of great value to students going abroad for further study.

9. THE FOLLOW-UP SERVICE

Nature of Follow-up

It is the review or systematic evaluation carried out to find out whether guidance service in particular and educational programme in general satisfy the needs of the students. It has to be observed to what extent have the students been able to achieve according to their abilities and aptitudes, to what extent curricular and co-curricular choices have been wise, and how are the students adjusting with the part-time or whole-time jobs. In order to determine the nature and extent of their need for assistance the students need to be followed.

Techniques of Follow-up

The follow up techniques include — *interview, post-card survey, or questionnaire.* Each technique has certain advantages and limitations. For example, while the interview provide the most valid information it is time-consuming and expensive. While the post-card survey is inexpensive and easy to conduct, its results re extremely limited. The questionnaire accomplishes some of the objectives of the other techniques and also overcomes their limitations in part.

The follow-up service can be maintained by follow-up interviews with the student and those involved in his new setting *e.g.*, his employers, follow-up questionnaires to the student asking his degree of satisfaction in his new setting and follow-up guidance bulletins giving him relevant information helpful in achieving self-actualisation in his new environment.

Importance of Follow-up

Information obtained through follow-up techniques can be used for improving the curriculum, stimulating better teaching, increasing the value of the guidance services and establishing better college/university and community relationships.

All the members of the staff should join hands for the success of this service. There should also be some means of bringing about coordination in follow-up activities.

10. THE RESEARCH SERVICE

One of the most important guidance services, Research is needed for a better understanding of students as well as for a working knowledge of college/university needs and resources and for evaluation of achievement in relation to goals. Its findings form the basis for curricular enrichment and/or redirection and also reorientation of other services.

Objectives of Research

Research service is intended to examine both the personal in the college/university guidance programme and the techniques of guidance used by them so as to discover their strong and weak points and ultimately strengthen the whole of the programme.

Advantages of Research

Research can give the guidance staff greater psychological security because of a knowledge of the effectiveness of its efforts. It can also provide a basis for guidance development programme.

It should be a continuous process as it cannot be "done" and "forgotten". It is advisable that one part of a student counselling centre should function exclusively on research activities.

11. THE EVALUATION SERVICE

The evaluation service finalises the entire process of guidance. It evaluates the use and application of information to established activities in order to determine their effectiveness (*i.e.*, the degree to which they satisfy needs) and their efficiency (*i.e.*, how well time, money and personnel are utilised).

Information Needed for Evaluation

(i) Degree of harmony between educational and vocational plans and capacity of the students.

(ii) Agreement between subjects taken or planned and the entrance requirements of the college/university the student plans to enter.

(iii) Extent of participation of students in co-curricular activities.

(iv) Extent and nature of shifts in vocational choices.

(v) Amount of maladjustment among students.

(vi) Extent to which students are aware of the type of information to be considered in making an occupational choice and the source of such information, etc.

Guidance and counselling programme in a college/university can work effectively if all these above mentioned services are organised well and implemented effectively, to facilitate good teaching and efficient learning. Thus these prove necessary supplements to academic achievement which is the primary responsibility of educational institutions. They also help in decreasing wastage, improving student performance, checking lower class absenteeism, creating favourable faculty opinion, eliminating student indiscipline and unrest and, creating congenial atmosphere in the institution. However, due to various human and material limitations all the service may not be instituted simultaneously. However, attempt should be made to start as many services as possible.

QUESTIONS FOR EXERCISE

1. Critically discuss the role of counselling service in universities.
2. Describe in brief the major guidance services in a college.

17

The Guidance and Counselling Personnel

Guidance is an all-inclusive programme, intended to help the students achieve their optimum potential. It is both a *generalised* and a *specialised* service. Therefore, the *total needs* of the students should be met by the *total staff.* One cannot assign the teaching-learning relationship to the teacher, the counselling relationship to the counselling officer and the smooth functioning relationship to the administrator. Hence the guidance should be a cooperative responsibility of all the members of the staff — professionally and technically qualified counselling officers and Deans, and administrators, teachers, advisers, wardens, physical instructors, doctors, librarians, parents, etc. Everybody who comes into contact with the student, contributes in one way or the other in his growth and development according to his capabilities and training.

1. THE ADMINISTRATOR

The administrator occupies a key position in the guidance programme. He should assume proper leadership and be a source of inspiration to the personnel engaged in guidance work. He should give it the status of an important service. He should prepare a yearly plan of guidance work. In consultation with the counselling/liaison officer and other members of the staff. He should take general policy decisions regarding phasing of the programme, make provisions of time and allocate duties to the members of the staff. Finally, he should create congenial atmosphere for guidance programme to be an integral part of the whole educational effort in the institution.

Functions of Administrator

(i) Providing suitable accommodation and facilities for the guidance service.

(ii) Arranging time schedule in such a manner that all students could benefit, provided there is whole time counselling officer.

(iii) If there is part-time counselling/liaison officer, allowing a relief of at least six periods in his teaching load so that at least the admission, orientation, student information and occupational information services are possible.

(iv) Making adequate provision in the budget for carrying on the guidance programme; by considering it a fit charge on the student amalgamated fund.

(v) Establishing and maintaining a cumulative record system.

(vi) Sending teachers for inservice training.

(vii) Giving desirable publicity to the programme to improve relation of institution with home, community and world of work.

(viii) Offering special inducements and recognition to the members who make solid contribution to the programme.

(ix) Evaluating the guidance programme in cooperation with the staff to determine and promote its effectiveness and evolve measures to strengthen it still further.

Importance of Administrator

Programme of guidance will succeed in proportion to the zeal and enthusiasm shown by the administrator. As is the administrator so will be the guidance programme in an institution.

2. THE DEAN

The Radhakrishnan Report (1942) recommended the title of Dean of Student Welfare to work as a coordinating agent of Indian college and university campuses. The Education Commission (1964-66) also recommended the appointment of a Dean of Student Welfare for the administration of complex and many-sided student welfare services.

Functions of the Dean

(i) Establishing rapport with students through personal contacts, public address system, group meetings, written communication, etc.

(ii) Organising and administering services such as orientation for new students, counselling services, financial aid to the needy, remedial services, etc.

(iii) Coordinating the various student activities so that every activity gets adequate time and finances.

(iv) Acting as an advocate of students in policy making bodies of the institution.

(v) Initiating policy regarding behaviour of students during their spare time.

(vi) Playing the role of a liaison officer between students and faculty and students and management. Whenever there is a communication problem, students should be able to depend on the Dean.

(vii) Keeping a two-directional relationship with all student services and activities : (a) To encourage, support and coordinate, including representation of and to the Vice-Chancellor and the Syndicate in the universities and to the Principals in colleges : (b) To receive information from the directors of different services and counselling/liaison officer etc. so that he is completely informed about everything taking place on the campus.

(viii) Assisting the university in understanding the needs and problems of students, guiding the youth in rational behaviour and in giving positive guidance to their future plans and aspirations, also creating for students and atmosphere of rich opportunities, of friendly community living, an ambition for realising their true selves, for attaining excellence.

(ix) Keeping in touch with the various public organisations such as the Rotary Club, Lions Club, etc., and enlist their cooperation in student welfare activities.

(x) Keeping adequate and uptodate records to increase the effectiveness.

(xi) Creating confidence in the students so that they confide in him feel free to express their grievances and misunderstandings openly and have the confidence that the Dean could help them solve their problems and straighten their misunderstandings to the best of his ability.

(xii) Coming down from his ivory tower to the level of the student and considering him as an equal human being, listening to what they have to say, offering encouragement for their ideas, suggesting other ideas in place to those he cannot encourage and stimulating the group to thinking and action listening more, talking less and helping rather than prescribing and evading.

(xiii) Ensuring optimum utilisation of resources, human and material and creating congenial atmosphere on the campus.

(xiv) Keeping his doors open to the parents also so that the uneducated as well as educated parents visit his office for a word of comfort, encouragement and understanding.

Mode of Functioning

In doing his duties the Dean is advised by a committee consisting of the heads or personnel in-charge of various services and also by the students, executive. This joint committee should be advised by experts drawn from the faculties such as psychologists, doctors, counsellors, educators, social workers. It should work out an administrative machinery for the coordination of the existing facilities and services through experienced staff employed for the purpose. He should have high professional standing a pleasant personality, charming manners, fluent speech, good command over language, quick wit and humour, crisp and cheerful responses. He should be an academician and administrator, an educator and a counsellor, a diplomat and a public relations man, a coordinator and a guardian, a humanitarian and a sage — all rolled into one.

3. THE COUNSELLING OFFICER

In a university or a college the Counselling officer is the nerve centre of the guidance programme. He should be a trained in at least one year's full time course in Guidance and Counselling from a University. In the words of Williamson, "The counsellor should be clearly more than a competent technician; he should be viewed as a broadly informed and cultivated educator." He should have a well-balanced lovable personality, a broad outlook, an understanding attitude, a genuine interest in helping students.

Functions of Counselling Officer

(i) Arranging orientation programmes for the teachers to enlist their cooperation.

(ii) Arranging orientation programmes for freshers and also for those passing through the transition period.

(iii) Preparing an uptodate list of the resources — informational, referral and energy — available to him and the proper method for calling on each particular resource and classify and fill the information properly.

(iv) Organising the Guidance Committee.

(v) Setting up an educational and occupational information centre.

(vi) Displaying the information collected in an attractive way.

(vii) Disseminating the information through educational and career talks, group discussions and film shows, etc.

(viii) Arranging talks by experts from different fields.

(ix) Organising career days, career weeks, career conferences, parents' days, etc.

(x) Educating students regarding proper study habits and assist them in their development.

(xi) Introducing Cumulative Record cards and get them maintained with the cooperation for other members of the faculty and use these cards in guiding the students.

(xii) Arranging individual discussions with students and their parents for giving the educational and occupational information.

(xiii) Arranging visits to places of work like industries, business establishments, offices, higher educational institutions, etc.

(xiv) Maintaining an active relationship with schools, colleges, university and other regional, national and social agencies like Indian Council for Cultural Relations, United States Educational Foundation in India, Principal of Colleges, Heads of Departments of the University, University Employment and

Information and Guidance Bureau, Employment Exchanges, University Health Centres, Medical Research Institutions, etc.

(xv) Maintaining an active liaison with clubs like Lions Club and Rotary Club.

(xvi) Referring the serious mental cases to clinical psychologists, psychiatrists or university health centres where the services of the clinicians are available.

(xvii) Maintaining total secrecy about the discussion between him and the client.

(xviii) Administering psychological tests.

(xix) Providing counselling service to his students.

(xx) Helping in the placement of students.

(xxi) Taking up research projects relating to the field of educational, vocational and personal-social guidance in the colleges and universities and convey the findings to important relevant agencies.

(xxii) Preparing guidance leaflets, brochures and monographs and get them printed for distribution to the students.

Qualities of Counselling Officer

The major qualities of the counselling officer are: belief in each individual; respect for individual human values; alertness to the world; open-mindedness; understanding of self; and professional commitment.

4. THE LIAISON OFFICER

Liaison Officer is a part-time guidance worker. In a small college he can be appointed from the rank of teachers. In single or groups as convenient to respective colleges, he can take charge of the guidance programme in a college. He should be a guidance-minded person with specialised training in guidance for at least three months. His duties are the same as that of the counselling officer.

The progress and efficiency of the guidance services in colleges depends on the ability, enthusiasm and dedication of liaison officers and the attitude of the administrators and teachers to them and to their work. The time can be fixed for the liaison officer depending upon the number of students and the load of work.

5. THE TEACHER

The teachers are the most useful allies of the counselling/liaison officers. As they have the closest, the most frequent and the most extended contacts with students in a natural situation guidance service can never become an integral part of any educational programme. Without their co-operation is inevitable.

According to Traxler and North the teachers and counsellors should join hands for an effective guidance programme. To quote actual words,

"Teachers and counsellors need to combine their efforts to help young people to understand themselves, to see the subject-matter of each field in relation to their own strengths and limitations, and to appreciate the need for developing broad abilities and skills to meet the vocational demands of tomorrow as hundreds of new occupations are developing to meet the new needs, and hundreds of other are rendered obsolete or relegated to places of minor importance. This is primarily a learning situation and the teacher, more than anyone else, can open doors through which the students may glimpse his own future."[1]

Objectives of the teachers

(i) To play a primary role in advising and orientation, in making known to the students the requirements and future job possibilities connected with their particular subjects.

(ii) To provide vocational motivation to the subjects taught by them.

(iii) To assess the achievements of the students and thus enabling them to know better their strengths and weaknesses in certain subjects.

(iv) To enable the students to explore and develop interest by integrating the curricular and co-curricular activities and thus orienting them towards worthy goals.

(v) To co-ordinate the efforts of various agencies, parents and guidance workers and thus raising guidance to a scientific level.

(vi) To detect early symptoms of any abnormality in the students' make up and drawing the counselling or liaison officer's attention.

(vii) To render "mental hygiene first-aid" and helping students remain on the right track.

Functions of the Teachers

(i) Studying the needs, interests, abilities and problems of each students in his class.

(ii) Winning the confidence of the students and helping them in every possible way to evaluate their own growth.

(iii) Getting acquainted with the parents and taking an active part in Parent Teacher Association.

(iv) Instructing the students in appropriate methods of applying for posts.

(v) Co-operating with placement organisations in their task of making specific suggestions and finding suitable openings.

(vi) Following-up the students they advise by obtaining progress reports on their satisfaction.

1. Arthur E. Traxler and Robert D. North, Techniques of Guidance, p. 289.

(vii) Assisting the students conserve their native capacities and investing and using the same so as to bring greatest satisfaction to themselves and benefit to society.

6. THE TUTOR

Different meanings. Tutoring means different things in different colleges and universities. In some it refers to an academic relation between one teacher and one student concerned primarily with academic subject matter, not personal problems or extra-curricular matters. It may also cover matters like housing and other information.

Tutor-Guardianship Scheme

At some universities there is the tutor-guardianship scheme close to a student advisory system. The tutor here is a synonym for a teacher, and 'guardianship' implies a caring or helping relation to a ward.

The tutor is the first line of reference on guidance matters in colleges. He is usually a teacher who does not actually teach the members of his tutorial group so that guidance is kept separate from the academic setting and it is made possible for a tutor to help with personal guidance without being hampered by any specific teaching relationship or overtones from the class-room situation. Thus the tutor develops a 'guidance' relationship with students. He does not teach in a limited weekly tutorial period.

Functions of the Tutor

(i) He orients the members of his group regarding the curricular, co-curricular facilities and ancillary services available in the institution.

(ii) He collects different types of information about the student and assisting in the compiling of this information in the cumulative record.

(iii) He informs the members of his group regarding the occupational openings.

(iv) He arranges discussions on educational problems.

(v) He orients the members of his group regarding the facility of scholarships, grants loans, freeships and concessions available, their eligibility and how to apply for them.

(vi) He recommends the genuine cases for help.

(vii) He acquaints the members with proper study habits and assisting them in their development.

(viii) He meets the parents for solving the problems of the students.

(ix) He arranges visits to places of work like industries, business establishments, offices, higher educational institutions, etc.

(x) He detects symptoms of abnormality in the students make-up and drawing the counselling or liaison officers, attention.

(xi) He renders "mental hygiene first-aid" and helping the students remain on the right track.

(xii) He refers the serious cases to clinicians or psychiatrists.

7. THE ADVISER

Advisers support and supplement the guidance and counselling programme in a college or university. The teachers who are assigned some specifically guidance duties are called *advisers* in some colleges and universities. Advisers duties may be assigned to all members of the faculty, a panel of advisers be available to students who may wish to consult its members; or selected faculty members known as tutors or seminar leaders.

The boys and girls coming from the high school atmosphere of security to the free atmosphere of college/university require a place where they can belong, someone they can go to and talk their heart out with. This determines the role of the adviser.

Functions of the Adviser

(i) Showing personal friendship to the new student, demonstrating concern and respect for abilities and ambitions of each of his advisers and thus creating a sense of belongingness, in the freshers.

(ii) Explaining the general programme of curricular and extra-curricular activities to the advisers.

(iii) Helping the student in the selection of subjects.

(iv) Serving as a "faculty friend" by being a personal friend to the student, by reacting sympathetically and in an understanding manner.

(v) Serving as a liaison between the student and the departmental heads, the administration and the Dean of students and Counselling/Liaison Officer and thus helping to solve the academic and administrative problems of the student.

(vi) Assisting in the work of selecting students for admission through interviews.

(vii) Arranging pre-registration conferences with students living in the vicinity of the college.

(viii) Helping in the maintenance of records in respect of his advice.

(ix) Helping in general orientation programme.

(x) Encouraging cultural interests which may help students integrate their studies and new vocational cultural and recreational interests and activities.

(xi) Helping by listening, by suggesting certain ideas and by working individually with students or if need be, in groups.

(xii) Accepting reasonable requests for information from students and helping to meet these demands by adequate briefing in the group meetings.

(xiii) Adjusting his programme according to the seasonal developments in the academic calendar, and the corresponding changes in students concern and anxiety.

(xiv) Referring students with more difficult problems to the counselling centre or to other officers on the campus.

(xv) Arranging follow-up conferences to ensure that advisers are not meeting undue difficulty in adjusting to their academic programmes.

(xvi) Assuring students of his readiness to talk with them whenever they are worried or uncertain as to future plans or available resources in large or small emergencies.

Qualities of Adviser

Adviser is the heart of the guidance and counselling programme. He should enjoy personal contacts, and be interested in students as individuals outside the classroom. He should have a good grounding of technical requirements of courses and other matters and should be well conversant with the various occupations and vocations. Finally he should have devotion to this cause.

8. THE WARDEN

An important link in the process of guidance and counselling, the warden ensures that hostel is not just a place for passing the night, but is also a place of education with a reputation for promoting scholarship as well as a place for making good leaders and good citizens.

Students coming to college from the rural areas, where experience in college is vast impersonalism particularly on university campuses. Life in the hostel may provide a bridge from the closer and personal environment of the house to the recognisably less personal one of the educational institution. With an increasing number of students knocking at the doors of higher education, the hostel warden can play a crucial role. He/she may provide recognition and love to the inmate, help him/her build up self-confidence and self-reliance. He/she can establish rapport through directness of approach, friendliness in manner, voice and sympathy. He/she may create in the residents a much-needed sense of belongingness to an institution.

Hostel is not to be an island isolated from the other counselling or cultural or social functions of the campus. Rather it should be an integral part of both the curricular and extra-curricular activities of an institution.

Functions of the Warden

(i) Orienting the students regarding the customs and expectations of the hostel and helping them to anticipate some of the problems of group living and indicating the availability of help in the hostel so as to enable them to reach a satisfactory solution.

(ii) Providing help to students handicapped by the lack of emotional stability or psychological resources needed to function well as students.

(iii) Collecting all types of information regarding the resident in cumulative record and coordinating and use the information for the benefit of the student.

(iv) Taking care of natural therapies which include day-to-day relations of residents in their rooms, in the mess and in co-curricular involvements.

(v) Establishing a good communication system so that the students could express freely and participate in the activities without any reservation.

(vi) Encouraging participation of students to develop self-discipline, initiative, sharing of common tasks within the framework of hostel to become well-adjusted residents.

(vii) Creating a sense of belongingness among the residents through cultural programmes, informal evenings, dinner nights, celebration of days in the hostel.

(viii) Offering the students opportunity to achieve the freedom, responsibility and skills promising maturity and making the hostel a place *par excellence* for achieving the adult role.

(ix) Protecting the weak, tempering the strong, encouraging the shy, bringing out latent talents of the residents, stimulating self-discipline and serving as an interpreter of administrative policies of the institution.

(x) Providing sound advice recognising the needs of security, recognition and love of the students.

(xi) Referring residents to experts when the occasion demands it.

The warden may easily know the aptitudes and interests of the words in co-curricular activities, emotional maturity, financial adequacy and ability to handle finances, ability to take individual responsibility, family background, social development and social maturity, vocational development, special talent like singing, dancing, sports, etc. He may use this information in "seeing through" the students and helping him/her "see himself/herself through." Thus, in the entire superstructure of guidance and counselling warden is a very important person. He should have the essential qualities of politeness, patience and concern for the wards so that the latter may develop an essential respect for him/her.

9. THE PHYSICAL INSTRUCTOR

The physical instructor is an important link in the chain of guidance personnel as physical health is an important part of the make-up of a student. Physical efficiency is one of the basic requirements in so many careers such as Medicine, Engineering, etc.

Functions of Physical Instructor

(i) He provides the necessary data regarding the physical efficiency of the student, his performance in the physical efficiency tests, games and sports for the cumulative record.

(ii) He discovers the potentiality of the student in a particular game and arranging special training facilities for developing the same.

(iii) He brings to the notice of the doctor the students with physical problems and handicaps for treatment.

(iv) He arranges coaching classes and demonstrations for the promising players.

10. THE LIBRARIAN

In the overall guidance programme the librarian plays an important role by the following :

(i) He circulates the latest information material among the teachers and students.

(ii) He provides right type of books on educational, vocational and personal guidance to both teachers and students.

(iii) He helps the counselling and the liaison officers in the classification, and filing of the occupational information material.

(iv) He displays the material received from time to time in an attractive manner.

11. THE MEDICAL STAFF

Neither the teacher nor the counselling or liaison officer is a fit person to deal with health problems. Medical assistance needs to be provided, for the smooth progress of the student. The medical staff can contribute to the guidance programme in an institution as follows :

(i) It provides entrance and periodic medical examination for all students.

(ii) It reports physical limitations to teachers and parents.

(iii) It develops a programme of helping students in physical hygiene.

(iv) It ensures that information supplied about the health of students is utilised in the guidance programme.

(v) It maintains the health record of all students which should contain all information regarding medical examinations and check-ups held, any treatment suggested, any changes or improvements resulting from treatment correspondence with parents regarding treatment and their reactions, and reports from teachers.

12. THE PARENTS

The parents are the principal counsellors of the students. The favourable upbringing, the special help in the form of praise, admonition, reproof, and advice in difficult situations provided by parents contribute significantly to the guidance process.

Parents Role in Guidance

(i) They get maximum information regarding the educational and vocational possibilities for their children in the decades ahead.

(ii) They use good principles of mental hygiene and right living in their families.

(iii) They help the children in developing effective study habits, plan their activities and budget their time for maximum achievement.

(iv) They show the children how to postpone immediate pleasure in favour of latter gratification.

(v) They get sorts of information regarding the facilities available and helping their children in utilising the same.

(vi) They help their children in discovering, developing and directing all of the inherent potentialities.

Measures to improve Parent's Role in Guidance

An All India Study (1960-61) Report points out, "It is probably true that the parents themselves became the students' greatest problems by expecting them to perform at much higher level than they are capable of. If these expectations are not realistic and are not based upon the knowledge of the ability and aptitudes of the young people, they may become a source of misunderstanding between the parents and the child and a cause of despair and frustration to the student." Therefore, parents should be guidance-conscious. Parents' Clubs, Parents' Forums may be formed to achieve the objective. Parents' Days may be organised. Parents' Group Conferences may be held from time to time. Parents' Bulletins and Reports may be issued to keep them in touch with current happenings.

QUESTIONS FOR EXERCISE

1. Who are the guidance and counselling personnel? Describe the role of Administrator, Dean and the Teacher in providing guidance.
2. Explain the functions of the counselling officer and the liaison officer in providing counselling in universities.

3. What is the role of the parents in providing counselling and guidance?
4. Write short note on guidance services rendered by any one of following :
   (i) Hostel warden,
   (ii) Tutor,
   (iii) Physical instructor,
   (iv) Adviser.

18

Collection, Filing and Dissemination of Occupational Information

According to Hoppock "Choice always involves knowledge, one cannot choose what one does not know...one may stumble into an appropriate occupation by sheer luck, but the wise choice of an occupation requires accurate information about what occupations are available, what they require and what they offer..." A large amount of accurate, up-to-date information is vital to the success of any guidance and counselling programme. It is regarding educational and professional institutions, jobs and industries, occupational patterns, occupational fields, training facilities, educational, professional and technical courses, newly emerging occupations, job specifications, wage structure, changes in required skills, employment trends, employment patterns, etc. A counsellor may be trained in counselling technique, but without adequate educational and occupational information his interview may be empty. Information is an indispensable tool with the counsellor to enable him to bring about better adjustment between himself and his environment. Guidance, without information, is quackery.

Need of Occupational Information

1. To make guidance informative. Students need to know the jobs, work processes, where the training institutions are situated, the content of training, the avenues of employment after training, the average income, status of the work, future prospects, etc. Without adequate and accurate realistic and work-oriented information, it is not possible for a guidance worker to help the individual evaluate his abilities and aptitudes in terms of the requirements of a course or career.

2. To enable the students to acquire the image of occupations and society's evaluation of different occupations and cross check or interpret the suitability or validity of their own tentative decisions. Occupational pattern is rapidly changing. Most of today's occupations and skills did not exist a century ago. The proportion of the population engaged in various occupations is also shifting dramatically. From the agrarian society in which two-third of the work force laboured on farms, we have metamorphosed through an industrially-dominated work era to a period in which white-collared occupations are predominating.

Tomorrow's industries and occupations are likely to be quite different from those now familiar to us. The pattern of occupational opportunities for young people and the qualifications and skills required of youth are likely to change beyond recognition. All these require that occupational information is made an essential part of guidance programme.

3. To help in educational and vocational planning. Realistic information about jobs and the trends can go a long way in helping in educational and vocational planning. The glut in courses and careers can be averted by timely information. It may remove the disharmony between the employment opportunities and the resources of the personnel.

4. To help revise the old courses and develop the new ones. An analysis of the long-range occupational and industrial trends may prove helpful in redesigning the courses and starting the new ones.

Thus adequate up-to-date information should be available to guidance worker, to make the service *informative, motivational, exploratory, evaluative* and *adjustive* and thus *helpful* for the students.

A very important aspect of guidance work is collection, classification, filing and dissemination of information. This information needs to be collected, processed and used with the same degree of accuracy and care that are characteristic of any scientific investigation in the field of social sciences.

Scope of Occupational Information

Occupational information includes facts on the nature of work, occupational relationships, working conditions, educational requirements (including personal requirements, training and experience requirements, and entrance requirements) and the employment opportunities.

Occupational information can be generally categorised into the following types :

1. Information on job opportunities.
2. Information on educational/training facilities.
3. Information on apprenticeship and on-the-job training facilities.
4. Information on scholarships and fellowships.
5. Information on trends, patterns and growth of educational, training and employment opportunities.

Sources of Occupational Information

1. *Information on job openings*

(i) Advertisements inserted in newspapers, gazettes, etc. by the Union Public Service Commission, State Public Service Commissions and individual establishments and institutions;

(ii) Vacancies notified and circulated at different levels in the Employment Service and

(iii) Career literature brought out by the DGE and T, NCERT, State Educational and Vocational Guidance Bureaux, various voluntary organisations in the field of guidance like YMCA, etc.

2. *Information on educational and training facilities*

(i) Prospectuses of various educational and training institutions and universities.

(ii) Directories of training institutions such as those brought out by different ministries, departments, Inter-University Board and professional and voluntary organisations.

(iii) Handbooks on training facilities in different states brought out by DGE and T.

3. *Information on apprenticeship and on-the-job training facilities*

(i) Advertisements inserted in newspapers, magazines, etc. by various establishments and institutions.

(ii) Central/regional/state assistant apprenticeship advisors, principals of ITIs, qualified architects, industrial establishments.

4. *Information on scholarships and fellowships*

(i) Advertisements issued by organisations, institutions like CSIR, UGC, universities, central/state governments, ministries and departments, international organisations and community trusts and

(ii) Schemes for financial and other assistance formulated by banks, community trusts and voluntary organisations like YMCA, Rotary Club, Lions Club, etc.

5. *Information on trends, patterns and growth of educational, training and employment opportunities*

(i) Census reports, fact books and special reports/reviews brought out by CSIR, IAMR, IAER, CSO, Planning Commission, DGE and T, year books, State Department of Statistics, etc.

(ii) Annual reports of banks, companies and administrative reports of government departments.

(iii) Schemes of self-employment and related assistance of small industries, service institutes, industrial departments, banks and professional organisations; and

(iv) Career literature brought out by the Employment Service at different levels.

COLLECTION OF OCCUPATIONAL INFORMATION

The needs and backgrounds of the students determine the type and amount of information collected. It should normally cover all those occupations which the students of a college or university have been entering in the previous years and are likely to enter in future. It should also cover information about the new openings which are rapidly coming up.

Collection of information should be a continuous process. The requirements change, the information changes, the context may alter or the individual query may be different in its composition. The continuous flow of information helps review and revise the information and make it up-to-date. The old and obsolete information should be weeded out.

METHODS OF COLLECTING INFORMATION

1. Want ads survey.
2. Alumni follow-up survey.
3. Community survey.

1. A want ad survey. It is one of the cheapest and the easiest methods of collecting information. The 'Situations Vacant' advertisements which have appeared in newspapers over a period of six months or a year are collected and information contained in them is analysed and tabulated. This is a good method as it provides current information about many kinds of jobs.

2. Alumni follow-up survey. In it the students of a college or university are contacted personally or by mail and are requested to provide information in the form of answers to specific questions asked. Through this method, information can be obtained about those occupations only in which the old students of a particular college or university are engaged.

3. Community survey. In it the employing agencies and the educational, training and professional institutions existing in the community served by the institutions are contacted personally or through mail. The method provides the latest information regarding the requirement and trends but is more expensive than a want ad survey or an alumni follow-up survey.

METHODS OF FILING THE INFORMATION

It is not enough to collect information. A mechanism needs to be developed to put the collected information in a usableform. This work has a technical aspect. It is usually associated with libraries. The procurement, study, storage, referencing, indexing, display and dissemination are the five main stages which require a constant study of the techniques and ways of implementation. All these deserve the greatest consideration. Only these will result in effective use of the information collected. Information must be able to meet the original as well as supplementary queries of the students, and be so stored/ arranged as to make it easily accessible. Out of date information should be weeded out to avoid the problem of storage as well as ensuring easy access.

Ordinarily, it is a good practice to review and scrutinise the information available at the beginning of every academic year, delete the irrelevant information and add amendments if any.

Some method of filing the information has to be followed to ensure easy availability and effective use. The use of a particular method will depend upon the technical competence and time available for guidance work.

The liaison officer who is a part-time guidance worker can follow the simpler methods as :

1. Filing in the alphabetical order. It is useful where the information is small. The cross references have to be given in this method.

2. Filing according to the subjects offered in a college. Here, information is filed subject-wise. A separate file for each subject can be prepared and, if required, sub-groups may be arranged and files provided. If there is any information relating to two subjects e.g. Economics and Mathematics, either two copies of occupational information be provided or in the sheet attached for cross reference of one of the files its reference may be made and a copy of occupational information may be attached in the other file.

3. Filing information on the pattern of division of occupations suggested by Dr. M.P. Mehta. Former Director of Vocational Guidance Bureau in the Labour Ministry, Dr. Mehta has suggested following 23 groups for classifying the occupational material :

1. Engineers and technicians at all levels.
2. Physical scientists.
3. Biological scientists.
4. Physicians, surgeons and dentists.
5. Nurses and other health workers.
6. Teachers for all types and levels.
7. Jurists.
8. Accountants.
9. Economists.
10. Social workers at all levels.
11. Psychologists — guidance personnel.
12. Journalists.
13. Artists of all types and levels.
14. Administrative, executive and managerial workers.
15. Clerical and related workers.
16. Sales workers.
17. Farmers.
18. Fishermen.
19. Miners.
20. Forestry workers.
21. Transport workers.

22. Communication workers.
23. Defence and police workers.

4. Filing according to national classification of occupations. A qualified counsellor should try to file the information according to the national classification of occupations :

(i) *Filing of information pertaining to occupations*

Information pertaining to occupations, apprenticeship and on-the-job training facilities should be filed under family heads of the NCO *i.e.*, information about all occupations in a family should be filed at one place. The following steps should be undertaken for this purpose :

(a) As there are 95 groups under he seven divisions of the NCO (excluding X divisions), 95 loose leaf files should be opened. Each file should contain information pertaining to a group of the NCO. Name and number of the file should be entered on the face of the file as shown below :

Group	00
Name	Physical Scientists

(b) If a filing cabinet with cradles and folders is available for the purpose, the number and name of the group need not be entered on the face of the file. They should be entered on the top fixed on the top of the folder. The file should be placed inside the folder which rests on cradles.

(c) According to the NCO, a group of occupations consists of certain number of families. For example, Group 00 consists of five families and group 13 consists of nine families. Hence Group File should contain as many family sheets as there are families in that particular group. Group File 00, for instance, will have five sheets and Group File 13, nine sheets. These sheets should be filed in the same serial order as in the NCO.

(d) Occupational information collected from employers and other sources should be extracted and recorded in the column of the relevant family sheets. For example, information pertaining to an occupation in the family of physicists should be entered in the file 00 and sheet 000. In the remarks column of the proforma, a cross reference about the source from which the information is extracted should be recorded. In the case of information about apprenticeship/on the job training facilities also an appropriate entry should be made in the remarks column. If one sheet is not sufficient for any family of occupations, more sheets should be added. In such cases, pages should be numbered for each family.

(ii) *Filing of information pertaining to training courses*

(a) Information pertaining to educational and training facilities should be filed according to guidance code numbers. A Guidance

Code Number is an indication of an applicant's interests and educational level. A file with this number should contain all relevant information about the courses.

(b) Each file should contain information collected from prospectuses and other sources.

(c) If the prospectus or other sources from where the information is extracted are in the shape of leaflets or booklets, they may be filed at the back of the relevant file for reference. In case the source is a bound book, it may be given a serial number and a cross reference to that serial number made in the remarks columns of the proforma.

(iii) *Filing information pertaining to scholarships*

Information on scholarships and fellowships should be filed in a separate folder and a cross reference to the relevant job on training opportunity file made in the remarks column of the proforma.

REFERENCE CARDS

In order to be able to locate all the information in the files useful for a particular type of applicant, it is necessary to maintain reference cards. For example, if a graduate seeks individual guidance, the Counselling/Liaison officer should be able to locate information about all the opportunities open to him.

Reference cards should be prepared according to educational levels and kept in a tray. For each level two cards should be prepared — one for occupations and the other for training facilities.

The reference cards for graduate-occupations, will contain an exhaustive list of all occupations open to a graduate. In the third column of the card, family number of the occupations should be entered so that for details the relevant occupational information file and the family sheet can be referred to without wasting time.

Similarly, Reference Card for training should also be maintained according to the educational level. For example, Reference card for Graduate Training should contain an exhaustive list of all the courses open to graduates. Here also, in the third column, file number and page number should be noted.

OCCUPATIONAL CLASSIFICATION SYSTEMS

There are two types of classifications in use in India — National Industrial Classification (NIC) and National Classification of Occupations (NCO).

1. National industrial classification (1970). It has been prepared by the Government of India in order that information regarding employment and unemployment in various sectors of economy be more specifically known by its various fact-finding agencies.

Industry means that sector of economic activity in which the earner is, or was, engaged e.g. textile industry, automobile industry, etc.

Code numbers have been devised for each industrial group on what is known as 'the digit' system for use in employment exchange records. This system is related to the international usage as recommended by the International Labour Office.

2. National classification of occupations (1968). It has been prepared by the Government of India on the basis of an international classification system recommended by ILO. It classifies, defines and describes the various occupations available in the country giving the standard and alternative occupational titles. The international code structure for classifying occupations has, to some extent, been modified by a committee of experts to suit Indian conditions.

The definitions in the NCO give the overall functions and operations performed by the worker in the order of sequence including the tasks which the worker may do in addition to his normal duties. They also indicate the special knowledge regarding the particular as well as allied occupations which the worker in that occupation may possess by virtue of his professional qualifications and experience. Further, below each definition, a record portion is provided to give guidelines for recording relevant details of applicants and vacancies. All this information is of particular help to employment officers.

USE OF NCO TO EMPLOYMENT OFFICERS

1. In classifying applicants who call for employment assistance;
2. In classifying vacancies notified by employers;
3. In matching suitable applicants against demands;
4. In assessing the comparative skill and knowledge of workers within the same occupation;
5. In recording special qualifications against item 15 of index card (X.1);
6. In reporting statistical data concerning the employment market and
7. In classifying occupational literature.

The occupational classification system is also of great importance in the analysis of data relating to employment, unemployment, under-employment, labour force statistics, migration, training, wage comparison, work injury, occupational disease, etc.

USE OF NCO TO OTHER AGENCIES

Apart from the use made of the NCO by the Employment Service, other agencies use it such as the Registrar General of India, Planning Commission, National Sample Survey, Central Statistical Organisation, Institute of Applied Man Power Research, etc. and industrial establishments. The occupational hierarchy in this classification system runs upwards from occupation to families, groups and divisions. A number of similar occupations are grouped under one family. A number of families of allied occupations are combined into groups and a number of related groups are assigned to divisions. The National Classification of Occupations has at present 8 divisions consisting of 95 occupational groups, divided into 462 families : under each family is a number of individual occupations, which at present comes to 2,484 occupations.

CODE STRUCTURE OF NCO

In numerical coding system adopted in the NCO, the code number of each occupation consists of 5 digits, formed in the following manner :

1. Each division is assigned a single digit code number as 0, 1, 2. etc. In the eighth division, which is a supplementary division for workers not classified by occupations, the code given is 'X'.
2. As each division is divided into a number of groups, each of these groups within the division has a two digit code number. As the groups have been further divided into families, each family has got a three digit code number.
3. For occupation, within the Family, two more digits are added, thus making a five digit code number. The allocation of a five-digit code number for an occupation is illustrated below :

Division	Sales workers	Code number
Group within the division	Salesmen, shop assistants and related workers	43
Family within the group	Salesmen, shop assistants and demonstrators	430
Occupation within the family	Salesman, wholesaler	430.10

4. The last two digits of the code number for individual occupations within a family are numbered in sequence like 10, 15, 20, 25 etc. usually, leaving intervals of five or ten between numbers depending on the number of occupations to be accommodated within the family.

Concept of Occupation

The 6th International Conference of Labour Statistics adopted the following definition of an occupation :

"An occupation is a trade, profession or type of work performed by an individual irrespective of the branch of the economic activity to which he is attached."

The same concept of an *occupation* has been adopted in the NCO.

According to it, the occupation of any person is the kind of work which an individual performs. The nature of the factory, business or service in which the person is employed has, however, no bearing upon the classification of the occupation. It is a person's occupation, independent of his industrial association, that is important in an occupational classification. There is, therefore, a clear distinction between an occupational classification and an industrial classification. The former embraces what an individual does, while the latter shows the position of the worker in the economic structure of the industry. A man's occupation is the type of work he performs. His industry is the type of commodities/services which his employer produces. For instance, a carpenter may work in the ship building industry, the food processing industry or a steel plant, but by occupation he will be a carpenter.

METHODS OF DISSEMINATING INFORMATION

There are two chief methods of disseminating occupational information to students :

(a) Group method.

(b) Individual method.

Under the present conditions group method of disseminating occupational information is most suitable. Besides, the group method has following advantages :

1. Orientation can be given to all students.
2. Information of common interest and value can be economically imparted.
3. Experiences of a number of individuals can be pooled for the benefit of each member of the group.
4. Individuals in need of individual counselling can be discovered.

GROUP TECHNIQUES OF IMPARTING OCCUPATIONAL INFORMATION

1. Through subjects. A subject teacher can show the relationship between his subject-matter and occupations, as well as the vocational implications of the subject-matter.

2. Career education. It can be given to students through a systematic teaching of occupations.

3. Career talks. These are talks on specific fields of occupations, training etc. appropriate to groups of particular educational levels, emphasising the importance of vocational planning. This is one of the best ways of giving first-hand information about the merits and limitations of a particular occupation. Talks may be arranged for students of particular faculties in a college. The subject-matter may range from how and why of career planning to disseminating information about broad and specific fields of opportunities. The students should be encouraged to ask questions after the talk to clarify doubts, etc.

4. Career conferences. These are meetings or series of meetings in which various professional experts in different occupations participate and make available their intimate knowledge of the requirements and opportunities in their fields of work.

The programme of a conference should be well-drawn up. The most suitable time for such conferences is the beginning of the academic session. Parents, too, can be invited.

5. Tutorials. These also provide a very good occasion for imparting occupational information. As the group is usually small, different problems regarding the different fields of occupations can be discussed informally.

6. Work-sample projects. The students may spend a day or two on the job of their choice. This will give them familiarity with working condition in particular industries, etc. not possible through reading.

7. Visits to places of work. Visits to the places of work, factories or business establishments can also prove useful as the pupils can get first-hand knowledge about the working conditions.

8. Films and film strips. Films and film strips help to arouse interest in the study of occupations.

9. Dramatisation. If students take up the writing and production of one act plays to teach something about occupations, it proves a very interesting way of disseminating occupational information. For example, the ideas of right and wrong way to apply for a job, right and wrong way to appear for an interview can prove very useful and interesting. Certain dramatised radio and TV programmes can also prove useful.

10. Career exhibitions. These are organised displays of materials of occupational interest. Although it is usually not possible to give detailed information through a display, certain basic ideas can be presented simply and clearly and at the same time, it can also be useful in directing students to other sources of information. Students should play an active role in planning and organising career exhibitions.

11. Bulletin board announcements and other devices. These may be used to call attention to the information available. Copies of handouts received from DGE and T, UGC, different ministries and social agencies, University Employment Information and Guidance Bureaux could also be displayed with advantage. A special notice board or bulletin board bearing the name 'Vocational Guidance' may help students in knowing where to look for the information. Students may also be encouraged to collect information which can be displayed with advantage.

Important news-cuttings may be displayed on the boards under heads as — advertisements of various State Public Service Commissions; Union Public Service Commission; Subordinate Service Selection Boards; Railway Service Cormmission; Posts and Telegraphs; information regarding competitive examinations, Scholarships, Apprenticeships; Admission Notices; New Courses; Miscellaneous.

The Counselling/Liaison Officer should also select from various studies important facts and assemble them for bulletin board display.

12. Special card catalogue. The Counselling/Liaison Officer should prepare a special card catalogue of the most useful occupational studies from books, pamphlets and magazines for ready reference. These cards should contain not only the usual information of author, title, publisher, etc. but also a careful analysis and evaluation of the study. Such a collection of cards can be of great assistance to the Counselling/Liaison Officer and, if carefully made, will save much time.

13. Library. Rich reference materials, easily available, help in informing the students about occupations and their requirements. A separate section should be organised in the library on occupational information. Prospectuses of various institutions may also be included in it with advantage. The publications should be both authentic and uptodate. The books and pamphlets in the library should cover a wide range of occupations for men and women. The library should also contain maps showing Training and Educational facilities in the country; posters and pamphlets prepared by various agencies; charts prepared by the Counselling/Liaison Officer, etc.

INDIVIDUAL TECHNIQUE OF IMPARTING OCCUPATIONAL INFORMATION

Students can see the Counselling/Liaison officer to seek his help in planning his career, choosing a course of study or training or career or apprenticeship. He may seek an interview or the Counselling/Liaison officer may write to him.

The individual technique, of course, is the best for disseminating information but due to the paucity of guidance personnel and large number of students to be guided, it may not be possible to arrange such interviews for every student.

LIST OF AGENCIES PUBLISHING CAREER LITERATURE AND OCCUPATIONAL INFORMATION MATERIALS

1. Central Institute for Research and Training in Employment Service (Career Study Centre), DGE & T, Pusa, New Delhi.
2. Ministry of Education and Social Welfare, Shastri Bhawan, New Delhi.
3. Directorate General of Health Services (Ministry of Health, Family Planning, Works, Housing & Urban Development), New Delhi.
4. National Council of Educational Research and Training, Sri Aurobindo Marg, New Delhi.
5. Institute of Vocational Guidance and Selection, 3, Mahapalika Marg, Bombay-1.
6. University Grants Commission, Bahadur Shah Zaffar Marg, New Delhi.

7. Association of Indian Universities, Rouse Avenue, New Delhi.
8. Central Statistical Organisation, Sardar Patel Bhawan, Parliament Street, New Delhi.
9. Council of Scientific and Industrial Research, Rafi Marg, New Delhi.
10. Indian Council of Agricultural Research, Krishi Bhawan, New Delhi.
11. Inter-University Board of India, Dyal Singh Library Building, Deen Dayal Upadhyaya Marg, New Delhi.
12. Union Public Service Commission, Dholpur House, New Delhi.
13. State Guidance Bureaux in the country.
14. University Employment Information and Guidance Bureaux.
15. Delhi Administration, Delhi.
16. Ministry of Information and Broadcasting, New Delhi.
17. Personnel Services Directorate, Naval Head Quarters, New Delhi.
18. The Institute of Chartered Accountants of India, Indraprastha Marg, New Delhi.
19. State Directorates of Employment and Training.

LIST OF AGENCIES PUBLISHING PSYCHOLOGICAL TESTS

1. Mansayan, Centre for Psychological Materials, 32, Netaji Subhas Marg, New Delhi-110002.
2. National Psychological Corporation, Hotel Dharamlok Building, Raja Mandi, Agra.
3. The Psychological Corporation, 304 East 45th Street, New York, 17, N.Y.
4. Purohit and Purohit, Shukrawar Peth, Poona-2.
5. Psycho Centre, T-22, Green Park, New Delhi-110016.
6. Educational Psychology Unit, NCERT, Sri Aurobindo Marg, New Delhi-110016.
7. State Central Pedagogical Institute, Allahabad.
8. A.B. Teachers' College, Ahmedabad-9.
9. M/s Bharat Prakashan, 44, Kalyan Bhawan, Tilak Road, Ahmedabad-1.
10. Manovigyan Shala, Allahabad, U.P.
11. Princeton : University Press, Humphrey Milford London, Oxford University Press.
12. Bureau of Educational and Vocational Guidance, No. 27, V Block, Kumara Park West Extension, Bangalore-20.
13. Bureau of Educational & Psychological Research, David Hare Training College, Calcutta-19.

14. Faculty of Education and Psychology, M.S. University, Baroda.
15. Educational and Vocational Guidance Bureau, Bihar, Patna.
16. Institute of Vocational Guidance, 3, Cruickshank Road, Bombay-1.
17. Slate Bureau of Educational and Vocational Guidance, Bangalore.
18. Central Institute of Education, 33, Chhatra Marg, Delhi-110007.
19. Atma Ram and Sons, Kashmere Gate, Delhi.
20. Vidya Bhavvan Teachers College, Udaipur.
21. Department of Education, Gorakhpur University, Gorakhpur, U.P.
22. Agra Psychological Research Cell, Tiwari Kothi, Belanganj, Agra-282004.
23. Department of Psychology, University of Madras, Madras.
24. Inter Trade Publications (I) Pvt. Ltd., 55, Gariahat Road, Post Box 102101, Calcutta-19.
25. Rupa Psychological Centre, B 19/60-B, Deoriabir, Bhelupura, Varanasi-221001.

19

Psychological Aspects of Vocation

Great is the importance of vocation in the life of an individual. "One's job is the watershed down which the rest of one's life tends to flow" has been so well said by Robert S. Lynd and Helen M. Lynd.

VOCATIONAL CHOICE

The choice of vocation is one of the very important decisions a person makes for himself. It is a long process rather than a simple incident. Vocational interests and choices do not appear all of a sudden during adolescence. They appear as a result of developmental process. A number of theories have been advanced by psychologists and occupational analysts on occupational choice.

Theory of Ginzberg and Others

Ginzberg and others studied the problem of vocational choices by investigating how occupational choices are made. They concluded that an individual never reaches the ultimate decision at a single moment in time, but through a series of decisions over a period of many years. They divided the process of occupational decision-making into three distinct periods. They said "the period during which the individual makes what can be described as a *fantasy choice*; the period during which he is making a *tentative choice*; and the period when he makes a *realistic choice*. The first (the period of fantasy choice) coincides in general with the latency period, between six and eleven, although residual elements of fantasy choice frequently carry over into pre-adolescent years. The second (the period of tentative choice) coincides, by and large, with early and late adolescence; with few exceptions, realistic choices are made in early childhood".

Three Basic Elements

Regarding occupational choice there are three basic elements suggested by Ginzberg and others as follows :

1. Developmental process. Occupational choice is a developmental process; It is not a single decision made over a period of years — a process which takes place over a minimum of six or seven years, and more typically over ten years or more.

2. Irreversible process. The process of decision-making is basically irreversible since each decision during adolescence is related to one's experience upto that point, and in turn has an influence on the future.

3. Compromise. The crystallisation of occupational choice inevitable has the quality of a compromise since occupational choice involves the balancing of a series of subjective elements with opportunities and limitations of reality.

Vocational choices take place as a result of a developmental process. It has been traced to the early days of the individual's life. This development can also be traced to the influences exerted before birth. Child development studies have proved the powerful influence which the thwarted ambitions and frustrations of the parents have on the vocational choice of the individual. Vocation is the implementation of the self-concept. When the parents fail to achieve it during their own career, they seek it through the choice of career for their children. They force their own unfulfilled career choice on their children. Sometimes, this works, at other times it leads to dissatisfaction for the child, often a revolt and a change of vocational choice. This involves frustration for the growing adult, waste of energy, money and precious time.

VOCATIONAL DEVELOPMENT

Vocational development may be conceived of as beginning early in life and as proceeding along a curve late in life. While four year old child who plays the policeman or soldier is in a very early stage of vocational development, the old man of sixty who does not work for money but still keeps himself busy with writing books in the field of his specialisation is going through the late stage of vocational development.

Vocational development follows the general pattern of developments. It can be conceived of as a continuum with definite life stages which can be defined through their peculiar characteristics.

VOCATIONAL LIFE STAGES

Buehler has classified the vocational life stages as :

1. Growth (birth to 14 years).

2. Explanatory (15 to 24 years). It has a sub-stages of fantasy which may be tentative or realistic with appropriate attitudes towards work and occupation.

3. Establishment (24 to 44 years). It begins with trial and progressing into a stable position as the individual begins to make his place in the world of work.

4. Maintenance stage (45 to 64 years). It is characterised by stability in the field in which establishment has taken place earlier in life.

5. The decline stage (65 onwards). It is characterised by deceleration during the early part and progressing into one of retirement.

Thus, the process of vocational development is a series of 5 life-stages characterised as those of growth, exploration, maintenance and decline. These stages may in turn be sub-divided into (a) the fantasy, tentative and realistic phases of the exploratory stage, and (b) the trial and stable phases of the establishment stage.

Nature of Development Process

The process of vocational development is continuous and ongoing. It is essentially that of developing and implementing a self-concept. It is a compromise process in which the self-concept is a product of the inter-action of inherited aptitudes, neural and endocrinal make-up, opportunity to play various roles, and evaluations of the extent to which the results of role playing meet with the approval of supervisors and fellows.

Process of Compromise

The process of compromise between individual and social factors, between self-concept and reality is one of role-playing whether the role is played in fantasy, in the counselling interviews, or in real life activities, such as school classes, clubs, part-time work and entry jobs. The opportunities of exploring the occupational roles available in the world of work through actual participation are obviously limited. While part-time and trial jobs offer some real experience, only a very few occupational roles can be sampled in this way. The majority of all exploratory activities involve rehearsing those roles which the individual wants to try in imaginary situations and test them against the self-concept. The material for these role playing activities can be games from a number of sources : the home, peers, friends and acquaintances who are in employment, the mass media, school/college/university, the career masters, counsellors, recruitment literature and so on. The inadequacies of these indirect sources and the unrealistic occupational perceptions gained from them often frustrate the most determined attempts to achieve a realistic compromise. Work satisfaction and life satisfactions depend upon the extent to which the individual finds adequate outlets for his abilities, interests, personality traits and values. They depend upon his establishment in a type of work or work situations and a way of life in which he can play the kind of role which his growth and explanatory experiences have led him to consider congenial and appropriate. Vocational preferences and competencies work in the situations in which people live and work. Hence, their self-concepts change with time and experience, making choice and adjustment a continuous process. "The vocational preferences of the developing child are subject to continual change. For the young child, the chosen occupation is often one which is identified with adults. Stated preferences may be the child's identification with that part of the adult world which he or she sees as being most pleasurable. As the child develops a greater degree of individuality and as a growing awareness of the self evolves, interests, capacities and values begin to influence preferences. At a later stage the need to face the reality of the occupational world and to find a place therein may again significantly influence choice."

The process of occupational choice and adjustment does not end when a youngster enters his or her first job. Occupational expectations are rarely fully realised and some adjustment to the unexpected is necessary. Even when such adjustment is achieved, the process is not complete. Regular work activities may facilitate the development of latent skills which the individual may subsequently utilise more fully. A growing awareness of the world of work and the opportunities available may also motivate the individual to seek out what to perceive in better jobs. Even where a person remains in the same job for much of his life, a series of adjustments are necessary to meet with the individual's changing concept of himself.

Features of Vocational Development

1. How does the individual reach the stage where he starts thinking of taking up a vocation?

2. How and when does he show definite attitudes towards occupation and a vocation?

3. Do his attitudes differ at different age limits?

4. What kinds of attitudes should be considered normal for an age and which should be unusual or abnormal?

FACTORS GOVERNING VOCATIONAL DEVELOPMENT

Occupational choice and subsequent vocational development is greatly influenced by the experience a child undergoes. The individual is a product of his environment, his inherent aptitudes and neural endocrinal make-up. The nature of the career pattern is determined by the individual's parental socio-economic level, mental ability, and personality characteristic and by the opportunities to which he is exposed.

1. The family. Of all the social systems which impinge upon the individual and influence his development, the family is the most important. Beginning in early childhood and continuing into the late years of life, the vocational development of the individual, which is a continuous process, appears to be as much influenced by his family as are other aspects of his development.

(i) *Hereditary factors* : The abilities, interests, physique and personality of the individual, which play such an important role in his vocational development, are partly determined by hereditary factors and the particular constellations of genes which the individual inherits depends upon his parents and ancestors. Thus the family as a biological unit begins to influence the vocational development of the individual before his birth, from the moment of his conception.

(ii) *Physical factors* : These include the geographical location of the home. The physical conditions prevailing in the home, and the health of various members of the family may, at times, have a significant effect on the vocational development of the individual. A boy coming from a home in a remote village has much more difficulty in obtaining a college education than a boy residing in a town. A person residing in a town which does not offer facilities for specialisation in a particular has to seek admission in another town, which obviously involves additional expenditure on board and lodging. If the family budget cannot accommodate this extra expenditure, the student has to change his educational — vocational aim and specialise in a different field or compromise by taking up a course of training at a lower level in the same field, if such training is available in his home town.

(iii) *The location of the family residence* : It also determines the type of vocational activities which the individual may take up. A person who has spent the formative years of his life in a project area — which is the centre of engineering activity — is likely to have more information about engineering, develop an interest in it, and see himself as playing a role in it, than a person who has lived far away from such type of activity. He is also likely to enter this profession as he has contacts with the people working in this profession.

(iv) *Physical conditions in the family* : These include over-crowding, noise, lack of proper light and ventilation, and an inadequate diet all of which have an injurious effect on the health of the individual as well as on his ability to concentrate on studies or work, and thus may adversely affect his vocational development.

(v) *The health of the members of the family* : It may also have an indirect effect on vocational development. Crippling, ill-health or death of the bread-winner of the family may make it necessary for a youngster to discontinue his studies, no matter how bright he may be, and take up the first available job, whether it is suitable or not. Similarly, ill-health or death of the mother may make it necessary for a girl to spend so much of her time on household chores, that her studies or job are neglected, or even to relinquish her studies or job altogether.

(vi) *The socio-economic level of the family* : It appears to exercise the most potent influence of all. The level and quality of education available and aspired to, as well as the level of work aspired to and accessible, are greatly affected by the family's finances and social contacts. Upper and middle class parents tend to have higher educational and vocational aspirations for their children than do lower-class parents. Thus, their children have higher aspirations either as a result of pressure from the parents or as a result of internalising parental pressures or both. If their intellectual endowment is good, their higher level of aspiration may be achieved. But if intellectual endowment is not commensurate with level of aspiration, conflict may arise. The individual may not be able to have an integrated self-concept, and vocational maladjustment is likely to follow. At times, however, the reverse is true. Among very affluent families, the level of educational and vocational aspirations may be low. A person with good abilities may not be sufficiently motivated to concentrate on studies and strike out a vocational path for himself, thus failing to actualise his potentialities.

Persons who belong to families from the *higher socio-economic strata* also have better chances of finding employment at a higher level because their parents, and they themselves, have more contacts with people who are well-to-do and influential, people who are employers rather than employees. In setting up a professional practice or business, too, individuals from the higher socio-economic strata are at an advantage because of the capital available to them as well as the well-to-do friends and acquaintances who are potential clients.

(vii) *The occupational information* : The occupational information which a person picks up from his family influence his vocational thinking and eventual choice of occupation. The types of occupations concerning which a family can provide information vary with its socio-economic level. A person from a higher level family is in a better position to obtain more information about professional, business and administrative work, and one from a lower level family about skilled, semi-skilled and unskilled work.

(viii) *Cultural Stimulation* : The types of cultural stimulation prevalent in the family, and the types of equipment available, play a part in facilitating or hindering the development of the youngster's abilities and interests in certain directions, providing or failing to provide him with opportunities to test his self-concept through explanatory activities. *Identification of the individual with the socio-economic class to which his family belongs may also influence his self-concept.* A person from a higher class family may find it difficult to work as a peon or clerk; while a person from a lower class family tends to see himself in these or similar roles — if his vocational thinking is reality-oriented and not dominated by fantasy. He may find it difficult to see himself as a professional man or businessman; an administrator or manager.

(ix) *The family as a mediator of culture* : It also influences vocational development. Caste and religion, mediated through the family, at times have a profound influence on vocational development.

(a) *Caste* : Caste often restricts the occupations open to its members. This restrictive effect plays a greater part in the vocational development of a person who comes from an orthodox family in which conformity and obedience have been stressed than in the vocational development of a person whose family is unconventional and regards its membership of a particular caste as a chance factor to which no importance need be attached.

(b) *Religion* : The family's religion too at times gives a bias to the choice of occupation. For example, the frequent choice of martial career by the Sikhs appears to be related to the militant nature of their religion.

(x) *Development of attitudes and values* : The family is also instrumental in helping the individuals develop attitudes and values. It has been proved through researches that children are not born with attitudes but they acquire them gradually through various experiences and influences. Wittingly or unwittingly parents transmit attitudes and values to children. Attitudes towards various types of occupations as well as towards work itself are learnt in the home. These play their part in developing in the individual preference for certain occupations and dislike for others. This is how people come to consider occupations as ranking high or low in prestige, as clean or dirty, as safe or risky, as purposeful or frivolous. For example, the individual who has grown up in a home where manual work is looked down upon as being uncultured and dirty, is likely to develop the attitude that manual work is beneath his dignity and to think that society will set less score by him if he takes up an occupation which involves manual work. This single factor is responsible for most of the people in India seeking white collar jobs, and remaining unemployed while jobs requiring skilled and semi-skilled work go.

(xi) *Work ethics* : Similarly, work ethics learned in the family can have a far reaching effect on vocational choice and adjustment. For example, if concern for the welfare of people has permeated a home, the personality of an individual growing up in such a home will be influenced by it, and he is likely to seek and find fulfilment in one of the social welfare occupations. If, on the other hand, monetary considerations have been predominant in his family, he tends to go in for a type of work in which the monetary rewards are attractive. A family in which aesthetic values play their part in daily living, children prefer artistic occupations. Children who come from a family, in which intellectual activities and achievements are valued, are likely to be drawn towards intellectual pursuits in adulthood. Children who come from a home in which intellectual activities are not valued tend not to be attracted towards such activities. If there be an attraction on account of high intellectual abilities seeking an outlet, the attraction will not be without conflict.

(xii) *Emotional currents in the family* : These also have a subtle influence on vocational development. Inter-personal relations prevailing within the family, particularly during the individual's formative years, play a great role in shaping his personality and behaviour, including vocational behaviour. Conditions such as parental neglect or rejections, over-protection, parental disharmony or intense sibling rivalry create insecure, unintegrated persons who find it difficult to make a good vocational adjustment; they find it difficult to make vocational decisions.

Even when they make decisions, they are often unwise, and unstable. They have work inhibitions or an overbearing urge to achieve which defeats its own purpose. They also find difficulty in getting alongwith other people. Researchers have shown that personality difficulties are the most frequent cause of vocational inefficiency and dissatisfaction and also of discharge from environment.

(xiii) *Emotional needs fostered in the early interpersonal relations in the family* : These tend to motivate the individual to seek their satisfaction through vocational activities. For instance, a child who has been over-protected by his family and grows up to have a strong need for security and dependence, tends to avoid occupations involving outdoor life, leadership, taking risks, etc. He tends to gravitate towards occupations in which the work is safe and holds little challenge. He is not likely to leave his home town. Another person whose needs for self-expression and recognition have not been gratified within his family, may either seek a vocational situation in which needs can be gratified or he may become so cowed down and lacking in confidence that he may choose an occupation considerably below his ability level, or even drift into an occupation without planning. Again, an exaggerated need of independence, developed in the course of his relationships with his parents, may make it difficult for a person to accept any salaried employment and impel him towards setting up his own business or go into some other independent venture.

(xiv) *Provision of adult role models* : The family provides the earliest adult role models with whom the individual may identify or whom he may reject. Normally the boy wants to be like his father and incorporates within himself the characteristics of the father, including his occupational role, work values and attitudes. As a child, he plays games in which he acts out the occupational role of the father, and later he wishes to take up the same occupation in earnest. Similarly, the girl normally patterns herself after the mother. While, for the girl, the mother is a sex model rather than an occupational model, whereas for the boy the father is both a sex model and an occupational model. A bright girl aiming at a career thus often finds a suitable feminine occupational model lacking in her family. She may then identify with some female outside the family or with her father, or other male member of the family. In the latter event, the conflicting (male and female) identifications may cause maladjustment in the vocational as well as in the personal-social sphere. Frequently, such a girl compulsively seeks fulfilment through a career and is unable to seek fulfilment in the normal psycho-biological female roles of wife and mother. The boy, too, at times has conflicts arising out of identification with his mother as well as his father.

(xv) *self Concept* : The individual's self-concept emerges from and is greatly influenced by his family. Their judgement of his capacities and characteristics, the status and role he experiences in his relations with them, their acceptance or rejection of him as a person; from a myriad of such perceptions the individual develops a concept of himself as a worker which he tries to implement in the course of his vocational development.

(xvi) *Influence of (in-laws)* : When the individual grows up, his/her vocational development is influenced by two families in addition to his/her parental family, *viz.* his spouse's family, and the new family of which he/she himself/herself is the head.

Thus, the family wields a great deal of influence on the vocational development of the individual, no matter from which point of view one looks at it.

2. Ability. Adolescents with higher ability tend to seek and prepare for jobs which require higher kind of intelligence, while the ones with lower mental ability go in for semi-skilled jobs and continue in positions of almost no importance. The individuals who do not choose their careers according to their level of ability, land in failure because of poor competence. Though no systematic and thorough study made on Indian samples is available, some foreign studies have produced results to illustrate the difference in vocational success of the intelligent and dull individuals. In one of the studies were followed up eight individuals who had been diagnosed as feeble-minded or of borderline intelligence. Some eighteen years earlier, when their vocational achievement was studies, two of them were working as truck drivers; another was a taxi driver; a welder; a shipping clerk; a train repair man, and an assembler at an air plane factory. All of these persons were earning meagre money but each one of them a self-supporting and productive citizen. On the other hand, a group of above average intelligence was followed up for a considerably long period. The members were found occupying positions of significant importance. Eighty per cent of those had graduated from college; 75 per cent were employed in professional or semi-professional positions. Many of them were university teachers, physicians, lawyers, architects, authors, engineers and artists.

3. Personality. Personality of the individual affects his vocational interests just as it does his general interests and their development. A social and an extrovert personality would make a successful public relations officer but not a scholar or a librarian. Similarly, a quiet and an introvert person would be unhappy if placed on the job of a salesman.

(i) *Job specifications* : Every job can be described in terms of the personality characteristics it requires for the person to be happy and satisfied in it. For example, good teachers are usually social, communicative, self-confident, self-sufficient and aggressive. Bankers, dentists and musicians are more conservative, self-contained and less aggressive.

(ii) *Interest patterns* : Attempts have been made to measure people's personal suitability to a particular job through the study of their interest patterns, through their responses to questions in interest inventories and interest blanks.

(iii) *Profiles of successful persons* : Prediction of the most suitable career for an individual is based on the numerous profiles of successful individuals in various jobs. The profile of the individual wanting guidance can be compared with those who have already been successful in that particular field. The similarity and divergence between their personal qualities is a reliable guide for prediction of a career for the individual tested. Studies of reliability of these predictions have proved that young people changing a particular career have interest profiles markedly similar to those of the successful persons in that particular line.

Study made by Norton has shown that persons most stable in their jobs showed interest patterns most suitable to work of their choice.

(iv) *Earnings* : Besides, a significant difference has been found in the earnings of persons in jobs most suited to their personality characteristics and the ones who have been placed in jobs not suited to their interest patterns.

(v) *Drive* : In addition to the job satisfaction, suitable personality and interest patterns provide the individual with an opportunity for the development of vocational drive. Mere work skills and abilities are not the sole determinants of success of the individual on the job; good personal adjustment and skills of inter-personal communication are also a must.

4. Economic factors. (i) *Prestige* : Economic factors plays an important role in the vocational choice and development of an individual. While planning the career, the individual avoids the vocations with low wages and low prestige even though these may be the ones in which he is interested the most.

(ii) *Business cycle* : Business cycle is another economic factor affecting the vocational development of young persons as well as the vocational pattern and adjustment of older adults. Business completes a cycle of success and failure. The business expands and brings the society to the condition of complete prosperity followed by another period of prosperity. This cycle has definite effects on the vocational development and employment of the individual. A young adult who completes his education during depression is faced with the strain of scarcity of employment which is unfamiliar to another young man who may have passed college during more prosperous times. The two are forced to make very different vocational adjustment. During depressions, there is a general downgrading which results in dissatisfaction among the workers. During prosperous times, on the other hand, there is scarcity of suitable individuals, so there is a trend of upgrading. Persons with ordinary qualifications are able to secure good and above-expectation jobs. This process can be painful because by putting people in strange situations and ways of life unknown to them, it calls for readjustments which cause considerable amount of strain on the individual.

5. Industrialisation. Industrialisation influences vocational development of an individual. Many new jobs come up due to industrialisation. The people are not usually familiar with these jobs. They had never aspired for them neither have they had the opportunity to explore their interests and aptitudes for these jobs. Industrialisation also effects the workers already settled in jobs. For many it may mean getting uprooted and looking for the main jobs; for the others it may mean acquiring new skills to fit into the positions requiring skilled labour.

6. Public policy. It has its effect on the vocational development of the individual. Reservations both in admission and jobs proves an important factor for scheduled castes to go in for particular vocations — inspire of the fact that they are not well-qualified. Similarly, those from other castes may not be able to go in for medicine or engineering in spite of fairly good merit as compared to the Scheduled Castes. Hence change in vocations in spite of interest, aptitude and ability for these lines.

State patronage for a particular industry in a backward area acts as a boost while similar industry in an advanced area may suffer an obvious setback.

MEANING OF VOCATIONAL ADJUSTMENT

Vocational adjustment has been regarded as the aim of all vocational guidance programmes and activities.

In adjustment to a vocation it is necessary that the individual should have a pleasant feeling and tone while doing his occupational work and that he should acquire a reasonable amount of facility in that work.

In case of some individuals vocational adjustment also means that the individual is able to express his personality adequately through his work. Moreover, the occupation provides him with enough remuneration to meet his economic needs. The work may also enable him to enjoy some social status and allow him to play a certain type of role in society in conformity with his values and personality needs.

FACTORS OF VOCATIONAL ADJUSTMENT

1. Total adjustment. Vocational adjustment cannot be judged merely by satisfaction and facility in work. Such criteria of adjustment tend to be narrow and neglect the "global" aspects of adjustment. Vocational adjustment means adjustment not only to work involved in the occupation but to all social, economic and physical situations connected with the occupation. An occupation brings with it many social relationships with colleagues, superiors, subordinates and the public. It also creates for the individual a social atmosphere in which he lives and works. Hence vocational adjustment means adjustment not only to work but to these social relationships and the social atmosphere prevailing in the place of work. A good deal of satisfaction is derived from social relationships. A worker may be very good in his work but if he is not adjusted to the social atmosphere, he should be considered as vocationally maladjusted. Conversely, a worker may not be quite competent by virtue of his aptitudes in the work but if he is able to derive satisfaction from the social relationships he may be well-adjusted to the work situation as a whole. *Social status* is more important in occupational adjustment than economic gain.

2. Competence. Professional and technical competence is not enough for vocational success or adjustment. There are many occupations — professional and technical in nature — which call for the qualities and competencies other than those required in the technical execution of work. People lose positions or fail to attain positions even when they are competent to perform the technical duties involved in their jobs. Conversely, technically incompetent persons may be retained or achieve advancement because other qualities offset the lack of technical competency.

3. Sell realisation. Vocational adjustment also involves the implementation of a part of the individual's self-concept in the world of work. By self-concept is meant the complex of ideas arid attitudes which an individual has about himself and to the world around him. Thus, self-concept defines the locus of the individual in the field of his relations to the social and physical world. It is the picture of the individual as it appears to him or the way he looks at himself. In his memorable article "Vocational Adjustment — Implementing a Self-Concept" Super explains how the self-concept is involved in vocational adjustment. He redefines vocational guidance in terms of self-concept when he says, "vocational guidance is the process of helping a person to develop and accept an integrated and adequate picture of himself and of his role in the world of work, to test this concept against reality, and to convert it into a reality, with satisfaction to himself and benefit to society."

Individuals vary in the degree of need for implementation of their self-concept in the occupational world, with the result that at the lower extreme, there would be individuals who could obtain satisfaction from several types of work within the range of their capacity.

4. Fulfilment of emotional needs of the individual. This is in his occupational world and the role of emotional needs in vocational choice. Gratification of these needs is the psycho-dynamic factor in vocational choice and adjustment. It may be felt by the individual consciously or may operate from the unconscious as an impelling force. Needs stated by Murray, are abasement, achievement, acquisition, affiliation, aggression, autonomy, cognizance, escape, nurturance, recreation, succourance, etc. It may be assumed that the persons' interests are focused on activities which seem likely to permit the satisfaction of their strongest need. If so, it may further be presumed that adjustment in a particular occupation involves the satisfaction of a particular need or a particular combination of needs. However, it seems that different individuals tend to satisfy the same need in different occupations. For example, the need for achievement may be satisfied by one individual in medicine whereas the same need may be satisfied by another individual in a technical occupation. Conversely, it may be stated that different individuals or different types of individuals gratify different needs in the same occupation.

5. The need for creativity. It plays an important part in vocational choice and adjustment. By creativity we mean the need to create new objects, maintaining and fostering them. Different individuals seek different ways of gratifying this need. Some may gratify this need in creating new patterns and designs in clothes, machinery, etc. some in working out a project, some in organising an office, some in teaching, some in treating the diseased, some in writing articles. The mode of gratification of this need which is related to the personality organisation of the individual, plays a significant part in vocational choice and adjustment. If the occupation does not give scope for the gratification of this need, the individual finds himself vocationally unadjusted. For many who do not seek gratification of this need in vocational life, other factors such as economic gain, social status and skill and capacity to do the work are more important factors in adjustment.

VOCATIONAL MATURITY

When we ask how suitable an individual is for taking up a vocation, we are talking of vocational maturity. Vocational maturity is in question when we try to evaluate the vocational choice that he has made and the adjustment that he is making in that vocation. Vocational maturity denotes the level of vocational development of individual. If we follow the stages of vocational development then vocational maturity would indicate whether the person is at the explanatory stage or has successfully gone through the stages of vocational maturity and come to the decline stage.

QUESTIONS FOR EXERCISE

1. Explain elements of vocational choice.
2. What factors govern vocational development?
3. What is the meaning of vocational adjustment? Describe factors involved in it.
4. Write short note on Vocational Maturity.

20

VOCATIONALISATION

Meaning of Vocationalisation

Vocational education has been defined by UNESCO as "comprehensive term embracing those aspects of the educational process involving, in addition to general education, the study of technologies and related sciences and the acquisition of practical skills, attitudes, understanding and knowledge relating to occupations in the various sectors of economic and social life. Such an education would be an integral part of general education and a means of preparing for an occupational field and as aspect of continuing education."

Vocationalisation implies that vocational subjects should be given a place in the curriculum so that the students may become competent to earn their living after completing their education. Vocationalisation means to provide self-dependence to the student in life. Vocationalised education develops the total personality of child. It is organised according to the individual aptitudes of the students. After ascertaining his various aptitudes and interests a good vocational capacity may be developed in the child. The Secondary Education Commission (1952-53) recommended that multi-purpose schools should include the education in various vocational subjects along with education in general subjects. Kothari Commission (1964-66) emphasised work-experience in education to promote the much-sided development of the individual. Vocationalisation of higher secondary education aims at increasing the employment potential of the people through education for self-employment, emphasis on agricultural and related occupations, including miniature small, cottage and agro-industries and through preparation for specific competencies in different vacations.

ALLOCATION IN TIME-TABLE

The Higher Secondary education has two spectra — the General Education spectrum and the Vocationalised spectrum.

Time-Table for General Education Spectrum

1. Languages. 15%
2. Socially Useful Productive Work (SUPW). 15%
3. Electives. 70%

Time-Table for Vocationalised Spectrum

1.	Languages.	15%
2.	General Education Course.	15%
3.	Elective Subjects.	70%

National Review Committee (Adiseshiah Report, 1978) gave the following recommendations about the teaching of vocational elective subjects :

1. 50% of weekly hours should be spent on practical work with certain amount of flexibility.

2. Special attention should be given to the self-employment factor.

3. Higher Secondary stage vocational education should not duplicate the training given at Industrial Training Institutes.

4. The main thrust of the proposed vocationalisation should be on rural agricultural and related vocations.

5. Courses in vocational areas should be drawn up in such a way that the employability of the students is enhanced.

6. In the formal system duration of a vocational course should normally be of two years. The courses requiring lesser duration than two years may be pursued through non-formal systems such as part-time and evening courses, correspondence courses, etc. The institutions should be free to offer such courses through non-formal channels.

VOCATIONAL ELECTIVES

Following are the vocational elective, which may be elected (chosen) by the students according to their capacity and traits :

1. Agriculture and Related Vocations.

2. Business and Office Management.

3. Para-Medical Courses.

4. Education Sciences.

5. Local Body and other Sciences.

6. Journalism.

7. Home Science and Related Vocation.

8. Commercial Art, Photography, Printing and Lithography, Ceramics, Pottery, Tourist Guides, etc.

ADVANTAGES OF VOCATIONALISATION

1. It helps in accelerating the economic growth of the country.

2. It gives a lead to society in the matter of self-employment.

3. It enlarges the supply of technical leadership at the grass-root level.

4. It puts an end to the mad rush for entrance into Universities, and the consequent deterioration in the standard of education.

Recommendations of National Review Committee (1978)

1. No rigid streaming of courses into the General Education and Vocationalised Education spectra. The student should be free to offer either the general education or vocationalised courses or a mix of the two, particularly in relation to the vocational courses as agriculture, and related vocations and other general sciences. There should be in-built elasticity in the choice of the general education or vocationalised subjects.

2. Learning must be based on work. It must be either through the Socially Useful Productive Work (SUPW) or through vocationalised courses.

3. Vocational courses. These should be provided in agricultural and related rural occupational areas and in managerial, commercial, health and para-medical vocations and not industrial and engineering occupations.

4. Books. These should be written on a priority basis to suit local conditions and should be made available to the schools, in order to impart instruction in vocational courses, in agricultural and related subjects.

5. Semester pattern and credit system. This may be introduced in higher secondary classes. Suitable steps may be undertaken for the orientation of teachers in this connection.

6. Teachers. To begin with, teachers with post-graduate qualifications need not be insisted. Persons who have had actual experience of on-the-job may be fruitfully utilised to reach vocational courses. Part-time teachers may also be appointed wherever necessary.

7. Pre-service and in-service teacher education. These should be organised in collaboration with Colleges of Education, SCERTs, NCERT, Agricultural Universities, ICAR, etc.

8. Survey. A vocational survey of the area-metropolitan, block, taluk, district or State should be undertaken.

9. Rural areas. All the new schools should be constructed in rural areas and should be adequately equipped as little or no vocationalised education facilities are readily available for rural students.

10. Shift system. It should be introduced wherever it is feasible.

11. Apprenticeship facilities. These should be extended to all the students who complete education in vocational streams if they desire to benefit from such training.

12. Vocationally qualified persons. These should be preferred to graduates and be entitled to the pay scales available to the graduates as long as the job performed are the same or similar.

13. National Council. A National Council of Vocational Education should be set up.

14. State council. At the State level, State Councils for Vocational Education be created and should function under the general guidance of the National Council of Vocational Education.

15. Local support. The vocationalisation of Education must be supported by the local community and other agencies, such as Panchayat, Union, Agricultural Co-operatives, the Small Scale Industries Corporation, Khadi and Village Industry Commission, Local branches of Nationalised and other Banks, etc.

IMPORTANCE OF VOCATIONALISATION

1. Complimentary role. General education alone leaves an individual unemployed and dependent on others for economic assistance. Vocationalised education may bring more fullness in life. However, while vocationalised education may make a child skilful worker in some area, it cannot make him a fully developed individual. Hence, it should be complemented in general education.

2. Capacity to earn. Vocationalised education gives a capacity to earn ones living. In the absence of sufficient vocationalised education, India is facing the problem of unemployment of youths.

3. Economic development. Though India has enough natural resources she could not yet exploit them fully due to lack of vocational education. Therefore, she is behind many other countries in production. Vocationalised education creates the trait of productiveness in the individual and teaches him how to exploit the natural resources intelligently. This may ultimately lead to the economic development of the nation and society.

4. Spirit of self-dependence. Vocationalised education creates a spirit of self-dependence in the individual as through this education he begins to earn even during his school or college career. Thus, he becomes a useful member of the society.

5. Satisfaction of psychological tendencies. Through vocationalised education an individual may satisfy his instincts of construction and self-display. Many of his latent interests may get full play. He acquires abilities and develops his talents. He is not a passive listener but becomes an active partner in the very process of his education. He learns by doing things. Therefore, various types of vocations should be incorporated in a vocationalised curriculum to cater to the varying needs, interests and aptitudes of students.

6. Dignity of labour. As in the vocationalised education one has to do some manual work for learning some vocational skill, it develops in him a sense of dignity of labour, which is not possible through purely general and academic education.

NEGLECT OF VOCATIONAL EDUCATION IN INDIA

Hitherto in India all the Committees and Commissions on education have recommended for vocationalisation of education. In the countries where education has been vocationalised, there is no acute problems of unemployment or the over-crowding in colleges and universities. The Kothari Commission (1964-66) observed that in India only 9 per cent of the students are able to get education through vocationalised curriculum. In comparison to that in many foreign countries this percentage is very low. The following may be the causes of this low percentage :

1. The Government has not taken up the problem of vocationalisation of education with due seriousness.

2. Lack of teachers for imparting instruction according to the vocationalised aspects incorporated in the general curriculum.

3. As Education Department of the Government has not been able to receive guidance for determining the exact nature of the vocationalised curriculum, the vocationalised education programme could not be formulated according to the social and national needs.

4. Due to lack of necessary facilities in schools and training colleges, Laboratories and Workshops have not been satisfactorily organised and the required number of trained teachers is not available.

5. The Universities neglected altogether the programmes pertaining to physical work and social service. These could not get adequate encouragement from schools, colleges and universities.

6. There has been a lack of co-operation between labour, industries and education departments of the Government. No department wholly took the responsibility of vocationalised education on its own.

7. The public remained altogether indifferent to vocationalised education as its utility has not been fully explained to people.

DEVELOPMENT OF TECHNICAL AND VOCATIONAL EDUCATION IN INDIA

In India the issue of technical and vocational education has already been there since ancient days. With the changes in time, ideas, circumstances and needs of life its shape has been changing. One may understand the technical and vocational education in India in the following two periods :

1. Ancient period and
2. Modern period.

1. Ancient Period

The development of technical and vocational education of the ancient period may be understood in the following periods :

(i) Vedic period.
(ii) Post-Vedic period.
(iii) Buddha period.
(iv) Muslim period.
(v) British period.

(i) Vedic period. Vedas are the oldest literature of the world. One find reference to technical and vocational education in the *Rigveda* and *Atharvaveda.* In the *Rigveda* one finds vivid descriptions of construction of canals, bunds and bridges, vehicles incorporating fast speed and beautiful palaces. *Ayurveda* is a branch of Atharvaveda. Therein one finds elaborate discussion of medical sciences. In the Vedic literature one finds ample discussion of manufacture of cotton, silken and woollen cloths, agricultural implements and arms and ammunitions.

(ii) Post-Vedic period. During this period the technical and vocational education continued as prevalent in the Vedic age. This is the epic (*Ramayana* and *Mahabharata*) period. In the *Ramayana,* the epic written by Valmiki, one finds frequent references of Rama's journey by Pushpak Viman and construction of bridge for going across the sea *i.e.* to Lanka, for conquering Ravana. In the *Mahabharata* one finds mention of houses made of wax and houses parks of which appear to be having water and other portions dry. The ruins of Mohanjodaro and Harappa remind us of technical and vocational skills of that period. One finds descriptions of means of fast transport for going from one place to another. One also finds description of various types of weapons and fire-arms used in wars.

(iii) Buddhist Period. During the Buddhist period the Vedic literature was also studied along with the Buddhist religious scriptures. The vocational study of Ayurveda (science of medicine), Dhanurveda (science of war) and Gandharvaveda (art of music) developed much during this period. The science of medicine, architecture, painting, sculpture, veterinary and chemistry are some of the chief contributions of this period.

(iv) The Muslim Period. During this period the art of making various types of silken, woollen and cotton cloths, wood work, architecture, drawing and ornaments developed remarkably. Imperial palaces, mosques, carpets, utencils and embroideries of this period have been of world fame. Vocational education during this period was not organised. The trainees used to learn the art under strict personal control and supervision of the artisans concerned.

(v) The British Period. After establishment of the British rule in India, the Britishers engaged themselves in consolidating it. For this purpose, they needed various types of workers. They felt the need of technicians in various areas. As it was very costly to borrow these expert workers from abroad, so they decided to start some technical and vocational colleges :

1847 to 1902. In 1847 an Engineering College was started at Roorkee. Afterwards, engineering colleges were started at Calcutta, Madras and Poona. The Wood's Despatch of 1854 emphasised the importance of making Indian education useful of life. By 1902 about 80 technical and vocational schools were established in the country. Lord Curzon took keen interest in expansion of technical and vocational education. He established an agriculture department in each province. He emphasised the need of establishing agricultural colleges. Agriculture was included as a subject for classes VI to X.

From 1902 to 1921. During this period also, the Government of India did not pay any attention towards technical and professional education. However, the recommendations of Indian Education Commission were accepted and technical and vocational subjects were included in the curricula of high schools in different provinces.

From 1921 to 1937. After the establishment of the dual rule in 1921, demand of the people for technical and vocational education received great momentum. A special Committee under the Chairmanship of Lord Lytton was entrusted this work in order to take a decision in this matter. This committee studied the problems and difficulties of the Indian students studying in foreign countries. It made many suggestions to remove them. The most important suggestion of the Committee was that the technical, vocational and industrial institutions should be established in India. Provision should be made for imparting higher education to Indians in their own country. Following institutions were established in consequence of this recommendation :

1. Harcourt Butler Technological Institute, Kanpur.
2. College of Engineering and Technology, Jadavpur.
3. Government School of Technology, Madras.

In 1937, there were nearly 535 technical, vocational and industrial schools in India.

From 1937 to 1947. After 1937, vocational and technical education was expanded with great speed due to the following reasons :

1. Up to the Second World War, the demand of persons with technical education increased.

2. New industries were established in India for the production of war material. Industrial persons having received technical education were required for these industries.

3. The demand of persons having received technical education increased for implementing the post-development schemes prepared by the Central and the Provincial Government.

In 1941-42 only 264 students were studying in graduate courses of technical education and 22 students in chemical technology respectively.

2. Modern Period after Independence

From 1947 to 1969. The post-independent period witnessed the tremendous progress in the field in technical and vocational education along with the rapid growth of industrialisation in the country. Earlier, there was the provision of imparting vocational and technical education to only 6,600 students. This number increased to 4,35,796 in the year 1963. Besides this, facilities were also provided to 25,000 students for engineering and technical degree and to 49,000 for diploma in the year 1966.

(i) First Five Year Plan. In the First Five Year Plan it was decided to develop Indian Institute of Science, Bangalore, to establish 14 colleges of engineering to make provision of teaching of some special vocational subjects and to establish guidance centres for the students receiving professional and technical education. Schemes were prepared for the establishment of industrial, technical and professional schools, conversion of crafts schools into junior technical high schools, establishment of junior multi-purpose schools, development of general secondary schools into technical high schools, giving of proper place to agricultural education in the curriculum, conversion of commercial, vocational and technical schools into colleges and grant of scholarships to the students for receiving higher education in foreign countries. Provisions was made for providing more facilities to impart training to the artists and craftsmen and to establish training centres in villages.

(ii) Second Five Year Plan. Due to the increasing demand of the technical and vocational workers, a special importance was given to the expansion of vocational and technical education during the Second Five Year Plan. 48 crores of rupees were allotted for technical and vocational education in the Second Five Year Plan. The Indian Institute of Technology, Kharagpur was developed for graduate and post-graduate studies. Provision was made for the study of graduate courses of 1,200 students and post-graduate and research work for 600 students. The Institute of Science, Bangalore was developed for Air and Naval Engineering, Power Engineering, Internal Combustion, Metallurgy and Electrical Research and other types of vocational and technical education.

In the centres already established for vocational and technical education under the First Five Year Plan, provision was made for the post-graduate course in engineering, technology and research work. Higher institutions of vocational and technical education were established in western, northern, southern regions of the country. Two of such types of institutions were established at Bombay and Kanpur.

Facilities for the education of engineering and technology in Delhi Polytechnic were expanded. Besides this, 9 other institutions of degree stage and 20 institutions of diploma stage were established in other parts of the country. The scheme of training of foremen was implemented with the co-operation of industrial institutions. The number of scholarships were increased from 630 to 800. Some seats were reserved for meritorious students in technical and vocational institutions. Hostels were provided for 13,000 technical students and for 3,300 students of Junior technical schools. Indian School of Science and Applied Geology, Dhanbad was further developed and expanded. Therefore, by the end of the year 1960-61, 57,000 graduates and 6,800 diploma holders in engineering and technical education were made available to the country.

(iii) Third Five Year Plan. It was envisaged that 45,000 graduates and 80,000 diploma holders would be required during the Third Five-Year Plan. A sum of rupees 142 crores was allotted for implementing the programme of the development of the technical and vocational education. During the period of the Third Five Year Plan, the number of students admitted annually in the degree courses was increased by 6,000 by admitting of 5,000 in engineering colleges part-time of correspondence courses. The number of students admitted every year increased from 13,200 in 1961 to 19,200 in 1966. Likewise, the number of students admitted in diploma courses was also increased by 15,000 by admitting 10,000 students in Polytechnic and education of rest of 5,000 students through part-time or correspondence courses. Thus the number of the students, which was 24,000 at the end of the Second Five-Year Plan increased to 9,000 at the end of the Third Five Year Plan.

(iv) Fourth Five Year Plan. An additional capacity of 4,000 seats for degree and 3,400 for diploma courses was created during the Fourth Five Year Plan.

(v) Fifth Five Year Plan. Top priority was given to vocational and technical education in the Fifth Plan. The proposed plan outlay for technical education was Rs. 164 crores.

Its aim was to provide technical education to 25,000 students at degree level and 50,000 at diploma level. It was said, in the draft of the plan, "The main stress will continue to be on the consolidation and improvement of the quality of the technical education system."

The following table shows the progress in the field of higher technical education under the First Six Five Year Plans in India :

Year	No. of schools	No. of students	No. of teachers	Exp. (in crore Rs.)
1961-62	3,751	4,08,443	28,657	12.80
1962-63	3,846	4,24,264	29,847	13.04
1963-64	4,137	4,57,350	33,494	16.24
1964-65	3,147	2,69,096	17,380	7.39
1965-66	2,755	2,47,021	17,785	7.66
1966-67	2,754	2,45,148	18,383	8.27
1970-71	2,764	2,52,412	18,745	9.32
1980-81	2,972	5,16,722	18,972	13.04
1985-86	3,102	8,12,517	19,394	35.00

(vi) Sixth Five Year Plan. The Janta Government under the Sixth Five Year Plan (1978—83) allocated Rs. 150 crores for the expansion of technical and vocational education. In its revised draft the Congress Government allocated Rs. 278 crores for its expansion under the Sixth Plan.

THE PROBLEMS OF VOCATIONALISATION

The Main Problems

1. Form and organisation of education. What should be the form of vocational education and how shall it be determined? These questions are concerned with the form of vocational education.

2. Organisation of the curriculum. This includes the problem of how to harmonise the vocational courses, with the general courses.

3. Training of teachers. The vocationalised education will require special type of teachers who can impart vocational education along with instruction in general education. It will mean change in the current set-up of teachers' training institutions like multi-purpose schools. The vocationalisation of education will fail in absence of suitable teachers.

4. Bringing in changes in the instructional procedures. Vocationalised education requires an integrated teaching procedure in which a certain vocation will have to be accepted as a nucleus and the various subjects will be taught around it in a correlated manner. However, all the subjects of general education cannot be taught in this manner. Only those subjects can be taught which may be correlated with the vocation concerned.

5. Laboratories and other equipments. Each school will require some workshop, laboratory and other physical facilities and equipments after vocationalisation of education. This will mean enough money. But due to want of financial resources even traditional schools lack the required facilities.

6. Selection of vocation at the time of admission of students. At the time of admission it is difficult for the student to choose a vocation. His aptitude should be ascertained through aptitude tests. Educational and vocational guidance services should be organised in schools. These services help the students in identifying their aptitudes and interests. Training in a particular vocation may be given accordingly.

7. Administration and control. General education has been under the control of Government education department uptill now. After vocationalisation the Government education department alone cannot control education. The co-operation of the departments of industries, agriculture and other ones will be necessary.

RECOMMENDATIONS OF COMMITTEES AND COMMISSIONS

Pre-Independence

Committees and Commissions of education were appointed keeping in view the problems arising out of vocationalisation of education. These Committees and Commissions have given following suggestions for vocationalisation of education :

1. Indian Education Commission (1882). It suggested that vocational subjects should be given due place in the current curriculum. But the government made no effort to implement this suggestion.

2. Hartog Committee (1929). It suggested that after passing the middle school examination a student should be given an opportunity to study industrial and commercial courses.

3. Sapru Committee (1934). It suggested that various types of vocational courses should be taught at high school level.

4. Basic Education Scheme (1936-37). A number of basic school were opened under this scheme. An attempt was made to teach a number of subjects around a certain craft with the interest of the student.

5. Abbot-Wood Committee (1937). It submitted its report on vocational education. This report emphasised the introduction of vocational courses for removing unemployment.

6. Sargent Scheme (1944-45). It recommended the continuance of the Basic Scheme. It suggested to incorporate local crafts and industries in the curriculum.

After Independence

1. Secondary Education Commission (1952-53). It recommended the incorporation of vocational courses in the secondary school curriculum as follows :

(i) Multi-purpose schools should be established. The current secondary schools should be gradually converted into multi-purpose schools. Till then vocational courses should be taught in them according to the varying interests of students. The whole curriculum was sub-divided into seven parts. Every student should study at least one of these parts according to his interest. Each student should study some vocational subject to develop a sense of respect for manual work. The Commission emphasised the need of educational and vocational guidance services in each school.

(ii) Each student should be given an opportunity to do some productive work in the school. The courses should be diversified to make many alternatives available for the students. It will enable each student to choose some manual work according to his interest.

(iii) The student should be given theoretical knowledge and practical training in agriculture. Such vocations as gardening, animal husbandry, veterinary science and bee-keeping, etc., may be encouraged in schools. These vocations were considered more useful for rural children. The rural school should function as community centre also.

(iv) Technical education should be provided in secondary schools. The student may choose some technical subject as his hobby. Some industrial tax may also be levied for acquiring some funds for technical education. The Central Government should annually give financial grant to State Government. A federal board for technical education should be established. Multi-purpose schools should be opened at some places.

2. University Commission (1948-49). It emphasised the need of establishing rural universities for teaching agriculture and allied subjects. It also recommended for making more progressive medical education, teachers' training and education in law.

3. Kothari Commission (1964-66). It emphasised the utility of vocational education and gave the following suggestions :

(a) We have not yet fully emphasised vocational education at the secondary stage. Secondary education must be vocationalised according to the means available to us.

(b) Vocational education should be sub-divided into the following stages according to the curriculum :

(i) *Junior secondary stage* : The students who have passed seventh or eighth class should be admitted in Industrial Training Institutes (I.T.I.). The admission age should be reduced to 14 years of age. This may also benefit the primary school passed student. Part-time education should be arranged for industrial training to benefit those children who are mostly engaged in domestic work. The students should be given training in agriculture and domestic science.

(ii) *Higher secondary stage* : Polytechnical institutions should be established for those students who have passed secondary school classes. Part-time training or Correspondence Courses may also be arranged for such students. In health, commerce, administration and small industries varying courses of six months to three years duration should be instituted.

(iii) Separate Committees and Sub-committees should be organised within the jurisdiction of the Education Department of Government for giving training in their respective vocation. These committees will look after part-time training and correspondence courses in their respective areas. First of all the man-power available for the various vocations should be ascertained. Then the training for the same should be organised. The firms which may absorb the trained hands should also be consulted about the trained hands that they would require.

(iv) The Central Government should give adequate financial assistance to the various States for vocational and technical education. In U.S.A. it was due to the federal assistance that secondary education could be vocationalised. This practice should be adopted in India also.

(v) The current facilities for vocational and technical education should be further extended. The training of workmen should be grouped into two parts : semi-skilled and skilled. The number of vocational and technical institutions should be increased. The private and State trade schools should be encouraged by giving financial help.

(vi) People have no interest in vocational curriculum as they do not understand its utility. Government should try to create interest in the people for vocational and technical training. Vocational courses should be made more interesting. Vocational Guidance Committee should be organised in school to give psychological vocational guidance to the students.

PROBLEMS AND REMEDIES OF TECHNICAL AND VOCATIONAL EDUCATION

1. The Problem of Qualitative Improvement

Education should be both quantitative and qualitative. While India has made quantitative improvement in technical and vocational education, we have not yet paid adequate attention to its qualitative side. Many technical and vocational institutions are being run in a very bad condition. There are no good workshops, laboratories, libraries and buildings. Well trained teachers are very few.

Remedy : Technical and vocational institutions which do not fulfil the minimum conditions should be closed. Those which are well managed and organised should be given adequate financial assistance for organising good workshops, laboratories and libraries. They should have close relationship with the relevant local industries. The trainees should be sent to these industries to obtain some practical experience.

2. The Problem of Creating Favourable Attitude Towards Manual Work

In India, the person engaged in manual work is looked down. A labourer does not enjoy that respect in our society which a teacher, advocate or doctor does. Hence, trainees in technical and vocational institutions do not like to engage themselves in those operations which require manual work. They do not get adequate practical experience. Technical and vocational institutions are not producing good skilled workers. No reform in technical and vocational education will yield the expected result unless this situation is changed.

Remedy : Opportunities should be given to students and teachers in schools, colleges and universities for doing various types of creative manual work. Workshops should be organised to give enough practical experience to each trainee. More time should be allowed in the time-table for practical work. It should be corresponding to capacity and interests.

3. The Problem of Defective Curriculum

The following defects are found in the curriculum of technical and vocational institutions :

1. It does not fulfil the local needs. For example, in the agriculturally predominant area, agriculture is not given a prominent place in the curriculum.

2. It has lack of productivity.

3. It does not develop in the student a love for manual work.

4. It lacks in variety. It does not have many purposes which should be a special feature of technical institution.

Remedy : It should be estimated as to how many teachers and guides are required for a particular stage of technical and vocational education. The arrangement for the equipment should be made on the basis of this estimate. The teachers and guides should be given attractive salaries and other facilities. The four regional committees established in the country should take the responsibility of doing the needful in this matter.

4. The Problem of Medium in the Technical and Vocational Education

The mother tongue has been accepted as the medium of instruction in India up to the secondary stage. After passing this stage, when the student takes admission in some technical institution, he is given the training through English, because good books are not available on the subject in his mother-tongue. This creates a great difficulty for the trainee. He has to devote much time to the study of English at the neglect of the technical subjects. Hence, many capable students are left behind.

Remedy : Regional languages should be accepted as the medium of instruction in the technical and vocational institutions. The trainee should be compelled to acquire proficiency in English, unless he himself insists for the same. Before making regional languages the medium of instruction, it is necessary to produce standard books in regional languages in the various areas of technical and vocational education.

The teachers and guides for technical and vocational institutions should be so trained that they may be able to impart the training through the medium of the regional language concerned.

5. The Problem of Administration and Control

The Education Ministry of Government of India is not responsible for technical and vocational education in the States of the Union. In States separate departments of the education, at some places two departments together, carry the responsibility for this education. At certain places labour department, industry, or agriculture departments is made responsible for this education. At some other place a university is entrusted with its responsibility. This situation has created the problem of administration and control.

Remedy : Many problems of technical and vocational education will be automatically solved by solving the problem of its administration and control. The Education Ministry of the Government of India should take up the responsibility of technical and vocational education in the same way as it looks after general education. A Council of technical and vocational education may also be organised for looking after the various implied issues. Suitable persons from various relevant departments may be requested to serve on this Council. The setting up of such a Council should be done at the Central and State levels. This will bring in a uniformity in administration and control of technical and vocational education.

6. The Problem Relating to Research

The Government of India has emphasised the problem of research in technical and vocational education in the various Five Year Plans but we have not yet become self-dependent in this respect and we have still to copy the Western pattern. Process and research styles should be according to our needs in the country. The foreign styles cannot meet our Indian needs. We have not yet succeeded in making such researches on the basis of which we may profitably use our full manpower. In many European countries and in the United States of America, there is a lack of adequate manpower because of the population being thinner. So in place of manpower they use machines as substitutes. But our Indian condition is entirely different from the conditions prevailing in the above foreign lands. As we are still manufacturing such machines which may be used as substitutes for manpower, a major portion of our manpower lies idle and unemployed.

Remedy : The research work in the field of technical and vocational education should be carried out according to the needs and conditions in the country. The Government should set up various types of experimental laboratories and research centres. The researchers should be given handsome stipends in order that capable persons may be attracted towards the same.

7. The Problem of Post-Technical Education and Training

After getting the training, if the trainee remains unemployed for some time, he forgets all that he has learned in the technical field concerned. And those who are lucky enough to get some employment continue working for years according to the old method that they learnt several years ago. They do not get any chance for acquainting themselves with the latest devices and technique. They forget even the theoretical aspect of the training that they obtained. In foreign countries an attempt is made to familiarise the old workers with the latest researches, techniques and inventions in their relevant areas. This develops their skills and accelerates the rate of production as well.

Remedy : The problem of post-education and training may be solved through any of the following measures :

(i) Correspondence courses.

(ii) Part-time course.

(iii) Close contact with the technical institutions and industries.

(iv) Short-term courses.

(v) Refresher courses.

(i) *The correspondence courses* : These may be organised for those workers who need enough orientation in latest theoretical principles. For in-service workers this is a good device. They already continue their workshop practice. So for 15 or 20 days they may be invited at a certain centre for reorientation.

(ii) *The part-time courses* : These develop the theoretical knowledge and skill of the in-service workers. But the part-time courses may be possible only at some technical institution. Morning or evening classes may be arranged for this purpose.

(iii) *Close contact* : According to the recommendations of the Kothari Commission (1964-66) the training for in-service may be arranged by establishing a close relationship between the technical institution and the concerned industries. This arrangement is likely to benefit both the in-service workers and the trainees.

(iv) *Short-term courses* : The in-service workers are invited to attend certain courses for two or three weeks at some technical institution. This programme may be conveniently arranged during the holidays of some relevant industries.

(v) *Refreshers courses* : The in-service workers may be trained in latest techniques and devices. This may be arranged at some technical education centre.

8. The Problem of Modernisation of Technology

Technology has been modernised in U.S.A., U.S.S.R. and other Western countries. Blindly following their method situation has created the following problems in India :

1. By modernisation we have begun to understand Westernisation. As our needs are different from the Western ones, so we have to modernise the technology according to our Indian needs.

2. The technology dependent upon the invested capital is creating a misunderstanding between the labourers and the owner. The one is the exploiter and the other is the exploited. So a gap is being created between the two.

3. Under the influence of modernisation we forget our Indian social values and circumstances. This has an adverse impact on the society.

Remedy : No doubt, India should modernise her technologies, but she will have to Indianise them as well according to her own conditions and needs. The technologies should be modernised in such a way as to obtain the maximum production by using the minimum manpower, capital and raw materials. The manpower should be properly utilised and the maximum number of people should get employment. The difference of rich and poor, owner and labourer and the exploiter and the exploited should be eliminated.

9. The Problem of Co-ordination between Training Facilities and Job Opportunities

Through our Five Year Plans India have developed opportunities for technical and vocational education. But the development of these opportunities has created the problems of unemployment of technical hands. At the same time, in some technical areas there were no trained hands.

Remedy : An estimate of the manpower needed for the various areas should be made for obtaining a balance and co-ordination between the technical facilities and job opportunities. According to this estimate technical and vocational education should be given to a few selected persons. The technical and vocational institutions should be closely related to the relevant industries, as it is these industries that the trained hands are to be employed. Its programme should be prepared by the various States according to their own specific needs.

QUESTIONS FOR EXERCISE

1. Discuss the meaning and importance of vocationalisation of education?
2. What have been the causes of slow progress of vocationalisation of education in our country? How can we remove them?
3. What have been the recommendations for vocational of education given by the Kothari Commission?
4. How has the Secondary Education Commission of 1952-53 tried to solve the problem of vocationalisation of education?

5. Give a brief critical account of development of technical and vocational education in India.
6. Describe the development of technical and vocational education in India after Independence.
7. Explain the main problems of technical and vocational education in India suggesting remedies.

21

Vocational Guidance

DEFINITION OF VOCATIONAL GUIDANCE

1. The General Conference of International Labour Organisation. "Vocational Guidance" as "assistance given to an individual in solving problems related to occupational choice and progress with due regard for the individual's characteristics and their relation to occupational opportunity."

2. National Vocational Guidance Association, U.S.A. (1937). "Vocational Guidance is the process of assisting the individual to choose an occupation, prepare for it, enter upon and progress in it."

3. UNESCO (1974). It is a "Comprehensive term embracing those aspects of educational process involving, in addition to general education, the study of technologies and related sciences and the acquisition of practical skills, attitudes, understanding and knowledge relating to occupations in various sectors of economic and social life. Such an education would be an integral part of general education and a means of preparing for an occupational field and an aspect of continuing education. Technical and vocational education should further contribute to the achievement of society's goals of greater demoralization and social, cultural and economic development, while at the same time developing the potential of the individuals for active participation in the establishment and implementation of these goals. It should lead to an understanding of the scientific and technological aspects of contemporary civilisation in such a way that men comprehend their environment and are capable of acting upon it while taking a critical view of the social, political and environmental implications of scientific and technological change. Given the necessity for new relationship between education, working life and community as a whole, technical and vocational education should exist as a part of system of lifelong education adapted to the needs of each particular country."

4. Prof. G.E. Myers. "Vocational guidance is fundamentally an effort to conserve the priceless native capacities of youth and the costly training provided for youth in the schools. It seeks to conserve these richest of all human resources by aiding the individual of invest and use them where they will bring greatest satisfaction and success to himself and greatest benefit to society."

5. Super. "Vocational guidance is the process of helping a person to develop and accept an integrated and adequate picture of himself, and of his role in the world of work to test this concept against reality and to convert it into a reality with satisfaction to himself and benefit to society."

NEED OF VOCATIONAL GUIDANCE

1. Individual differences. The fundamental reason why guidance is needed is that there are differences among individuals and differences among courses of action open to them.

2. Thrift. As many young people enter many occupations by chance and not in accordance with their suitability, there is an economic loss to the young workers. A lot of money is being spent unnecessarily in the preparation of two vocations rather than one. The individual takes a longer time to adjust himself to the proper occupation and loses money that he might have earned if he would have continued working in his previous occupation.

3. Financial loss to the employers. Changes in occupations are much more common with younger than with old workers and are also much more expensive than mere changes in the places of employment, both to the employers and the workers themselves. Industry and business incur heavy loses if an electrician's apprentice decides to leave his job and becomes an automobile mechanic. The new worker takes time to gain proficiency to the point attained by one who has left. The quality and the quantity of work suffers. The time spent on the selection and appointment of the previous work is also wasted.

4. Financial Loss to the society. D.D. Eisenhower has said, "The wealth of the world is created by the work of skilled hands on raw material." Ultimately it is the society that suffers all the costs of these wasteful methods of entering occupations. Inferior goods at a higher cost are made available to the society.

5. Adverse effect on health. Wrong choice of occupations adversely affects the health of the workers. A delicate eye-sight is injured by work which greatly affects the eye-sight. Nervous system is shattered by making efforts to maintain a speed of production beyond one's capacity and so on. Therefore, vocational guidance is very much needed.

6. Satisfaction of personal and social values. Super writes, "Occupation is not merely a means of earning a livelihood but also a way of life, a social role." Happiness of the worker, satisfaction in his work, are involved his personal growth and his contribution to human welfare. In the choice of an occupation a frustrated and dissatisfied worker is curse to himself and to the society. Failure in an occupation has a great demoralising effect on an individual. In the words of G.E. Myers, "Each failure in the experience of a young worker increases the probability of another."

7. Utilisation of human potentialities. The society loses much through its failure to discover potential genius. A great deal of genius remains undiscovered in every generation in absence of vocational guidance.

8. Fulfilment of needs of a complex society. Today, far-reaching changes have taken place in economic, political and social structure of the country. Even country requires scientists, engineers, technicians and technologists, to man the industrial and commercial establishment. New and altogether new occupations are coming to the forefront. An expanding economic structure intensifies the need for help to individuals through vocational guidance.

9. Information concerning individuals. Modern new methods of studying the individuals help us to understand the individual in more scientific and comprehensive way. This factor is of great assistance to a guidance worker in guiding an individual in the matter of making a choice.

HISTORICAL OUTLINE

Vocational guidance was defined by the 1954 Committee of the International Labour Organisation in its suggestions concerning vocational guidance, as assistance rendered by an individual to another in the latter's solving of problems related to his progress and vocational selection, keeping in mind the individual's peculiarities or special abilities and their relations with his occupational opportunity. In this manner, the objective of vocational guidance is the proper and complete utilisation of a nation's man-power through helping the individual to achieve his development and satisfaction in his profession. An individual should choose a profession that suits his abilities in order that both he and the nation may profit. It is not possible for any one individual to be capable of doing every job. Special kinds of job require particular kinds of skill and special know-how. It is possible that it may be asked why guidance thereby becomes necessary since every individual can tell the kind of skill he has and choose a profession accordingly. But if the situation is objectively viewed it will be found that it is not precisely of this nature, as only few people are able to gauge their own abilities and capabilities. A large majority of persons are wrong in their estimate of their own capabilities, many of them over estimating while a fair number denigrating themselves. It is not possible for the proverbial human eye to see the very grit that is in it, it being implied that the human eye rarely lights upon the individual's own defects. If one were to go to any student doing post-graduate work in the university and ask him as to what he proposes to do after obtaining the degree, the most likely reply would be that he would take one of the competitive examinations, preferably the administrative service, and if not fortunate enough to be selected, carry on to do research and finally become a teacher. The audacity and over-weaning self confidence of the student is stupendous. If you were to ask him as to what he will do if neither of these contingencies comes about, then it will only be a regard for your social standing that will prevent him from denouncing you on the spot. The implication is that very few of the students who fail in these and other competitive examinations realise that they do not possess requisite qualities. When they fail, they turn their wrath upon the examiner while the more charitable abuse only their bad luck. There will hardly be one student who will acquiesce in the knowledge that it was he himself who was lacking in the qualities required in the job. Again, to prevent unnecessary meanings being read into these statements it must be pointed out that the competitive examinations held in the present era can hardly be considered sufficient to gauge an individual's inherent merit. The sole intention of introducing this example is to point out the fact that young men and women do not think rationally and scientifically when faced with the choice of a profession. Vocational guidance helps in the solution of no other than this problem. Scientific testing reveals all that there is to know of the individual to the guide, who then advises the former as to the profession most suitable for him. Experiments have succeeded in pointing out roughly the qualities that a particular kind of profession requires of the individual. For example, efforts were made to establish the intelligence level required for various kinds of jobs. The following table states the intelligence quotient that a person should possess in order to go in for one or the other profession :

S.No.	Professional Class	I.Q.
1.	Administrative work and high level professional work	150 or more
2.	Low level professional and technical work	130 to 150
3.	Clerical or high level skilled labour	115 to 130
4.	Skilled work	100 to 115
5.	Semi-skilled work	85 to 100
6.	Work not requiring intelligence	70 to 85
7.	Labour work	50 to 70

Similarly, other tests and experiments have been conducted to establish some relation between vocation and other mental abilities. For example, engineering and other industrial work requires mechanical skill in the individual, with the result that persons who possess it in a slight degree cannot in the normal course be expected to become successful engineers or skilled technicians. Some kinds of work, for example, the repair of chronometers and surgery, require the ability to do minute accurate work skilfully. Lacking this quality no individual can become a good surgeon, watch repairer or experimenter or research worker. In much the same manner other industries and professions require different kinds of expertise and skill.

The above description makes evident the importance inherent in vocational guidance. But this hardly means that the guide pays no attention to the person's aptitude. Aptitude is one of the bases of guidance, but one thing that is beyond questions is that no individual can attain much success on the sole basis of aptitude. Accordingly, the guide has to collect elaborate and detailed information concerning the individual's aptitudes and capabilities, and give guidance on the basis of such information. Vocational guidance does not involve categorical declarations that one shall be doctor while such another shall be a clerk or an engineer. It is only a hypothesis and a suggestion that has its own limitations. What the guide says is simply that such and such a person possesses certain qualities in abundance that fit for him for such a profession, and there is much greater possibility of success in that profession then in any other for that individual.

Personnel Selection

It was the National Institute of Industrial Psychology that commenced research on matters concerning vocational guidance, and its results have been used much by all the big industries. Every productive unit has large variety of functions which can best be performed by individuals having different kinds of ability and training. Now, the selection of separate individuals for each of these jobs is what is called personal selection. And this personnel selection is based upon vocational guidance. Here, it is essential that the distinction between personnel selection and vocational guidance be well marked and known. In both it is essential that the qualities fit for different jobs be present in the person being considered for selection or guidance, as the case may be. But, in personnel selection, the qualify required for some particular function is remarked, and one person out of many applicants is selected to perform that function, of course, care being taken that the best of the applicants is thereby selected. In vocational guidance, the qualities of a person are gauged and he is accordingly advised to take up some vocational training or adopt a particular profession that suits him and is likely to bring him satisfaction. Vocational guidance and personnel selection are two branches of vocational psychology. Both these branches are interdependent since the provision of the right man for the right job and right job for the man requires, on the one hand, analysis of the individual, and an analysis of the job on the other.

PROGRESS OF VOCATIONAL GUIDANCE

The Western nations have done much work concerning vocational guidance, particularly in the United States of America personnel selection is itself a specialised job now. Considerable moderation and improvement work is being earned on there to improve the collection of information regarding the professions and the method of selection. A Dictionary of Occupational Titles has been prepared to search for and thereby provide information concerning vocations that are open to individuals. Then, an Occupational Code has been prepared by classifying the vocations according to the qualities that they require in the man as well as according to their different levels. Detailed information regarding every profession is collected. Job description, which is an important organ of the information concerning every profession, provides a detailed and exhaustive account of the various factors such as conditions of work, wages, responsibility, etc., that are operative in the industry or vocation. The first dictionary included details of 75 per cent vocations and occupations, and it comprehended some 90 per cent of working population of that country. This dictionary went through additional and improved editions in 1942, 1944 and 1945 while in its 1959 revised version some 40,40,023 professions were detailed. And job analysis in 1942 has been confined to 16 professions.

Vocational Guidance in India

In India, vocational guidance is not easily available, as are few other technical and specialised services. In 1945, the Training and Employment Service Organisation Committee headed by Shri B. Shivarao suggested that occupational information be selected and published. As a result, during the Second Five Year Plan period a project was prepared to set up 50 vocational guidance centres to supplement the efforts of the employment exchanges in their personnel selection. There have been certain appointments in this connection but the actual achievement is not very noticeable. And the books on occupations that have been published are no scientific research material but merely constitute a description. Besides the efforts of the Government of India, the state governments have also opened some centres, while this in turn has been supplemented by certain non-governmental agencies. Among them the Y.M.C.A. and the Rotary Club have achieved things that deserve mention. As is apparent from the above rather short account, progress in the direction of vocational guidance for a large country like India, is not worthy of praise. It need hardly be pointed out that much of this failure is to be attributed to the lack of organisation.

List of Abilities and Traits

Much important research and modification work has been carried on in connection with finding out the qualities and traits required for different professions. The National Institute of Industrial Psychology of England has prepared a list of approximately 20 psychological abilities and traits. On the basis of this list an industrial survey was undertaken. In this survey, the specialists and senior officers working in the different occupations were requested to supply information as to the qualities and traits required for their respective functions. Specialists of different occupations effected a rating from three standpoints — average, high level, and very high level. Now the specialists of National Institute took the average of the ratings made available from some 80 occupations. This average was categorised in the form of a table. And on the basis of this table it is possible to determine whether a particular individual is suitable for a specific profession or not. For example, this table clarifies the qualities that are requisites for the medical and the legal professions and the qualities that are quite desirable.

Another bit of important research work in connection with various professions and mental abilities was carried on by R.B. Cattell.[1] Cattell tested some 100 adult persons and found out their average intelligence level. This average indicates the approximate level of intelligence required by a person wishing to join some particular profession. This is made apparent in the following table :

Sl.No.	Professions	No. of trained people	Average I.Q.
1.	Teachers of universities and inter-colleges	30	151
2.	Doctors and surgeons	25	146.5
3.	Teacher of government schools	50	145
4.	Civil engineers	20	142
5.	Mechanical engineers	18	140
6.	Teachers of primary schools	90	137
7.	Managers of industry	20	137
8.	Stenographers	57	129
9.	Clerks	54	127
10.	Travelling representatives	24	123
11.	Nurses	250	122
12.	Telephone department employees	52	115
13.	Workers doing minute work	19	114
14.	Workers doing gross work	—	106 to 78

Tests by Dvorak and Dodge

Dvorak and Dodge also conducted tests upon employees of different professions, of persons successful and unsuccessful within one profession, of people working in the same profession but in differing capacities. This testing was based upon a wide variety of authentic psychological testing techniques. These tests revealed considerable difference between the abilities of motor mechanics, successful or unsuccessful clerks, and other people. But these tests were neither extensive and comprehensive to be applied to a majority of professions nor concentrated enough to have completely distinguished one profession from another. In this manner, it is essential to exercise the greatest care in applying the conclusions in these tests. Dodge himself has acknowledged this fact.

1. Cattell, R.B., Occupational norms of intelligence and standardisation of adult Intelligence Test, *British Journal of Psychology*, Vol. XXV, July 1954.

Minnesota Occupational Rating Scales

In Minnesota University six mental abilities and their extent were determined for 30 professions and occupations. And even in this the ability was individually divided into four categories — a, b, c, d. These six mental abilities were Verbal, Mechanical, Sociability, Clerical, Musical and Artistic. And, these six abilities where divided into four classes each for different professions. For example, the Minnesota occupational rating scale concerning the ability of verbal efficacy can be understood from the following table:

	Class Level of Intelligence	Necessary ability	Example
(a)	High level	Highest university education creative ability and power of argument.	Professors, authors, scientists, advocates, etc.
(b)	Higher than average	High school and college level of education.	Clerks, photographers, foremen, etc.
(c)	Average level	High school level of education.	Typists, mechanics, etc.
(d)	Below average	Junior high school or eighth grade education.	Labourers, porters, etc.

PROCESS OF VOCATIONAL GUIDANCE

The preceding description of vocational guidance must have made it apparent that it requires two kinds of information or subject matter to be collected, the first concerning indispensable information about the individual, and the second pertaining to knowledge of the industrial or occupational aspect. In this manner, vocational guidance has two aspects :

(A) Study of the individual.

(B) Study of the occupation or professional sphere.

(A) Study of the Individual

Before any vocational guidance can be rendered to an individual, it is essential that adequate information concerning his education, level of intelligence, mental abilities, aptitudes, interests, physical development, health, nature, personality characteristics and economic status be gathered, because variations in any of them will necessarily require change in guidance.

1. Education. Individuals need differing levels of education in order to enter into and succeed in different professions, as for example, the highest education is required for advocates, professors, engineers, doctors, and other such professions, whereas a general and lower level of education can serve the purpose if the profession is clerk, overseer, mechanic, compounder, teacher, etc. Besides these there are certain other occupations in which the medium level of education suffices *e.g.*, business salesmanship such in professions only the basic necessities of literacy must be fulfilled, as much else depends upon practice. It is only because of this importance of various levels of education being relative and relevant to different professions that most advertisements for applications for job contain specific instructions regarding the educational qualifications. For example, a person teaching students at the high school and Intermediate level need only be a graduate while no more graduate can teach the college or graduate level. Doctors require medical degrees while in order to qualify as an engineer it is essential that one passes an engineering examination.

2. Training. Education does not merely imply the degree obtained at the end of a session by passing a prescribed examination. Now-a-days, most occupational units make it obligatory on all new entrants to be trained in addition to being educated, and this is being carried to the extent that only a trained individual is allowed to fill the post of a high school teacher. Certain occupations need training inevitably, for example, the occupations of an electrician, stenographer, chemist, compounder, etc. As it is the tendency to employ trained personnel in industry and other occupations is catching on. In certain professions, the individual after having entered it is oriented for a period of few weeks, and only then is he allowed to handle work on his own responsibility.

3. Level of intelligence. Besides difference in education, different professions require differing levels of intelligence. For example, the medical, technical, legal, teaching and administrative professions require the highest intelligence level, while on the other hand, the peon and the domestic worker can be selected from people with a much lower level of intelligence. Other professions require only the average level of intelligence, so that evidently, before a person can be told of the profession that suits his natural endowments, it is essential to know the level of intelligence to which he belongs.

4. Special mental abilities. Individuals differ not only in respect of their intelligence but also in respect of their special mental abilities. For example, all people do not possess mechanical ability to the same degree and neither is verbal felicity shared by all in equal degree. Different professions require differing mental abilities, verbal ability being required by advocates and teachers, etc., mechanical ability by doctors and engineers, etc. Hence, prior to the selection of a profession it is essential for the individual to be aware of his mental abilities.

5. Aptitudes. Success in a particular profession seems to depend to some extent upon one's aptitude for it. If a person lacks artistic and creative aptitude, there is not much likelihood of his succeeding in the role of an artist, and one need not expect it. As a general rule, it is advisable for every person to join the profession for which he has any natural aptitude. Hence, knowledge of a person's aptitudes is also essential before he can be given any vocational guidance.

6. Interests. Interest helps to increase the possibility of success in a profession. Interesting work is done enthusiastically and patiently while uninteresting work tends to fall upon most men, and requires very conscious application to be carried through. Success in work requires that serious interest be taken in the work, or that interest in that kind of work be created, and this is possible. Interests are mutable, and it is possible to create interest in work that was once repugnant. But if the individual is originally endowed with interest for a particular occupation and is also possessed of the requisite mental abilities, then he would be best advised to adopt it. It need hardly be respected, as a slogan is, that a knowledge of the person's interest in essential before any vocational guidance can be rendered.

7. Health and physical development. As a general rule proper health and physical development are necessarily taken into consideration in every profession, but in certain other occupations success depends almost solely upon these factors. For success in the armed forces or in the police department health and good physical development are quite indispensable. In the absence of these factors the presence of no other qualities of ability will bring success to the individual. Hence, physical development, constitution and health are additional factors that must be taken into consideration when the question of vocational guidance comes up for consideration.

8. Nature. Different people show very pertinent and obvious difference in their nature, some being introverted while others more extroverted. And, different kinds of people can successfully settle down only in some specific professions that suit their nature. An extroverted personality, for example, is an essential if one wants to succeed as a salesman, agent, administrator or even as a leader, while on the other hand, gifted introverts make great artists, authors, scholars, scientists, specialists, etc. If choice of profession is contrary to one's natural inclination, it goes against the grain and deprives the individual's life of happiness and contentment, and the profession becomes a burden. While, if the profession conforms to one's nature, then one is happy and enthusiastic in his work, and these conditions are conducive to progress and success. Hence, before vocational guidance can be ventured upon, it is necessary to judge a person's nature also.

9. Personality characteristics. It is a fact generally known that different qualities of the personality are required in such widely separated professions as teaching, artistic creation, selling, labour work, etc. Hence choice of profession should also be made with a due regard for the qualities of the person's personality.

10. Financial status. As a general rule, it is improper and unnecessary to take into consideration a person's financial status before making a choice of profession, but in a country like India where scholarships are hard to come by, the economic status of the students also plays an important part in his choice of the future that he wants to shape for himself. Now a person with middle class status is in no position to afford a technical or medical education for his child because either of these two special courses involve the expenditure of a considerable amount of money. And it is unnecessary and improper to advice poor and needy person to go in for higher education when he cannot afford it. It is equally useless to advise such a person to choose a profession in which high education and specialised qualifications are desired. Hence, a person should be recommended only to that profession for which he can afford to gain education and any training that may be essential. He must have the means to gain such training. It must also be remembered that economic or financial status can be a bar to earning some profession only under certain circumstances. There are many examples of people who came from poor families having gained very high education and improved their lot in life. The truth or crux of the matter is that instead of discouraging a student from entertaining thoughts of a profession for which he apparently has not the economic means, the psychologist should expend his effort in arranging scholarships or other facilities whereby he may be able to attain the goal for which the former is striving, as he stands great chances of success. In India, these things are still unexplored, and many individuals fail to gain satisfying and rewarding positions in life that conform to their abilities, interests and aptitudes, for no reason other than they were born in poor families.

11. Other important factors. In addition to all elements pointed out above it is necessary to keep in mind certain other factors concerning the individual before giving vocational guidance. Age of the person, for example, is another factor that must be taken into account since many jobs and occupations set the maximum and minimum age limits on all applicants, so that people not qualifying for them in this respect cannot enter these services. Hence, there is hardly any point in advising them to take up such a profession. Sex of the person is another consideration in vocational guidance upon which much depends because some occupations are more suitable to the male individual while others are within the capacities of the female, and for these she is eminently suitable. Nursing and caring for the diseased in hospitals is one function that can safely and even desirably be allocated to women, while in the armed forces and the police most of the jobs with very few exceptions, are suitable only for the male.

(B) Study of Professional World

Having collected all the necessary and desired information regarding the individual under consideration, it is necessary to turn to another aspect of vocational guidance, that of studying the professional world. While the psychologist must necessarily have enough information concerning the person to whom he is imparting vocational guidance, it is equally important that he be well informed on its professional and occupational aspect. Only then can he provide proper and effective assistance. It is enough for the psychologist to be knowing the number and kinds of professions but also the kind of education, training, intelligence, mental abilities, interests, aptitudes, personality, qualities, etc., that are desired as well as the conditions of work that prevail therein.

Classification of occupations

Occupations have been classified in different ways, according to the viewpoint adopted in doing so. Classification is beneficial because the individual comes to know all the professions from one point of view and can select from among them. This has the two-fold advantage to narrowing down the range from which the selection is to be made while at the same time it provides a number of alternatives. It will be advantageous now to glance at these various professions.

(A) Classification according to interest. Professions have been divided into the following classes on the basis of interest :

(1) Occupations concerned with child life,
(2) Mechanical occupations,
(3) Computational occupations,
(4) Scientific occupations,
(5) Occupations concerned with change,
(6) Artistic occupations,
(7) Literary occupations,
(8) Musical occupations,
(9) Occupations concerned with social service,
(10) Clerical occupations.

In each of these classes there are professions belonging to five levels, depicted in the following classification :

(B) Classification on the basis of educational level, mental ability or skill, training, age and social respect. This classification of the professions is the work of Beckman,[2] as follows :

1. Executive, Managerial and Professional. This class includes the following three kinds of occupations :

(i) *Verbal* : such as advocate, judge, editor, auditor, professor, etc.
(ii) *Scientific* : such as doctor, engineer, scientist, accountant, etc.
(iii) *Executive or managerial* : such as the various kinds of managers and executives, etc.

2. Business and sub-professional. This class includes the following two kinds :

2. Beckman, R.O., A new scale for gauging occupational rank. *Personnel Journal*, (1954), pp. 233-235.

(i) *Business* : such as trader, salesman, agent, etc.

(ii) *Sub-professional* : such as actor, photographer, designer, etc.

3. Skilled occupation. This class includes the following two kinds of occupations :

(i) *Physical labour* : such as electrician, dyer, machineman, and press mechanic, etc.

(ii) *Intellectual* : such as clerk, supervisor, stenographer, cashier, etc.

4. Semi-skilled occupation. Such as policeman, bus conductor, driver, guard, etc.

5. Unskilled occupation. Such as labourer, peon, night watchman, etc.

(C) Classification according to the form of work. Professions have been divided into the following four classes according to the nature of work done by them :

1. Social occupations. These professions require that the person be possessed of social qualities and a high degree of sociability because he comes into contact with very many individuals. Examples of such professions are advocate, leader, salesman, agent, administrator, manager, teacher, etc.

2. Occupations of mental skill. In these professions tools are used for work that requires a high degree of manual skill, examples being carpenter, mechanic, mason, binder, overseer, engineer, etc.

3. Occupations concerned with offices. This class includes all people concerned with office organisations such as clerks, cashiers, peons, etc.

4. Intellectual and scholarly occupation. In this class come the professions that require intellectual acumen and love of academic work of the individual, examples of which are philosopher, author, inventor, poet, scientist, etc.

Job families

From the above classification of occupations it becomes evident that there are many professions that are similar in respect of their nature of work done, conditions of work, desired skill, interest, mental abilities and personality qualities, etc. When such similar families are put together, a job family is constituted. In one job family the work can carried on different levels such as high, medium or low. Evidently; then, the individual will first have to select a job family, and then level of that family on which he is capable of functioning.

Sources of information regarding occupations

The question that may justifiably intrigue the beginner is the source of all this comprehensive information regarding a profession. The following are the sources from which such information is forthcoming and can be gathered :

(1) Through papers and magazines.
(2) Through information published by government organisations.
(3) Through radio discussions.
(4) From employment exchanges.
(5) From information broadcast by industrial and commercial institutions.
(6) Through lectures delivered by specialists.
(7) Through examination of factories and people working in them.
(8) By working on any particular profession.
(9) From guidance psychologist and vocational adviser.

Significant facts in vocational selection

After gathering information regarding the profession from one or more of the above mentioned sources it is possible to select one's profession, but before committing oneself finally, as has been pointed out before, the following thing must be taken into consideration and made a note of :

(1) Nature of work which includes the kind of work, charge, responsibility, duty, interest, etc.
(2) Working conditions, which include both psychological and physical needs.
(3) Necessary personality traits such as nature, adepts in behaviour, power of leadership, etc.
(4) Level of intelligence.
(5) Mental abilities.
(6) Interest and aptitudes.
(7) Necessary education and training.
(8) Income, chances of promotion, permanency of work.
(9) Procedure of entrance.
(10) Necessary physical development and health.
(11) Social prestige.
(12) Demand of the job.

In this manner, a profession is chosen after analysing the individual on the one hand, and the various occupations upon the other. Analysis of the individual reveals the abilities and qualities present in him while analysis of the job or profession reveals the desired qualities and abilities. Now, all that remains to be done is that the person who possesses abilities and qualities requisite for a particular profession should be prompted to join it.

STEPS OF THE VOCATIONAL GUIDANCE METHOD

Vocational guidance, as in the case of all other forms of guidance, can be given by two methods — the individual method, and the collective method. And, in these methods, the steps are the same as were described in the case of educational guidance. In this manner, vocational guidance will involve the following steps :

(1) Orientation talks.

(2) Psychological testing.

(3) Collection of data from the school.

(4) Collection of data from the family.

(5) Interview.

(6) Formation of profile.

(7) Achievement besides the above important steps in vocational guidance, which means that the psychologist, along with providing vocational guidance, also helps the individual to attain to the desired profession. For this he keeps in contact with employment exchange offices and social workers.

(8) Follow up studies.

Vocational Guidance at Different Stages

1. Primary school stage. Following are the qualities and skills which have great vocational significance and which can be very conveniently developed at the primary stage :

(1) Dignity of manual work.

(2) Training in the use of hands.

(3) Good eye-hand co-ordination.

(4) Neat and systematic work.

(5) Orderly arrangements of materials.

(6) Spirit of team work.

(7) Sharing the gains with others.

(8) Appraisal of one's own product.

(9) Good inter-personal relationships.

(10) A desire to do better work.

(11) Development of sales skills.

2. Secondary school stage. Its main purposes would be the following :

(1) To help pupils to know themselves.

(2) To help pupils to know the child at work — adequate information about various jobs, skills, opportunities.

(3) To help pupils to make a right choice.

(4) To help pupils to get suitable jobs in their chosen field — placement service.

(5) To help pupils to think seriously whether to go to college or not.

3. The college level. Following are the specific functions of guidance programme at the college stage :

(1) Helping students to relate their studies to the vocations that would be open to them at the end of their college career.

(2) Helping them to make a detailed study of the careers which they would like to pursue.

(3) Helping them to acquaint themselves with the different avenues of work.

(4) Helping them to acquaint themselves with avenues for higher studies.

(5) Helping them to know about the various programmes of financial assistance — scholarships, fellowships — for improving their prospects.

AIMS AND OBJECTIVES OF VOCATIONAL GUIDANCE

Jones has stated the following specific aims of vocational guidance :

1. To assist the student to acquire knowledge of the characteristics and functions, the duties and rewards of the group of occupations within which will probably lie his choice.

2. To enable him to find what general and specific abilities, skills, etc., are required for the group of occupations under consideration and what are the qualifications of age, preparation, sex, etc., for entering them.

3. To provide opportunity for experiences in school (try-out courses) and out of school (after-school and vocation jobs) which may give such information about conditions of work as may assist the individual to discover his own abilities and help in the development of wider interests.

4. To help the individual realise that all honest labour is worthwhile and that the most important bases for choice of an occupation are : (i) the special service that the individual can render to society, (ii) personal satisfaction in the occupation, and (iii) aptitude for the work required.

5. To assist the individual to acquire a technique of analysis of occupational information and to develop the habit of analysing such information before making a final choice.

6. To assist the individual to secure such information about himself, his abilities, general and specific, his interests and his powers as he may need fair wise choice.

7. To assist economically handicapped children above the compulsory attendance age to secure financial assistance through public or private

funds, scholarships or other means so that they may have opportunities for further education in accordance with their vocational plans.

8. To assist the students to secure a knowledge of the facilities offered by various educational institutions for vocational training and the requirements for admission to them, the length of training offered and the cost of attendance.

9. To help the worker to adjust himself to the occupation in which he is engaged; to assist him to understand his relationships to workers in his own related occupations and to society as a whole.

10. To enable the student to secure reliable information about the risk of alluring short-cuts to fortune.

Common Mistakes in Choosing a Career

Dr. J.A. Humphreys and A.E. Traxler point out the following mistakes which are generally made in choosing a career :

1. Selecting an occupation that requires mental ability above that of the individual.

2. Choosing an occupation that has limited employment potentials.

3. Choosing an occupation for which the individual does not possess essential skills in tool subject.

4. Choosing an occupation for which the required level of skill cannot be attained by the individual.

5. Choosing an occupation for which the individual does not have the appropriate characteristics of personality.

6. Choosing an occupation without the physical strength and endurance required by it.

7. Choosing an occupation because of its glamour.

8. Choosing an occupation without giving due attention to its financial aspects.

9. Choosing an occupation which is already overflooded.

10. Choosing an occupation on the basis of parent's wishes and ambitions.

RESPONSIBILITY OF THE SCHOOL FOR VOCATIONAL GUIDANCE

1. **Age.** It is at the adolescence stage that the children begin to think more seriously of their future career and they are in attendance in the school at this stage.

2. **Data.** The schools are in a better position to collect comprehensive and reliable information concerning an individual — his health and scholastic records, general intelligence ratings, records of his social and moral qualities, etc.

3. **Genuine service.** The public faith and confidence in its schools and also feels that the schools render a genuinely fair-minded and disinterested service.

4. Integration. At present vocational guidance is not an integral part of an adequate programme of education and as such it must become an integral part of school education.

CO-OPERATION OF MANY AGENCIES IN GUIDANCE

G.E. Myers stresses that acting as a responsible leader the school should seek and obtain the co-operation of many other social agencies and see the fulfilment of the following :

1. A list of all possible co-operating agencies is prepared.

2. The ways in which each such agency can render its contribution are studied.

3. A plan is chalked out in which each agency can make its contribution.

4. This co-operation continues to function successfully and effectively.

SERVICE RENDERED BY VOCATIONAL GUIDANCE PROGRAMME

According to G.E. Myers, "A comprehensive programme of Vocational Guidance in Secondary Schools is concerned with eight different services :

1. Vocational information service.
2. Self-inventory service.
3. Personal data collecting service.
4. Counsellor service.
5. Vocational preparatory service.
6. Placement or employment service.
7. Follow-up or adjustment service.
8. Research service."

1. The vocational information service (requirements of different vocations). A school should supply the following types of information concerning occupations to children according to their aptitudes, temperament, etc. :

(i) Importance of the occupation.
(ii) Nature of the work.
(iii) Working conditions.
(iv) Personal qualities needed.
(v) Preparation needed.
(vi) Opportunities for advancement.
(vii) Remuneration.
(viii) Advantages and disadvantages.

The above information may be given by these methods : (i) Information through school subjects. (ii) Information through field trips and visits to the places of work. (iii) Information by organising career conferences. (iv) Information through the use of library. (v) Information through inviting specialists. (vi) Information through charts. (vii) Information through films. (viii) Information through organising various co-curricular activities. (ix) Information through special talks on occupations by teachers or the school counsellor. (x) Information through organising surveys of the various occupations available in the locality. (xi) Information through radio and television.

2. The self-inventory service. The self-inventory service assists the child know his personal assets and liabilities without which he cannot take a wise selection of an occupation. It aims at assisting an individual to take stock of his abilities, aptitudes, personally traits; etc. It includes :

(i) *Exploratory experiences* : The number of specific occupations for which part time, after school and during vocation exploratory experiences can be provided is extremely limited in India at present. This method provides the exploration under actual working conditions and is very useful in vocational guidance. However, it cannot be made use of due to the inadequacy of the occupations which can provide such experiences.

(ii) *Try out experiences* : In science, laboratory periods can furnish try out experiences for the youngsters who think that they are interested in becoming a chemist, a physicist or a biologist. Since these same courses are related to other scientific careers, such as medicine, they serve as partial try-outs for these careers also.

(iii) *Self analysis* : Know Thyself, is a famous saying of Socrates. Self-analysis is knowing oneself. The students should be provided enough opportunities to discover themselves. In America numerous blanks or forms have been devised for use in self-rating with the help of which students make an estimate of their strengths and weaknesses.

3. Personal data collecting service. Six kinds of data concerning each student are needed for use in programme of vocational guidance : (i) General data. (ii) Physical data. (iii) Psychological data. (iv) Social environment data. (v) Achievement data. (vi) Data concerning the individual's educational and vocational plans.

4. The vocational counselling service. According to Myers, "Counselling implies a confidential relationship between two individuals. The vocational counsellor assists the counselled to marshal pertinent facts and to evaluate them in relation to the latter's vocational plans."

5. The vocational preparatory service. The Secondary Education Commission recommends, "Apprenticeship training being an important part of the training needed, suitable legislation should be passed making it obligatory for the industry to afford facilities to students for practical training." Vocational Preparatory Service means the service that is rendered to an individual in assisting him in receiving training before entrance upon regular full time employment. The individual's vocational success depends upon the quality and completeness of his preparation as well as upon suitable choice of an occupation. Vocational preparation should make provision for the following :

(i) *Preparation before employment begins* : Many American schools assist students in training for a group of occupations before preparation for a specific employment begins. Correspondence schools have been established in America which assist students in pre-employment training.

(ii) *Preparation in connection with employment* : This is of three types : (a) Apprenticeship training for those who spend one-half time in school and the other half at work. (b) Training for those who spend only a few hours per week in the school. (c) Training for those who obtain their apprenticeship wholly on the job.

(iii) *Preparation for change of occupation* : As there are many occasions when an individual seeks to change his occupation, there should be provision for change. Occasions which necessitate change are : (a) Technological employment. (b) Voluntary changes of occupation. (c) Dismissals on account of depression conditions or for other reasons.

6. The placement service. According to Myers vocational guidance programme is incomplete without placement. He says, "Entering occupational life advantageously, getting off to a good start, is quite as important as choosing and preparing for a suitable occupation. The placement office of a school system helps youth to sell their services in a favourable market. Well administered, it strengthens the rest of the programme and builds up the prestige of the schools in the community."

7. The adjustment service. The school authorities should keep themselves in close touch whether or not the young worker are making satisfactory progress. Following methods may be employed for this purpose :

(i) Obtaining written reports from the employers and the young workers.

(ii) Telephone and personal calls at the place of employment by a representative of the placement office.

(iii) Calls made by the youth on his former school counsellor.

The adjustment needs of the youth are the following : (a) Assistance in obtaining a new job. (b) Help in removing causes of dissatisfaction. (c) Help in determining what additional preparation should be obtained and how and where to obtain it. (d) Help in planning suitable cultural, recreational and community service activities. (e) Help in meeting the discouragement of prolonged employment.

8. The research service. Its chief function is to bring about improvement in the effectiveness of the other services and of the programme as a whole. It makes new experiments for finding out new techniques of collecting data and keeping it up-to-date and complete in all respects. It furnishes the necessary information when required by other agencies interested in child welfare.

PRINCIPLES OF VOCATIONAL GUIDANCE

1. Client-Centred Principles

(i) Making guidance available without interruption.
(ii) Guidance covering all clients.
(iii) Making guidance programme client-centred.
(iv) Guidance services meeting the varied and extensive needs of the individual.
(v) Making choice by the client himself.

2. Vocational Guidance Personnel-Centred Principles

(i) Accepting genuine responsibility to guide clients.
(ii) Professional efficiency.
(iii) In-service training.
(iv) Using all available information about the client.
(v) Observing a strict code of professional ethics.
(vi) Collecting external factors about the client.
(vii) Using varied methods and techniques.
(viii) Using research finding.

3. Organisation-Centred Principles

(i) Helping up-to-date records about the clients.
(ii) Making adequate budget provision.
(iii) Framing an independent guidance programme.
(iv) Making adequate time available to guidance workers.
(v) Making adequate space available for guidance workers.
(vi) Allowing field workers to undertake follow-up studies.
(vii) Offering placement services.
(viii) Making provision for individual and group guidance programmes.
(ix) Seeking cooperation from similar organisations.
(x) Making adequate supply of materials.
(xi) Responsiveness to guidance programme.

4. General Public-Centred Principles

(i) Mobilising public opinion.

(ii) Making public receptive to guidance programme.

(iii) Making public conscious of the careers of young members of the society.

(iv) Cooperation to the guidance worker.

(v) Identifying their needs by the people and bringing these to the notice of the guidance personnel.

(vi) Appreciation and constructive criticism of the work of the guidance personnel by the public.

QUESTIONS FOR EXERCISE

1. Explain the term 'Vocational Guidance'. Justify for an organised programme of vocational guidance.
2. The theory of individual differences is basic to the development of vocational guidance. Discuss.
3. Bertrand Russell has said, "Give a man the right kinds of skill and he will be virtuous. Give him wrong kinds, or none at all and he will be wicked." Discuss and bring out clearly the importance of vocational guidance.
4. "In its final analysis, all guidance is vocational guidance." Elucidate.
5. Explain the basic needs and aims of vocational guidance.
6. Describe the methods, services and organisation of vocational guidance in Indian schools.
7. What is vocational development? Is educational and vocational guidance inseparable at the secondary stage of schooling?

22

The World of Work and Occupations

SOME DEFINITIONS

1. Work. It has been defined by Miller and Form as a "general activity centring around subsistence and the specific routines of this activity as occupations."

2. Occupation. Shartle offers the following definition. An 'occupation' is a group of similar jobs in several establishments.

3. Job. A 'job' is a group of similar positions in one plant, business, institution or other work place.

4. Position. A 'position' is set of tasks performed by one person. There are as many positions as there are workers but there may be one or a number of persons employed on the same job.

5. World of work. The world of work is fast changing with the times. Some fields of work are growing and others are declining. New professions are emerging and many old ones are disappearing. While the occupational structure of world is not permanent, one can determine the trend of various professions at a particular time.

In the dictionary of occupational titles developed by the United States Employment Service 22,000 jobs have been defined.

The world of work in India may also continue to be complex as new discoveries and inventions begin to pile up giving birth to new occupations.

Work selected according to the needs of the individual may turn out to be a source of satisfaction and creativity. If wrongly selected it may make the individual an unhappy man. Therefore, it is necessary that proper selection of occupation should be a primary focus of society.

6. Families groups and divisions of occupations. For the sake of simplicity, various 'occupations' have been classified under 'families'; families are combined into 'groups' and 'groups' are assigned to 'divisions'. In India National Classification of Occupations as prepared in 1959 by the Occupational Unit of the Directorate General of Resettlement and Employment has 11 divisions consisting of 75 Groups divided into 331 families under which the individual occupations are classified. The main divisions are the following :

(i) Professional, Technical and Related Workers.
(ii) Administrative, Executive and Managerial Workers.
(iii) Classical and Related Workers.
(iv) Sales Workers.
(v) Farmers, Fishermen, Hunters, Loggers and Related Workers.
(vi) Miners, Quarrymen and Related Workers.
(vii) Workers in Transport and Communication Occupations.
(viii) Craftsmen, Production Process Workers.
(ix) Service, Sport and Recreation Workers.
(x) Workers not classified by occupation.

Each of these groups of occupations requires different types of intelligence aptitude, scholastic attainment, personally traits and predispositions.

OCCUPATIONAL INFORMATION

Meaning. C.E. Shartle defines occupational information as the "accurate and usable information about jobs and occupations". It includes facts concerning the importance of an occupation, entrance requirements, opportunities for promotion, health and accident hazards compensations and other working conditions that are usually found in specific occupations or related group of occupations.

Need for Occupational Information

In the field of occupations seeks to assist the pupils in securing educational experiences through understanding his role in the field of work. In efficient guidance knowledge of occupations is absolutely essential. A counsellor may be trained in counselling techniques but his work will not carry any significant weight without vocational content. One of the responsibilities of the school is to bring the complex reality into focus and to help the individual to evaluate both his opportunities and his limitations.

The pupils should be provided with accurate and usable information before leaving school. This will remove the disharmony between the employment opportunities and the resources of personnel. Occupational information assists pupils to gain maturity in vocational understanding and develop attitudes according to the modern and ever-changing demands of our social and economic life. It assists the pupils to make a realistic vocational selection.

To organise an effective guidance programme, occupational information should be disseminated from the early stages. Educational programmes should be geared to the actual requirements found in jobs. Schools and colleges should take upon themselves the responsibility of disseminating occupational information. Careful vocational counselling is needed in the light of authentic information about jobs and opportunities otherwise the vast programme of expanded educational facilities will produce a great deal of dissatisfaction.

Types of Information to be imparted at the Secondary Stage

1. About various jobs.
2. About various industries.
3. About training facilities.
4. About placement facilities.
5. About common errors in choosing an occupation.
6. About various items to be considered in choosing an occupation.
7. About sources of information about occupations.
8. Regarding one's own abilities and interests.

Contents of the Occupational Information

1. History. The history of the occupation, how it developed and how long a history does it have.

2. Importance. The importance of the occupation and the contribution it makes to the development of society.

3. Number. The number of people working in the occupation.

4. Structure. The pattern of employment, the number of workers employed and the possibility of future employment.

5. Duties.

(i) Specific task, other occupations with which this work may be related or combined, nature of work, tools, machines and materials used.

(ii) Definition of the job as described by the law and official organisations.

6. Requirements. Qualifications, sex, age, community; special physical, mental, social and moral qualities; skills and the use of special tools and equipment required to work on the job.

7. Preparation. It includes general education, special training and schools or institutions offering special training.

8. Duration of training. It is the time required to acquire the skills necessary for the job.

9. Methods of entering the job. It concerns special agencies like the Employment Exchanges and the State Public Service Commissions through which the job must be sought.

10. Advancement. It shows the line of promotion and opportunity for advancement.

11. Progress. Other occupations with better prospects to which the present job may lead.

12. Emoluments. Starting salary, average earnings and the maximum earnings throughout the career.

13. Time tables. Hours of work the worker expected to put in, the procedure of overtime, vocations and other requirements.

14. Yearly duration of work. Whether it is a permanent work throughout the year or it closes down during certain months, its busy months and comparatively easy months.

15. Risk. Health and accident risk.

16. Places of employment. It is important for the worker to know whether he is to be placed in an office, a shop or a factory.

17. Understanding. Providing the pupil with better understanding of various occupations and the workers in these occupations.

18. Choice. Helping the pupil in making a wise choice of a career and in preparing him for the chosen occupation.

KINDS OF INFORMATION CONCERNING OCCUPATIONS

George E. Myers has suggested the following outline for the study of an occupation :

1. Importance of the occupation. How does it serve society? How many people does it employ? Is it widely distributed or localised?

2. Nature of the work. What does the worker do? Is the work highly repetitive or quite varied?

3. Working conditions. Is the work indoors or outdoors? Does the worker stand or sit? What are the working hours?

4. Personal qualities needed. What personal traits, etc., are important?

5. Preparation needed. What general education and special training are needed?

6. Opportunities for advancement. What are the principal related occupations in which one might seek advancement?

7. Compensation. What annual earnings may one expect? What are retirement benefits etc.?

8. Advantages and disadvantages. Important features that do not fit under other headings may be placed here.

CLASSIFICATION OF OCCUPATIONAL INFORMATION MATERIAL

1. Career pamphlets or occupational monographs. These give an all-round picture of a single occupation.

2. General occupational survey records. These give information about a number of occupations in a single volume.

3. Prospectuses. These concern educational, vocational and training institutions.

4. Handbook. These depict educational, vocational and training facilities.

5. Literature. It is brought about by professional organisations regarding various courses and examinations conducted by them.

6. Dictionaries. These are on occupations and industries giving codified and classified lists of occupations or industries with definitions.

7. Directories. These provide details and addresses of occupations, industries and organisations.

8. Employment market. Literature on employment market trends.

9. Occupational choice. Literature on occupational choice and adjustment.

10. Audio-visual aids. These include films, filmstrips, charts and posters.

SOURCES OF OCCUPATIONAL INFORMATION MATERIAL

1. Direct sources. There are various commercial and industrial establishments which students, teachers and counsellors visit to collect occupational information.

2. Indirect sources. These include various types of information booklets, etc., published by various institutions and organisations.

METHODS OF CLASSIFYING AND SORTING OCCUPATIONAL INFORMATION

(A) Classification of Area

1. Administrative, executive and managerial.

2. Agricultural, including horticulture, sericulture, veterinary, animal husbandry, fishery and forestry.

3. Clerical and secretarial.

4. Communication and transport.

5. Defence services.

6. Fine arts, like dance, drama, music, painting, photography and sculpture.

7. Health services.

8. Journalism.

9. Literature.

10. Mining, quarrying and related occupations.

11. Research.

12. Service occupations like house-building, hostels and restaurants, insurance and travel agency.

13. Social work.

14. Teaching.

15. Technical crafts.
16. Trade and commerce.
17. Miscellaneous.
18. The use of code plan or code number.

(B) Methods of Disseminating Information

1. Through individual contacts such as counselling interview.

2. Through group contacts or group guidance. These include :

(i) Imparting occupational information as a regular subject.
(ii) Occupational information through career conferences.
(iii) Through special subjects.
(iv) Through school clubs.
(v) Through home rooms or tutorials.
(vi) Through class talks.
(vii) Occupational talks by specialists in the occupations.
(viii) Occupational information through work experience projects.
(ix) Through visits to places of work.
(x) Through dramatisation.
(xi) Through films and film strips.
(xii) Through displays or exhibitions.
(xiii) Through Bulletin Board announcements.
(xiv) Through library.
(xv) Through booklets.
(xvi) Through co-curricular activities.
(xvii) Through display corner.
(xviii) Through Radio and Television.

SOURCES OF OCCUPATIONAL MATERIAL IN INDIA

1. Directorate-General of Employment and Training, Shram Shakti Bhawan, New Delhi.

2. National Council of Educational Research and Training, Mehrauli Road, New Delhi.

3. Vocational Counselling Bureau, Y.M.C.A., Indore.

4. Y.M.C.A. Publishing House, 5, Russell Street, Calcutta-700 016.

5. Manovigyan Shala, U.P., Allahabad.

6. Ministry of Scientific Research, Government of India, New Delhi.

7. Directorate-General of Health Services, Ministry of Health, New Delhi.

8. Government of Maharashtra, Institute of Vocational Guidance and Selection, 3, Cruickshank Road, Bombay-400 001.

9. Ministry of Railways (Railway Board) Government of India, Rail Bhawan, New Delhi-110 001.

10. Bureau of Educational Research, Ewing Christian College, Allahabad-3.

11. Rotary International, Rotary Club, Hyderabad (Andhra Pradesh).

12. College of Educational Psychology and Guidance, Jabalpur (M.P.).

13. Faculty of Education and Psychology, Maharaja Sayajirao University of Baroda, Baroda.

14. Offices of the Employment Exchanges in all States.

15. University Employment Bureaus attached to the universities.

16. Ministry of Education, Information Section, Shastri Bhawan, New Delhi.

17. Association of Indian Universities, Kotla Road, New Delhi.

18. Public Service Commissions of Union Territories and States.

19. Staff Selection Board, CGO Complex, Lodhi Road, New Delhi.

20. All State Bureaus of Educational and Vocational Guidance.

FACTORS DETERMINING OCCUPATIONAL CHOICES

1. Psychological Factors

(i) Intelligence.
(ii) Aptitude.
(iii) Interest.
(iv) Personality traits.

2. Physical Factors

(i) Height.
(ii) Weight.
(iii) Chest measurement.
(iv) Eyesight.
(v) Face, etc.

3. Job Values

(i) Leadership qualities required or possessed by the job.
(ii) Esteem of the job.
(iii) Interesting experiences of the job.
(iv) Power inherent in the job.
(v) Status of job.
(vi) Fame of the job.
(vii) Security of job.
(viii) Profit or emoluments in the job.

(ix) Self-expression outlets available in the job.
(x) Independence in the job.

4. Economic Factors

(i) Demand and supply of the job.
(ii) Business cycle.
(iii) Technical change and automation.
(iv) Taste and style.
(v) Public policies.
(vi) Unionisation.
(vii) Organisation of establishments.

5. Family Factors

(i) Behaviourable patterns of parents, brothers or sisters.
(ii) Cultural background of the family.
(iii) Educational background of the family.
(iv) Monetary position of the family.
(v) Political affiliations of the family.
(vi) Property holdings of the family.
(vii) Religious feelings of the family.
(viii) Social status of the family.
(ix) Traditions of the family.

6. Contingent Factors

(i) Conditions of work.
(ii) Occupational opportunities available.
(iii) Training facilities available.

7. Social Factors

(i) Fulfilment of social needs.
(ii) Social taboos if any on a particular job.

8. Individual Differences

(i) Differences of sex, temperament, etc.
(ii) Occupational differences.

9. Educational Factors

(i) Qualifications needed for a job.
(ii) Education received from a public, private or government institution.
(iii) Certificates, diplomas or degree acquired through regular study or private study.

10. Decisional Factors

(i) Who makes the choice — student, counsellor, parents or friends.

(ii) Equal proficiency in some jobs and the issue of making choice for them.

(iii) Timing of a career plan.

11. Problematic Factors

(i) Lack of information about occupational world.

(ii) Lack of knowledge about self.

12. Philosophical Factors

(i) Does not occupation provide opportunities to serve people and society?

(ii) Can one follow virtues like honesty while pursuing the occupation?

(iii) The profession subversive of the society? Professions like that of smugglers, bootleggers or dacoits come under this category.

13. Chance or Accident Factors

(i) Unexpected inheritance of money or property.

(ii) Outbreak of war and new occupations or openings.

(iii) Change remarks of a friend, whims of a relative, ease of getting a particular job.

(iv) Chance of quick earnings, attractions or glamour of a job.

(v) Contraction of serious diseases.

(vi) Gains from gambling or lottery.

(vii) Failure of business ventures.

FACTORS DETERMINING VOCATIONAL ADJUSTMENT

1. Salary, other benefits and facilities.
2. Working conditions.
3. Rules and regulations of the management.
4. Physical environment.
5. Physical ability.
6. Performing assigned work properly.
7. Regularity and punctuality in doing a job.
8. Relations with co-workers.
9. Relations with the management.
10. Proper use of facilities.
11. Learning new techniques and trends.

PERSONALITY TRAITS IN CAREER DEVELOPMENT

1. **Emotional stability.** Not to be easily upset.
2. **Industriousness.** Willingness to work hard.
3. **Initiative.** Taking action without being told to do so.

4. Leadership. Ability to influence and direct others along constructive and worthwhile lines.

5. Responsibility. Tendency to complete work without supervision.

6. Seriousness of purpose. Striving to achieve goals.

7. Self-confidence. Trust in one's judgement and action.

8. Socialability. Ability to get along with others.

MAJOR GROUPS OF OCCUPATIONS

1. Professional, Technical and Related occupations.
2. Administrative, Executive and Managerial Workers.
3. Clerical and Related Workers.
4. Sale Workers.
5. Service Workers.
6. Farmers, Fishermen, Hunters, etc.
7. Production Workers.
8. Equipment Workers.

OCCUPATIONAL FIELD

1. Accountancy.
2. Administrative Services.
3. Agriculture.
4. Various Arts.
5. Banks.
6. Building Industry.
7. Data Processing (Computers, etc.).
8. Defence Services.
9. Educational Industry.
10. Film Industry.
11. Hotel Management.
12. Engineering.
13. Industry — Large Scale.
14. Industry — Small Scale.
15. Journalism.
16. Management.
17. Police.
18. Security Service.
19. Secretarial Assistance.
20. Social Services.
21. Printing.
22. Medicine.

SOURCES OF OCCUPATIONAL INFORMATION

(A) Sources

1. Particular boards, commissions, institutions and organisations.
2. Chambers of Commerce.
3. Company Reports.
4. Publications of Government Departments.
5. Trade Unions.
6. Voluntary agencies.
7. Employer's associations.
8. Licensing authorities.
9. Newspaper advertisements.
10. 'Employment News' published by the Department of Information, Government of India.
11. Employment Exchanges.
12. Government Departments.
13. Employment Market Reports.
14. Mass Media — Radio, Television and Cinema.

(B) Criteria for Suitable Occupational Information and Literature

1. Authenticity.
2. Availability.
3. Format (simple).
4. Inexpensive.
5. Information not easily available.
6. Motivational for further reading.
7. Objectivity.
8. Readability.
9. Recency.
10. Suitability.

(C) Areas in Career Occupational Information

1. Job opportunities.
2. Educational and training facilities.
3. Apprenticeship and on the job training.
4. Trends, patterns and growth of educational, training and employment opportunities.
5. Self-employment opportunities.

(D) Methods of Filing Occupational Information

1. Alphabetical order of occupations.

2. Industry-wise occupations.
3. Employment-wise occupations.
4. Interest pattern-wise occupations.
5. Subject-wise occupations.
6. NCO-wise (National Classification of Occupation).

QUESTIONS FOR EXERCISE

1. What do you understand by the term 'World of Work'? What is its significance from the point of view of guidance?
2. Discuss fully the need, sources and the methods of disseminating occupational information to the students.
3. Elucidate the group techniques of imparting information.
4. Explain the factors determining occupational chances.
5. What are the factors determining vocational adjustment? Describe the sources criteria and areas of occupational information.

23

Institutions of Higher Learning and the World of Work

Today the traditional forms and processes of teaching and learning are changing rapidly. The ancient ideal of the institutions of higher learning was a kind of *cloister or an ashram* where seekers of knowledge could abstract themselves from the persistent problems of daily life, and concentrate on higher values and principles, is no longer meaningful. Today, the institutions of higher learning have shed the habit of the cloister — and went forth into the market place in order to grapple with the complex problems of contemporary life. Hence, the need of a drastic restructuring of the entire concept and functioning of institutions of higher learning.

EARN WHILE YOU LEARN

An important aim of institutions of higher learning is to prepare the youth for work, to equip them for occupations, as well as to prepare them for cultivated intellectual and human lives. The universities and colleges, come into contact with students in the formative stages of their life. The students study the prescribed syllabus and acquire the intellectual equipment with which they face the problems of life. A persistent life problem before them is to enter into the world of work. Even though preparation for employment is not the sole objective of higher education, it is one of the main objectives. The delaying of work until after completion of education creates among the young an occupational illiteracy where they know little about the world of work, though work is still the psychological way that youth come of age. The isolation of students from work is a dangerous phenomenon. Institutions of higher learning will succeed in the task of preparing personnel for employment only if they are in constant touch with the huge and vast and fastly expanding world of work.

EDUCATION SUITABLE FOR MARKET

In the new industrial and technological era, institutions of higher learning have to ensure that their products suit adequately to the needs of the labour market which constantly requires higher levels of education, skill development and professional specialisation. They have also to ensure that their products are employable. Therefore, all levels of education, must quickly move to assume greater responsibilities for preparing men and women into the changed and changing world of technological work...Technology has created a new relationship between man, his education and his work, in which education is placed squarely between man and his work. Technology today dictates the role that education must play in preparing man for work.

Link between Education and Work

The link between higher education and work at the highest occupational level is recognised every where. In the research and development field, for example, the line between *education* and *work* is very thin.... The professions, it has long been agreed, are a proper subject of academic attention, and preparation for them should take place within a formal educational framework. We know that technology has advanced many occupations on the technical, skilled, semi-skilled and semi-professional levels to a point where they require higher levels of specialisation and related knowledge that are best obtained within educational frameworks. The demand for higher education is becoming greater and greater because both the technology and industry are demanding workers with a degree of training and related education that can best be offered in a system of higher education only.

Industry Oriented Courses

It is being increasingly felt that all engineering, technical and vocational courses need to be made industry-oriented. Courses should not be just institution-based, rather the professional trainees should be given the feel of work. The Education Commission (1964-66) recommended : "Practical training for full time degree students should commence from the third year of the course, and should be properly prepared and supervised in cooperation with the industry. Wherever possible sandwich type of courses should be adopted."

"For colleges and institutes of technology to become more concerned with the needs of the industry, research design projects sponsored by industry or government should be made a part of the curriculum."[1]

NEED OF APPLIED RESEARCH

Institutions of higher learning cannot confine their sphere to pure (basic) research, leaving applied research and development in all branches of science to other institutions. Applied research such as developing important new techniques or designing and fabricating special instruments or apparatus is very much the field of work of the universities and professional institutions. There has to be a marriage of industrial establishments and institutions of higher learning for a speedier development of economy.

1. Education Commission Report, p. 383.

CONTROL OF LOPSIDEDNESS

A linkage and working arrangement between education and the world of work is also necessary to control lopsided development of educational facilities. This would enable us to make education an effective instrument for occupational preparation of the labour market entrants and harness manpower resources effectively. Future development of educational facilities in agriculture, science, engineering and technology and expansion of other vocational and technical courses needs to be so planned as to meet the requirements of employment market and the new technology.

CHALLENGE OF SUPER INDUSTRIALISM

There should be close coordination between the institutions of higher learning and the world of work due to the challenge posed by super-industrialism and tremendous increase in the rate of scientific activity which necessitate estimating and forecasting technical man-power requirements at all levels. The development of science and technology, new fields of knowledge such as electronics, instrument technology, aeronautics and astronautics and nuclear power generation, and advanced research in various areas need careful planning for which institutions of higher learning and world of work must join hands.

We cannot get away from the idea that good higher education is one of the stepping stones to a good world of work. Institutions of higher learning have to shoulder the responsibility of feeding the entire economic system in a country, coordinate education with man-power requirements, estimate and forecast the future requirements, plan and adjust its plans and programmes to suit the present and emerging requirements. They cannot afford to remain in the ivory towers quite oblivious of what is needed for the changing world of work.

EXPANDING WORLD OF WORK

The world of work is fast expanding. The total number of occupations available in a country is a reliable index of any country's stage of development and industrialisation. The American *Dictionary of Occupational Titles* (DOT), 1965 lists 21,741 occupations consisting of 35,550 job titles and now their number have increased a lot. This is due to the very high degree of specialisation achieved in the U.S.A. at all stages of assembly-line operation. According to the National Classification of Occupations (NCO), 1968 in India, we have 2,484 occupations consisting of six to seven thousand job titles. Here, too, there must have been a good increase by now. Due to the scientific and technological developments in the twentieth century, there has been a great increase in the number of occupations.

Government Institutions

During the past few decades there has been tremendous scientific development in our country. A number of scientific research organisations as the Indian Council of Agricultural Research (1929), The Council of Scientific and Industrial Research (1942), The Department of Atomic Energy (1954), The Defence Research and Development Organisation (1958) etc. have been set up. These research facilities have created innumerable well-staffed hierarchies of scientific workers. These national laboratories are a source of gainful careers to qualified scientists.

Private Institutions

A number of research organisations financed by private endowments, industry, professional associations, universities and centres of advanced learning, too, have been occupied with scientific research. Typical examples are : The Tata Institute of Fundamental Research (TIFR), Bombay; The Bose Institute, Calcutta; The Birbal Sahni Institute of Palaeo-botany, Lucknow; The Ahmedabad Textile Industry's Research Association, Bombay; The South Indian Textile Research Association, Coimbatore; The Indian Jute Industries Research Association, Calcutta; The Maharashtra Association for Cultivation of Science, Poona; The Sri Ram Institute for Industrial Research, Delhi, etc. All these are offering jobs to outstanding youngmen and women.

New Occupational Outlets

This tremendous technological and scientific development and growth is throwing up new occupational outlets. More and more persons are specialising in the rapidly expanding new fields like Nuclear Physics, and Nuclear Power Generation, Electronics Engineering, Computerisation etc.

Rapid Industrialisation

During the past three decades there has been tremendous technological development resulting in huge industrial growth and expansion. Today, India is producing its own supersonic fighter aircraft, heavy electrical transmission equipment, railway engines, sophisticated instruments and equipment, engineering goods and machinery, light and heavy armaments, etc. India has, in fact, come a long way in the field of industrialisation.

Industrialisation has created innumerable new job opportunities. It has also thrown up new occupations, in the wake of development of improved technological processes and new raw materials. Fuel and gas, petroleum, chemical and plastics, technologies and electronics, agriculture, forging and heat treatment, hydraulics and dam engineering and naval architecture, etc. have developed into distinct specialisations as a result of these developments.

Green and White Revolutions

Green and White Revolutions have caused a number of occupational changes. Agriculture has been mechanised. It has required application of technical know-how and use of new agricultural machinery and implements. Agricultural research, development and extension work is offering employment to numerous graduates and specialists in various fields of agriculture as agronomy, agricultural botany/chemistry/economics/entomology/microbiology/marketing/extension/sociology, mycology and plant pathology, plant breeding and genetics, plant physiology, etc., horticulture, floriculture, fisheries, veterinary science and animal husbandry, animal nutrition, animal pathology, dairy science, warehousing, water conservation, soil science, poultry farming, etc. etc.

Agricultural revolution has opened up new and steadily expanding avenues of self-employment — agro-service centres, customs service units, agro industries, rural industries, forest based industries, etc.

Increasing Urbanisation

Increasing urbanisation has resulted in greater housing, educational, transport and recreational activities. It is throwing up innumerable service industries and occupations to cater to the demand of the urban population. There is a steady growth in the number of workers in transport, catering and hoteliering, construction, education and service occupations. The establishment and seemingly unending growth of local transport, electricity, water, milk, gas, petroleum and petroleum products and food and food products supply system and public health, sanitary and fire services are the necessary off-shoots of urbanisation. Then, there are numerous other 'social' services to tackle sociological problems arising from urbanisation; law and order, magistracy and judiciary, housing and slum clearance, town planning and development, delinquency and vagrancy, beggary and immoral traffic, unemployment, labour unrest and disputes, etc. — all these offer various career openings.

New Occupations

The break up of occupations and jobs has created new occupations at the national level. Three decades ago, there were not many engineering occupations other than those of the popular civil, mechanical and electrical engineers. The National Classification of Occupations (NCO), 1968 lists 82 occupations of engineers and technologists at the degree and specialisation level. And by the time, this book is being written, some new branches might have emerged.

Thus, the occupational pattern is fast changing. New occupations are emerging, some old ones are disappearing. It is obligatory for the institutions of higher learning to keep themselves posted with the latest information regarding the developments in occupational pattern, and the surplus and shortage occupations to avoid the imbalance in demand and supply; to predict the occupational outlook; to forecast the man-power requirement and plan and adjust the educational facilities accordingly.

Institutions of higher learning should also keep a close contact with the Directorate General of Employment and Training, Institute of Applied Man Power Research, Planning Commission, Directorate of Man Power, etc. to keep themselves equipped with research on occupational outlook, manpower forecasting and manpower projection and demands.

DEFECTS IN HIGHER EDUCATION

1. Passive knowledge. In India, today the contact between institutions of higher learning and those responsible for using their products is not effective. The institutions do not know where to modify their programmes in more functional directions. The passive absorption of knowledge and the uncertainty of being able to use it in a career is unwelcome to young people of intelligence anywhere. The underlying unease amongst students does not help them to get the most from institutions of higher learning nor does it enable them to make a rational and constructive contribution to the economy.

2. Prestige symbol. Besides, higher education is considered a prestige symbol. People are placing a high value on the growth of facilities for higher education. Due to political pressures, the facilities are expanding. No body is bothering to understand what scope the economy has for absorbing its products.

3. Lack of balance. The lack of balance between supply of personnel by institutions of higher learning and demand by different sectors of economy is another serious problem.

4. Inadequate products. There is also the lacuna as far as the products of institutions of higher learning are concerned. Employers complain that their products are inadequately equipped. The graduates even in specialised subjects are unable to cope with their work without substantial further training, and graduates recruited for responsible jobs lack the qualities and skills of good management. Some ex-students also complain that they were taught much that is of no use to them!

NEED OF CLOSE LIAISON

Close liaison between institutions of higher learning and the World of Work is needed for following objectives :

1. To help students to understand the world of work and to appreciate where they are likely to stand in it;
2. To help students to enter appropriate employment;
3. To help employers to pick suitable young workers;
4. To reveal the quantitative and qualitative needs of the world of work to students and the faculty;

5. To bring the work of institutions into as practical a relationship as possible with the needs of the economy;
6. To ensure the proper quality of products;
7. To involve and associate employers in the work of the educational establishments which, in the end, will provide them with their key staff and
8. To check the imbalance between supply and demand in various sectors of economy.

GUIDELINES FOR CLOSE LIAISON

Institutions of higher learning and world of work should be brought closer and there exist a two-way traffic between the two.

1. Industry-university interaction. There is an urgent need for improving the mutual confidence at various levels between Industry and Universities. The following points of contact need to be established to achieve this objective :

(i) *Representation* : It should be given to people from Industry and Government — on various academic bodies like Board of Studies and Research Boards. Besides, individuals from each side should interact frequently, discuss and identify areas of mutual interest.

(ii) *Visiting committees* : University science and engineering departments should establish visiting committees with strong participation of industrial research and development managers. These committees could advise on research in curricula, industrial openings for staff and post-graduate students, summer openings, etc.

(iii) *Interaction between people from both sides in teaching and research programmes* : Some courses should be tailored to the needs of industry and offered at the post-graduate level. These courses should be over and above the core or basic courses which are a must for every post-graduate student. Talent from industry should be used for teaching such courses in situations where the industry has competent persons. Competent persons from industry should be appointed as visiting professors so as to enable them to participate in the teaching programmes of the university.

(iv) *Fellowships* : Industries should be motivated to offer fellowships to post-graduate students who take specially designed courses or do thesis research in fields of importance to the industry.

(v) *Contracts* : Contracts in the major and medium size industry in the public and private sector can play very important role in developing progress of mutual interest and benefit. The universities should make available their facilities to industry at a reasonable charge.

(vi) *Industrial research centres* : Students should be allowed to work in industrial research centres/laboratories for post-graduate research degrees, provided appropriate facilities are available.

(vii) *Sponsored research projects* : Universities should explore all avenues for securing sponsored research projects from industry in areas of mutual interest.

2. Development and research. The institutions of higher learning are supposed to conduct research of a *pure and fundamental* nature; while the industrial establishments mostly conduct *applied* research. They can join hands to the benefit of both. For instance, an engineering college having certain facilities which the industry may not have, may even design and develop prototypes for the industry. Universities and professional institutions are generally equipped with sophisticated apparatus which can be utilised for industrial advancement. They can carry out performance tests on the products of industries. The information collected can prove useful for applied research and fundamental investigations. The institutions of higher learning may also enter into the field of technical and general consultancy and may take up assignments like job evaluation, analysis of wage structure, incentive schemes etc.

3. Research on manpower problems and requirements. Such studies are being conducted by a number of universities in foreign countries. These studies can be of immense use to manpower planners in our country also. Institutions of higher learning like universities, institutes of technology, various institutes of Research can undertake studies and research projects on behalf of government agencies, industrial establishments, government undertakings and also send the members of their faculty on deputation to serve in them for short terms. The research in manpower requirements will enable them to make reliable manpower estimates, forecasts and projections and thus the cobwebs, which at present blur the understanding, can be removed.

4. Analysis of productivity, skill and occupational composition of labour force. Institutions of higher learning should analyse the levels of productivity and manpower composition in various industries and their units. This will help build up reliable national estimates of productivity, skill composition and other related matters in the different sectors of the economy. A detailed micro-analysis on productivity manpower mix may provide a firm and dependable basis for manpower planning. It can provide valuable data regarding the ratio between technical and non-technical personnel in various sectors and levels of employment, the preparation of various categories of manpower to total employment in different sectors and the extent to which manpower availability has been affected by in and out migration of personnel. The institutions of higher learning are in the best position to take up these studies.

5. Collecting data about employment trends of their products. The student enrolment in the field of higher education has risen. India has achieved the third place in the world in terms of college enrolment. It is immediately following the United States and the U.S.S.R. There have been significant changes in the pattern of enrolment of students. These changes are due to the tremendous demand for educational facilities that is building up in the country. If institutions of higher learning build up reliable statistics regarding the employment history of their alumni, it will be helpful to determine from time to time the emerging pattern of the utilisation of educated manpower in the country. This information will provide valuable guidelines for manpower and educational planners. The regular flow of such information would serve as an early warning signal indicating the manpower categories which the economy is finding difficult to absorb.

6. Formation of an apex body at national level. In relation to manpower requirements an apex body should be set up at the national level at the earliest. It may be formed under the aegis and guidance of DGE and T without prejudice to its autonomy. It may consist of the representatives of DGE and T, UGC, ICAR, 1CMR, NCERT, national laboratories etc. The data regarding manpower requirements be speedily circulated to colleges and universities for curricular adjustment and future planning.

7. Creating a sense of dedication and commitment. Institutions of higher learning must educate and train high level and middle level manpower; inculcate in their products a sense of dedication and commitment so essential for successful completion of plans and projects so ambitiously launched by the country.

8. Redesigning the courses of studies. The institutions of higher learning must make provision of new courses to meet the emerging needs, redesign the old ones to suit the new requirements so that the products of these institutions get the intellectual equipment to meet the contemporary challenge. The employing agencies may also make conscious evaluation of the adequacy of their employers' educational qualifications with reference to job requirements and they may take the initiative and approach the institutions for formulating special courses, and modify the existing ones.

9. Sandwich courses or work-experience. The campus theoretical studies need to be supplemented with practical and mechanical reference and thus raise the theoretical appreciation of the tasks. There should be an effective link between institutions of higher learning and the vast world of work so that the institutions can give practical slant to their courses, and employers can help their workers gain the much needed theoretical base for their jobs. The system of 'cooperative courses' under which a student will obtain practical experience by actually working in an industry for specified period should be extended to as many fields of technical education as possible.

10. Compulsory vocational paper. A compulsory vocational paper may be introduced in the colleges to pave the way for graduates to take the advantage of self-employment schemes.

11. Research projects. Institutions of higher learning may undertake research projects on problems arising in the various fields of world of work. Market research, application of modern mathematical techniques into business planning, ergonomics, industrial relations, incentive schemes, selection techniques, etc. might be taken up. Such projects could produce results of great commercial value for which leading firms would be prepared to pay. Thus both the institutions and the students involved would benefit.

12. Job studies. Institutions of higher learning may take up job studies to help prepare the youngmen and women for the world of work. These studies should include information on what people do in their jobs, what decisions they make and what knowledge and techniques they use. First hand studies of jobs can prove of immense use for familiarising the students with the world of work and ultimately help in proper choices.

13. Employment surveys. Institutions of higher learning may undertake employment surveys to find out the following number :

(i) Students who found jobs within one year of graduation either by direct selection or through competitive examination;

(ii) Students who found jobs after securing additional skills outside the institutes and

(iii) Students unemployed in each category.

This information may prove of immense use to manpower planners. It may also enable the institutions to judge the extent to which the various kinds of courses command value in the labour market. It is likely that institutions may discover new intake and training needs and as a result feel the need for starting new courses. These surveys may also indicate to employers genuine concern on the part of the institutions to seek the real needs of the economy.

Discussions should be arranged with members of Chambers of Commerce — Rotary clubs, Lion clubs, etc. to make the surveys comprehensive and useful.

14. Entrepreneurial development courses. These should be introduced at the college and university level with active cooperation of financial institutions and banks, government departments and promotional agencies.

15. Inclusion of case histories of successful entrepreneurs in the courses. Case histories of successful big, medium and small entrepreneurs should be included in the courses of studies to serve as beacon lights and motivate the young students for venturing into new paths.

16. Self-employment cells. These should be opened in colleges and universities to provide students with necessary information on self-employment opportunities. In the changing economy, it is necessary that the youth is weaned away from illusive 'glamour' of white-collared jobs. A sizable fraction of enterprising youth need to be initiated into careers of self-development. Efforts need to be made to make self-employment an acceptable and worthwhile proposition to our young-men, identify the deserving cases fit to take up self-employment, educate them on how to proceed about the job of setting up a venture, help them through the cooperation of the concerned agencies in this sphere to prepare technically sound and economically viable projects, sponsor their cases to the batiks for loan assistance, and guide them to overcome the teething troubles through effective follow-up after the commencement of venture.

17. Continuing education. Facilities for continuing education should be provided in the institutions of higher learning to those engaged in the labour force. Refresher courses, seminars, workshops, advanced courses may be arranged for the labour force like the engineers, technologists, scientists, medical specialists, etc. Facilities should be offered for persons in employment who desire to acquire additional knowledge which has been found necessary in the light of their experience in employment. For example, an engineer may undergo an advanced course in Mathematics and a Mathematician that of economics. Besides, they can make provision for specialised courses to satisfy the requirements of the users of manpower.

18. Setting up of information centres. A chain of information centres in terms of procedures, policies, economic information, statistical data, technical library facilities should be set up in each state at the state headquarters, at the industry concentration centres, and colleges, so that the students could get the latest and most reliable information.

19. Recruitment on the campus. Liaison between institutions of higher learning and the world may be established by encouraging employers to visit the institutions to interview students either to fill specific vacancies or to review applications from students interested in employment in their firms. Facilities may be arranged by the authorities. The occasion might also serve for informal talks by the employers with heads of departments and discussions with the faculty, etc.

There is also the practice of visit to the institutions of higher learning by recruiting and selection teams of the leading firms to select boys and girls of recognised and proven ability. Thus, the most brilliant and meritorious get into good jobs without any difficulty.

20. Meetings. Meetings of staff of institutions and employers can also go a long way in bringing them closer.

QUESTIONS FOR EXERCISE

1. What are the defects in present higher education? How can these be removed?
2. What are the objectives of liaison between Institutions of Higher learning and world of work? How can close liaison be achieved?

24

Job Analysis

Job analysis is a detailed and systematic study of jobs to know the nature and characteristics of the people to be employed on various jobs. It involves collections of necessary facts regarding job and their analysis.

DEFINITION OF JOB ANALYSIS

1. **John A. Shbim.** "Job analysis is the methodical compilation and study of work data in order to define and characterise each occupation, in such a manner as to distinguish it from all others."

2. **Scott Clothier and Spriegal.** "Job analysis is the process of critically evaluating the operations, duties and responsibilities of the job."

3. **Edwin B. Flippo.** "Job analysis is the process of studying and collecting information relating to the operations and responsibilities of a specific job."

4. **Michael J. Jucius.** "Job analysis refers to the process of studying the operations, duties and organisational aspects of jobs in order to derive specifications, or as they are called by some, Job descriptions."

5. **Dale Yeder.** "Job analysis is the procedure by which the facts with respect to each job are systematically discovered and noted.... A job description is a systematic outline of information gained from notes taken and recorded in the job analysis report."

Thus, job analysis is a process by which job, duties and responsibilities are defined and the information of various factors relating to jobs are collected and compiled to determine the work conditions, nature of work, qualities of person to be employed on job, position of the job, opportunities available and authorities and privileges to be given on the job, etc. Its purpose is to describe and define the distinctions among various jobs in the organisation and their relationship.

Job Description and Job Specification

The requirements of job are known as Job description and the qualities demanded from the job holder are termed as Job specifications.

Thus, job description and job specification are two products of job analysis.

JOB ANALYSIS PROCESS

1. Collection of factual material. The first step in job analysis process is to collect the factual information relating to job. The four currently most popular approaches utilised in studying a job are : (i) questionnaires, (ii) narrative descriptions, (iii) observations and (iv) interviews. Two types of information are collected, *i.e.,* (i) information regarding job such as its physical environment (temperature, noise, dirt, comforts and dangers, etc.) its social environment (whether job is in teams, shifts or isolated), financial conditions (wages, bonus, incentive schemes of fringe benefits, etc.) and (ii) information relating to qualities of persons holding the job *i.e.,* his physical demands (muscular energy, hours of work, travel, etc.), intellectual demands (university, technical or professional degrees and problem solving abilities required). Skills experience and personality factors required on the job.

2. Completing job description blank. After collecting information the job analysis puts such information in a standard job description form as a comprehensive draft. It is a statement showing full details of the activities of the job. Separate job description forms may be used for various activities in the job and may be compiled later on. The job analysis is made with the help of these job description forms which may be used as references for the future.

3. Preparation of job specification. Job specifications are prepared on the basis of information collected. It is a statement of minimum acceptable qualities of the person to be placed on job. It specifies the standard by which the qualities of the person are measured. Job analyst prepares such statement taking into consideration the skills, required in performing the job properly.

4. Preparation of report. The job analyst prepares a report on the basis of information collected mentioning the analysis of various activities on the job and the qualities of the individual to be placed on the job. Report will be presented before the supervisor and the personnel manager for suggestions and comments. The analyst should revise the original report in the light of the suggestions or comments given by the supervisor or the personnel manager to make it more correct and informative.

5. Approval. The complete draft presented by the analyst and approved by the supervisor and personnel manager may now be received by the top executive. If union officials have ideas for making changes, management should consider them as suggestions and incorporate such changes, if possible, in the job description and job specification. The final draft should be approved by the top line executive or by the personnel manager who is responsible for making final decisions on the matter.

SIGNIFICANCE OR USES OF JOB ANALYSIS

1. Manpower planning. Job analysis is the qualitative aspect of manpower requirements because it determines the demands of the job in terms of responsibilities and duties and then translate these demands in terms of skills, qualities and other human attributes. It also determines the quantum of work which an average person can perform on the job in a day. It facilitates the division of work into different jobs. Thus, it is an essential element of manpower planning because it matches jobs with men.

2. Recruitment, selection and placement. In order to hire a right person on the job, it is essential to know the requirements of the job and the qualities of the individual who will perform it. This information is procured from job description and job specifications respectively and help the management in matching as closely as possible the job requirements with workers' aptitudes, abilities, interests, etc., to facilitate the execution of employment programme.

3. Training and development. Job analysis determines the levels of standard of job performance. It helps administering the training development programme. If the contents of job descriptions and job specifications are known to the employees, they will try to their level best to achieve the skills, and knowledge required to perform the task assigned to them efficiently. They may also prepare themselves for the higher post. The same information may be used by those who administer the training and development programmes by determining the contents and subject matter needed in such programmes.

4. Job evaluation. Job analysis provides a basis for job evaluation. Job evaluation aims at determining the relative worth of the job which in turn helps in determining the compensation of job. An accurate and comprehensive set of job descriptions and job specifications forms a factual basis for evaluating the worth of the job.

5. Performance appraisal. Job analysis data provide a clear-cut standard of performance for every job. The performance of employee can be appraised objectively with the standard of job performance so established. A supervisor can very easily compare the contribution of each man with the set standards.

6. Job designing. Industrial engineers use the job analysis information in designing the job by making the comprehensive study of the job elements. It helps in time and motion study, work specifications, methods and work-place improvement and work-measurement. Human engineering activities such as physical, mental and psychological are studied with the help of job analysis information.

7. Safety and health. The job analysis process uncovers the hazardous and unhealthy environmental factors such as heat, noise, fumes, dust, etc. The management can take corrective measures to minimise the chances of various risks to ensure safety to workers and to avoid unhealthy conditions.

8. Discipline. Job analysis provides the information regarding characteristics of various jobs and the job-holders. It studies the failure of the workman to meet the required standard of performance. Corrective measures may be taken in time to avoid untoward situation. In this way it helps in maintaining the discipline in industry.

ADVANTAGES OF JOB ANALYSIS

On the basis of 401 essays concerned with job analysis, Zerga pointed out twenty advantages and utilities of job analysis. One is the increase in efficiency, as well as increase in the mutual feelings of workers since everyone is happy to be employed in the job he cherishes. Job analysis can help to determine the salary or wages accruing to the employee for a particular function performed by him. Job analysis helps in the classification of professions and occupations, it thereby becoming possible to determine the qualities and abilities required for them. Through job analysis it also becomes possible to determine the extent of training necessary for a specific individual to be given a particular job of work. Job analysis determines the duty of everyone in his own job by determining the responsibility inherent in any kind of work.

Various Components of a Job

Now, the first thing to be mentioned in connection with job analysis is the presence of various components in a job. Headings of information collected in this connection are the following :

1. Identification of the Job.
2. Number Employed.
3. Statement of Duties.
4. Machines Used.
5. Analysis of Operations.
6. Conditions of Work.
7. Pay and Incentives.
8. Relation to Other Allied Jobs.
9. Opportunities for Transfer and Promotion.
10. Time and Nature of Training.
11. Personal Requirement :
    (a) General — Age, Sex, Nationality, Marital Status.
    (b) Physical.
    (c) Educational.
    (d) Previous Experience.
    (e) General and Special Abilities.
    (f) Temperamental and Character Requirements.

As is evident from the above list, there is extensive collection of data regarding job analysis.

Methods of Job Analysis

Of the many methods employed in job analysis, the main are the following :

1. Individual Psychographic Method.
2. Questionnaire Method.
3. Job Psychographic Method.
4. Job Analysis by Text.
5. Motion Study Method.

These methods will now be described in brief as follows :

1. Individual psychographic method. In this method, the mental peculiarities of an individual successful in a particular kind of job are examined, a list of these peculiarities prepared and this list transcribed in figure form on graph. This provides some standard of judgement in future recruitment for the same job.

2. Questionnaire method. A list of questions is prepared on the basis of the different qualities of personality concerned with the job. This list is then provided to the individuals doing that job, and they are asked to answer these questions. An analysis of the answers received helps to reveal the special qualities necessary for the job, a list of which can now be prepared. This, too, helps in the future selection of candidates for the job in question.

3. Job psychographic method. According to Viteles, there are three things essential of job psychographic method :

(a) accurate classification of mental qualities,

(b) valid method of evaluation,

(c) direct examination or analysis by trained examiners.

In this manner, in this method, some specialist analysists study the work, and they evolve a valid and standard method of evaluation. They prepare a very accurate list in which the various mental qualities required for the job are properly and reliably classified. A graph of these qualities is prepared so that selection of candidates for the job may become easier.

4. Job analysis by test. In the test method, some reliable and valid tests are performed on the basis of essential qualities and abilities; the candidates are tested for selection and suitability by these tests.

5. Motion study method. Under this method, the speed of an individual worker in performing some job and the time consumed therein are both noted. Similar examinations being performed on other individuals doing the same work, the results obtained are compared.

Such a study of speed and time helps in job analysis and classification of the workers.

Job analysis can be done by any one or more of these methods, the choice of method being governed by the situation or circumstances.

Job Families

Jobs can be grouped according to the extent to education required, the income they bring for the worker or the interest of the persons in those jobs. Given below is a list of ten job families and the kind of jobs that fall within each family :

Job Family	Kind of Jobs
1. Agricultural Worker	Farmer, dairy worker, Forest ranger.
2. Athletic	Athletic coach, games teacher, director physical education/teacher.
3. Artistic-Musical	Actor, commercial artist, music teacher, textile designer.
4. Clerical	Bank clerk, officer clerk, book-keeper, accounts clerk.
5. Literary	Critic, editor, reporter, writer.
6. Mechanical	Draughtsman, engineer, tool-maker, welder.
7. Personal Service	Aeroplane hostess, hair dresser, hotel manager, receptionist.
8. Persuasive	Advertising worker, lawyer, politician, salesman.
9. Scientific	Biologist, bacteriologist, chemist, physicist, doctor.
10. Social Service	Social worker, school counsellor, teacher.

BASIC OUTLINE OF JOB ANALYSIS

1. History of the occupation.

2. Importance of the occupation and its relation to society.

3. Number of workers engaged in the occupation.

4. Need for workers' trends.

5. Duties.

(i) *Specific tasks* : This includes other occupations with which this work may be combined nature, of work, tools, machines, and material used.

(ii) *Definition of the occupation* : This is as given by laws, as determined by official organisations, carefully formulated definition acceptable to those in the occupation.

6. Qualifications. This is concern with sex, age, race, special physical, mental, social and moral qualities, skills, special tools and equipment; legislation affecting workers.

7. Preparation. This includes general education; special training, required and desirable, schools, etc., offering training; experience.

8. Methods of entering; use of special employment agencies.

9. Length of time before skill is obtained.

10. Advancement. This includes line of promotion; opportunity for advancement.

11. Related occupation to which the job may lead.

12. Earnings. This pertains to beginning, most common, maximum, regulations.

13. Hours. This is in terms daily, weekly, overtime, shifts, vocation, regulations.

14. Regularity of Employment. This includes normal months, busy months, dull months, shut-down of plants, cyclical unemployment.

15. Health and accident hazards.

16. Organisations — employers, employees.

17. Typical places of employment.

18. Supplementary information. This is suggested readings, magazines, films, information.

TYPES OF JOB ANALYSIS

According to F. Meine, job analysis can be classified into following four types with respect to purpose :

1. Job analysis for improving working methods and processes.
2. Job analysis for protecting health and safety.
3. Job analysis for training employees.
4. Job analysis for employment purposes, *i.e.*,
   (i) in guiding pupils in selecting proper vocation;
   (ii) in helping employees to select, transfer and promote employees;
   (iii) in establishing salary schedule.

PURPOSES OF JOB ANALYSIS

1. To assist in knowing the personnel specifications for various jobs.

2. To help in bringing together the right worker for the right job.

3. To help in job satisfaction and job efficiency.

4. To assist in the accurate determination of job opportunities for various types of manpower in the industries.

5. To help in planning appropriate training programmes.

6. To define labour needs in specific terms.

SOURCES OF INFORMATION IN JOB ANALYSIS

1. Employees on the job.
2. Other employees including supervisors who know these jobs.
3. Independent observers who watch employees performing their jobs.

SCOPE OF JOB ANALYSIS

1. Methods and Process of Work

(i) Duties and tasks performed by the workers.
(ii) Materials and the supplies used by the workers.
(iii) Equipment, machines and tools used by the workers.
(iv) Description of the place of work.
(v) Methods and procedures employed in carrying out the work.
(vi) Responsibilities of the workers.
(vii) Supervision exercised.
(viii) Standard of output.

2. Work Environment (Physical Conditions)

(i) Place of work (Inside or outside).
(ii) Condition of illumination.
(iii) Condition of ventilation.
(iv) Condition of noise.
(v) Cleanliness.
(vi) Any dangerous and unhealthful aspect.
(vii) Congestion.
(viii) Accessibility (transport) to the place of work.

3. Conditions of Employment

(i) Methods of selection of employees.
(ii) Use of interviews and tests, etc.
(iii) Transfers from one job to another.
(iv) Working hours.
(v) Remuneration and its methods of payment.
(vi) Permanent or otherwise nature of the job.
(vii) Opportunities of advancement and promotion.

4. General Environment

(i) Relationships among the workers.
(ii) Behaviour of the management, *i.e.,* autocratic or humanistic.

5. Relation of Job to Other Jobs

(i) Relation of job to other jobs.
(ii) Coordination of work of the job with other jobs.

JOB DESCRIPTION

Definition

1. **Date Yoder.** "Job description is the sum total of the facts relating to what is being done on the job and what type of employees are needed."

2. **Dictionary of occupational titles.** "A job description is a definition of a particular job. The definition is divided into four parts : first, the main job title; second, identification of the industry in which the job occurs; third, occupational code number and fourth, the job description, what actually a worker does."

3. **Edwin B. Flippo.** "The first and immediate product of the job analysis is the job description. As its title indicates, this document is basically descriptive in nature and constitutes a record of existing and pertinent job facts."

4. **Pigors and Myres.** "Job description is a pertinent picture (in writing) of the organisational relationship, responsibilities and specific duties that constitute a given job or position. It defines a scope of responsibility and continuing work assignment that are sufficiently different from those of other job to warrant a specific title."

The job description document discloses what, how and why it is to be done. It classifies the job into various sub-jobs and analyse the nature of each such sub-jobs.

Contents of Job Description

1. **Proper job title.** The job title should be short, definite and suggestive of the nature of the job. The desirable qualities of job-holder should also be clear from the title so that every job should be distinguished from one another. Commerce and industry nomenclature, wherever applicable should always be considered in phrasing meaningful job titles.

2. **Job summary.** The findings of the job analysis should be summarised so that all the necessary facts may be incorporated in paragraphs to make it convenient to identify the job. It would clear the nature of the job. Primary, secondary and other duties to be performed, on the job should clearly be indicated separately.

3. **Job location.** It should also be given in the description where the job is to be performed *i.e.,* in what department.

4. **Duties and responsibilities.** These are to be performed on the job with proper classification as primary, secondary and other duties should clearly be written in the job description. Time taken in performing the job and sub-jobs should also be mentioned. The duties and responsibilities, as far as possible should be arranged in chronological order.

5. **Nature of supervision.** The degree of supervision required on each job should also be mentioned. While unskilled jobs require close

supervision other jobs like skilled or supervisory or managerial job require less supervision or no supervision.

6. Machines, tools and materials. The machines, tools, equipment and material required in the performance of each job included in job description will indicate the nature and complexity of the job and will help devising the training programmes.

7. Relation to other jobs. It intensifies the vertical relationship of promotion and horizontal relationship of work-flow and procedures.

8. Working conditions. The working conditions on the job hazards and physical surroundings within the working area should be described to help in job evaluation.

9. Elasticity. It should be elastic enough as to incorporates from time to time to make it uptodate.

10. The policies of the job-holder. These should be mentioned clearly.

In preparing the job description all points should be described in short but complete in all respects. Every item should be exactly worded.

Preparing Job Description

Job description provides the data of the job in terms of duties and responsibilities. In order to prepare the documents, the detailed information is collected about job title, job summary, duties and responsibilities, etc., through any of the techniques of the job analysis and compiled in a well-designed bank in an organised manner. Separate blanks are filled for each job. Blank is a descriptive document mentioning each and every aspect of the job in detail. It is a precis of the details collected by the job-analyst. It is a record for future reference and guidance.

Characteristics of a Good Job Description

1. Uptodate. Necessary amendments and adjustments should be made from time to time.

2. Job title. It should be short, definite and suggestive as to indicate the nature of the work.

3. Primary, secondary and other duties and responsibilities should clearly be defined.

4. Clear Job specifications. It should be clearly mentioned.

5. Descriptive but short. Limitations of each and sub-job should be spelt out clearly in order to meet the objectives of the job.

6. Understandable. All employees must know the contents of the job description.

Job acceptable should be easily understandable special work conditions and special qualifications of the job should be clearly explained in job description.

JOB SPECIFICATION

Job specification is also the product of job analysis. It is a statement of acceptable human qualities necessary to perform the job. It specifies the type of person required in terms of educational qualifications, experience, aptitude, etc., on the job and further assists in the selection of appropriate personnel by outlining the particular working conditions to be encountered on the job. Job specification has been defined by various authors as follows :

1. Edwin B. Flippo. "A job specification is a statement of minimum acceptable human qualities necessary to perform a job properly."

2. Dale Voder. "The job specification, as such a summary popularly described, is thus a specialised job description, emphasising personal requirement and designed especially to facilitate selection and placement."

It is clear from the above definitions that job specification is a statement of summary of personnel requirements for a job. It may also be called 'standard of personnel for the selection'.

JOB IDENTIFICATION

In this classification an effort is made to identify the job without describing the duties in detail. It includes the title of the job and the department of an organisation in which it is included.

It may also incorporate the job classification code number. Usually two types of code numbers are being used. NCO is very popular. According to it, occupations are divided into the following categories :

(i) The Industrial Classification of the Labour (ICL).

(ii) The National Classification of Occupation (NCO).

Occupational Division		Description of Occupation
0	———	Professional, Technical.
1	———	Administrative, Executive.
2	———	Clerical and Related Worker.
3	———	Skilled Workers.
4	———	Farmers and Fishermen.
5	———	Mineman and Quarryman.
6	———	Workers in Transport and Communication.
7 & 8	———	Craftsman and Production Process Workers.
9	———	Services, Sports and Production Process Workers.
10	———	Unskilled Workers.

JOB SUMMARY

The job summary provides a brief of the entire job. It gives the scope and purpose of the job. It gives an overall statement about the duties. It performs a very important function in connection with an understanding of the job description as a whole. It must be drafted very carefully and in accordance with the procedure laid down :

1. **The statement.** It should be brief and precise.

2. **Meaning.** It should mean only one thing at a time.

3. **Vocabulary.** It should be selected very carefully and scientifically.

4. **The language.** It should be such as differentiates very carefully one job from other jobs.

5. **The purpose of the job.** It should be clearly mentioned.

6. **The important functions performed on the job.** These should be brought out in detail so as to make them clearly distinct from other jobs.

7. **What, how and why.** It must be in conformity with the what, how and why of the job analysis formula.

8. **General terms.** Use of the general terms which can be interpreted in many ways should be avoided.

9. **Final.** Job summary should be written when all parts of the job description are completed first.

10. **Methods.** Different methods are used in preparing job summaries in a specific firm for a specific job and in an industry.

JOB REQUIREMENTS

According to Jones, following are the important elements that should be taken into consideration in making a choice of job :

1. Suitability for the occupation, involving ability, physical, and mental characteristics and aptitude.

   (i) What standard of physical qualities like strength, endurance, hearing, eyesight, etc., are needed for the job?

   (ii) What is the minimum requirement I.Q. needed?

   (iii) What is the minimum requirement of the job as regards emotional stability?

   (iv) To what extent are the qualities like leadership, etc., needed?

2. Service to society.

3. Interest in the occupation.

4. Satisfaction in the work.

5. Financial returns, immediate and future.

6. Opportunity for employment.

7. Opportunity for advancement.

8. Health conditions.
9. Social conditions.
10. Nature of the work.

1. Service to society. The child should be trained not to be selfish, not to get his own way and not to think only for himself so that we may expect him to choose an occupation for service. If he is trained in this way, his choice will not surely be primarily for financial gains. There is a great need for the development of this attitude in the prospective worker.

2. Job satisfaction. It may be satisfaction, with pay, the general surroundings, the social position, or all of these combined. Actually job satisfaction can come only after one has entered in the job.

3. Financial returns. This is the only or dominant reason for choice of an occupation in the present materialistic society. Sufficient stress should be laid so that ultimate rather than immediate financial returns of an occupation are taken into consideration. "All that glitters is not gold," is an old proverb and should be needed to in the choice of an occupation.

4. Opportunity for employment. It is not advisable to choose an occupation which has limited employment opportunities. Under exceptional circumstances when an individual is favourably placed, the choice of an occupation when the opportunity is very small may be justified.

5. Opportunity for advancement. In the choice of an occupation it is important whether or not an individual can have the opportunities of going from lower ranks to higher ranks. There are occupations in which departmental examinations are conducted which afford opportunities to the enterprising employees to go up. Such occupation should be preferred.

6. Health conditions. The health conditions of the environment in which an individual has to work and also the health of the individual should be taken into consideration before making a choice.

7. Social environment. The type of locality and the social surrounding should also influence the choice. Other things remaining the same, an individual would like to work where people speak the same language, have same manners, customs, traditions, etc.

8. Suitable nature of work. (1) Is the work repetitive or varied? (2) What is the moral duty of the worker? (3) Is the work mental or physical or both? (4) Is the work mainly indoor or outdoor or both? (5) Does the work involve sitting, standing, etc.?

9. Timing of choice. Divergent opinions have been expressed as to when the choice of an occupation is to be made, *i.e.*, whether it is to be made before entering high school, college or before finishing college education. No rigid rule can be laid down but choice should be made before the child leaves school. The child should be advised not to rush the choice : he should rather go slow and very cautiously.

WHY IS A PERSON REJECTED?

1. Poor personal appearance.
2. Over-aggressive, 'know-it-all' attitude.
3. Inability to express oneself clearly — poor voice, etc.
4. Lack of interest and enthusiasm.
5. Lack of confidence and poise.
6. Poor scholastic record.
7. Lack of maturity.
8. Lack of courtesy.
9. Condemnation of past employers.
10. Lack of vitality.
11. Failure to look interviewer in the eye.
12. Indecision.
13. Sloppy application blank.
14. Wanting job only for a short time.
15. Little sense of humour.
16. Lack of knowledge in field of specialisation.
17. Unwillingness to go where sent.
18. Overcritical of others.
19. Inability to take criticism.
20. Late to interview without good reason.
21. Indefinite response to questions.

HOW TO HOLD THE JOB?

1. Take a genuine interest in the job.
2. Learn it completely.
3. Perform duties efficiently.
4. Be a willing worker.
5. Be friendly with co-workers.
6. Show loyalty and allegiance to the employer.
7. Be regular and punctual in performing duty.
8. Do not criticise fellow-workers or superiors.
9. Follow the directions given by the officers.
10. Offer suggestions only when asked for.

RATING FOR SELECTING A JOB

After an individual has collected information about a job if he is holding any or another job if he has to decide between the two jobs, a sort of 3-point rating scale given below will facilitate to rate the two jobs. Out of three words in column II, one is to be retained, and the other two deleted. In column III the same procedure is to be followed.

I Item	II About the Job	III For Comparison
	Outstanding, Satisfactory, Unsatisfactory	Better/Same/Worse
1. Nature of Duties.		
2. Working Conditions (Physical).		
3. Working Conditions (Social).		
4. Income (pay, allowances and other benefits).		
5. Promotions (without adding to qualifications).		
6. Promotions (adding qualifications or by passing departmental examination).		
7. Stability of the employer and possibilities of expansion of department of organisation.		

JOB SATISFACTION

Job satisfaction is the whole matrix of job factors that make a person 'like' his work situation and be 'willing' to head for it without distaste at the beginning of his work day.

Characteristics of job satisfaction

1. Liking and enjoying the job.
2. Going to one's with head erect and with smiles.
3. Successful adjustment in the following three areas :
   (i) Adjustment to Self.
   (ii) Adjustment to Society.
   (iii) Adjustment to Work.

1. Personal Factors

(i) *Sex* : Generally women are more satisfied with their jobs than men due to the fact that women's financial needs and ambitions are less.

(ii) *Number of dependants* : The more the dependents the lesser the job satisfaction.

(iii) *Age* : Age has little relationship with job satisfaction.

(iv) *Time on job* : According to Hall and Kolstad, the highest morale is reached after the 20th year.

(v) *Intelligence* : Better level of one's intelligence more in the job satisfaction.

(vi) *Education* : Right placement of workers in the light of their professional education leads to job satisfaction.

(vii) *Personality* : Personality maladjustment is the source of job dissatisfaction.

2. Factors Inherent in the Job

(i) Types of work.

(ii) Skills required.

(iii) Occupational status.

(iv) Size of plant.

3. Factors Controlled by Management Authority (Government)

(i) Security.

(ii) Pay.

(iii) Fringe benefits.

(iv) Opportunities for advancement.

(v) Working conditions.

(vi) Co-workers.

QUESTIONS FOR EXERCISE

1. What is job analysis? Show its significance in a guidance programme.
2. What factors should be kept in view while entering into an occupation?
3. On what factors does job satisfaction depend?
4. Explain the following :
   (i) Job.
   (ii) Job families.
   (iii) Job description.
   (iv) Job identification.
5. State the factors on which the choice of a job depends.
6. Write short note on Job satisfaction.
7. What is job analysis? How should it be performed? Evaluate its significance in personnel management.
8. "Job analysis is the process of critically evaluating the operations, duties and relationship of the job." Elucidate this statement.

25

EDUCATIONAL GUIDANCE

DEFINITION OF EDUCATIONAL GUIDANCE

1. Arthur E. Traxler. "Guidance enables each individual to understand his abilities, interests, and personality traits, to develop them as well as possible to relate them to his life goals and finally to reach a state of complete and mature self-guidance as desirable citizen of a democratic social order. Guidance is thus vitally related to every aspect of the school, the curriculum, the methods of instruction, the supervision of instruction, disciplinary procedure, attendance problems of scheduling, the extra-curricular, the health and physical fitness programme, and home and community relating."

2. Brewer. "Educational guidance is a conscious effort to assist in the intellectual growth of individual — anything that has to do with instruction or with learning may come under the term of guidance."

3. Dunsmoor and Miller. "Guidance as a form of systematic assistance whereby students are aided in achieving satisfactory adjustment of school and life."

4. Dr. K.G. Rama Rao. "Guidance in the wider context of a total curriculum and embracing education of everyone of the basic activity pattern — intellectual as well as social, economic as well as artistic, moral as well as spiritual, domestic as well as physical — becomes all inclusive as well as competes with instructional and testing or examining functions of the school in preparing the school-leavers for work and life in general."

5. G.E. Myers. "Educational guidance is a process concerned with bringing about between an individual pupil with his distinctive characteristics on the one hand, and differing groups of opportunities and requirements on the other, a favourable setting for the individual's development or education. If there is a single group, of opportunities and requirements, as is the case with a fixed curriculum, the problem is simply one of the education by the best methods possible in a setting already determined and not of educational guidance."

6. Jones. "Educational guidance is the assistance given to the pupils in their choices and adjustments with relation to schools, curriculums, courses and school life."

7. Ruth Strong. "Educational guidance is positive. It is a developmental programme concerned with the questions. What is this boy or girl good for? What kind of education will reveal his capacities and help him to develop them? Educational guidance is intended to aid the individual in choosing an appropriate programme and in making progress in it. This involves (1) knowledge of the abilities and interests of the individual, (2) awareness of wide range of educational opportunities and (3) programmes and counselling which help the individual to choose wisely on the basis of these two kinds of knowledge."

8. Shirley, Hamrin and Clifforde Erickson. "Guidance in the secondary school refers to that aspect of the education programme which is concerned especially with helping the pupil to become adjusted to his present situation and to plan his future in line with his interests, abilities and social needs. Guidance or personal work represents an organised effort on the part of the school, equipped with both a knowledge of the pupil and information as to opportunities, of an educational, a social and vocational character to help the individual pupil become adjusted to his present situation in such a way as to provide the greatest development for him and to aid him in planning for his future. It is rightly said that this programme helps John see through himself and then to assist him in seeing himself through."

STAGES OF EDUCATIONAL GUIDANCE

1. Kindergarten stage. According to Jones, "The more comprehensive view of guidance makes it imperative that guidance be incorporated in the educational programme beginning with kindergarten." School guidance work should not be considered chiefly a function of the high and higher secondary schools. It is equally important in the early life of the child.

The chief functions of educational guidance at the kindergarten stage is to help the child adjust himself to the new life of the school which is regimented and not as free as the home life. Guidance is directed towards the development of personality, social behaviour and problems concerning learning. The classroom teacher acts both the teacher and the counsellor. He discovers the children who are dependent, shy, easily frightened, over-aggressive, quarrelsome, gifted or otherwise. By organising activities and by contact with home the teacher gradually helps the shy and over dependent child to overcome his handicaps. "Every teacher is a guidance worker" and guidance occurs minute by minute, hour by hour, and day by day in every classroom of every school.

2. Elementary and middle school stages. At this stage 'Guidance in Schools' (1978) a publication of NCERT has explained the role of guidance in these words, "Nothing gives a better realisation of the close relationship between education and guidance than a study of its functions at the elementary stage. Educationists from time immemorial have emphasised the importance of the early years of child's life in the development of habits, attitudes, interests, and personality qualities, which would be required to live a healthy and well-balanced personal-social-life. The foundations of the future personality, it is said, are laid during the first few years of the child's life. A comprehensive educational programmed at this stage must, therefore, include besides instruction, in the narrower sense, those programmes which are directed in a conscious manner towards the development of good habits and right attitudes. This is not the task of instruction *per se* but that of guidance which alone can fulfil these purposes of education par excellence. A programme of education which will help the child explore his talents, and thus improve his understanding of himself, is the sine qua non of all future guidance. The child has also to be oriented to new modes of living and thinking which will become the corner-stone of his habits and attitudes. Further, he has to be helped to adjust himself to an expanding environment both within the school and outside. He has also to be helped through a varied programmed of conicular and co-curricular activities to develop, in systematic way, his basic potentialities which would be important from the point of view of the individual as well as from that of the society. It may be mentioned here that potentialities either do not develop or have a stunted in a restricted and poor environment. A less intelligent child is often one who has been derived of those opportunities in his environment, which are basic to an optimum development of intelligence. Difficulties in reading, writing and computation are often due to faulty development of these basic skills at home and in school. A carefully thought out programme of guidance has to be introduced at the elementary stage so that the development needs of the child are adequately met."

FUNCTIONS OF EDUCATIONAL GUIDANCE

1. Making a good beginning. At the primary stage of education, pupils need guidance to help them making a good beginning. Some pupils drop out at the end of the primary or the middle stage, because of the lack of incentive for further studies. They do not blow the possibilities that a good and complete education can open before them. A good educational guidance programme in elementary schools prevents these children from early leaving and thus paves the way for a better utilisation of human resources.

2. Planning intelligently. Each child has to make his choice of subjects when he enters the higher secondary stage. It is essential that each child prepare well for this important step in life during the middle school years. Enough opportunity has to be afforded to each child to try out and explore his abilities, aptitudes and interests, and to relate them to the type of courses available in the secondary school. An intelligent understanding of the nature of these courses and their vocational implications is necessary before final choice is made at the end of the middle school stage. With a knowledge of the vocational implications of these courses, the child may relate his educational choices to his vocational goals and aspirations which are often at variance.

3. Getting the best out of education. Sometimes some specific difficulties are at the root of poor achievement. Some diagnostic devices will have to be used for the purpose. Guidance at this stage is not a special service programme. It permeates the work of every teacher.

4. Secondary stage. It acquaints students with the nature and purpose of the higher/senior secondary school curriculum through : (i) class talks, (ii) exploratory and try-out courses where possible. It assists them in making an appraisal of their own abilities, skills and interests, and to relate them with the curricular courses in the higher secondary school. It acquaints them with the vocational implications of the various courses of study. It informs them of the schools in the locality or region which offer some particular course or courses not available in the school in question. It provide information about polytechnical or university education which the school leavers may like to take up.

5. Higher/senior secondary stage. There is a marked difference in the curriculum of an elementary and secondary school and that of a higher secondary school. Curriculum of a Higher Secondary School is a diversified one which involves the problem of selecting subjects in class XI. Important decisions are to be made in class XI and class XII. In class XI the selection of subjects is largely influenced by vocational requirements. Help is needed when the students are about to leave the school either to secure jobs or to go to college or to some other types of further training.

Objectives at the Secondary School Level

1. To assist him to secure information regarding the possibility and desirability of further schooling.

2. To help him to know the purpose and functions of the different types of schools.

3. To enable him to know in detail the offering of the school that he might attend.

4. To assist him to know the requirements for entrance into the school of his choice.

5. To help him to adjust himself to the curriculum, the school and the social life connected with it. This help is given in the following areas :

(i) The selection of subjects.

(ii) The selection of books for each subject.

(iii) In developing study habits.

(iv) In making satisfactory progress in various school subjects.
(v) In selecting hobbies.
(vi) In the selection of co-curricular activities.
(vii) In knowing the availability of scholarships, loans, etc.
(viii) To find out his tastes, aptitudes and interests.
(ix) To build good social relationships.

6. To help him in the selection of a vocation.

7. To acquaint him about the various openings available after finishing the school career.

8. To help him to find out his physical, mental and emotional handicaps and then to treat them.

RECOMMENDATIONS OF THE EDUCATION COMMISSION

1. Aim and scope of guidance services. Guidance services have a much wider scope and function than merely assisting students in making educational and vocational choices. Their aims are both adjustive and developmental. They help the student in making the best possible adjustment to the situations in the educational institution and in the home. They facilitate the development of all aspects of his personality. Guidance as an integral part of education and not a special psychological or social service peripheral to educational purposes. It is meant for all students, not just for those who deviate from the norm in one direction or the other. It is a continuous process aimed at assisting the individual to make decisions and adjustments from time to time.

2. Guidance in primary school. Guidance should begin from the lowest class of the primary school for helping pupils to make a satisfactory transition from home to school for diagnosing difficulties in the learning of basic educational skills; in identifying pupils in need of special education (*e.g.*, the gifted, the backward, the physically handicapped); for helping potential drop-outs to stay in school; in guiding pupils to develop insight into the world of work and favourable attitudes towards work; and for assisting in plans for their further education or training. Little has been done so far in the shape of guidance services at the primary stage because of the large numbers of institutions involved, the poor qualifications of the teachers and the absence of resources. It would, therefore, be unrealistic for a long time to come to think of providing qualified counsellors on these schools. Some guidance functions can, however, be performed by well-trained primary school teachers. Community resources can also be mobilised to meet some of the guidance needs of the young pupils. Following suggestions may be used making a beginning in guidance in the primary school :

(i) *Training programme* : The training programme for primary school teachers should include familiarising them with simple diagnostic testing and with the problem of individual differences and the implications of these differences for classroom practices.

(ii) *Lecturer* : There should be at least one lecturer in the training school who should be able to deal with the subject of principles of guidance and mental hygiene.

(iii) *Training school* : Guidance services should be introduced in the training institutions and schools attached to the institutions so that the trainees may get first-hand knowledge of the problems involved in their organisation.

(iv) *Short in-service courses* : Wherever possible, short in-service courses in guidance should be provided for the primary school teachers.

(v) *Literature* : Simple literature for the occupational orientation of children may be prepared and made available in the regional languages.

At the end of primary stage, children and parents should be helped in the selection of courses for further education and the selection should be based on the examination results alone.

3. Guidance in secondary education. The main function of guidance at the secondary level is to aid in the identification and development of the abilities and interests of adolescent pupils. It helps pupils to understand their own strengths and limitations and to do scholastic work at the level of their ability; to gain information about educational and vocational opportunities and requirements; to make realistic educational and vocational choices and plan based on a consideration of all relevant factors; and to find solution to their problems of personal and social adjustments in the school and the home. It also helps headmasters and teachers to understand their students as individuals and to create situations in which the students can learn more effectively.

4. The role of the counsellor in the education of the talented. With his detailed knowledge of each talented student the counsellor is in a unique position formulate a programme of enrichment for him and to suggest the necessary modifications in the curricular and extra-curricular requirements. This task will fall on the teachers where special counsellor are not available. It is, therefore, necessary to train teachers for this responsibility through in-service seminars and special courses. The classroom atmosphere and the attitudes of teachers is of considerable importance. The first requirement for the promotion of talent is for the teachers to create an atmosphere of free expression in the class and to provide opportunities for creative work.

5. Guidance and the education of the backward. Guidance and counselling services have an important role to play in the education of the backward, with regard to identification of the group, diagnosis of their special defects and planning for their education and future occupation. The essential factor for the success of the programme is the co-ordinated approach that the entire school faculty should make to the problem of these children with a degree of sympathy and understanding and with an insight into child psychology born out of long experience. The teacher should be able to give some help to the under-achievers. Parent-teacher associations should be mobilised for enlisting cooperation of parents in dealings with special cases. There should be at least one adequately staffed child guidance clinic in each major town. Serious cases of backwardness should be referred to these clinics for diagnosis and remedial help.

6. At the college stage. A guidance and counselling programme, assisting the students in the choice of courses, indicating the lines of remedial action and helping in dealing with educational and psychological problem is an integral part of the educational facilities provided in institutions of higher education. It would be necessary to have at least one counsellor for every one thousand students on the roll. Smaller institutions may share a counsellor who may work in each of the institutions on a part-time basis. The organisation of such a service requires a large number of professionally trained counsellors. Hence a project for their training should be organised in some university competent to do so.

The employment, information and guidance bureaux of the National Employment Service have been collecting, compiling and making available to the students occupational and employment market information, information regarding preparation for different careers, training facilities, apprenticeships, scholarships, etc. They have also been placing students in employment. In the absence of counselling services with fully qualified counsellors, they have also been offering advice and help to the students in planning their careers. The student advisory bureaux originally set up by the Ministry of Education to provide information regarding facilities for higher education abroad, are now providing information regarding facilities in India. Since educational and occupational information is closely inter-linked, it is recommended that these bureaus may be combined to form an information and employment centre which should function directly under the supervision of the Dean of students.

NATURE OF EDUCATIONAL GUIDANCE

1. Educational guidance is administered to students. Out of the many problems that the students is often faced with, there are some that he fails to solve of his own accord, and these do not even admit of any fruitful assistance from the teachers or the parents. Solution of these problems calls for the intervention of the specialist, and this specialist is none other than the psychologist.

2. Intended for educational selection. One part of the student's education consists in making a variety of selections, the first of them being the kind of college or school in which he would like to be educated. Then he has to follow this in the selection of the curriculum that he imagines will be suitable for him. Another problem that confronts him is the choice of the subjects that he wishes to study. It must also be remembered in this connection that normal kind of curriculum is not suitable for either morons, brilliant children or for the backward children. The child himself has normally no way to telling whether he is moron, a brilliant chap or a backward person. This is something that the psychologist alone can discover through his psychological examination. Hence, the need of guidance in this respect.

3. Rendered for adjustment in education. A student finds a peculiar atmosphere in the college, the like of which he cannot find outside, and he has to adjust himself to this atmosphere. This atmosphere is a composite of his friends, teachers, daily routine of the institution, method of teaching, curriculum, subjects taught, extra-curricular programmes, etc. This environment is the same for every individual students, whatever his personal capability or drawback. Evidently, and, as a result, problems of adjustment arise. One student finds the teaching terribly dull while his more enterprising partner runs away from school. Another child might find himself tired most of the time while another is constantly bored stiff. Some of them indulge in systematically destroying discipline while others turn of crime and delinquency. Educational guidance is rendered for the solution of such problems that arise in the educative process.

INDIVIDUAL EDUCATIONAL GUIDANCE

The following information concerning the individual is required in the individual educational guidance method :

1. Scholastic attainments. As a general rule, if one is to discover these holistic achievements of the students all that is necessary is to secure the results obtained in the various tests or examinations taken by him. But sometimes attainment tests are also given to secure more reliable information on this point.

2. Personality characteristics. Problems of adjustment and selection concerning education are influenced in an important way by personality characteristics. Hence the psychologist gathers facts of this through astute testing.

3. Interest. Selection in connection with important elements in education such as curriculum, subjects, extra-curricular programmes, etc., depends upon the individual's interests. Hence, in educational guidance, interests of the individual are determined through tests and lists of interests.

4. Level of intelligence. Different subjects required differing levels in intelligence for successful study. Hence, intelligence tests are given to the student to discover his level of intelligence.

5. Special mental abilities. Selection of curricular subjects requires that attention be paid not only to the level of intelligence but also to special mental abilities. For example, literal subjects require verbal felicity, memory, mathematical ability, logic, flow of thought, etc., while creative subjects require speed in perception, spatial ability, artistic ability, etc. Different tests have been devised to discover different mental abilities.

6. Aptitude. Educational guidance requires that the student's aptitude also be known.

7. Health and physical development. Many of the problems of adjustment that arise, in fact, originate in problematic health and physical development. Hence, it is essential that the selection of curriculum, subjects and extra-curricular activities for the student should take into account his health and physical development. For example, students taking up the study of agriculture should be study of body and strong of will.

8. Family background and economic condition. Many of the problem of adjustment that appear in the college are in fact born in the family. Hence guidance concerning them requires knowledge of the family background. Similarly, many of the educational problems that arise have an intimate relation with the student's economic condition. It is within the pale of possibility that a student may not have been able to select a desirable and suitable curriculum only because of his economic condition. In such conditions a scholarship should be provided, if the student be deserving.

Having gathered the above mentioned variety and quantity of information concerning the student, the next step in educational guidance is to collect useful information about the curriculum, subjects taught, the college and other allied matters. A psychologist keeps fairly extensive information concerning these things at his disposal. Nowadays colleges specialise in the teaching of specific subjects. Agricultural colleges impart knowledge of agricultural techniques and all that there is to know on the subject while technical institutions or colleges impart technical training. Engineering and medical colleges teach their respective subjects. Besides these, there are some multipurpose colleges that take up the simultaneous teaching of technical subjects along with the sciences as well as humanities. The psychologist keeps extensive information concerning all such colleges, their individual curriculum, their subjects and atmosphere, etc. In educational guidance his function is to help the student to make a choice of curriculum, subjects to be studied and a college, according to his abilities and aptitudes.

GROUP EDUCATIONAL GUIDANCE

Besides individual guidance, educational guidance is also rendered in the form of group guidance. Following are the steps in group guidance :

1. Orientation talks. These talks or lectures, as is apparent from the term, establish a proper orientation for guidance. Before turning to actual group guidance the psychologist first lectures the group on the importance of guidance and encourages them to collect information on the various adjuncts of educational guidance to be rendered.

2. Psychological testing. Following the lecture, the members of the group are then subjected to psychological testing in order to gain some data on their general and individual intelligence, mental abilities, interests, aptitudes and personality.

3. Collection of data from the school. A considerable fund of useful information concerning the child is normally available from his school. His scholarly achievement is usually epitomised in the marks that he obtains in the various regular tests held in the class, while interview with the teachers reveals much of the child's general behaviour, interest, personality, etc. And in most cases, teacher is the only reliable source of such information. The small confined circle that child has in school is a mine and treasure of information for the psychologist.

4. Collection of data from the family. The next step is consolidation of information by applying to the child's family. Parents and other members of the family have usually been with the child ever since his birth, and are thereby in a position to reveal many very interesting and unique facts to the psychologist, he being able to make much of them. And for them it is a personal matter as they are anxious to solve the child's difficulties. In addition to the report of the child's nature given to him by the parents and relatives, the psychologist also tries to discover the family's economic, cultural and educational status. And, in fact, many of the child's problems have their origin in his relations with his parents. Hence, it is very necessary for the psychologist to have adequate knowledge of this relationship.

5. Interview with the child. Finally, the psychologist personally interviews the child occasionally and finds out his views on his past, present and the future that he looks forward to. Self-inventory can be of much help in this respect.

6. Formation of profile. Consolidating and integrating all the above information that the psychologist has compiled a profile of the child is now constructed which supplies a good view of all the aspects of the child. Educational guidance can now be rendered on the basis of this profile.

7. Follow-up studies. Educational guidance does not end with the actual giving of advice but proceeds one step further to the follow up study of the child. Having provided the guidance and advice the psychologist keeps an eye on the child to make sure that the child is in fact benefiting from his labour. If the child fails to show any appreciable progress then he is given more tests and the necessary changes in guidance are affected.

In this manner, what educational guidance amounts to is the personal advice given by the psychologist to the child for solving various problems connected with the process of education. Educational guidance forms the basis of vocational guidance, since, the vocation that the child will ultimately select depends much upon the subjects that he chose in his period of education. Now, a person who has never studied science has the worst possible prospect for an engineer or overseer. But the process being one of reciprocity, educational guidance also depends upon vocational guidance since, once, the matriculation level of education has been attained through a more or less general pattern, choice of subjects at the intermediate and university level is determined by the profession to be followed later by the student. Thus, educational and vocational guidance are interdependent.

FUNCTIONS OF EDUCATIONAL GUIDANCE

The objective of guidance in respect of education is the solution of educational problems, helping the student select his curriculum, and to impart to him the ability to adjust to school surroundings and conditions. Mainly, the following can be said to be the objectives of educational guidance :

(1) Selection of curriculum according to ability and capability.

(2) Improvement in the method of study.

(3) Arrangement of a special method of education for the backward child.

(4) Creation of special education programmes for the gifted children.

(5) Consideration and solution of failures at examinations.

(6) Encouraging the child's inspiration to study.

(7) Removing weakness in particular subjects.

In order to clarify the outlines of educational guidance, it would be useful to go into a detailed description of the above mentioned problems.

1. Selection of curriculum according to ability and capability. Researches in psychology have established that success in education depends upon the student's judicious choice of a study curriculum that suits his capability and aptitude. In this, two factors are at work and have to be established. The first is that the student's abilities should be tested and evaluated and the second that the subjects conforming to those abilities determined. To take a simple example, it is essential that the qualities required for the study of mathematics should be known and found to exist in the student before any educational guidance can be rendered. Some definite and reliable knowledge of the various mental abilities required for the study of different distinct subjects has been established through psychological research. Now, the main thing that is to be done is to test the student and find the mental abilities that he happens of possess. This test of the student is designed to reveal his memory, intelligence, power of reasoning imagination, skill in manual work, special interests and his personality. All these various tests have been described at adequate length in the preceding chapters. In this examination while some tests are resorted to, study of the student's living environment is also undertaken. In this manner, the psychologist tests each individual case, and then advises the young student as to the educational course he should profitably pursue. Experiments have shown that advice of this nature, concerning the selection of curriculum, has not only resulted in marked improvement in examination results but has also had the effect of appreciably improving the child's or student's chances of gaining a real ability in his sphere. Educational guidance is normally required at the 8th or 10th class level. The high school or school leaving stage is divided into four courses, one in sciences, the others in the arts, agriculture and commerce. The particular course that a student is to take up has to be determined by the 8th class, by reason of which this class has been called the Delta class. As a general rule the subject that a student chooses in the 10th class is also continued late, but renewed guidance is required at this stage. In India, in particular, this is all the more necessary since at this stage the student has to decide the profession that he intends to follow and to choose a course to suit that profession. In giving educational guidance at this level, the psychologist has to keep in mind the guidance that he rendered to the same student when the latter was in the 8th class.

In rendering advice besides paying attention to the results of various tests performed upon the student it is essential to pay attention to his progress in school as well. Much information concerning school progress takes the form of annual, bi-annual and monthly test scores, educational habits regarding general discussion and play, and the teacher's evaluation of the student's personality and ability. All this information is collected in the cumulative record, which is prepared either by the teacher or by the school psychologist.

Besides the cumulative record, another source of valuable information is the Guardian's Schedule in which the parents of the students record important facts concerning the student. Besides, the student himself is required to furnish information regarding himself and the subjects that he would prefer to study at a higher level. In this manner, the student prepares a self-inventory in which he includes mention of the subjects that he prefers and others that he does not and besides mentions the profession that he finds attractive and suitable. Generally, subjects are chosen from among the following classification of a general nature :

(1) Literary,
(2) Scientific,
(3) Agricultural,
(4) Commercial,
(5) Technical,
(6) Constructive,
(7) Aesthetic.

Making use of the cumulative record, the guardian's schedule and the self-inventory, the psychologist prepares an information record, following which he interviews the student. In this interview the psychologist may also invite the parent or guardian. Following this interview the guide or psychologist offers his advice to the student. Educational guidance at the delta class level is available to almost all students in the Western countries, but, unfortunately, in India at present only a few students are in a position to benefit by this scheme of things. And the paucity of such advice is evident from the fact that a state of the size and population of Uttar Pradesh has only 25 schools that provide facilities for such guidance.

One major difference between the guidance at the 8th class level and the 10th class level is that in the former case the guidance is limited solely to the concerns of curriculum selection while in the latter stage it must also be concerned with the need for future selection of profession and career. In this manner, the educational guidance after the 10th is more of an educational, vocational nature and hence it naturally requires more information. In this, in addition to the student's educational career records such as the cumulative record, guardian's schedule and self-inventory, the teacher's rating is also solicited, and finally the student is again interviewed. What usually happens is that confronted with all this information in the form of a profile the student is himself able to choose a suitable profession and curriculum, but if for some reasons he is unable to sort out his way, the psychologist has to intervene and offer his assistance.

2. Improvement in the method of study. The other important aspect is the improvement in the study method of the individual. The study method is comprised of such factors as mode of taking notes, mode of reading, ability to summarise, method of memorising, proper division of time, arrangements for test, etc. It would be useful to go into a slightly detailed account of these factors :

(i) *Mode of taking notes* : Charles Bird has sagaciously observed that study improves if notes are taken, but taking notes on an art that is not given equally to all men. Taking notes does not involve taking down all that the teacher says or in omitting the important points. In fact, taking notes implies taking down in brief all that is said. Signs can be used as in the case of shorthand. Notes should not be so brief as to be incomprehensible on a second reading and neither should they be so extensive as to be difficult to memorising. Notes should be so designed that all important facts mentioned should be noted all extraneous or detailed explanatory matter excluded.

(ii) *Mode of reading* : Considerable research has been made in psychology concerning the mode of reading. For example, the various conditions under which and the degree to which either the whole or the part method is useful have been discovered. Reading quietly or reading aloud have their own qualities and these too have been discovered. When reading it is essential that sufficient light be available and that least disturbance be present. Speed of reading can be improved by practice and effort.

(iii) *Method of memorising* : Considerable research on the memorising of facts have been made, the following conclusions are available concerning the various methods of memorising recommended :

(a) *Recitation* : Recitation does not mean reading a piece of matter over and over again but its repetition. This has advantages over rote learning and over numerous readings. But this does not mean that making more than one reading has no advantage. In fact, recitation and repetition should go on side by side.

(b) *Part and whole methods* : In the part method the matter to be learned is divided into suitable pieces while in the whole method it is learnt as one piece. And the method that is to be used in a particular case depends upon the quantity, kind and nature of the matter as well as upon the capability of the learner. A small poem can be learnt whole but if the poem is long it is best to use the part method. Similarly, the whole method is advisable when the matter is difficult as this helps in the understanding of the various individual parts of the matter. But it is perhaps best to use both methods. In practical life, a student has to decide for himself but in choosing between the two methods he must be aware of his own capacity to learn and remember. Individuals who tire of the whole method should use the part method while others who only warm up after a short period of study would probably benefit by using the whole method.

(c) *Spaced and unspaced methods* : In the spaced method, as is evident from the name, memorising is done with intervals introduced between pieces. Contrary to this, in the unspaced method, the entire subject is tackled in single sitting. As to which method will prove more efficacious depends upon the learner's ability and the extent and nature of the subject being tackled. A small poem with no more than ten or fifteen lines can conveniently be memorised in a single sitting, but if the poem has something like 200 lines it is usually found more practicable to distribute the burden over more than one sitting.

And, there is no definite rule as to the space or time period that should be provided between two successive sittings. Roughly speaking, the only thing that can definitely be said is that the second meeting should commence only when the exhaustion of the first is completely removed, and memory impressions of it have had a chance to become permanent. In fact, the spaced method has many advantages. It not only provides opportunity for removing fatigue and creates chance for mental consideration of what has been memorised, it also reduces monotony and helps to concentrate attention upon the work in hand.

(d) *Active and passive methods* : Memorising by reading out aloud is called the active method while learning quietly without any external aid is known as the passive method. Experiments have indicated that in the active method, as compared with the passive method, attention is disturbed much less, a pattern of the subject if formed in the mind, and the various parts of it establish relations with each other. The learner is aware of all that he has in fact learned and the desire and effort of learning are retained. Yet, it may sometimes be more convenient and profitable to precede the loud reading, with a quiet reading of the subject matter.

(e) *Rote and intelligent methods* : In the rote or mechanical method the learner memorises without understanding what he is learning, whereas in the intelligent method the learner understands its meaning and comprehends it along with memorising it. Experiments and tests have shown almost conclusively that the intelligent method of learning is almost invariably better than the rote method. In it thoughts from definite associations, the subject matter sinks into the brain, and the memorising is more permanent and longer lasting. When the above methods of learning and memorising are supplemented with grouping, association and rhythmic learning it becomes possible to be much more expansive when writing on the subject. The importance to learning poetry by rhyming is known to one and all. Association helps the newly memorised subject matter to be related to that which is already in the mind and hence improves its retention. Besides, self-confidence is another important factor in memorising. Memory is further helped by mental set. The objective in learning a piece also helps its successful retention in the mind. Attention is quite essential as without it memorising is impossible. Mental commentary also helps memory. In this process the subject matter learnt is repeated in mind. Finally, apperception, or mixing newly learnt with that which is present in the mind, helps the process of memorising.

(f) *Method of summary* : Another aspect of learning that is very important is the method of summarising. The main thing in this is perception of the heart of the matter, and selection of terms that succinctly sum up all that has been said in the minimum possible number of words.

(g) *Division of time* : As has been pointed out, much benefit is to be derived by reading over divided periods of time rather than continuously. Division is also two fold — division between periods of study and rest, and division of study period according to the subject to be studied. Division of both kinds is essential.

(h) *Provision of rest* : If one rests after having read for some-time the fatigue caused thereby is relieved, boredom is obviated, and all that has been read gets a chance to sink into the mind. Experiments have shown that if one sleeps after reading, all that is read in that period is retained for far greater time than any other material read under differing circumstances. This occurs because sleep provides complete rest to the brain. The extent of rest required after reading a book depends not only upon the capacity of the student himself, but also upon the material read because if the subject is difficult rest will be needed only after a short reading, whereas in the case of a simple or light subject much reading can be done before fatigue sets in.

From the above analysis of the results of psychological investigation in study methods, students can discover the faults and advantages of their own methods and can also effect improvements in them. Students who cannot do this stand in need of a psychologist's guidance. And in giving such guidance and advice the psychologist should find out the complete capacity and capability of the students, as this is intimately related to the method of study.

3. Provision of a special method of education for the backward child. One specific aspect of educational guidance is the guidance concerning backward children. This category includes children who usually fail at examinations, or show signs of indiscipline, running away from school, juvenile delinquency, or other defects of such nature. Backwardness in education can be caused by personal causes as well as by the method of teaching or external factors. The advisor must be able to gather all possible relevant information regarding the backward child whom he is called upon to guide. In this besides getting hold of the cumulative record and guardian's schedule, or the self-inventory it is necessary to gather information from the parents and teachers. It is only on the basis of such information that any advise for the solution of educational problems can be given. In case a child is intellectually of a lower level or suffers from some mental defect, then he requires a special curriculum and a special method of teaching to suit his needs. Psychologists can advise on this matter also. If it is observed that the backward child fails to show any progress despite persistent effort then he would be best advised to go into some technical profession requiring training rather than mental acumen. If the child's backwardness is due to family conditions or the school environment then the psychologist should advise his parents and teachers. Sometimes backwardness can be the result of some mental disease. In such a case the child stands in need of medical treatment rather than guidance. Briefly, the psychologist and the adviser must individually consider the case of each child and give private and separate advice to each patient.

4. Provision of special educational programmes for the gifted children. While backward children require guidance and care, the unusually gifted children also require a special educational arrangement as otherwise there is fear of their falling into bad activities. A gifted child does not find the ordinary programme that satisfies and invigorates the average child, satisfying and helpful. The psychologist discovers such exceptional children, gathers all available information regarding them and guides their parents and teachers as to the manner in which the child should be treated. Guidance of such cases more usually concerns suggestions for some special extra-curricular programmes that can help the child develop properly and in accordance with his special gifts. Putting it briefly, it can be said that the psychologist arranges a curriculum that suits well with the child's gifts.

5. Consideration of failures at examinations. In the intermediate and high school examinations held every year by the U.P. Board of High School and Intermediate examination, the results are almost invariably below 50 per cent. More than half the students that appear for the examinations fail to pass them. And while one hears a few odd cases of suicide that are the result of this failure there are many more individuals who become discouraged and give up their educational career when it has just begun. Some of the more enterprising turn to anti-social activity, others lose their mental balance, while a major portion of them become morose and frustrated. Almost all educationists are of the view that as a result of this very high rate of failures, the nation's wealth and strength are being greatly undermined. On the face of it, it is a national problem or at best the fault of the state's faulty educational methods and educational organisation that admits of almost no interference on the psychologist's part, but he can nevertheless resolve the factors that lead children of failure in examinations through his guidance.

6. Encouragement to the child's inspiration to study. Another problem that makes itself felt to the psychologists is when a particular child evinces lack of inspiration and enthusiasm to study. Causes of this lack of motivation may both the personal as well as related to the environment whether social, family or school. Among the personal reasons can be physical factors such as a weak constitution or mental reasons such as anxiety and irritation. Environmental factors are concerned either with the home or the school. As far as the school is concerned it may produce a variety of causes such as uninteresting curriculum and routine, the method of education or teaching being anything but psychological, absence of extra-curricular programmes, etc. The psychologist sifts all these factors and causes, and then advises the child to create motivation in him. In fact, this can be achieved more by removing causes that destroy motivation than by any guidance. For this the psychologist guides either the teacher or the parents. The parents, teachers and the psychologist can jointly exert themselves to create a condition in which the student will take an interest in his education of his own volition. Then, and only then, can the child be inspired to take an interest in the study of his subjects

7. Removal of weakness in particular subjects. Yet another problem confronts the psychologist when a student shows signs of being weak in some particular subject or subjects. English, for example, is one subject is which most students in Uttar Pradesh are lamentably weak. A major portion of college students failing is of those who fail in the English language papers. Some students evade some subjects as if they were running for the safety of their very lives. Mathematics, for example, is another subject that is something of burden for many people, equalled perhaps only by grammar for the dread it causes. Weakness in a particular subject is not due to lack of the required ability in the students, but more often because the student fails to take a keen interest in that subject. Through tests and observation the psychologist can locate the individual cause that is responsible for the weakness. If it is the study of that subject as soon as possible, or if some ability can possibly be injected into the students, efforts should be made to create it in him. If the cause of weakness is something else, then in that case teachers, parents, the psychologist and the student can cooperate to put an end to the meaningless weakness threatening the student's progress.

QUESTIONS FOR EXERCISE

1. What do you understand by the term educational guidance? What are the aims and purposes?
2. What are the important factors that suggest the introduction of guidance programme in education?
3. Discuss the aims and values of educational and vocational guidance.
4. Discuss the scope of guidance at different stages in the educational ladder.

26

SOLVING EDUCATIONAL PROBLEMS

According to K.G. Saiyidain, "A student who could have done brilliantly in the Humanties may, for want of proper guidance, take up science or *vice versa,* and be put down as a dud, not only in school but even in later life if this results in wrong choice of a career. If the choice had been correctly made, his whole life pattern may have been quite different." The success or the failure of students in school and later in life depends of a considerable extent on the selection of suitable subjects, which has assumed all the more importance in the new pattern of education.

Conditions for Effective Working of the New Scheme

1. **More than two practical courses.** The schools should offer more than two practical courses as far as possible so that the students may have sufficient scope to select subjects suitable according to their ability, interest and aptitude.

2. **A comprehensive programme of guidance.** It should exist in the schools to guide the students on the right lines in the selection of suitable courses and careers.

3. **Laboratories and workshops.** The schools should have well-equipped laboratories and workshops for practical work.

4. **Co-ordination.** There should be co-ordination between the school and the industrial establishments. This will facilitate the problem of getting expert advice.

5. **Tutorial system.** The importance of giving individual attention to the students implies the introduction of some sort of tutorial system.

Criteria for Electives

1. Pupil's ability, aptitude, talents and interests.

2. Parent's wishes.

3. Availability of place in school.

4. Facilities for further education after passing the Higher Secondary Examination.

5. Employment opportunities.

Curricula Guidance

The Working Conference on Educational and Vocational Guidance in Multipurpose Schools discussed the problem of Curricula Guidance under following four headings and made useful recommendations :

1. Preparing the Parents

(i) *Parent-teacher association* : Every school should have a Parent-Teacher Association to facilitate contacts with parents, especially parents of pupils in Standard X, XI and XII.

(ii) *Personal contacts with parents* : Attempts should be made by the teacher to establish personal contacts with parents through home visits, periodical meetings and conferences and correspondence.

(iii) *Model literature* : In collaboration with State Bureaus of Education and State Institutes of Education the N.C.E.R.T. should prepare model literature in the form of brochures and short pamphlets for orientation of parents in regard to the aims and objectives of the new pattern, and the situation of choice of curricula in the "Delta" class faced by their children. The scheme of educational and vocational guidance in relation to Secondary and Higher Education may be discussed and guidelines given. State Bureaus should adapt them with suitable change, if found necessary, for use in their respective regions.

(iv) *Broadcasts* : Broadcasts for parents and employees should be organised by All India Radio in collaboration with the State Bureaus.

(v) *Group contacts* : These should be established with parents and employers for general orientation through career conferences to be organised by the school at least once a year. The programme should include talks, exhibitions, film shows, etc.

2. Preparation of Pupils for Curricular Guidance

(i) *Orientation talks* : These help pupils choose wisely the optional group of curricular subjects. These should be organised in the "Delta" class at least once in a week, forming part of social studies syllabus in the long-term programme for guidance. At present they may be organised as separate topic of guidance within the school day.

(ii) *Extra-curricular activities* : In order to develop and explore the interests of pupils in the senior classes a programme of varied activities integrated with the curriculum should be provided in the school, organised the relation to the diversified courses available at the Higher Secondary School of the region. These should form part of the regular school time-table. Provision should be made to devote three hours per week or to concentrate them into two periods of one-and-a-half hours duration each. The following is an illustrative list of hobbies and leisure-time activities which can organised for this purpose :

(1) **Art club.** Drawing, Clay-modelling, Photography, Sign painting, Decorating.

(2) **Music group.** Instrumental, Dramatics, Stage-craft, Folk dancing.
(3) **Wood work.** Carving, Picture framing.
(4) **Textiles.** Weaving, Costuming, Felt work.
(5) **Trades.** Bookbinding, Painting, Radio, Electric Wiring.
(6) **Outdoor sports.** Camping, Fishing, Scouting, Forestry.
(7) **Personal service.** Laundry, Hair-dressing, Library.
(8) **Gardening.** Flower shows, Plant study, Farming.
(9) **Cookery.** Candy making, Cooking.
(10) **Animal care.** Bee-keeping, Pigeon-raising, Small animals.
(11) **Scientific society.**
(12) **Model making.** Airplanes, Furniture, Papier-mache.
(13) **School publications.**
(14) **World affairs Forum.**
(15) **Student government.**

3. The School broadcasting service. In collaboration with All India Radio and States Bureaus the School Broadcasting service should arrange broadcasts for the orientation of pupils to the "Hobby" hour and the new experiences to which it is an introduction. Talks should be short and preferably given once a week during the last term in "Delta" class after preliminary orientation work in the school.

4. Permanent guidance corner. Provision should be made for a permanent guidance corner in each school for orientation through visual aids suet as posters and charts, employment news, etc.

5. Career conferences. Career conferences including talks, exhibitions and film shows for pupils may be organised along with those meant for parent.

6. Visits. Class visits to work sites and educational institutions preceded by preparation through study and should be arranged for developing interests and acquiring information through realistic situations and personal contacts.

7. Interview. Every pupil should have at least one individual interview with the teacher-counsellor before the end of the year.

METHODS AND PRINCIPLES OF ADMITTING STUDENTS TO THE DIFFERENT COURSES IN HIGHER SECONDARY SCHOOLS

Instead of relying on one or two sources only the following types of data should be used for serving the basis for selection and choice of different courses :

1. Questionnaire. Information should be obtained from each child about his interests and plans through a questionnaire or form prepared for this purpose.

2. Relevant information about the child and his plans. It should be gathered from the parents through a separate questionnaire or form.

3. Cumulative records. These should be maintained for all pupils. The following items should be included in the cumulative record card :

(i) School achievement data.

(ii) Physique and health data.

(iii) Interests.

(iv) Personality data.

4. Psychological tests. Tests of intelligence, relevant aptitudes and interests should be used. Objective Tests should be used for assessing achievement in school subjects.

HINTS FOR EDUCATIONAL AND VOCATIONAL ORIENTATION IN STANDARD X, XI AND XII

1. Observation. Pupils should be closely observed and studied by their teachers through the Higher Secondary School years.

2. The school programme. It should be flexible during the first six months in a Higher Secondary School to make necessary changes possible.

3. Individual interviews. These should be arranged in Classes IX and XI wherever necessary in order to help pupils in adjusting to the new curriculum and to enable them to make necessary change of courses when it is needed. Individual interviews should be arranged in Classes X, XI and XII for each school leaver.

4. Work on hobbies. It should be continued but not necessarily as part of the school time-table.

5. School-leaving report. It should be prepared on the basis of the available data.

RECOMMENDATIONS FOR DEVELOPING STUDY HABITS AMONG CHILDREN

The following recommendations were made by the Summer Camp of Delhi Principals held at Pahalgam in 1956 :

1. Library and reading room. The school library and reading room should be well equipped, tastefully furnished, well lighted and ventilated so that the students may be attracted and encouraged to take advantage of it. It should be spacious enough and should be located in a quiet place.

2. Books and periodicals. These should be easily accessible to the students — the open shelf system is recommended.

3. New arrivals. These should be suitably displayed to attract attention of students and teachers.

4. Class libraries. Classlibraries containing sufficient number of books on suitable topics be organised. Adequate library grant should be given for the purpose by the managements and the Government. Parents can also help in equipping the library by donating books, periodicals, etc.

5. Time-table. Time-table should be so framed that each class get at least two periods every week for extra reading. These periods should be utilised for (a) silent reading of periodicals and books, (b) guiding pupils with regard to reading material and ascertaining whether they have gone through the books, and (c) reporting and discussing in the class about the books and periodicals read by the students.

6. Record of reading. A proper record of extra books read by each student should be maintained by allotting one page to each student in the library issue register or by making entries on the individual cards. This record should be periodically entered in the student's progress report books.

7. Guidance by librarian. The librarian should be trained, well-read, and interested in children so that the requisite guidance, encouragement and help may be available to the students. In a large school there should be library assistant to help him. In the absence of trained librarian the services of a senior teacher interested in reading should be utilised to organise the work of the library.

Responsibility of the Teachers

1. Love of reading. They should develop their own love of reading which will stimulate the students to develop reading habits.

2. Children literature. They should be well-versed in children's literature so that they may suggest suitable books for the students. Generally speaking, teachers do not read children's literature with the result that they are quite ignorant of the reading needs of the students.

3. Methods of teaching. They should adopt such methods of teaching and give assignments in such a way as the students may be encouraged to supplement their class work by extra reading.

PRINCIPLES OF DEVELOPING GOOD STUDY HABITS

Following principles were enumerated by the participants of the Summer Camp of Delhi Principals :

1. The study programme. It should be purposeful pleasant and interesting to the child. It is unless the programme is enjoyable and meaningful, the child will develop a distaste for studies.

2. Easy goal. The goal set before the child should be well within his reach. This is necessary in order to develop in him a sense of self-confidence and achievement.

3. The methods of instruction. These should be such as to stimulate a real desire for discovery.

4. The study material. It should be properly graded and plentiful.

5. The study programme. It should be such as to encourage initiative and independent thinking.

6. Progress report. The child should be allowed to know his progress and be encouraged to make further improvement by competing with himself.

METHODS OF DEVELOPING GOOD STUDY HABIT

1. Telling stories and recitation. From the very beginning of their school career, the children should be stimulated to create a taste for reading by telling stories and recitation of children's poems.

2. Study material. Bold-typed, illustrated and attractive books, charts and other material arouse their interest in reading.

3. Specific periods. Some specific periods for looking at pictures, picture books and story books should be provided.

4. Credit for extra-reading. Some credit for extra-reading should be given to the students. This fact may be mentioned in their progress report.

5. Dictionary and reference books. In the Higher Secondary classes the students should be encouraged to use dictionary and reference books. They should be asked off and on to write down the difficult words and their meanings from the textbooks as their home assignment.

6. Tools. In the regular class periods, it should be stressed that the students must be equipped with the necessary tools, *e.g.*, pencil, note-book, etc.

7. Declamation contests and debates. These should be organised from time to time so that the students may consult books or other material for preparing themselves.

8. Essay competitions. These should be held off and on.

9. Postures. The students should also be instructed to pay due attention to their postures when they study books.

10. Class-room library. Apart from central library, class-room libraries may be organised.

11. Note-book for summary. The students should be asked to prepare a notebook in which summary of the books read by them should be recorded.

HEALTH GUIDANCE

According to Robert H. Knapp, an adequate school health programme should cover four important areas :

(1) The creation and maintenance of a health and sanitary school environment which fosters the physical and mental health of the individual.

(2) An adequate school health instruction programme.

(3) Adequate health services.

(4) The provision of a recreational and physical-education programme which has as its purpose the building of strong bodies and healthy minds.

QUESTIONS FOR EXERCISE

1. How can guidance help the students in the selection of proper subjects? Discuss.
2. What are the different methods of selecting students to the different courses? Explain.
3. Suggest an educational and vocational orientation programme.
4. What are the principles and methods of developing good study habits among students? Narrate.
5. Discuss the importance of health guidance for the students.

27

Pupil Personnel Work in Indian Schools

Main Objectives of a Guidance Programme

1. To decide upon and carry out certain functions in simplified.

2. To determine the needs of the students more accurately.

3. To accommodate more students with a fewer guidance personnel.

4. To define individual responsibilities with a fair degree of accuracy and to motivate the staff more readily accept the responsibilities.

5. To put proper persons at the proper place, in the proper manner and at the proper time.

6. To avoid duplication of efforts.

7. To plan the programme co-operatively and carving promise for success and motivation.

8. To make use of resources — both human and material.

9. To give necessary information and proper guidance to students.

10. To co-ordinate all activities suitably.

11. To obtain the services of competent guidance personnel.

12. To attain objectives more readily.

13. To provide specific personnel services. These are as follows :

(i) Assisting students in selecting a course or an institution.

(ii) Maintenance of student records.

(iii) Orientation of students to new institution, courses, etc.

(iv) Counselling the individual in achieving his best educational, vocational and personal adjustment.

(v) Provision of a co-ordinated programme of school activities.

(vi) Provision of appropriate physical and mental health services.

(vii) Provision of remedial services.

(viii) Placement function *i.e.,* rendering assistance to the students in finding appropriate employment when leaving school and assistance also in gaining admission to the post-graduate school of their choice.

IMPLICATIONS OF ORGANISING GUIDANCE SERVICES

Jones observes, "Guidance is not something that can be separated from the general life of the school, nor is it something that can be located only in some particular part of the school; it cannot be tucked away in the office of the counsellor or in the employment bureau. It is a part of every school activity, some form of guidance is the duty and the responsibility of every teacher in the system. It is, then, a function that is shared by all and should be so administered." The organisation of guidance services has the following implications :

1. Laying down objectives in clear terms.
2. Mustering of resources and utilising them in the best possible manner.
3. Systematic planning of guidance work.
4. Co-ordination and conduct of certain activities within an administrative framework.
5. Allocation of duties and responsibilities.
6. Provision of minimum essentials.
7. An able leadership to co-ordinate, supervise and direct activities.
8. Working of various guidance personnel as a team.

ADVANTAGES OF ORGANISING GUIDANCE SERVICES

1. **Facilitation.** It facilitates the use of skill, training and interests of staff members.

2. **Organisation.** It co-ordinates the work of all persons engaged in the guidance programme.

3. **Economy.** A well-organised programme economises time, money and effort.

4. **Good relationships.** It helps in developing good human relationships.

5. **Understanding need.** It helps to understand the physical, social, emotional and intellectual characteristics and the needs of all human beings.

6. **Understanding individual differences.** It helps teachers to understand the individual differences of children in various spheres.

7. **Efficiency.** It promotes efficiency in providing adequate, reliable and scientific data.

8. **Community resources.** It utilises community resources.

PRINCIPLES OF ORGANISING GUIDANCE SERVICES

1. **Serving interests, needs and purposes.** In any programme of educational guidance service in the school, the interests, need and purposes of the students which it serves should be the guiding factors.

The guidance programme may be different in an industrial school from that of an agricultural school.

2. Universal. The guidance services should serve all the students.

3. Integral. The guidance services should treat the individual as a whole.

4. Environmental. The guidance service should consider the total environment of the child.

5. Solution of problems. It should also meet the specific needs and problems of the child.

6. Early solution. Problems should be dealt with before they become serious.

7. Information. Adequate information regarding occupational and educational requirements and opportunities should be secured.

8. Staff cooperation. The interest and effort of every member of the staff should be enlisted.

9. Agencies cooperation. It should co-operate with all the agencies of education and provide for leadership.

10. Simplicity. It should be as simple as possible.

11. Self direction. It should be directed towards improved pupil self-knowledge and self-direction.

12. Testing. Adequate provision should be made for testing tools.

13. Follow-up. There should be a well-organised plan for following in individuals after they leave the school.

Guidance work — a job of the specialists or teacher. There is no hard and fast rule to allocate exactly the role to be played by the teachers and the role played by the specialists.

The pattern of guidance may differ from school to school. It would depend upon the size or type of a school and the facilities available therein. In some school it may not be possible to engage a whole-time counsellor. One member of the staff may work as a teacher-counsellor. A guidance scheme cannot be launched on the same pattern m a small school as in a large school.

ORGANISATION OF GUIDANCE IN A SENIOR SECONDARY SCHOOL

1. Teacher counsellor. A qualified teacher who is well-versed and interested in guidance should be made the in-charge of the guidance unit of the school. He may then become the part-time school counsellor. The special subject teachers can render a useful help in the guidance programme.

2. Venue. A separate room should be provided for the counsellor to enable him to put his relevant materials about the records of the students, information materials concerning educational and vocational choices and the conduct interviews without any disturbance by taking the students into confidence.

3. Library. A small library containing books giving information regarding hobbies and different vocations may be set up in the counsellor's room. Books should be issued by counsellor to the students in accordance with their capabilities and aptitudes.

4. Guidance committee. Guidance Committee may be formed in the school with the counsellor as its secretary. Composed largely of teacher, the Guidance Committee is in a better position to study the needs, purposes and procedures essentials to the development of guidance service and to set necessary guidance policy. It is also expected to play an important role in impressing upon the teachers the necessity of maintaining accurate records about the all-around growth of an individual.

FUNCTIONS OF THE COUNSELLOR

1. Testing. To administer psychological tests.

2. Interpretation. To interpret the results of the psychological tests.

3. Information about courses. To collect and give information about different types of courses at school and in technical training institutes.

4. Information about occupations. To give information about different occupations.

5. Individual counselling. To give individual counselling to students who have difficulty in choosing or in taking up employment on leaving school.

6. Stimulation. To stimulate students to put forth maximum efforts.

7. Assisting teachers. To assist teachers with pupil problems which the teachers find difficult.

8. Placement. To assist youth employment services in the placement of pupils in various jobs.

9. Follow-up. To take up follow-up work with a view to assessing the outcome of guidance services in regard to students who have received guidance.

10. Familiarisation. To assist in familiarising new class-room teachers and other school personnel with guidance services available.

11. School records. To explain school records with which the students are not familiar.

12. Measurement. To obtain as much of an objective measurement of a pupil's abilities, interests, aptitudes and physical characteristics as possible.

13. Interviews. To give assistance and counselling through interviews with each pupil to enable him to understand himself and his problems.

14. Contact. To maintain close contact with the school doctor in all health problems of students.

15. Knowledge of home. To obtain a knowledge of the relevant aspects of a student's home environment, economic status and personality.

16. Contact with parents. To confer with parents and arrange group meetings of parents as needs arise.

17. Emotional crises. To be constantly alert to signs of emotional difficulties.

18. Specialists. To refer difficulties to available specialists.

19. Educational guidance. To provide counselling for a pupil relative to educational problems or plans.

20. Excursions. To arrange excursions for pupils with a view to providing them with realistic educational and occupational information.

21. Career conferences. To arrange career conferences when considered appropriate.

22. Vocational guidance. To assist students in making vocational choices commensurate with their ability and skill.

23. Personal guidance. To arrange case conferences about an individual student who is experiencing some type of difficulty.

24. Self-direction. To assist pupils to develop initiative and independence so that they may progress in self-direction.

25. Help to drop-outs. To aid potential drop-outs to make the school experience as profitable as possible.

26. Group guidance. To arrange for group guidance through class meetings, sessions with guest speakers, films, and activities to promote social adjustment.

CHARACTERISTICS OF SCHOOL COUNSELLOR

A Committee on Educational and Vocational Guidance in USA suggested the following traits required for the post of a counsellor :

1. Stable and well-adjusted personality.
2. High degree of intellectual capacity.
3. Fundamental liking for persons.
4. Sympathetic and objective understanding of people.
5. Facility in establishing wholesome, effective, personal and social relations, including ability to work co-operatively with other people.
6. Ability to stimulate students and colleagues and to challenge their best efforts in working for ends that they come to accept as desirable.

7. Ability to see and understand the total situation and the separate parts in relation to the whole.

8. Understanding and appreciation of one's own limitations in dealing with certain areas of problems and with certain individuals.

9. Broad general knowledge and wide interests.

10. Understanding of class-room conditions, teaching responsibilities, and pupil relationships.

11. Understanding of working conditions and employer-employee relationships in jobs outside the educational work and in non-professional vocational life.

12. Understanding of social and economic conditions and influences — general and local.

Walter B. Jones has given the following characteristics of a counsellor :

1. Breadth of interest. (i) Ability to get the business point of view. (ii) Sympathetic with prospective drop-outs as well as with college preparatory pupils. (iii) Interested in various types of people. (iv) Interested in pupil's home and school life.

2. Co-operation. (i) Doing extra work in a cheerful manner. (ii) Living for mankind. (iii) Co-operating with employers.

3. Refinement. (i) Not dominating or dictatorial. (ii) Not too cock-sure of the wisdom of his own judgment.

4. Magnetism. (i) Putting others at ease. (ii) Inspiring confidence at interview. (iii) Makes pupils feel that they are always welcome to see him and that they will be given help.

5. Considerateness. (i) Appreciating the difficulties of the teachers in working out student adjustments. (ii) Exhibiting human understanding of those less fortunate. (iii) Having real love for the fellowmen without being sentimental.

According to Ruth Strang, "The counsellor is like a gardener who prepares the soil and does everything he can to help each plant grow in its own best way." At another place, Strang writes, "If he is emotionally mature and feels fairly secure in his social and professional relationships, he is able to convey a certain sense of confidence to the counselee."

According to the Secondary Education Commission "A good guidance officer possess many good qualities. He has an understanding of young people and their problems based on scientific knowledge but inspired with sympathy and the ability to look at life through the eyes of boys and girls. He has special training in good counselling methods, mental hygiene and in the discriminating use of tests and school records. In the field of vocational guidance, he has an accurate knowledge of occupational opportunities and requirements. He has ample time for conferences with pupils, parents and employers. He is fully familiar with the purpose and programme of the school. He has the capacity to work in close cooperation with the teachers."

AREAS OF KNOWLEDGE NEEDED BY COUNSELLORS

1. Human behaviour. Area as the individuals are not like machines to be regulated mechanical adjustment, they must be motivated as persons. A competent counsellor constantly enlarges his knowledge of psychology of motivation and his understanding of behaviour.

2. Child psychology and the adolescent group. The counsellor should be a specialist in handling the young persons with whom he deals. He should fully understand the characteristics of different age groups.

3. Individual child. A competent counsellor collects all available and pertinent information about the counselee before the first interview.

4. Resources. The counsellor has at his command a considerable knowledge about the school, recreational facilities, job opportunities or other facilities of various sorts.

5. Counselling process. The counselling process includes 'all the means' by which the counselee and the counsellor together marshal the counselee's resources and the resources of his present and future situations.

6. Human relationships. A competent counsellor establishes cordial relations with all the participants of the guidance programme *i.e.,* the counselee, the administrators, the teacher, the students, the parents, the employers, other schools and the other agencies and the community. This is as follows :

(a) His competency to work with the staff members includes the ability :

(i) To gain the confidence and respect of the teaching staff.

(ii) To co-operate with others responsible for non-instructional services.

(iii) To provide leadership in guidance committee work.

(iv) To conduct teacher group conferences of problems related to guidance services.

(v) To organise and carry out a programme of in-service programme.

(vi) To assist individual teachers with specific pupil problems.

(vii) To conduct research on all phases of the guidance programme.

(b) His competency to work with the parents includes the ability :

(i) To conduct effective home visits.

(ii) To gain the confidence and respect of the parents.

(iii) To enlist the co-operation of the parents in the solution of pupil adjustment problems.

(iv) To organise and direct parent conference.

(c) His competency to work with the community includes his ability :

(i) To know when and how to make referrals.

(ii) To participate effectively in number of community activities.

(iii) To explain the significance of the entire school programme.

(iv) To develop effective relationships with employers and other community groups and utilise their services.

(v) To plan and direct community occupational surveys.

ROLE OF A TEACHER IN GUIDANCE

According to L.L. Bojkin, "The principal area of student personnel work is teacher-student relationship, not occasional interviews with specialised counsellor." As stated by Gordon, "The major task of the teacher is the study of student." Bojkin says, "Good teaching has emotional and moral as well as intellectual objectives. It aims at the growth of the whole person as well as the mastery of the subject in hand."

Areas of Guidance Work by the Teacher

1. Needs of the students. He primarily concerned with the problems and needs of their students.

2. Maladjustment. He should try to detect the emerging maladjustment of pupils.

3. Development. He should provide situations for the maximum development of the pupil.

4. Implementation. He should implement in right earnest the decisions made due to the pupils' contacts with counsellors.

5. Information. He should make use of every opportunity of acquiring information and many insights about pupils and their experiences.

6. Contact with parents. He should find opportunities of developing contacts with parents and community agencies which have many possibilities in the complete guidance programme.

7. Contact with students. He should develop personal contacts with students.

8. Testing. He should construct and administer tests in their regular academic courses.

9. Notes. He should guide their students in the taking of notes.

10. Talks. He should guide students in giving short talks.

11. Library. He should guide students in the proper use of the school or college library.

12. Fields of students. He should acquaint the students with the fields in which their subjects are related to.

13. Reporting. He should report about students who are experiencing special difficulties to the school counsellor.

14. Co-curricular activities. He should assume responsibilities for the organisation of the co-curricular activities which are closely allied to their subject-matter fields.

PRINCIPLES GOVERNING TEACHERS ROLE

1. Gaining understanding of every pupil in his class. This is done through daily observation, listening to what pupils say, talking with them and their parents, visiting their homes and using some form of cumulative record which he can also pass on to the next teacher to give him background in understanding each new class.

2. Accepting children as they are and to look for the best in them. When a student gets up to recite and gives a confused answer, the teacher should help him/her to think through the question more clearly himself/herself. And when he/she had done this successfully, the teacher should say, "I knew you could do it, if you kept on trying."

3. Providing the experiences each child needs. As the child grows older, he/her should have work experiences in school and outside of school that help him/her to discover what he can do best and what he/she likes to do. This is concerning school work that is meaningful to him/her in which he/she can succeed with reasonable effort, friendly relations with teacher and other pupils that give him/her social experiences, and encouragement to study at home on his/her own initiative.

4. Guiding as he teaches. This requires being constantly sensitive to the individuals and their interaction in the group. When a pupils gives the wrong answer the guidance-minded teacher, is more likely to ask : "How did you get that idea?" This helps him to understand children's misconceptions and to show them how to correct them. It also prevents a child feeling inferior from experiencing another failure. Instead, the child gains a little more self-confidence as a result of the teacher's emphasising whatever is positive in what he says and does.

5. Helping the older child make educational and vocational plans in line with his abilities.

ROLE OF CLASSROOM TEACHERS IN GUIDANCE

If the classroom teacher is in control of classroom environment of the youngsters he can play a very strategic role in manipulating the environment to bring about an improved adjustment of pupils, which cannot take place if the class-room environment is unsympathetic and does not cater to the needs of the individual pupil. A successful guidance programme is dependent upon the classroom teacher who is dependent upon the personnel workers to carry put the primary function of instruction. If he practises good mental health and willing to contribute to the specific services of a guidance programme he is an invaluable member of the guidance team. For this he must be acquainted with the following about the students :

1. The academic ability of each of his student.
2. Students reading ability.
3. The important details of student's past academic work.
4. Students, parents and home situations.
5. The results of other tests the student has taken.
6. Vocational plans of the student.
7. Educational goals of the student.
8. Student's likes and dislikes.
9. Student's condition of health.
10. Student's abilities and weaknesses.
11. Student's problems and frustration.
12. Student's social relationships — his friends, his group contacts.
13. Student's recreational activities.
14. Student's study habits and study conditions.
15. The unusual experiences student has had.
16. What other teachers think about the student.

According to Chisholm, "In the school in which the class-room teacher assumes responsibility for guidance, there is no forbidden ground dividing his instruction and guidance responsibilities. The teacher helps pupils study their own abilities, select work, appraise their own progress, and the other things necessary in an adequate programme of guidance. In the actual class-room work, then, the teacher is sensitive to and understands the level of interest and ability of the pupils and adapt the work to individual needs or helps the student revise his choice of school activities so as to get those experiences in harmony with his needs."

ROLE OF THE PRINCIPAL IN GUIDANCE

1. Understanding. He helps the members of the staff concentrate their attention on the problems, needs and characteristics of the students.

2. Leadership. He has the responsibility for providing constructive leadership in developing better guidance services.

3. Shared responsibility. He has the responsibility of helping the members of the staff understand the importance of the "shared responsibility" for pupil growth.

4. Time schedule and facilities. He has the responsibility of providing the time scheduling and facilities so that staff members can work more effectively.

5. Interpretation. He has the responsibility of interpreting the programme of guidance services to the school and to the community.

6. In-service training. He has the responsibility of providing in-service training facilities to the teachers and counsellors to acquire greater skill and security.

7. Organising guidance. He has the responsibility of helping the staff organise the guidance programme.

8. Selecting teacher counsellor. He has the responsibility of selecting competent teacher-counsellors and placing them in an educational setting so that they can operate effectively.

9. Whole-hearted support. According to a Manual of Educational and Vocational Guidance, issued by the Ministry of Education, "The Principal or the Headmaster is the keyman of the guidance programme within his school. He must be in sympathy with its purposes and give it his whole-hearted support."

ROLE OF THE ADMINISTRATOR IN GUIDANCE

The administrative support is an integral aspect of the entire guidance programme without which the success of the programme is doubtful. According to Froehlich the following are some of the functions of the administrator concerning guidance :

1. Recognising the need and importance of a comprehensive guidance programme and give it his personal support.

2. Making his staff cognizant of the value, functions, and problems of guidance.

3. Providing suitable quarters and facilities for the guidance service.

4. Arranging the school schedule so that counselling service is possible for all pupils.

5. Seeing that ample time is allowed for the counsellor.

6. Making adequate provision in the budget for carrying on the guidance programme.

7. Establishing and maintaining a cumulative record system.

8. Establishing a plan of in-service training for members of the staff.

9. Offering special inducements and recognition to counsellors in the guidance programme where extra services and training are required.

10. Working out and co-ordinating the guidance programme co-operatively with members of the staff.

11. Evaluating the guidance programme in co-operation with the staff to determine its effectiveness.

12. Giving desirable publicity to improve school, home, and community relationships.

ROLE OF AREA COUNSELLOR IN GUIDANCE

A Manual of the Ministry of Education suggests that one regional or area counsellor with two technical assistants in every district or for a maximum of 120 secondary schools is desirable until such time as every secondary school has a whole-time counsellor. The counsellors have to render all possible assistance to the teacher-counsellors and to co-operate with the State Bureau in research work and with local Regional Employment Exchanges for collecting vocational and educational information. The area counsellors will provide assistance to the feeder Middle Schools for giving educational and vocational orientation to the pupils.

ROLE OF PSYCHOLOGIST IN GUIDANCE

A psychologist attends to the emotional side and not to the vocational side of the child as does the counsellor. He gathers valuable information regarding an individual through administering psychological tests. He is concerned with the students, their teachers and parents. Sometimes even teachers or parents may become a problem for children. By meeting with the teachers and parents the psychologist impresses upon them the desirability of the problems of children in a particular way. The psychologist is a guidance worker at a level higher than that a counsellor.

ROLE OF HEALTH SPECIALIST IN GUIDANCE

As body and mind are two interdependent aspects of the living organism, physical troubles may lead to mental troubles and *vice versa*. If a school cannot engage a full-time doctor, it must make provision for the occasional visits of the physician for the medical examination of each child after a suitable interval. Complete records pertaining to the health of children should be properly maintained and utilised.

PREREQUISITES OF A GUIDANCE PROGRAMME

1. Assessment and data. A comprehensive system of pupil assessment and recording of pupil data.

2. Provision for work related to guidance. Adequate provision in the school time-table for work related to guidance — filling in student's cumulative records by teachers — holding class talks — organising group guidance activities.

3. Facilities for efficiency in guidance. Arrangements to provide facilities to teachers to become increasingly efficient in guidance work by :

(i) Providing up-to-date guidance literature.

(ii) Providing opportunities for attending seminars and short term courses in guidance.

(iii) Organising study groups to assess and evaluate pupil needs and the ways to meet them.

(iv) Enlisting the support and co-operation of the parents and introducing them to the idea of guidance.

(v) Enlisting the co-operation of the school staff in the implementation for guidance programme.

(vi) Making adequate budgetary provision.

PATTERNS OF GUIDANCE ORGANISATION

1. Centralised pattern. In it guidance is provided by specialised trained guidance counsellor. Directions/guidelines are issued to the teachers by the counsellor/central of the counsellor.

2. Decentralised pattern. In it the teachers and the guidance counsellor share the responsibility. Teachers play an active role in the guidance programme.

3. Mixed form. Explaining this form of guidance say Crow and Crow, "Services are organised in such a way that the purposes of programme are understood by the entire faculty. Certain responsibilities are delegated to the specialist, and others are assumed by teachers and other members of the school personnel — To be most effective the guidance programme should follow a plan that lies midway the extremes of centralisation and non-centralisation."

QUESTIONS FOR EXERCISE

1. Describe the main objectives of a guidance programme in a school. How can these objectives be obtained?
2. State the role of the various guidance personnel in the school.
3. Is the guidance work the job of the specialists or teacher? Explain.
4. Write short notes on the role of the following in guidance :
   (a) The Class Teacher,
   (b) The Teachers,
   (c) The Principal,
   (d) The Administrator.

28

New Pattern (10+2+3) of Education and Guidance Services

HISTORICAL REVIEW

1. **Sadler Commission.** In 1917, when the Calcutta University Commission, popularly known as the Sadler Commission, was appointed its deliberations led to the recommendation that the dividing line between the university and secondary courses could more realistically be drawn at the level of Intermediate Examination rather than that of Matriculation. Therefore, the Commission asked the Government to establish Intermediate Colleges to provide instructions in arts, science, medicine, engineering, etc.

2. **Hartog Committee.** In 1927, the Hartog Committee recommended division of more students to industrial and commercial careers at the end of the middle stage.

3. **Sapru Committee.** In 1934, the Sapru Committee recommended diversified courses at the secondary stage, one for entering University and the other for meeting vocational requirements.

4. **The University Education Commission.** In 1948-49, the first University Education Commission in independent India, regretted that the importance of Intermediate College in the educational system of India had not been realised and appreciated. It recommended that in order to raise the standard of university education admission to universities should be after 12 years of schooling.

This was followed by discussions by various committees and conferences of experts. The Conference of Vice-Chancellors (1962), the All India Council for Secondary Education (1963), the Conference of State Education Ministers and Vice-Chancellors, etc. (1963) and the Conference of State Education Ministers (1964) recommended a 12-year course of schooling before admission to a three-year degree course.

5. **The Education Commission of India** (1966). It underlined the need for a direct link between education, national development and prosperity. This was possible only when the national system of education is properly organised both qualitatively and quantitatively. It also

pointed out that the existing system of education was largely unrelated to life, needs and aspirations of the people. There was a wide gulf between its contents and purpose as well as the interest of national development. One of major weaknesses of the educational system was that secondary education prepared a boy for a college and almost made him unfit for everything else. Secondary education has two specific objectives in any well designed national system of education:

(i) to prepare a student for university,

(ii) to become really terminal and prepare a student for some vocation in life.

Therefore, realising that the total period of education course and the duration of its different stages have a direct bearing on the quality of education imparted for achieving the goal, the Education Commission recommended :

(i) a broadly uniform pattern of education,

(ii) extension in the period of schooling to bring about a general rise in the standard of attainment and

(iii) vocationalisation of education.

6. National Policy Statement. On the basis of the recommendation of the Education Commission the Government formulated a National Policy Statement on Education in 1968, which said it was convinced that a "radical reconstruction of education on the broad lines recommended by the Education Commission is essential for economic and cultural development of the country, for national integration and for realising the idea of a socialistic pattern of society." The policy statement stated that it will be advantageous to have broadly uniform educational structure the 10+2+3 in all parts of the country.

7. The Conference of Education Secretaries and Directors of Public Instruction. Held on September 15 and 16, 1972 it passed the following resolutions on the Adoption of Uniform Pattern of School and College Classes (10+2+3) :

(i) *Uniform pattern* : A uniform of education of 15 years duration leading to the first degree should be adopted by all States.

(ii) *Co-ordination* : There should be close co-ordination between the vocational courses attached to the higher secondary stage, the Industrial Training Institutes and the Polytechnics. Courses selected should have close affinity to the skills and services in demand in the locality. This will involve manpower studies and production centres as well as financing of the skilled personnel on co-operative or institutional pattern for self-employment or employment in production centres.

(iii) *Vocationalisation* : The scheme of vocationalisation of education as well as work experience deserves highest priority in the Plan and should be assisted fully.

(iv) *Vocational courses* : Vocational courses prescribed in institutions would need constant review and replacement as technology materials and demand change. They would have to keep pace with development of local industries also, particularly the small-scale, cottage and consumer industries.

8. The National Policy on Education 1986. It also favoured the adoption of 10+2+3 system.

SALIENT FEATURES OF THE NEW PATTERN OF EDUCATION

1. Common 10-year schooling.

2. 12 years of schooling in place of 11 which was the usual school pattern.

3. After 12 years of schooling the first degree course is of three years duration.

4. The first university degree is obtained after 15 years of study.

5. A selective approach in upgrading the existing higher secondary schools.

6. Compulsory teaching of Mathematics, Science, Social Studies, Trade or Craft, Moral Education in classes IX and X.

7. Two levels of courses in various subjects — advanced level and ordinary.

8. Taking care of individual differences of students by providing for grouping of students based on their attainment in different subject. It will be possible to have a student doing advanced level work in one subject and ordinary level work in another.

9. A close link between the school and the environment and modification of the present emphasis on theoretical aspect of education.

10. Appropriate opportunity to students to take up vocational courses.

11. Specialisational only after 10 years of schooling in classes XI and XII.

12. Reducing pressure on the universities by providing for alternative courses and training facilities at higher secondary stage.

13. Raising the standard of school education which in turn will help the universities to raise their first degree standard higher.

Advantages (Claimed) of the New Pattern of Education

1. Uniformity. A broadly uniform pattern all over the country will strengthen national integration.

2. Rationalisation. The new structure will rationalise and strengthen school education. This strengthening has been recommended by practically all committees, commissions and other organisations in the country.

3. Student quality. It will sent more knowledgeable and mature students to the universities.

4. Reduction in pressure. It will reduce pressure for admission on universities and other centres of higher education.

5. Vocationalisation. It will provide an opportunity and means to introduce appropriate vocationalisation at the higher secondary stage.

6. Modernisation. It will provide an opportunity and a means to modernise school curricula and to re-structure them on more scientific lines as well as to serve the social and economic needs of the adolescent in a better manner.

7. Implementation of educational programmes. A broadly uniform pattern in all States and Union territories will facilitate implementation of educational programmes such as production of books and reading material and teaching aids, training of teachers and their movement, reconstruction of syllabus and improvement in examination practices.

8. Removal of difficulties of mobile students. It will remove difficulties concerning education of children of the mobile population which is continuously increasing in the country.

9. Solution of problems of minorities. It will help solve educational problems of minorities at least in two ways :

(i) *Language books.* The minority language books produced in one area can be used in all other concerned areas.

(ii) *Affiliation.* The schools adopting the minority languages as media of institution in any State or Union Territory can be considered for affiliation to a Board of Secondary Education outside that State or territory. This would result in reduction on administrative costs and difficulties of some of the State Boards.

10. No early decision making. It will do away with the criticism that is generally levelled against the present higher secondary system that students are required to take a decision at too early an age about the particular course to be studied by them.

11. Raising general standard. It will contribute to raising the general standard and quality of education at all stages — school and university.

NEW PATTERN OF EDUCATION AND GUIDANCE SERVICES

In *The Curriculum for the Ten Year School,* a booklet prepared by the National Council of Educational Research and Training (1975) it has been pointed out that it is very necessary to provide adequate guidance services in educational institutions for the successful implementation of the New Pattern of Education. School counsellor should be made available for school or groups of schools. Teachers must be oriented to guidance activities. Cumulative records of the individual pupil's growth and development should be maintained.

Guidance Activities and Programmes

1. Students should be helped in the selection of courses and in making a vocational choice during the period of general education.

2. Students should be provided with information about the various vocational possibilities through career conferences and occupational corners of schools.

3. Students should be helped in developing a realistic self-concept through individual and group counselling.

4. Students with special talents should be identified and provided opportunities to develop them to the maximum possible extent.

5. Enriched programmes should be provided for the gifted.

6. The educational needs of the children coming from the weaker sections of society should be located and suitable provisions made to satisfy them.

7. Diagnostic testing and remedial instruction should be provided for slow learners.

8. In addition to problems related to achievement in various subjects personal adjustment problems should be identified and suitable remedial measures taken to overcome them.

CHARACTERISTIC FEATURE OF THE HIGHER SECONDARY STAGE

Higher Secondary Education and Its Vocationalisation. A Draft Paper prepared by NCERT states, "The characteristic feature of the last two years of schooling (called the higher secondary) is diversification so as to avoid forcing the students into the academic channel alone and to give them an opportunity to choose subjects and programmes of study in keeping with their aptitudes, interests and abilities which would in turn provide the society with personnel having a wide spectrum of knowledge and training for its own needs. If diversification does not take place we would be faced with the problem of having to greatly extend tertiary education of the academic kind, with consequent expenditure on the one hand and danger of unemployment on the other. Therefore, there is a great urgency for designing a diversified higher secondary education in which the academic stream would cater for not more than about 50% of the students at the higher secondary level. A necessary feature of the higher secondary education would, therefore, be the provision of a large number of vocational streams which would generally be terminal but the system itself would be so designed that one may transfer from the academic to the vocational stream without having to start in the other stream from the very beginning, with provisions for pursuing some of the study through part-time and correspondence courses."

VOCATIONAL GUIDANCE IN CLASSES XI AND XII

Objectives of Guidance

1. To help students discover their own abilities and aptitudes.

2. To find out what type of job situations will meet these aptitudes most adequately.

3. To make students realise that education does not lead only to any type of job, the entrance to which lies through university education, but that each of us possess abilities for which there are several situations in a growing economy like ours.

4. To establish a close link between the individual, his abilities and the employment situation obtaining in the country.

5. To give rise to a better adjusted youth who will think of some more gainful pursuits if higher education does not suit them.

6. To include activities which would help the child develop a kind of vocational maturity to enable him to look at life work from a more realistic standpoint.

7. To inculcate in him good work habits and develop proper work attitudes basic to work success and work satisfaction.

Need of Guidance

The need of guidance has been envisaged in *Higher Secondary Education and its Vocationalisation* (April 1976), published by NCERT as "Institutions would have to provide some kind of guidance and counselling for careers and courses to take the best advantages of such a situation. This means that higher secondary institutions will have to get at least some of their teachers trained in careers advisement so that they may help the parents and students to make the best choice of courses in the first instance, and later on to advise them about any proposed changes in the options."

TYPES OF GUIDANCE SERVICES IN THE SCHOOL

1. Individual inventory service. The first essential of every guidance programme in the school is the compilation of individual inventory in the form of a cumulative record giving detailed information about each student concerning his abilities and achievements of different areas. This information should be kept up-to-date to be used for the good of the student.

2. Information service. Students of higher secondary schools generally need three types of information to make decisions about various courses, occupations and institutions, (i) Information about colleges and training opportunities, (ii) Information about available occupations, and (iii) Information about scholarships and other financial help available during the training period. Thus, information may be collected from papers and magazines, government notifications and bulletins and information centres of the Employment Exchanges, etc. Its usefulness will be lost if it is not up-to-date. It may be supplemented by talks of people from different occupations.

3. Counselling service. Regarded as the 'heart' of the guidance programme this service must assist an individual in identifying understanding and solving problems that confront him by a well-trained counsellor.

4. Placement service. It helps the individual in obtaining employment. Placement service has three stages :

(i) *Assessing* the abilities, aptitudes and interests of the individual student.

(ii) *Analysing* several occupations, particularly the ones in which the student expresses his interest.

(iii) *Relating* occupations and abilities.

5. Follow-up service. A continuation of the guidance give to a particular individual follow-up service enables the authorities to check the worthwhileness or otherwise of the guidance services provided in the school. It can be generally done by issuing questionnaires and holding interviews from time to time.

A MINIMUM GUIDANCE PROGRAMME FOR HIGHER SECONDARY SCHOOLS

Objectives

1. To orient the pupils and parents with regard to the aims of guidance programme and its various activities.

2. To help the students in educational and personal adjustments.

3. To help the delta class pupils in selecting the electives.

4. To orient the pupils to the world of work and helping the school-leaving pupils in making educational and/or vocational plans.

5. To help students to develop a realistic self-concept of their strengths and weaknesses, their abilities, their interests, their educational achievements and the like.

SUGGESTED ACTIVITIES

I. General Activities in a Guidance Programme

(i) *Discussion of the plan with the Principal.*

(ii) *Orientation of the School Faculty.*

(iii) *Formation of the School Guidance Committee* : Headed by the Headmaster the Committee consists of the Career Masters, Physical Education Teacher and one representative from each of the streams. The Head Master is to be the President and one of the Career Masters, the Secretary.

(iv) *Student orientation :* Orienting the students with regard to the need for guidance and various activities to be organised under the Guidance Programme.

(v) *Parents Orientation.*

(vi) *Setting up of information centre.*

The above programmes except setting up of information centre may be carried out within a fortnight from the date of the reopening of the school. The dates and the time may be fixed by the Guidance Committee.

II. Specific Activities in a Guidance Programme for Middle Classes (VI to VIII)

1. Collection of Data

(i) Identifying data.

(ii) Home and family background data.

(iii) Scholastic achievement data.

2. Orientation Programme (Group Guidance) for Pupils

(i) Regarding the school environment.

(ii) Regarding the curriculum and special services including facilities available in the school.

(iii) Regarding regular study habits, use of leisure, etc.

(iv) Regarding social adjustment.

3. Orientation Programme for Parents of New Entrants

(i) Regarding the School.

(ii) Regarding the role of parents in the Guidance Programme.

4. Starting the cumulative record. If it has not been done in earlier classes it should be done now. The entries in the Cumulative Record will be made by the class teacher.

5. Intelligence tests. Administering two group tests of Intelligence — one verbal and another non-verbal.

6. Identification. Identification of underachievers and likely dropouts.

7. Remedial programme. Providing assistance in organising remedial programme for the weak students and enrichment programme for the gifted ones.

8. Syntality. Understanding 'Syntality' of each class section.

9. Improvement. Steps to improve 'Climate for learning'.

10. Counselling. Referral to specialists should be keeping in view the problem.

Time Schedule

1. Activities (1) and (2). These are to be completed before the third week of first month after the reopening of the school.

2. Activity (3). It is to be taken up in the 2nd week of the first month.

3. Activity (5). It is to be taken up in the 4th week of the first month.

4. Activity (6). It may be taken up just after the first terminal examination.

5. Activity (7). It may be taken up after the underachievers and low achievers have been identified.

6. Activity (8). It may be undertaken in the last week of second month when the students would have known each other intimately.

Guidance Programme at Class IX

1. Orientation programme for new students and their parents.
2. Collection of data on aptitudes, interests, achievement and other psychological variables.
3. Programme for self-understanding — know yourself, know your abilities, know your personality, etc.
4. Programme for orienting to the world of work.
5. Field trips.
6. Career conferences and exhibitions.
7. Helping students in the choice of courses.
8. Referral of cases to counsellor and specialists keeping in view their problems.
9. Identification of underachievers and dropouts.
10. Providing assistance in organising remedial programmes for the weak students and enrichment programme for the gifted ones.

Time Schedule

1. Activity (1). It is to be completed within a fortnight from the date of reopening.

2. Activity (2). It is to be completed in the first two months.

3. Activities (3) to (6). These are to be taken up in the 3rd, 4th, and 5th months.

4. Activities (9 and 10). These are to be taken up after the first terminal examination.

Guidance Programme at Class X

Three options for students :

(1) They can enter the world of work. A teacher can create awareness among them regarding the development of knowledge and skills, effective work habits, and proper attitudes which can be helpful in the personal and vocational development of students.

(2) They can take up vocational courses. A teacher can help in the choice for vocational courses and socially useful productive work in the light of his future career plans.

(3) They can take up academic courses to study to prepare for first level degree courses in a college or university. A teacher can help in the choice of academic courses in the light of his future career plan.

Guidance Programme at Class XI

1. **Orientation programme.** This is for new students and their parents.

2. **Starting the cumulative record card.** This is if not already started in earlier classes or available from previous school. The entries will be made by the class teacher.

3. **Collection of data.** This is on aptitudes, interests, personality and other psychological variables for new entrants. Where there is no Counsellor, testing may be limited to two tests of General Intelligence — one verbal and another non-verbal, provided at least a few of the teachers have had special training in the use of tests.

4. **Identification.** This is concerning underachievers and potential dropouts.

5. **Providing guidance.** It is to students who desire a change in the stream.

6. **Remedial measures.** Providing assistance in organising remedial programme for the weak students and enrichment programme for the gifted ones.

7. **Learning skills.** Helping students in learning skills useful in studying effectively, good examinee behaviour, and the use of library resources.

8. **Syntality.** Understanding 'Syntality' of each class section.

9. **Improvement.** Steps to improve climate of learning.

10. **Counselling.** Counselling or referral to specialists, keeping in view the problem.

Time Schedule

Same as for class IX above.

Activity 5 should be taken up after the first terminal examination and should terminate after the half-yearly examination result.

Guidance Programme at Class XII

1. **Activities.** Continuing activities listed for Class XI. Activities 4 and 5 should be organised intensively.

2. **Data.** Collection of data on aptitudes, interests, personality and other psychological variables and preparation of profiles. Administration of two tests of intelligence — one verbal and another non-verbal is given where there is no Counsellor.

3. Self-understanding. Programme for self-understanding — know your abilities, know your interests and know your personality.

4. Understanding world of work. Programme for understanding world of work, organising class talks, field trips, career conferences, etc.

5. Guidance to parents. It is given through Parent-Teacher Association regarding vocations.

6. Individual counselling programme and complete psychological testing. It would be taken up only when the services of a Counsellor are available.

Facilities Required

1. Physical facilities. A separate room with necessary furniture for guidance activities.

2. Financial Facilities

(i) A non-recurring expenditure of Rs. 5000/- for the purchase of test materials and information material needed for the guidance programme every 5th year.

(ii) A recurring expenditure of Rs. 5/- per head p.a. for following items :

(a) Audio-visual material.

(b) Occupational information material.

(c) Organising field trips (Guidance).

(d) Career conferences and exhibitions.

(e) Films and film strips.

(f) Answer sheets for tests.

SUGGESTIONS FOR EFFECTIVE IMPLEMENTATION OF THE SCHEME

1. Career master. These should be one Career Master per 500 students for classes VI to X.

2. Periods. The Career Master should devote 6 periods a week to guidance work.

3. Allowance. An allowance of Rs. 100/- per month may be paid to the Career Master, as is already being done in case of teachers in charge of NCC, Audio-visual education, etc.

4. School staff. The school staff should be oriented towards guidance. Class teachers should be trained in filling Cumulative Record Cards and administration and scoring of Psychological Tests.

5. Training. There should be a trained Counsellor in every higher secondary school from classes XI and XII.

6. Services for All Pupils

(i) Orientation of new pupils.

(ii) Articulation of pupils from school to school and level to level.
(iii) Group guidance for all information regarding activities.

7. Services for Individual Pupils

(i) Counselling individual one to one or in groups.
(ii) Individual child study.
(iii) Information about environment.
(iv) Placement of the individual in groups for instruction.
(v) Placement of the individual in jobs.

8. Services for Teachers

(i) Referrals from teachers.
(ii) Participation with teachers.

9. Services for Administrators

(i) Curriculum development.
(ii) Community liaison (information only).

10. Research Services for School and Community

(i) Survey of the community for occupational information.
(ii) Follow-up of the individual students to evaluate effectiveness of the guidance programme.

SUGGESTIONS FOR SOLVING PROBLEMS CONCERNING GUIDANCE

1. Occupational orientation of pupils. Wise selection of a career is based on the realistic understanding of self and the world of work. The students need information about the various educational facilities and occupational opportunities. Following suggestions are offered in this connection :

(i) *The State bureaus* : These should draw up a minimum programme for the occupational orientation of pupils in schools and discuss the same in the meeting of the State Co-ordination Committee.
(ii) *Vocational guidance officers and career masters* : Their responsibility should be clearly defined so that every one knows what to do and when to do it.
(iii) *The Vocational guidance officers* : They should occasionally meet the Career Masters in groups so as to keep them informed about the latest position regarding job opportunities and occupational trends.
(iv) *Full time counsellor* : In the schools having full-time counsellors on the staff, at least one period a week in each of the classes IX, X, XI and XII should be provided in the time-table.
(v) *Part-time career masters* : In schools with part-time Career Masters one period a fortnight may be provided.

2. Assessment of pupil data for use in guidance

(i) *Counsellor* : The assessment of the abilities, interests and skills of the students would be the function of the Counsellor or Career Masters.

(ii) *Cumulative record cards* : It should be maintained for all students.

(iii) *Vocational guidance officer* : The schools should make available to him, on request the information about those students who seek the help of the Employment Exchange for placement.

3. Placement of youth. The placement of youth in training, apprenticeship or entry jobs should be the responsibility of the Employment Service.

4. Local Coordination

(i) A District Coordination Committee should be formed where it does not exist

(ii) Career conferences, career exhibitions, career weeks and career fortnights may be organised jointly with a view to arousing the interests of the general public in the guidance of the youth.

(iii) The Vocational Guidance Officers and the representatives of the State Bureaus should contribute articles on guidance to newspapers, give career talks on the radio and television, address parent-teacher associations and initiate discussion on the guidance problems in the meetings of the Principals' associations.

5. Evaluation of the guidance programme. Guidance programme in schools and the Employment Exchanges should be evaluated at regular intervals through the joint venture of the Employment Service and education authorities. A representative of the Education Department should be invited for the assessment of the guidance programme being offered at the Employment Exchanges. Vocational Guidance Officer may accompany the Education Officer of the school for the assessment of guidance programme in the school.

MODEL SCHEME FOR CONDUCT OF AREA SKILL SURVEY

Historical Background

The Conference of Chief Secretaries held in June 1970 while discussing Vocational Guidance programmes and Career Advising Service and Training Schemes recommended the launching of Area Skill Surveys has a method of determining current availability of skills and requirements in the foreseeable future. The project was discussed in a meeting held on 15 October, 1970, under the chairmanship of the Employment Commissioner. A working group comprising representatives from the Directorate of Manpower, I.A.M.R. and the

D.G.E.T. was constituted to formulate a Model Scheme for conduct of Area Skill Surveys. This Group met on 15th December, 1970, and on 16th March, 1971 formulated the Model Scheme for conduct of Area Skill Surveys.

Meaning. According to the working group an Area Skill Survey is basically a method of determining current availability of skills and requirements in the foreseeable future in respect of a given geographic area. Skill surveys seek to find an answer to such questions as : What are the characteristics of employed work force by age, sex, skill level, educational qualifications, wastage, turn-over, etc.? What are the factors that are likely to affect the existing and future composition of labour force? What are the skills needed in various occupations and industries and how will the situation be affected by the proposed economic development plan for the area? How does the output from the existing training and educational institutions balance with the current and future manpower requirements? What is or will be the scope for self-employment in an area?

Objectives

(i) To assist in translating economic goals set forth in a planned economy into manpower terms.

(ii) To provide specific information on changes that will be necessary in the size and quality of training and apprenticeship programme to meet future requirements.

(iii) To provide information for use in vocational guidance which depends for its success on a sound knowledge of changing job opportunities in different occupations in the areas.

(iv) To furnish details for use in job development and placement activities of the Employment Service.

(v) To provide area-wise information concerning manpower resources needed in connection with location and expansion of industries.

(vi) To supply information which will enable identification and development of avenues for self-employment.

Vocational Courses at 'plus two' Stage, Provision of Facilities for on-the-job Training

The NCERT's draft paper on "Higher Secondary Education and its Vocationalisation" recommends that each State should undertake a district-level survey for starting vocational courses keeping in mind the needs of the area. The Mathura survey has suggested that there would be no difficulty in finding employment in the district for those who take vocational courses relevant to such industries as book publishing and printing, fertiliser, coal tar, plastics, fabrication work, dairying, sugarcane crushing, animal husbandry, inland fishery, co-operative farming, agricultural extension services, food preservation and processing units and veterinary services.

As for self-employment opportunities, the survey team identified following areas as having considerable scope : agricultural implement manufacture and repairs, tractor repairs, motor-pump repairing, poultry, intensive cultivation to raise such crops as potatoes, vegetables and sugarcane. Regarding the possible expansion of small-scale industries, ancillary industrial units and the location of the oil refinery in Mathura, the team feels there is considerable scope for development of those trained as stenographers, salesmen and accounts clerks.

The Council has taken up surveys in the districts of Mysore in Karnataka, Berhampur in Orissa, Ganganagar in Rajasthan and Durg in Madhya Pradesh. It has recommended to the State Governments that such district survey work should be undertaken to identify employment opportunities so that suitable vocational courses could be offered there. This would minimise the rate of migration to urban areas.

The Role of the Teacher

The teacher has a key role to play in whole programme of guidance. His systematic and proper orientation would be necessary if he has to become increasingly efficient in guidance work. This could be done by providing him with special facilities to acquaint him with the basic purposes and functions of the guidance programme. In this connection, extension courses in guidance organised by the Extension Services Departments and State Institutes of Education would be useful. Further, they could be provided with up-to-date guidance literature written in a non-technical language and in concise form. As they become oriented to the new idea of guidance, they are not likely to be deterred from the task by the provision or otherwise of funds for the programme.

QUESTIONS FOR EXERCISE

1. Explain the significance of the New Pattern of Education. What benefits may be expected from this pattern?
2. What types of guidance services may be provided in a school for the successful implementation of the scheme?
3. 'Provision of Vocational Guidance is Fundamental to the New Scheme.' Explain.
4. Discuss the need and importance of Area Skill Survey for providing vocational guidance to the students.
5. Suggest a suitable programme of educational and vocational guidance in the context of 10+2+3 system of education.

29

Guidance and Counselling in Indian Colleges and Universities

STRUCTURE OF GUIDANCE IN COLLEGES IN UNIVERSITIES

Different structures of guidance will have to be planned to suit different set-ups in colleges and universities. This is as follows :

1. For Constituent Colleges on the Campus

(i) *If the number of students on rolls is 1,000* : A counselling officer assisted by the Guidance Committee can plan the programme according to their needs and implement it with the co-operation of the Deputy Chief of UEIGB and Academic Adviser of SAB.

(ii) *If the number of students is less than 1,000* : A Liaison officer may be appointed.

(iii) *If the number of students exceeds 1,000* : An assistant counselling officer may be appointed to assist the counselling officer. While the counselling officer may be appointed in the Reader's scale, the Assistant Counsellor may be appointed in the Lecturer's scale.

2. For Affiliated Colleges at a Distance

(i) *If the number of students on rolls is 1,000* : A counselling officer assisted by the Guidance Committee can plan the programme and implement it with the help of Vocational Guidance Officer.

(ii) *If the number of students is less than 1,000* : Liaison officer may be appointed.

(iii) *If the number of students exceeds 1,000* : An assistant counselling officer may be appointed to assist the counselling officer for every 1000 students or part thereof. Each university should have a specialist co-ordinator of Guidance Services to help the counselling officers or Liaison officers in different colleges.

3. For the Universities

(i) *If the number of students is below 1,000* : Deans of Students, specially assisted by the Heads of Departments of Psychology and Education, and the Guidance Committee with the Counselling Officer can plan the programme and implement it with the co-operation of the Deputy Chief of UEIGB and Academic Adviser of SAB.

(ii) *If the number of students exceeds 1000* : Assistant counselling officers may be appointed. One assistant counselling officer may be had for every 1,000 students. Some of these counselling officers may be taken from student leaders on some *adhoc* remuneration or with special rights and facilities including representation of different groups, or sections of students.

The Counselling Officer in the university should be in the Reader's grade while the Assistant Counselling Officer may be in the Lecturer's grade.

ESSENTIAL GUIDANCE ACTIVITIES IN COLLEGES/UNIVERSITIES

1. Guidance and counselling committee. A Guidance and Counselling Committee should be formed consisting of the Dean/Principal, Counselling/Liaison Officer, teachers representing different points of view, academic disciplines, interests and basic philosophies, student representatives, parents, Deputy Chief of UEIGB, Vocational Guidance Officer, etc. It should serve as an advisory committee or a policy making body for the programme. It can thrash out problems requiring group solution. It should plan monthly, quarterly and yearly programme, co-ordinate guidance activities and assess the work done.

It is necessary to determine the limits of responsibility of the guidance committee and identify the specific role to be assumed by each faculty and staff member.

2. Clerical assistance. It needs to be provided to the Counselling/ Liaison officer. A methodically organised guidance programme would require maintenance of a lot of record/information by a part time to whole time assistant depending upon the load of work.

3. Counselling centre. Every university and a big college should have a counselling centre headed by a trained professional counselling officer with a Ph.D. or Master's degree in Psychology and Counselling along with considerable counselling experience.

Functions

(i) Assisting individuals and small groups of students and staff members with special educational, vocational and personal problems.

(ii) Assisting the university and constituent colleges in developing, advising and counselling programmes and consultation on special psychological problems.

(iii) Providing psychological testing facilities for the university both for individuals and groups.

(iv) Carrying on research on the development of testing procedures and experimental programmes in counselling.

GUIDANCE AND COUNSELLING SET-UP IN COLLEGES

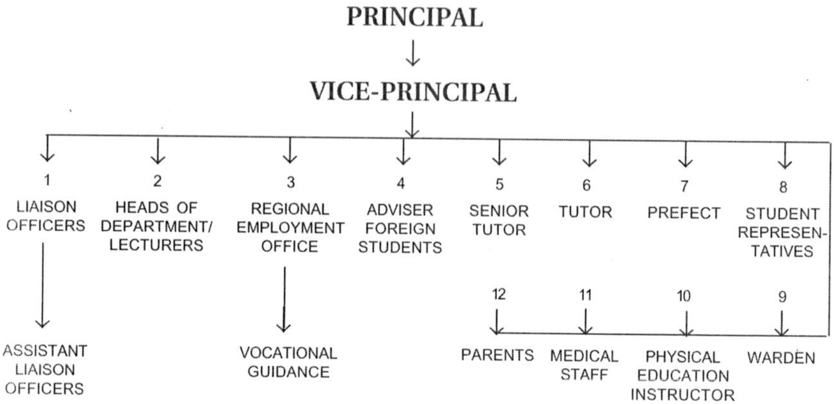

(v) Helping the training of post-graduate students in counselling and testing.

(vi) Developing confidence in the Counselling Services by meeting new students at the time of orientation, visiting the hostel and giving talks to assemblies.

The Counselling Centre include special clinics and laboratories for speech and hearing problems, study skills and reading improvement.

The Centre should be situated at convenient place so as to facilitate the provisions of counselling services for the whole university community, or at least the colleges in the immediate vicinity.

4. The Counselling officer/liaison officer's office. The Counselling officer/Liaison officer should be given a separate room with sufficient privacy and adequately furnished with a small desk or table with a chair for the Counselling/ Liaison officer and one or two extra chairs for the visitors, a small book-shelf, a filing cabinet, an almirah, curtains for the windows and doors, a flower vase of table lamp or even an attractive paper weight. The room should be made cheerful and pleasant, inviting, warm and attractive so that the students like to visit it and feel welcome and at home.

5. Occupational information room. Occupational information room to be set up in every college and university should have adequate arrangements for the seating of the students who may visit it for counselling the occupational information material sufficient space for conducting group discussions and other guidance activities and some provision for individual guidance. It should be distinct and prominently noticeable. If a separate room cannot be spared, a portion of a room or a verandah may be utilised for the purpose.

Suggestions for Display of Occupational Information

(i) Presentation of the information having relevance to the current needs of the students should be attractive and motivating.

(ii) Charts, posters and other visual aids should be at the eye level of the students.

(iii) Detailed information, if placed for reading, should be purposively arranged bearing close relationship with the materials displayed on the walls.

(iv) Materials should not be crowded in a particular place; but evenly distributed over places where students normally gather for receiving various services.

(v) Material displayed should be reviewed frequently in order to updating the contents as also highlighting specific aspects of the information.

6. Student record system. An effective guidance and counselling programme presupposes reliable, valid and comprehensive information about the individual which is possible only when the work of collecting information is done on a systematic basis. Maintenance of cumulative Record Card is necessary for good guidance programme. Counselling officer should maintain this record with the cooperation of other members of the faculty.

Contents of Students Cumulative Record

(i) Student's identification, family history, personal history, health condition, etc.

(ii) Test results.

(iii) Problems inside and outside the college/university, emotional and social problems.

(iv) Specific assets and limitations.

(v) Unusual talents.

(vi) Academic and co-curricular progress.

(vii) Placement.

(viii) Follow-up.

Activities of Counselling/Liaison Officer

1. Educational talks. Talks on educational topics may be given by the Counselling/Liaison Officer or the members of the Guidance Committee or some highly educated and experienced persons from the community or some neighbouring institution. Some suggestive themes are : adjustment with the institution, adjustment with peers, getting the best out of college/university education, studying effectively, preparation of notes, preparing and taking examinations, utilisation of library services, participation in co-curricular activities, good work habits, entry and success in a job, taking an interview, living in hostels, choosing your career.

2. Orientation talks. Orientation talks provide adequate information to the students regarding the courses of studies, the facilities available in the institution in the form of libraries, laboratories, workshops, playgrounds, hobbies, teaching personnel, freeships, fee concessions, stipends, scholarships, etc., information about courses and careers open to graduates/post-graduates, competitive examinations, correspondence courses, apprenticeship schemes, entry jobs which could be taken up fresh from the college/university without experience, courses and careers available abroad, changing occupational pattern, employment and occupational trends, guidance agencies at different levels, etc.

3. Career talks. Career talk, a talk about the details of a particular job maybe delivered on themes such as avenues open to graduates and post-graduates, self-employment schemes, government service, scope of employment, methods of recruitment, discovering vocational interests and aptitudes, exploring vocations which interest you, planning your vocational programme, etc.

GUIDANCE AND COUNSELLING SET-UP IN UNIVERSITIES

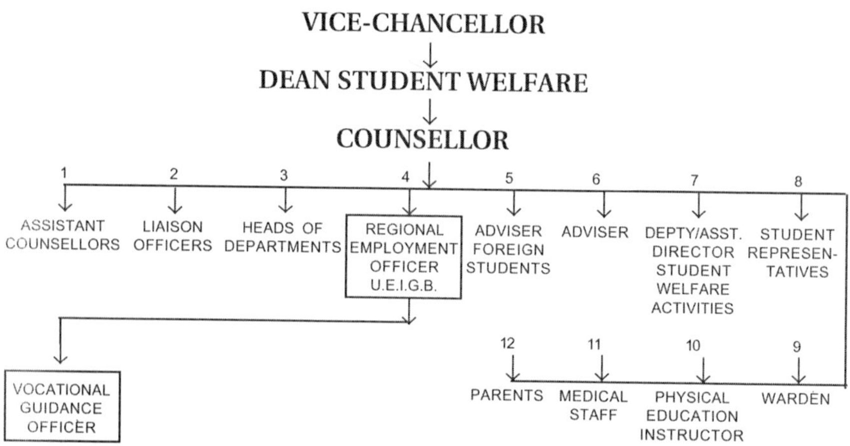

4. Career conferences. Career conference is a group activity organised for the purpose of providing occupational information of a preliminary or supplementary nature to a large number of students in a small or a big group. In it several speakers belonging to different professions come and deliver talks about their own fields to groups of students. Career conferences may be organised twice a year.

5. Plant tours. Visits to commercial establishment, industries, professional colleges, research institutions, etc., should be arranged to provide the students with direct and first hand experience of the work done and its physical and social environment. The students should be prepared well in advance so that they know what to observe, which questions to ask and how to behave during the visit. A visit is more useful when followed by a group discussion in which students talk about, what they have seen and exchange ideas.

6. Screening of films and film-strips. Film shows followed by group discussions are important means of disseminating information.

A TENTATIVE SCHEDULE OF GUIDANCE FOR VARIOUS CLASSES

(A) T.D.C. I class in colleges and M.A./M.Sc. I Year

(l) Collection of data about

(i) the home and family background of the students,

(ii) the educational achievement of the students,

(iii) the achievement of the students in co-curricular activities,

(iv) any special feature of limitation.

(2) Orientation programme for the students

(i) *Institution orientation* : Familiarising with the college/university organisation, past achievement, present plans and programmes and future plans and perspectives, the policies in respect of admissions, changes of courses, participation in activities.

(ii) *Courses orientation* : Familiarising with the varied courses and combinations allowed, the arrangement of co-curricular activities, hobbies, etc.

(iii) *Facility orientation* : Familiarising with the facility of freeships fee concessions scholarships, loans, part-time jobs, fellowships — how and when and to whom to apply and through whom the applications are to be routed.

(iv) *Testing.* Arranging testing programme to help + 12 students in the selection of T.D.C. subjects.

(v) *Educational talks* : Giving educational talks on how to study effectively for maximum gain, budgeting time, taking class-room notes, using leisure profitably, getting the best out of college/university education, adjusting with college/university teachers, class-mates, senior and junior students, choosing friends of the right type, living in hostels, etc.

(vi) *Films shows* : Some films may be shown on the running of some famous colleges and universities.

These activities should be completed during the first month of the beginning of the academic session.

(3) Orientation programme for the parents/guardians of the students. Efforts should be made to invite as many parents as possible for the orientation programme to tell. What does a university/college offer and how their wards can benefit. This will help the students.

This activity may be taken up in the second week of the first month.

(4) Starting the cumulative record card. Cumulative Record Card contains different types of information regarding the student. Its entries can be made by the tutor or adviser, in the college and teachers or advisers in the universities in the third week of the first month of the academic session.

(5) Identification of low and high achievers and students with speech, hearing and reading handicaps. This may be taken up after life first terminal test or first semester examination so that they may be given special attention and guidance for a purposeful career.

(6) Identification of problem students. This can done during the first three months.

(7) Personality counselling for low achievers and students with other problems or sending them to specialists. This is to enable them to make a satisfactory adjustment to the demands of college/university life and to assist them to obtain deeper insight into their own personalities through which they may resolve personality conflicts, and lower the level of anxiety and improve performance.

(B) T.D.C. II Class in colleges

(1) Collection of data about new students

(a) The home and family background of the students.

(b) The educational achievement of the students.

(c) The achievement of the student in co-curricular activities.

(d) Any special feature or limitation.

(2) Supplementary orientation programme. Familiarising the students regarding any change in courses, policies regarding admission and evaluation, fee concessions, etc. in the first two weeks of the new academic session.

(3) Remedial programmes for the weak and enrichment programme for the talented. This may be done in second month of the new academic session.

(C) TDC III Year — M.A./M.Sc. Final and other final classes

Orientation Programme

This programme may be taken up at the beginning and at the end of the session, when the counselling officer meets the parents by appointment. It contain the following activities :

1. Giving information regarding the courses/careers open to these students.

2. Giving information regarding the world of work.

3. Organising field trips.

4. Arranging career conferences and exhibitions. These activities may be spread over during the last term.

5. Arranging remedial programmes for the under-achievers.

6. Helping students in learning the skills which will help them in effective study, use of library resources, etc.

7. Sending the students to the expert according to the problem. These activities may be taken up when the need arises.

8. Guiding parents about the careers through P.T.As.

Requisites

For the implementation of the above programme following requisites need to be provided in addition to the required trained personnel :

1. Funds for activities. At least 5 per cent of the students' amalgamated fund should be earmarked for meeting the expenditure on activities related to guidance and counselling as :

(i) Audio-visual material.
(ii) Field trips.
(iii) Career conferences and exhibitions.
(iv) Answer sheets or the psychological tests.
(v) Purchase of occupational information and educational guidance and counselling literature.

2. Patronage and support of the Administrator.

QUESTIONS FOR EXERCISE

1. Describe the essential guidance activities in colleges/universities.
2. Give a tentative schedule of guidance for various classes.

30

THE UNIVERSITY EMPLOYMENT INFORMATION AND GUIDANCE BUREAUX (UEIGB) AND UNIVERSITY STUDENTS ADVISORY BUREAUX (USAB)

U.E.I.G.B.

Historical Background

1. Foundation. In 1956, a study group on Educated Unemployed recommended the establishment of the Bureaux in the universities to provide their alumni with employment information and career guidance. In 1957, the scheme for the setting up of the Bureaux was prepared by the Directorate General of Employment and Training envisaging bureaux to be primarily employment counselling agencies which could also function as placement agencies for professional and highly qualified persons and cater to the needs of all students of the universities whether still pursuing studies or about to leave after completing their education.

2. First Bureau. The first University Employment Information and Guidance Bureau was set up in 1958 at the University of Delhi. As the experiment was successful, bureaux were set up in almost all the universities of the country as an integral part of the National Employment Service functioning according to the procedures and policies laid down by it.

3. Financial assistance. At its meeting held on 5th May, 1971, the University Grants Commission considered the question of giving financial assistance to universities for their University Employment Information-cum-Advisory Bureaux and Career Advising Units in selected affiliated colleges, U.G.C. to provide financial assistance up to the end of the Fourth Plan period to 41 bureaux and 75 career advising units whose proposals were approved by the Commission.

4. Recommendations. The Review Committee appointed by the University Grants Commission on September 2, 1976, recommended the following :

(i) *Association of authorities* : The Vice-Chancellor and other university authorities as well as different faculties and departments should be actively associated with the activities of the bureau.

(ii) *Projects programme and studies* : The bureaux should initiate research projects programmes and studies to be conducted in collaboration with various concerned departments of the university/colleges on local and regional basis for estimation of manpower requirements in various categories in the context of the developmental outlay in a district/region/state. The UGC should provide necessary financial assistance for such programmes, and projects on priority basis. COHSIP colleges (College of Humanities and Social Sciences Improvement Programme) could be fruitfully involved for data collection and surveys.

(iii) *Policies, procedures and guidelines* : The DGE and T should continue to be responsible for framing policies, procedures, general guidelines and norms for the functioning of the Guidance Bureaux.

(iv) *National apex body* : An apex body should be set up at the national level under the aegis and guidance of the DGE and T, without prejudice to its autonomy to collect data regarding manpower requirements. It may consist of the representatives of the DGE and T, UGC, Indian Council of Agriculture Research (ICAR), Indian Council of Medical Research (ICMR), NCERT, National Laboratories, etc.

(v) *District bureaux* : Considering the requirements of universities and colleges and taking into account the number of students involved, in future separate bureaux, in district headquarters where there is a cluster of colleges, be organised under the aegis of the main university bureau.

Organisation

The bureau is an integral part of the National Employment Service. It functions according to the procedures and policies laid down by the service. It has an advisory committee with the Vice-Chancellor as its chairman to gear the working of the bureau to the needs of the university. Among others, the committee consists of heads of departments, principals of colleges, representatives of employers, the state and central governments, director of employment and training, deputy secretary to government, labour and employment department; deputy chief of UEIGB, representative of Director General of Employment and Training; Ministry of Labour, Government of India; President of Rotary Club or his nominee, student representatives and Liaison officers of the colleges, etc. The bureau functions under the guidance of the Vice-Chancellor of the university. A senior member of the teaching staff of the university is responsible to the Vice-Chancellor for the day-to-day work of the bureau works on a part-time basis and is paid Rs. 200/- p.m. for this service by the state government. Provided by the State Department of Employment the staff for bureau consists of 1 Divisional or Regional Employment Officer or Deputy Chief, 1 Technical Assistant, 2 Clerks, 1 Steno Typist, 2 Peons, while the university provides accommodation and furniture to the bureau at its own cost, the rest of the expenditure is borne by the state government.

Venue

The bureau maintains a Career Information Room for use of the visitors where guidance literature and other material considered useful for university students is displayed along with a visitor's register to keep a record of those who use this room.

Functions of the Bureaux

(i) Giving employment information and advice to the university alumni.

(ii) Collecting and disseminating information on higher education, technical and professional courses in India and abroad.

(iii) Providing help for admission in foreign universities.

(iv) Rendering employment assistance of graduates in professional and post-graduate courses and to answer enquiries regarding the availability of suitable applicants on its registers from employers and furnish particulars where called for.

(v) Providing information of scholarships, fellowships, grants and loans to students.

(vi) Assisting students in finding part time and vacation employment.

(vii) Arranging group guidance by faculty members on social adjustments and other problems of students.

(viii) Giving proper orientation to students to cultivate right attitudes towards work.

(ix) Arranging talks on employment opportunities to students of various faculties by specialists and employers.

(x) Mobilising community resources for making available guidance and employment to the students.

(xi) Arranging group programmes of vocational guidance.

(xii) Arranging visits of students for on-the-spot studies of occupations.

(xiii) Conducting surveys and research pertaining to guidance and manpower, etc.

Categories of Applications Registered

(i) Persons holding Bachelor's or higher degree or equivalent diploma in a professional or specialist course, such as Engineering, Medicine, Agriculture, Veterinary Science, Technology, Law, Education, etc.

(ii) Persons holding a Master's or higher degree or post-graduate diploma or equivalent in other subjects except B.A./B.Sc./B.T./B.Ed.

Other graduates can be registered but after registration their index cards are transferred to the local employment exchange where all further action is taken in respect of them.

(iii) National Register Card (C-1) is to be completed and sent to the CSIR in respect of the scientists and technical personnel who are eligible for registration in the special section of the National Register maintained by the CSIR.

(iv) University Employment Bureaux are to register not only their own alumni but also graduates of other universities resident in the area, who seek such registration.

PROCEDURE OF EMPLOYMENT

1. Circulation of vacancies. The Directorate General of Employment and Training and the State Appointments Branch officers concerned circulate to the University Employment Bureaux vacancies that are appropriate for those registered with them. The bureaux submit particulars of suitable candidates on their registers to the P and EO against vacancies notified by it. The P and EO considers these candidates for submission against notified vacancies at par with the candidates on its own register. The bureaux make direct submission against vacancies circulated to them by the Central Employment Exchange. The university bureaux may also submit particulars of suitable persons in response to specific enquiries addressed to them by private employers.

2. Forms and procedure. The University Employment Bureaux follow the same procedure and use the same forms as the National Employment Service. Modifications, if necessary, are made in consultation with the DGE and T and the university authorities.

3. Statistics of the work of bureaux. These are rendered in the forms prescribed for the purpose. If an applicant submitted by the bureau is placed against a vacancy circulated by the P and EO it is accounted for the POD placement by the P and EO and the bureau counts it as LOD placement.

4. Co-ordination. The DGE and T effects the necessary coordination at all India level in regard to registration and circulation of vacancies to University Employment Bureaux. At the state level, the State Appointments Branch Office (State Directorate of Employment Bureaux situated within the state) does this job.

COMMUNICATION BETWEEN BUREAUX AND THE COLLEGE

1. Liaison units. One of the channels of communication between bureaux and the college student community is the liaison units in colleges.

2. Career advising units. Many bureaux have assisted the constituent and affiliated colleges in their jurisdiction in establishing career advising units under the charge of a teacher of the colleges concerned. The bureaux regularly feed occupational information literature to these college units.

3. Training seminars. Bureaux organise training seminars for the Liaison Officers.

4. Conferences, talks and exhibitions. Bureaux also help them to arrange career and educational conferences, talks and exhibitions.

LIMITATIONS OF THE BUREAUX

Although the bureaux have been functioning in our country for about four decades, they have not fulfilled the objectives for which they were set up. The lukewarm attitude of the universities as well as the state governments, lack of proper accommodation, furniture and equipment, and only a meagre budget are stated to be some of the reasons for this state of affairs. They need to make special efforts so that they matter in the university life.

Suggestions for Improvement

(i) *Hobby clubs* : Bureaux should sponsor hobby clubs at the university and colleges which may be helpful in developing technical and professional skills of the students.

(ii) *Training* : Bureaux should give training for preparing the youth conduct mock interviews, organise periodic quiz contests regarding the questions set or topics commonly covered in the employment interview, hold sessions on how to face the interview, give guidance on how to prepare for competitive examinations. The National Employment Service should activate the Bureaux in its fold to render service on these lines.

(iii) *Awareness of importance* : Bureaux should endeavour to create an awareness, motivation and acceptance of the importance of guidance on education and employment given by them to the university and college students.

(iv) *Information* : Bureaux should supply detailed, latest and up-to-date information on occupations, training, admissions, higher studies, apprenticeship facilities, scholarships, study facilities abroad, employment information, general trends in job market situations, etc.

(v) *Data banks* : The bureaux should be veritable "data banks" on careers and courses of local, regional and national interest so that once a student visits the bureau, he finds something worthwhile to read, rather than be disappointed and goes frustrated, not to visit it again.

(vi) *Humanistic approach* : Bureaux should treat the students and job seekers calling for guidance not as mere cases but as 'individual personalities' passing through a crucial phase of life. They should honestly, sincerely and genuinely try to help the students and job-seekers in solving their problems.

(vii) *Library* : Bureaux should have a good reference library having information on the following aspects :

(a) Syllabi of all India universities.

(b) Facilities for research specialisation in different universities and research institutes in India and abroad.

(c) Scholarships available for specialised training courses.

(d) Facilities for study abroad.

(e) Relevant selected books and periodicals, etc.

(viii) *Talks and film shows* : Bureaux should arrange group talks and screen films on career counselling.

(ix) *Exhibitions* : Bureaux should arrange mobile exhibitions for the benefit of students in the rural and urban colleges.

(x) *Research* : Bureaux should undertake research projects, relevant to employment and unemployment aspects of the local area.

(xi) *Manpower planning* : Bureaux should provide scientific and imperial base for manpower planning by conducting studies and surveys on recruitment practices of employers, occupational aspirations of students, etc.

(xii) *Chiefs* : Bureux should have full time chiefs in the scale of university professor, designated as the Director of Bureau.

(xiii) *Liaison* : Bureaux should maintain liaison with state and central ministries, Indian Council for Cultural Relations, United State Educational Foundation in India, British Council, principals of the colleges, heads of the departments of the university and other organisations.

(xiv) *Dy. Chiefs* : The Deputy Chiefs of the UEIGBs should be well-motivated and fully trained persons having undergone a special orientation course so as to equip themselves regarding the relevant job requirements.

(xv) *Orientation courses* : Bureaux should arrange orientation courses for the principals as well as the liaison officers of the colleges where guidance facilities are provided so as to ensure the worthwhileness of the programme.

(xvi) *Earn while you Learn* : Bureaux should start, 'Earn While You Learn' programmes so that the students learn to use the leisure time in learning useful arts and crafts and develop dignity of labour.

(xvii) *Talent bank schemes* : The Bureaux should initiate Talent Bank Schemes to select talented students from various departments of the universities and prepare them through special coaching for taking up senior management and executive posts in big industrial houses.

(xviii) *Venue* : The Bureaux should be housed in proper buildings and should have adequate furniture and other equipment.

STUDENT ADVISORY BUREAUX (SAB)

Realising the need and importance of providing educational guidance for the deserving students, the Ministry of Education set up 13 Students Advisory Bureaux functioning at the various universities in India. These bureaux were set up to render service to the students pursuing higher studies in England for I.C.S., F.R.C.S., Bar at Law, etc. and such examinations. Later on their scope was widened to include other countries and the work of finding suitable employment for those who returned from foreign countries.

Functions of SAB

1. Helping in creating among the students keen desire to know and plan their future.

2. Encouraging them to increase their knowledge about educational developments, activities and facilities in India and abroad.

3. Disseminating information on higher education, research and training in India and abroad to the students.

4. Maintaining educational information libraries for the use of students.

5. Supplying application forms for admission into educational institutions and universities in foreign countries.

6. Holding orientation courses for the benefit of students passing out of the university.

The Education Commission recommended that the Student Advisory Bureaux and University Employment and Guidance Bureaux should be combined to form an information and employment centre functioning directly under the supervision of the Dean of students.

UNIVERSITIES AND INSTITUTIONS OF HIGHER LEARNING IN INDIA (STATE-WISE)

Andhra Pradesh

1. Acharya N.G. Ranga Agriculture University, Hyderabad
2. Andhra University, Visakhapatnam
3. Central Institute of English & Foreign Languages, Hyderabad
4. Dr. B.R. Ambedkar Open University, Hyderabad
5. Dravidian University, Kuppam
6. University of Hyderabad, Hyderabad
7. Jawaharlal Nehru Technological University, Hyderabad
8. Kakatiya University, Warangal

9. Maulana Azad National Urdu University, Hyderabad
10. Nagarjuna University, Guntur
11. Nizam's Institute of Medical Sciences, Hyderabad
12. NTR University of Health Sciences, Vijayawada
13. Osmania University, Hyderabad
14. Potti Sreeramulu Telugu University, Hyderabad
15. Rashtriya Sanskrit Vidyapeetha, Tirupati
16. Sri Krishnadevaraya University, Anantapur
17. Sri Padmavati Mahila Vishvavidyalayam, Tirupati
18. Sri Sathya Sai Institute of Higher Learning, Anantapur
19. Sri Venkateswara Institute of Medical Sciences, Tirupati
20. Sri Venkateswara University, Tirupati

Arunachal Pradesh

21. Arunachal University, Itanagar

Assam

22. Assam Agricultural University, Jorhat
23. Assam University, Silchar
24. Dibrugarh University, Dibrugarh
25. Guwahati University, Guwahati
26. Indian Institute of Technology, Guwahati
27. Tezpur University, Tezpur

Bihar

28. B.N. Mandal University, Madhepura
29. Babasaheb Bhimrao Ambedkar Bihar University, Muzaffarpur
30. Indian School of Mines, Dhanbad
31. Jai Prakash Vishwavidyalaya, Chapra
32. Kameshwar Singh Darbhanga Sanskrit University, Darbhanga
33. Lalit Narayan Mithila University, Darbhanga
34. Magadh University, Bodh Gaya
35. Nalanda Open University, Patna
36. Patna University, Patna
37. Rajendra Agricultural University, Pusa, Samastipur
38. Siddhu Kanhu University, Dumka
39. Tilka Manjhi Bhagalpur University, Bhagalpur
40. Veer Kunwar Singh University, Arrah
41. Vinoba Bhave University, Hazaribag

Jharkhand

42. Birla Institute of Technology, Ranchi
43. Birsa Agricultural University, Ranchi

44. Ranchi University, Ranchi

Chandigarh

45. Panjab University, Chandigarh
46. Postgraduate Institute of Medical Education & Research, Chandigarh

Delhi

47. All India Institute of Medical Sciences, New Delhi
48. University of Delhi, Delhi
49. Indian Agricultural Research Institute, New Delhi
50. Indian Institute of Technology, New Delhi
51. Indira Gandhi National Open University, New Delhi
52. Jamia Hamdard, New Delhi
53. Jamia Millia Islamia, New Delhi
54. Jawaharlal Nehru University, New Delhi
55. National Museum Institute of History of Art, Conservation & Museology, New Delhi
56. School of Planning & Architecture, New Delhi
57. Shri Lal Bahadur Shastri Rashtriya Sanskrit Vidyapeeth, New Delhi

Goa

58. Goa University, Goa

Gujarat

59. Bhavnagar University, Bhavnagar
60. Dr. Babasaheb Ambedkar Open University, Ahmedabad
61. Gujarat Agricultural University, Dantiwada
62. Gujarat Ayurved University, Jamnagar
63. Gujarat University, Ahmedabad
64. Gujarat Vidyapith, Ahmedabad
65. M.S. University of Baroda, Vadodara
66. North Gujarat University, Patna
67. Sardar Patel University, Vallabh Vidyanagar
68. Saurashtra University, Rajkot
69. South Gujarat University, Surat

Haryana

70. Chaudhary Charan Singh Haryana Agricultural University, Hisar
71. Guru Jambheshwar University, Hisar
72. Kurukshetra University, Kurukshetra
73. Maharshi Dayanand University, Rohtak
74. National Dairy Research Institute, Karnal

Himachal Pradesh

75. Dr. Y.S. Parmar University of Horticulture & Forestry, Solan
76. Himachal Pradesh Krishi Vishwavidyalaya, Palampur
77. Himachal Pradesh University, Shimla

J & K

78. University of Jammu, Jammu
79. University of Kashmir, Srinagar
80. She-e-Kashmir University of Agricultural Sciences & Technology, Srinagar

Karnataka

81. University of Agricultural Sciences, Bangalore
82. University of Agricultural Sciences, Dharwad
83. University of Bangalore, Bangalore
84. Gulbarga University, Gulbarga
85. Indian Institute of Science, Bangalore
86. Kannada University, Kamalapura
87. Karnataka State Open University, Mysore
88. Karnatak University, Dharwad
89. Kuvempu University, Shimoga
90. Mangalore University, Mangalore
91. Manipal Academy of Higher Education, Manipal
92. University of Mysore, Mysore
93. National Institute of Mental Health & Neuro Sciences, Bangalore
94. National Law School of India University, Bangalore
95. Rajiv Gandhi University of Health Sciences, Bangalore

Kerala

96. University of Calicut, Kozhikode
97. Cochin University of Science & Technology, Kochi
98. Kannur University, Kannur
99. University of Kerala, Thiruvananthapuram
100. Kerala Agricultural University, Thrissur
101. Mahatma Gandhi University, Kottayam
102. Sree Chitra Tirunal Institute for Medical Sciences & Technology, Thiruvananthapuram
103. Sree Shankaracharya University of Sanskrit, Kalady
104. Visveswaraiah Technological University, Belgaum

Madhya Pradesh

105. Awadhesh Pratap Singh University, Rewa
106. Barkatullah Vishwavidyalaya, Bhopal

107. Devi Ahilya Vishwavidyalaya, Indore
108. Dr. Harisingh Gour Vishwavidyalaya, Sagar
109. Guru Ghasidas University, Bilaspur
110. Indira Gandhi Krishi Vishwavidyalaya, Raipur
111. Indira Kala Sangit Vishwavidyalaya, Khairagarh
112. Jawaharlal Nehru Krishi Vishwavidyalaya, Jabalpur
113. Jiwaji University, Gwalior
114. Lakshmi Bai National Institute of Physical Education, Gwalior
115. Madhya Pradesh Bhoj University, Bhopal
116. Maharishi Mahesh Yogi Vedic Vishwavidalaya, Jabalpur
117. Mahatma Gandhi Gramodya Vishwavidyalaya, Chitrakoot
118. Makhanlal Chaturvedi National University of Journalism, Bhopal
119. Pandit Ravishankar Shukla University, Raipur
120. Rani Durgavati Vishwavidyalaya, Jabalpur
121. Vikram University, Ujjain

Maharashtra

122. Amravati University, Amravati
123. Bharati Vidyapeeth, Pune
124. Central Institute of Fisheries Education, Mumbai
125. Decan College Post Graduate & Research Institute, Pune
126. Dr. Babasaheb Ambedkar Marathwada University, Aurangabad
127. Dr. Babasaheb Ambedkar Technological University, Lonere
128. Dr. Panjabrao Deshmukh Krishi Vidyapeeth, Akola
129. Gokhale Institute of Politics & Economics, Pune
130. Indian Institute of Technology, Mumbai
131. Indira Gandhi Institute of Development Research, Mumbai
132. International Institute of Population Sciences, Mumbai
133. Kavikulguru Kalidas Sanskrit Vishwavidyalay, Ramtek
134. Konkan Krishi Vidyapeeth, Dapoli
135. Mahatma Gandhi Antarrashtriya Hindi Vishwavidalaya Wardha
136. Mahatma Phule Krishi Vidyapeeth, Rahuri
137. Marathwada Krishi Vidyapeeth, Parbhani
138. University of Mumbai, Mumbai
139. Nagpur University, Nagpur
140. North Maharashtra University, Jalgaon
141. University of Pune, Pune
142. Shivaji University, Kolhapur
143. SNDT Women's University, Mumbai
144. Swami Ramanand Teerth Marathwada University, Nanded

145. Tata Institute of Social Sciences, Mumbai
146. Tilak Maharashtra Vidyapeeth, Pune
147. Yashwantrao Chavan Maharashtra Open University, Nashik

Manipur

148. Central Agricultural University, Imphal
149. Manipur University, Imphal

Meghalaya

150. North Eastern Hill University, Shillong

Nagaland

151. Nagaland University, Kohima

Orissa

152. Berhampur University, Berhampur
153. Orissa University of Agriculture & Technology, Bhubaneswar
154. Sambalpur University, Sambalpur
155. Shri Jagannath Sanskrit Viswavidyalaya, Puri
156. Utkal University, Bhubaneswar

Pondicherry

157. Pondicherry University, Pondicherry

Punjab

158. Guru Nanak Dev University, Amritsar
159. Punjab Agricultural University, Ludhiana
160. Punjab Technical University, Jalandhar
161. Punjabi University, Patiala
162. Thapar Institute of Engineering & Technology, Patiala

Rajasthan

163. Banasthali Vidyapith, Banasthali
164. Birla Institute of Technology & Science, Pilani
165. Jai Narain Vyas University, Jodhpur
166. Jain Vishva Bharati Institute, Ladnun
167. Kota Open University, Kota
168. Maharshi Dayanand Saraswati University, Ajmer
169. Mohanlal Sukhadia University, Udaipur
170. Rajasthan Agricultural University, Bikaner
171. University of Rajasthan, Jaipur
172. Rajasthan Vidyapeeth, Udaipur

Sikkim

173. Sikkim-Manipal University of Health, Medical & Technological Sciences, Gangtok

Tamil Nadu

174. Alagappa University, Karaikudi
175. Anna University, Chennai
176. Annamalai University, Annamalainagar
177. Avinashilingam Institute for Home Science & Higher Education for Women, Coimbatore
178. Bharathiar University, Coimbatore
179. Bharathidasan University, Tiruchirapalli
180. Dakshina Bharat Hindi Prachar Sabha, Chennai
181. Gandhigram Rural Institute, Gandhigram
182. Indian Institute of Technology, Chennai
183. University of Madras, Chennai
184. Maduraj Kamaraj University, Madurai
185. Manonmaniam Sundaranar University, Tirunelveli
186. Mother Teresa Women's University, Kodaikanal
187. Periyar University, Salem
188. Sri Chandrasekhareadra Saraswati Viswa Maha Vidyalaya, Kancheepuram
189. Sri Ramachandra Medical College & Research Institute, Chennai
190. Tamil Nadu Agricultural University, Coimbatore
191. Tamil Nadu Dr. Ambedkar Law University, Chennai
192. Tamil Nadu Dr. M.G.R. Medical University, Chennai
193. Tamil Nadu Veterinary & Animal Sciences University, Chennai
194. Tamil University, Thanjavur

Tripura

195. Tripura University, Agartala

Uttar Pradesh

196. Aligarh Muslim University, Aligarh
197. University of Allahabad, Allahabad
198. Babasaheb Bhimrao Ambedkar University, Lucknow
199. Banaras Hindu University, Varanasi
200. University of Bundelkhand, Jhansi
201. Central Institute of Higher Tibetan Studies, Varanasi
202. Chaudhary Charan Singh University, Meerut
203. Chandra Shekhar Azad University of Agriculture & Technology, Kanpur
204. Chhatrapati Shahu Ki Maharaj Kanpur University, Kanpur
205. Dayallbagh Educational Institute, Agra
206. Deen Dayal Upadhyaya Gorakhpur University, Gorakhpur

207. Dr. Bhim Rao Ambedkar University, Agra
208. Dr. Ram Manohar Lohia Awadh University, Faizabad
209. Indian Institute of Technology, Kanpur
210. Indian Veterinary Research Institute, Izatnagar
211. University of Lucknow, Lucknow
212. Mahatma Gandhi Kashi Vidyapeeth, Varanasi
213. M.J.P. Rohilkhand University, Bareilly
214. Narendra Deva University of Agriculture and Technology, Faizabad
215. Purvanchal University, Jaunpur
216. Sampurnanand Sanskrit Vishwavidalaya, Varanasi
217. Sanjay Gandhi Postgraduate Postgraduate Institute of Medical Sciences, Lucknow

Uttaranchal

218. Hemwati Nandan Bahuguna Garhwal University, Srinagar
219. Govind Ballabh Pant University of Agriculture & Technology, Pantnagar
220. Forest Research Institute, Dehradun
221. Gurukula Kangri Vishwavidyalaya, Hardwar
222. Kumaun University, Nainital
223. University of Roorkee, Roorkee

West Bengal

224. Bengal Engineering College, Howrah
225. Bidhan Chandra Krishi Vishwavidyalaya, Mohanpur
226. University of Burdwan, Burdwan
227. University of Calcutta, Calcutta
228. Indian Institute of Technology, Kharagpur
229. Indian Statistical Institute, Calcutta
230. Jadavpur University, Calcutta
231. University of Kalyani, Kalyani
232. Netaji Subhash Open University, Calcutta
233. University of North Bengal, Darjeeling
234. Rabindra Bharati University, Calcutta
235. Vidyasagar University, Midnapore
236. Visva Bharati, Santiniketan
237. West Bengal University of Animal and Fisheries Science, Calcutta

STUDENTS ADVISORY BUREAUX IN INDIA

1. Andhra University, Waltair.
2. Banaras Hindu University, Ruiya Hostel, First Floor, Varanasi.
3. Faculty of Education & Psychology, Student Counselling Centre, M.S. University of Baroda, Baroda.
4. University of Burdwan, Rajbati, Burdwan (E. Rly.).
5. University of Calcutta, Senate House, Calcutta.
6. Gauhati University, P.O. Gauhati.
7. Jiwaji University, Sanatan Dharam Road, Gwalior.
8. Kameshwar Singh Darbhanga University, Darbhanaga.
9. Lucknow University, Lucknow.
10. Patna University, Patna.
11. University of Rajasthan, Jaipur.
12. Maharana Bhupal College, University Campus, Udaipur.
13. Utkal University, Vani Vihar, Bhubaneshwar. Distt. Puri.

QUESTIONS FOR EXERCISE

1. Write an essay on UGIGB in India explaining its organisation and function on national and state level.
2. Write shortnote on Student-Advisory Bureaux in India.

31

Personal Guidance

An important part of guidance is personal guidance, and it constitutes the personal and individual advice offered by a guide to an individual for the solution of latter's personal problems. This helps the person to adjust to circumstances in his life. As a general rule problems are a part and parcel of human life, but not every-one is able to solve the problems that arise in his life and ruffle the calm of existence. People who find no way out of the morass of problems need the guidance and opinions of a specialist and expert. And, a psychologist is the only one who can provide advice concerning the solving of personal psychological problems.

Need for Personal Guidance

There cannot be exact prescription of the number and kind of problems that can be called essentially personal, because while the same person may be faced with a wide variety of problems at different stages of his life, the same problems may assume a different shape when they plague another individual. In this manner, personal problems are so numerous and have so many incongruous and varying forms that it is well nigh impossible to indulge in a description of them, and yet, the main personal problems that beset the human animal can be distinguished. Roughly speaking, human problems of a personal nature can be of two kinds — (1) Personal or individual. (2) Social. Individual problems can also be divided into two classes : (1) Physiological problems such as health, disease, development and concerned problems. (2) Psychological problems such as sex problems, problems concerning the satisfaction of instinctive needs. Among the psychological problems those of emotional adjustment are very important because inability to solve them has very great debilitating influence upon the entire personality of the individual. And social more than the personal problems cause anxiety to the person. If the truth be required, it may be declared that human life, from the moment of birth to the time of death, is a continuous and ceaseless process of adjustment with social circumstances. These social condition keep on changing and being transmuted, with the result that new problems are constantly presented to the person for solution. Now, as to which of these problems is likely to cause disorganisation in his personality, it is not easy to say with any degree of certitude. It is the opinion of psychologists that most men need personal guidance at some or the other occasion in life when the cross that they have to bear becomes a mite too heavy for them. That life continues on its desultory path even without guidance is a mundane truth. Life continues even in strife, poverty, unemployment, disease and trial. But man wants to improve his lot in life with the help of science. The psychologist's guidance helps the individual to solve certain personal problems, the failure to attain which only increases the burden of life, stops all development and progress in the person, even though he may continue to exist and outwardly appear to be hale and hearty. There are many aspects of social adjustment and adaptation because there are more than one dimensions of man's social circumstances. Social problems are generally interpreted to include family problems of school and college if the individual is a student, vocational problems if he is an earning individual, moral and ideal problems. Of these, the family problems are the most prominent and varied, comprehending problems of relations between the child and his parents, relations between husband and wife, conjugal problems, relations between brothers and sisters, financial status of the family, mutual adaptations of the individual and others. And, anyone of these problems is herculean enough to destroy the peace and calm of an individual. Problems of conjugal love, for example, compel an infinity of couples to spend their life in utter misery and misunderstanding.

Very often the individual makes some slap dash trial and error efforts to solve his personal problems or turns to good friends for personal advice, or instead turns to the older family members or teachers. Though this advice may have some practical validity, yet scientifically it is difficult to find any justification for it. If we take up for consideration the problem of conjugal love and bliss, then, it will be seen that the advice rendered by the best friends and sages of the family is all based upon their personal experience, and cannot provide any real guidance for a person. The crux of the matter is that the conjugal relations between no two pairs are identical. The conjugal problem of one specific pair is a personal and particular problem. Examples from other persons and solutions can only provide some general suggestions but it is dangerous to emulate others without paying attention to the particular merits of one specific case, for which the solution is being sought. Evidently, then, the individual can tackle his own problem after making a comprehensive study and gathering considerable psychological knowledge, but if this psychological knowledge is present in him then why should that problem arise in the first place? Naturally, it is essential for the person to turn to the psychologist for expert advice. But it must be kept in mind that guidance and advice cannot solve the problem in its entirety. This advice is more of the nature of suggestions, is scientific, and has no qualities of hit and miss about it. If the individual is to profit from such suggestions, he must be possessed of understanding, sympathy and skill.

PROCESS OF PERSONAL GUIDANCE

The first condition of personal guidance is that the person to be guided be fully and completely understood. It is desirable that the individual should himself come forward with all relevant information in the form of life history, present condition, feelings, thoughts, activities and all main facts concerning his life, and pass it on to the psychologists. He should not try to conceal anything, irrespective of the inhibitions that may urge him to do so, for it has often been found that the root of the problems to be solved existed in things from which the person wanted to escape, that he not only did not want to reveal to others but of which he did not even want to think himself. Briefly stated, in personal guidance, the psychologist should, with the co-operation of the person himself as well as with the help of various tests, gather all relevant and necessary information concerning the person. Roughly, personal guidance has the following five steps :

(1) Gathering the facts,
(2) Diagnosis of the problem,
(3) Prognosis,
(4) Therapy,
(5) Follow-up studies.

1. Gathering the facts. Gathering of factual information is the first and most important step in personal guidance. These facts can be of two kinds — those connected with the particular problem, and those concerned with the general life history of the person. And, the facts concerned merely with the problem also can be of two kinds — The first concerned with the individual and his characteristic qualities, the second concerned with the external circumstances of the problem. And the need for knowing these facts compels the psychologist to turn to observation, interview and various tests that yield it. The person himself is not the only one interviewed, as much valuable information is forthcoming from the interviews of people nearest to him, such as friends and relatives. In an interview it is essential that the psychologist ventures to speak as little as possible, that he asks questions that elicit the correct and desired responses by allowing the interviewed person to carry on the bulk of the talking. As in the case of educational and vocational guidance, in personal guidance, the opportunity for interview arrives only after a profile has been formed from the available information. And for this profile, the school, family, and other sources are ransacked for information. This necessitates the use of the cumulative record, the guardian's schedule, the self inventory and the teacher's ratings, besides which a number of tests are also performed. The outline of the profile is something like what is described below :

(i) *Physical description* : Physical description includes the person's age, sex and physical health.

(ii) *Family description* : In family description are included facts concerning the family background and hereditary relationships, parents (whether real or step, living or dead), brothers and sisters (their mutual relationships), economic status of the family, social standard of the family, mutual relations between all the members of the family, etc.

(iii) *History of social development* : This class includes the student's relations with other members of his class, and with other friends outside the class. If the person requiring guidance is not a student, then his relations with his neighbours and relatives outside the family will be studied.

(iv) *History of college life* : This classification includes the student's history in his progress through the primary, secondary and college educational stages which is constituted by results of examinations and record of part taken in extra-curricular programmes. If the person being studied and guided is not a student, then his life outside the sphere of his family should be studied to provide equivalent information. If he is engaged in some professional pursuit, it is necessary that the information regarding level of income, conditions of work, relations with other members of the profession or institution, etc., is collected.

(v) *Mental abilities* : *By* means of various tests and examinations intended for the purpose, the psychologist gathers information concerning the individual's level of intelligence, mental abilities and aptitudes, etc.

(vi) *Qualities of personality* : Qualities of personality have an important part in the personal problems, hence the psychologist finds it incumbent to secure information concerning the person's interests, emotional maturity, motives, ambitions, objective and ideals, etc.

One very important part of gathering such information is the keeping of proper records so that the information be available in future. Even in interview it is desirable for the psychologist not to depend upon his memory too much but to take adequate notes so that the information revealed is permanently available to him when it is required. But this requires an attitude of co-operation on the subject's part and a reassuring approach on the psychologist's part so that the subject should not become suspicious. If a person finds any objection to his statements being recorded, then modern tape recording machines can be used without the person being informed of them. Facts which do not qualify for this kind can be recorded after the person has been informed of their importance. For example, the psychologist should encourage and praise the subject and lead him into believing that all that he says deserves to be recorded.

2. Diagnosis of the problem. Having gathered all the facts that he wanted to collect the psychologist is now ready to start his own work. He has to search and analyse this information in order to see some system in it as well as any pattern that will help to reveal the cause of the problem under consideration. Such a discovery of pattern is the diagnosis of the problem. And this diagnosis is the basis on which the problem is to be solved, and the trouble cured. The better and more accurate the diagnosis, the better will be the cure ultimately effected. And it would be no misnomer to state that with a proper and accurate diagnosis half the psychologist's work is over.

3. Prognosis. Prognosis consists in estimating the benefit or result of the guidance. A psychologist tries to visualise the extent to which he will be able to solve the person's problem or, in other words, to what extent is there hope of the problem being solved. For example, by seeing a person's past performance in mathematics and by measuring his mental abilities, it becomes possible to make some tentative estimate of what he will be able to achieve after the guidance is rendered.

4. Therapy. Now the time for therapy or cure has arrived, or, in other words it is the time for the psychologist to come forward with a satisfactory solution of the problem. Seeing the profile of the problem from all the information gathered about it as well as from the interviews with the psychologist, the counselee himself gains insight into the problem and sometimes even comes up with some sensible and practicable solution. The truth of the matter is that this in fact should be the aim of the psychologist for he should try to make the counselee see his problem and its pattern, and even to think up a solution for it. If this happens, he will on the one hand gain considerable pleasure from having solved the problem of his own accord, while on the other, he will have considerable enthusiasm in solving the problem, and he will exert himself to the maximum limit. Freud, who used to cure mental diseases by the psychoanalytic method, used this method very effectively. When his patients became aware of the unconscious cause of their trouble, much of the problem was solved, whereas if the psychologist insists on giving his own suggestions and advice, then it becomes possible that due to certain tendencies and motives the subject may choose to ignore it. But if the counselee fails to understand the therapeutic measures implied by the psychologists, then the latter has to take positive steps. And, in the event of such a condition being precipitated it is always best for the advice not to seem to be authoritative or sermon like, and neither should any of the person's shortcomings be mentioned. The counselee should be given some hope that his problem will be solved, and it should be so expressed that it may appear to have come from the counselee instead of the psychologist.

5. Follow-up studies. Personal guidance does not come to an end with therapeutic measures being introduced because the psychologist's job is not only to provide guidance, but also to see the actual success of his advice. Hence, even after the therapy he has to keep up contact with the subject and to make inquiries to find out the success that he has and in solving the problem originally entrusted to his care. This not only furthers the help rendered to the counselee but also adds to the experience and knowledge of the psychologist, because much of what is learnt in guidance is through trial and error. Human psychology is so complex that it cannot be tied down by any laws. Success in guidance depends upon the psychologist's own experience and insight, and as has been said before, he is assisted in acquiring these through follow up studies. It need hardly be emphasised at this stage that personal guidance is more or less incomplete without a follow-up study.

METHODS OF FOLLOW-UP STUDIES

The following methods are utilised in follow-up studies :

1. Follow-up through letters. As is evident from the term applied to this method, in this method the counselee is contacted through the medium of letters. Letters reveal only a small quantity of information, but they do contribute something positively to the study. And, if need be, these letters can be used to transit further guidance to the person or even meet him.

2. Questionnaire method. In the questionnaire method, the counselee is sent a questionnaire, and he is asked to answer it, and return it to the psychologist. Most questions selected for the purpose have the quality of requiring short, simple, concise and precise answers, most of them being in terms of positives and negatives. This questionnaire is concerned with various aspects of the progress of a problem concerning which the advice was given. Psychologist tries to find the extent to which he has succeeded in curing the person, and if not, why. The questionnaire method has the advantage of soliciting more varied and comprehensive information than mere letters. But the main disadvantage lies in the small number of questionnaires returned to the psychologists.

3. Card file method. In this method, details of an interview in terms of the name of counselee, age, address, purpose of interview and details of the problem are inscribed. This is kept in the central office of the guidance centre, so that the counselee can contact his guide at any time that he wishes. The file method also makes use of the ticklers file, in which the psychologist keeps an open file of the counselee within easy reach, which keeps details of the further contacts than have to be made. The file is so named because it tickles the guide into contacting the person guided.

The above three methods are prevalent and have beneficial results. There are some other methods also, in addition to these main ones, by means of which the contact between the psychologist and the counselee can be kept alive. Telephone, for example, is another instrument that is frequently used in U.S.A. for renewing such contacts and gathering fresh information from the subjects.

It would be very useful to present a realistic example of personal guidance before winding up a description of it. This will improve realisation of the actual causes that are confronted and the extent to which our state provides facilities for dealing with them.

A professor in a local college at Allahabad went to take a look at the central jail there, where he saw a young boy undergoing sentence for breaking in or affecting an entry and thieving, the term being six months. The professor had the boy released on probation and took him into his own household. The boy maltreated the professor and continued on his path of theft and crime. He was also often absent for a couple of days from home. Finally, the professor handed the boy over to the parents who were living within the college campus. The boy was sent to school where he was admitted to the sixth class, but his progress was not satisfactory by any standards. Psychological tests revealed that he was definitely below the average in mental traits and capacities. But his practical skill and ability was somewhat better than the average. His other faculties were definitely weak. He naturally did not pay any attention to his study, and took no interest in social activities. At times he was filled with feelings of guilt and remorse, but at other times he showed to be very aggressive and anti-social. This boy was brought to the bureau of psychology for personal guidance, where it was advised that the boy needed a change of environment. It was opined that an understanding and sympathetic person might help to improve his adjustment to life, and that there was no benefit to be derived from further study. He should turn to acquiring training in a mechanical trade. Psychologists also felt that the boy required regular mental treatment, but as the bureau was not able to provide this assistance not much could be done in this direction. Even then, the boy benefit somewhat from the guidance of the psychologists. He learned to understand some of his problems and this helped him in his adjustment.

QUESTIONS FOR EXERCISE

1. Write short note on Educational Guidance.
2. Explain personal guidance, give examples.

32

Individual Testing and Non-Testing Devices in Guidance

In the democratic system of education the curriculum is based on the needs and interests of children and youth. Children have individual differences in their needs and interests their number and intensity. Therefore, a study of the individual through testing and non-testing devices is a pre-requisite for guidance.

Advantages of the study of individuals

1. Measurement of progress. The measurement of the progress of the individual child towards the primary objective of the school is necessary to assist children to a happier, more satisfying life.

2. Measurement of success. Study of the individual helps to understand the success or lack of success individual children are experiencing in meeting their life goals.

3. Planning. It helps in planning appropriate classroom situations and experiences for particular children lessening the possibility of intensifying problems arisen on account of unrealistic demands.

4. Satisfaction of teachers. It helps in increasing satisfaction of teachers in the profession of teaching by keeping them ever on the alert for assisting the students in adjusting their behaviour and mode of adjustment to situations.

Postulates of the study of facts

(1) Any facts are better than no facts.

(2) Facts are better than opinions about facts.

(3) Facts valuable only in proportion to our ability to use them.

(4) Methods of collecting and recording must be perfect.

(5) Facts should be gathered from as many different sources as possible. "What the child does in school, in the classroom, and outside the classroom provides a very sound basis for observing the recording his behaviour."

TYPES OF DATA TO BE COLLECTED

1. General data. It includes name, address, age, date of birth, father's name and occupation which are helpful in locating the individual and in making contact with those responsible for the pupil.

2. Family and social environment. It includes the home environment and the social conditions existing in the neighbourhood educational attainment of family members living in home or closely associated with the child, residential history of family (rural, urban), method and amount of parental control, attitude of other members towards the child, special cultural pattern of the family, etc.

3. Physical health. It includes findings of medical examination, growth characteristics, nutrition and general health.

4. Achievement data. It includes progress in the past and in the present in terms of marks and also in terms of other objective, such as good work habits, appreciation, etc., attitude towards school subjects, likes and dislikes, special abilities and disabilities towards co-curricular activities, etc.

5. Psychological data. It includes general mental health, predominant mood, self-assertion and self-abasement, sense of self-confidence, attitude towards self, etc.

6. Educational and vocational plans data. The educational and vocational plans of an individual may reveal the extent to which his parents had a hand in his educational and vocational plans and extent to which is really interested.

The achievements of the pupils in school subjects and their comparative standing in various subjects is an indication of the trend of their interests which determines his educational plans and vocational training.

7. Social development. It includes participation in the co-curricular activities of the school, sociability, adaptability, etc. The hobbies and activities pursued by the student give a fair indication of his interests and aptitudes.

Sources of Data Collection

(1) The student himself.

(2) The parents and the family members.

(3) Classmates and peers of the students.

(4) Various school records relating to the individual.

(5) Teachers and other personal connected with students.

ANECDOTAL RECORD

Definition of Anecdotal Record

1. Randall. "A record of some significant item of conduct, a record of an episode in the life of the student; a word picture of the student in action...a word snapshot at the moment of the incident; any narration of events in which the student takes such a part as to reveal something which may be significant about his personality."

2. Raths Louis. "An anecdotal record is a report of a significant episode in the life of a student."

3. Brown and Martin. "Anecdotes are descriptive accounts of episodes or occurrences in the daily life of the student."

4. Zahn, D. Willard. "An anecdotal records is a simple statement of an incident deemed by the observer to be significant with respect to a given pupils."

5. Traxler. "This record, as the name implies, involves setting down an anecdote concerning some aspect of pupil behaviour which seems significant to the observer."

Thus, anecdotal record is a running cumulative description of actual examples of behaviour as observed by teachers and counsellor and followed by a comment by the teacher.

Example of Anecdote

Place. Hindi Class

Objective description. I have been finding Sarita reading magazines day after day in the library yet she never has time to correct error or to work carefully on English assignments.

Comment. Sarita does not like to write but likes to read. I have asked the librarian not to admit her during her free periods unless she hears from me that Sarita had done her work.

Principles of Keeping Anecdotal Record

1. There is no limit on the number of anecdotes to be recorded. It depends upon the time at the disposal of the teachers or guidance workers.

2. Anecdotal records are supplement to other records and not as substitutes.

3. The objective description of the behaviour should not coloured with the subjective comments.

4. Every significant behaviour should be recorded be it in the classroom, in the school or outside the school.

5. All behaviour, favourable, unfavourable and neither favourable nor unfavourable should be recorded.

6. The facts presented in all the anecdotes must be shifted and arranged in order to be studied in relation to one another.

7. The record should be confidential and should not fall into irresponsible hands.

A SPECIMEN OF AN ANECDOTAL RECORD

Name of the school

Name of pupil observed	Class ______
Observer	Date and place
Objective Description	

COMMENTS OF THE OBSERVER

Advantages of Anecdotal Records

1. **Description.** They provide specific and exact description of personality and minimise generalisations.

2. **Understanding.** They are helpful in understanding the child's behaviour in diverse situations.

3. **Continuous.** They provide a continuous record.

4. **Self appraisal.** They provide data for pupils to use in self-appraisal.

5. **Summary.** A summary of these records is forwarded with a pupil when he is transferred from one school to another.

6. **Acquaintance.** The new members of the staff may use these records and acquaint themselves with the student body.

7. **Clinical service.** These records are useful in clinical service.

8. **Stimulation.** Records stimulate teachers to use them for guidance.

Characteristics of Anecdotal Records

James M. Bradfied and H. Stewart Moredock have given the following characteristics of an anecdotal record :

1. Only that is written down in which was seen or heard. Inferences, guesses, assumptions are omitted unless clearly labelled as inferences, guesses or assumptions.

2. The observer determines what aspects of behaviours are related to the dimension being appraised. He observes these only and records them only.

3. If the record is to be cumulative, a plan of periodic observation and recording is established and adhered to.

4. Words and phrases are used whose meaning is clear, and so far as possible unequivocal.

5. Only those words and phrases are employed which are definable in terms of things rather than other words. Concrete statements are preferred to abstract ones.

6. Words and phrases with strong emotional connotations are avoided, such as love, hate, insolvent, courteous, loyal, dishonest, etc.

7. Words and phrases which express the observer's judgement, or his opinion, and not his perception are avoided. The following frequently encountered "judgemental terms" should be avoided :

(i) Well-behaved.
(ii) Delinquent.
(iii) Aggressive.
(iv) Didn't try.
(v) Industrious.
(vi) Nervous.
(vii) Happy.

PERSONAL DATA BLANK

The personal data blank seeks to check the accuracy of certain information items and to bring them up-to-date. Its form provides considerable information about the pupil's background, his present activities and his plans for the future.

The counsellor should try to enlist the co-operation of the students by explaining them the various items of the personal data blank and letting them know its purpose and explaining the confidential nature of their answers.

PERSONAL DATA BLANK

(For School Leaving Class)

Name of the student .... Date of birth ....
Class .... Section .... School Year ....
Father's Name .... Occupation ....
Address ....

1. Which school subjects do you like most?
2. Why do you like these subjects?
3. Which school subjects do you like least?
4. Why do you not like these subjects?
5. In what co-curricular activities do you take part?
6. To which out of school organisations do you belong to?
7. What are your special talents or abilities? Instrument....................... voice.............................drama................................dancing........................... art............................
8. Do you enjoy reading?
9. If so, what type of books do you prefer?
10. Who are your favourite authors?
11. What magazines do you read?
12. How often do you go to see pictures?
13. What kind of pictures do you like best?

14. Have you had any job experience?

15. Name the job.

16. Give reasons if, you had liked that.

17. What are you planning as your life occupation.

18. Write two or three activities which people in this job have to do.

19. What are the advantages of the occupation of your choice?

20. Are there some hindrances that might prevent you from following this occupation? If so, name them.

21. Considering these hindrances, have you thought of some other occupations? If so, name more than one in order of preference.

22. Do you think that the education that you are getting will help you in entering any of these occupations?

23. What is the opinion of your parents/guardians on your future after leaving school?

24. Note here any other information that may help the counsellor to help you.

PERSONAL DATA BLANK

(Delta Class)

Name of the School..
Name of the Student.................................... Class and Section.......................
Date of Birth...
Father's Name.. Occupation...........................
Address...

1. Which school subjects do you like the most?

2. Which school subjects do you like the least?

3. If you want to continue your studies, which subjects would you like to take up after class VIII?

4. If you want to leave school after class VIII, what will you do after that?

5. Have you planned to take up some job after completing your studies? If so, mention the job you like the most and if possible give more than one choice.

6. Mention the school activities you take part in — Drama, Music, Scouting, Games, Red Cross, etc.

7. What are your favourite hobbies?

8. How much time do you spend on your studies after school hours?

9. Do you do any domestic or any other sort of work? If so, name the work and tell how much time this work usually takes you.

10. Give any additional information that may help us to help you.

CASE HISTORY

According to Thorne, "An adequate case history clarifies etiological relationship, resolves controversial points, uncovers illogical thinking and misinformation and aids in the differentiation between functional and organic complaints. The client derives reassurance from the fact that such a careful study is being made of his difficulties and benefits from desensitisation, catharsis and abreaction. As the details of the case history are elicited and brought into perspective, the client perceives casual relationships and gains new insights concerning the total problem of the organism meeting the environment."

Scope of Case History

Jane Waiters writes, "Whether long or short, written in formal manner or in free description and narrative style, the case study should present as accurate and as objective an account and as complete and dynamic a picture as possible." The writer should, avoid technical terminology; make it a rule to shun loose generalisations. The study of Rotnney and Roens revealed that there was need for preparing case histories of following children :

1. Those of exceptionally high achievement.
2. Those who show exceptionally high ability in art.
3. Those who show exceptional skill in practical arts or painting.
4. Those who are persistent in striving for success.
5. Those who are trying very hard against great obstacles.
6. Those who show exceptionally high ability in music.
7. Those who constantly present behaviour problems in class.
8. Those who do not seem to be able to the work of the grade.
9. Those whose behaviour makes them appear to be 'model'.

Allport suggests that successful case study fall into three sections:

Present	*Past*	*Future*
1. Problem.	History of Problem.	Educational plans.
2. Educational status.	Educational history.	Prediction of ultimate level.
3. Intellectual status.	Intellectual development.	
4. Health and physical status.	Health and physical history.	Prediction of future health.
5. Maturity level.	Developmental history.	
6. Personality	Personality development.	
7. Social relations.	Social history.	
8. Vocations.	Vocational history.	Vocational plans.
9. Family relationships.	Family history (including home and neighbourhood).	

CASE HISTORY OUTLINE

1. Identity Data

(i) Name of the child, date of birth, age, class, sex.

(ii) Name of the father, occupation, address.

2. Types of problems

In school	**Out of school**
Scholastic	Delinquency
Conduct	Recreational needs
Health	Home conditions
Emotional	
Attendance	

3. Cases Referred to by

Principal Teachers Parents

4. Information

(1) ***Symptoms*** : Statements on the symptoms of the case should be recorded.

(2) ***Examination***

(i) *Psychological* : It includes vision, hearing, co-ordination and speech.

(ii) *Health* : It includes height and weight measurements, nutrition, teeth and general physical conditions,

(iii) Mental.

5. Family History

(i) *Father's occupation, his education — early life* : These include, social and economic status, attitude towards family, recreational interests.

(ii) *Mother* : It includes conditions of mother during pregnancy, nature of delivery, careful history of birth, her early life, attitude towards family and life, attitude towards society, maternal relationship.

(iii) *Sibling interrelationships* : It includes, locality, changes in residence if any from the birth of the child to present time, number of rooms, ventilation, space, orderliness, cleanliness, sleeping and studying arrangements, recreational facilities, and sanitation.

(iv) *Discipline of the home* : It includes control exercised by parents, grandfather or grandmother, methods employed to maintain discipline in the home — threats, bribes, deprivations; agreement or disagreement between parents in using these methods.

6. School history. It includes schools attended, age of entering school, child's attitude towards school, towards teachers, towards subjects; towards classmates, his status in his class, teacher's attitude towards him, his attitude towards co-curricular activities, promotions and non-promotions, any special difficulties in school subjects, future educational plans.

7. Health and physical history. It includes age, weaning, age of walking, talking, teaching, any physical defects like sense organ deficiencies, speech defects, etc., illness including duration and severity, convulsions, influenza, fainting spells, glandular, disturbance, serious injuries, his attitude towards his health and body, over-careful or careless.

8. Social history and contacts. It includes religious background, extent or his participation in social, cultural, religious, political activities, etc., gang affiliations.

9. Recreational interests. It includes participation in leisure time activities, hobbies and special interests.

10. Personality traits. It includes outbursts of rage and fears, aggressive or submissive, happy or unhappy, fantasies, attitude towards sex.

11. Vocational history. It includes job held, reasons for change, date of change, vocational interests and ambitions, special skills.

RATING SCALES

Definition

1. Ruth Strant. "Rating is, in essence, directed observation."

2. A.S. Barr and others. "Rating is a term applied to expression of opinion or judgment regarding some situation, object or character. Opinions are usually expressed on a scale or values. Rating techniques are devices by which such judgments may quantified."

Characteristics of a Rating Scale

(1) Description of the characteristics to be rated. (2) Some methods by which the quality, frequency or importance of each item to be rated may be given.

Advantages of Rating Scale

Rating scales are helpful in the following :

1. In writing reports to parents.
2. In filling out admission blanks for colleges.
3. In finding out students' needs.
4. In making recommendations to the employers.
5. In supplementing other sources of understanding about the child.

6. In their stimulating effect upon the individuals who are rated.

Limitations of Rating Scale

1. Some characteristics are more difficult to rate.
2. Subjectivity element is present.
3. Lack of opportunities to rate students.
4. Raters tend to be generally generous.

Principles Governing Rating Scales

1. The specific trait or mode of behaviour must be defined properly.

2. The scale should be clearly defined three, four or five-point scale. The teacher or the counsellor may rate each individual on each quality on a three-point, or five-point scale. In a five-point scale the description of the qualities of an individual may be 'Outstanding', 'Very good', 'Average' and 'Poor'.

3. The trait to be treated should be readily observable.

4. Uniform standards of rating scale should be observed.

5. The rater should observe the rates in different situations involving the trait to be rated.

6. The number of characteristics to be rated should be limited.

7. In the rating scale card, some space may be provided for the rater to write supplementary material.

8. The directions of using the rating scales should be clear and comprehensive.

9. Several judges may be employed to increase the reliability of any rating scale.

10. Well-informed and experienced persons should be selected for rating.

Errors in Rating

1. **Generosity error.** It occurs when raters would not like to run down their own people by giving them low ratings.

2. **Stringency error.** It is the opposite of generosity error. Some raters have tendency to rate all individuals low.

3. **The Halo error.** It occurs due to a tendency to rate in terms of general impressions about the rates formed on the basis of some previous performance.

4. **The error of central tendency.** It occurs because of a tendency in some observers to rate all or most of the raters near the mid-point of the scale. They would like to put most of the ratees as 'Average,' etc.

5. **The logical error.** It occurs when the characteristics or the trait to be rated is misunderstood.

Types of Rating Scales

1. Descriptive rate. In it the rater puts a check (√) in the blank before the characteristic or trait which is described in word or phrase.

Example — Has this pupil initiative?
— Shows marked originality.
— Willing to take initiative.
— Quite inventive.
— On the whole unenterprising.
— Very dependent on other.

2. Numerical scale. In it numbers are assigned to each trait. If it is a seven-point scale the number 7 represents the maximum amount of that trait in the individual; 4 represents the average amount.

3. The graphic scale. It is similar to the descriptive scale and the difference lies only in the way it is written. This is also called "Behavioural Statement Scale."

4. The percentage of group scale. In it the rater is asked to give the percentage of the group that possesses the trait on which the individual is rated.

5. Man to man scale. In it an individual is asked to rate the ratee by comparing him to the person mentioned on the Scale and assign the ratee his position. For example, A B C D E are the persons who have been already rated as very persistent, not easily stopped, work quite steadily, somewhat changeable, gives up easily.

PROJECITVE TECHNIQUE

Definition

1. Gates and others. "The label projective techniques has been applied to settings or material designed to give a person a chance to reveal his thoughts and feelings while seemingly responding to something in the external environment."

2. Ruth Strang. "Projective techniques are a method of understanding the inner world of the individual."

3. Rapport. "Projective techniques seek to elicit, to render observable, to record, and to communicate the psychological structure of the subject, as inherent to him at any given moment and without study of historical antecedents."

4. Murrary. "The purpose of this procedure is to stimulate literacy creativity and thereby evoke fantasies that reveal covert and unconscious complexes. The test is based on the well-recognised fact that when a person interprets an ambiguous social situation, he is apt to expose his own personality as much as the phenomenon to which he is attending."

GUIDE TO THE ASSESSMENT OF PERSONALITY TRAITS

(The Secondary Education Commission 1952-53)

Personality Traits	A	B	C	D	E
Initiative	Shows marked originality and independence.	Willing to take initiative.	Quite inventive, able to take initiative.	On the whole unenterprising.	Very dependent on others, diffident.
Integrity (Moral sense)	Completely trustworthy under all circumstances.	Of superior dependability, honest in face of punishment.	Usually dependable.	Questionable times.	Positively dishonest.
Persistence	Very persistent.	Not easily stopped.	Works quite steadily.	Somewhat changeable, restless.	Gives up easily.
Leadership	Much drive, mild, impressive, steady, convincing, wide influence, acceptable to group, sought after by the group and takes the group with him.	Ready to take the lead, works quietly for leadership, accepts responsibility.	Sometimes leads in minor affairs.	Satisfied to have others, lead.	Probably unable to lead his fellows.

Personality Traits	A	B	C	D	E
Self-confidence (Poise)	Very self-confident, very resourceful, willing to take reasonable risks.	Self-confident trust his own ability, well-adjusted to others.	Normally confident in familiar circumstances. Does not need special assurance.	Cannot work for long without demanding attention or responds after special encouragement.	Always draws attention to self. Afraid of being overlooked or afraid to open out in presence of others, very nervous.
Emotional Control	Unusual balance of responsiveness	Well-balanced.	Unually well-balanced.	Tends to be over-emotional.	Too easily moved to anger and fits of depression.
Social Attitude	Strongly altruistic, greater aesthetic sensibility.	Usually considerate of others, aesthetic sensibility.	Has no positive attitude, neutral, conscious of his rights and those of others or indifferent.	Self-centred	Anti-social.

5. Anne Anastasi. "It is expected that the test material of the projective techniques will serve as a sort of screen upon which the subject projects, his characteristic ideas, attitudes, aspirations, fears, worries, aggressions and the like."

"Typically, projective instruments also represent *disguised* testing procedures in so far as the subject is rarely aware of the type of psychological interpretation which will be made of his response. Projective techniques are likewise characterised by a global approach to the appraisal of personality. Attention is focused upon a composite picture of the whole personality rather than upon the measurement of separate traits."

6. L.K. Frank. 'Projective Technique' in an article that appeared in 1939 though such methods had been in use for many years prior to that date.

Kinds of Projective Techniques

1. Play situation. In play situation dolls are given to the child to play with the observation is made of his reactions. Dolls represent a father, a mother, a boy and a girl and provide the medium through which the child might act out or reveal his/her thoughts, impulses and feelings about himself/herself and others. Controlled play techniques are also used.

2. Story-telling and story completion. In it an incomplete story may be told to the child and he may be asked to complete it. While completing the story, the child may reveal something about his feelings and desires. The situation selected should touch the emotional life of the child whose personality traits we wish to assess. The child is likely to depict his innermost feelings, wishes and thoughts while he narrates the story.

This method is usually employed in the case of delinquent children.

3. Incomplete sentence technique. In it some incomplete sentences are presented to the child which he completes in any way he likes. By reading the individual's responses, the counsellor records observations which indicate unhealthy or conflicting, positive or healthy attitudes, etc. Stimulus in the form of the following words may be presented to the child :

	Sentence Completed
(i) A baby..................................	(i) is very lovely.
(ii) The world..........................	(ii) is full of cruel people.
(iii) My home..........................	(iii) is not a good place to live in.
(iv) My father..........................	(iv) is very cruel.
(v) Money..............................	(v) is everything in life.
(vi) My best friend................	(vi) is very poor.

Sentence completed

By going through these completions the psychologist may get some clue of the repressed wishes of the child.

4. Original drawings and paintings. Original drawings and paintings of the children give an idea of the personality of the child. An indication of the various traits of the personality of the child may be found in the theme or subject, the colour, the masses and the open spaces, the length, direction, curvature of the lines.

5. Free association and dream analysis. Freud used this method to find out the repressed unconscious desires, emotions and feelings of individual men and women. It has been recognised by many psychologists that dream have their roots in the person's private world.

In this method, the psychologist first develops rapport with the subject. The subject takes a comfortable position reclining on a sofa. He is encouraged to talk about his troubles freely. The psychologist or the psychoanalyst records his responses and interprets them.

6. The Rorschach Ink Blot Test. Rorschach was Swiss psychologist who experimented with the use of ink-blots as a means of diagnosing mental disorders in the basis of perceptual approach. The perception of an individual is influenced by the emotional and social make-up when he is asked to perceive a figure which is not well defined.

7. Thematic Appreciation Test (T.A.T.). It involves a systematic use of pictures representing a number of dramatic events.

SOCIOMETRIC TESTS

Definition

1. Jennings. "Stated briefly, sociometry may be described as a means of presenting simply and graphically the entire structure of relations existing at a given time among members of a given group. The major lines of communication or the pattern of attraction and rejection in its full scope, are made readily comprehensive at a glance."

2. William J. Goode and others. "These and other variants of sociometric techniques offer rather simple methods of ranking individuals on a continuum of 'acceptability' or 'outgoingness' on the part of group members. When their use is justified they may be powerful research tools since they meet the general problems of scaling very well."

Types of Tests

Sociometric studies have been made of many types of social groups including classroom groups. Being peer-rating rather than rating by superiors, sociometry adds another dimension to the understanding of social relationships.

QUESTIONS FOR EXERCISE

1. Describe types of Data required for guidance.
2. Explain Case History Method.
3. Describe Personal Data Blank for Guidance.
4. Explain the kinds and uses of Projective Techniques.

33

Guidance in Adolescence

The English word adolescence is a derivative of the Latin 'adolescere' which means to grow to maturity. This age begins from twelve and continues till the age of twenty. In the words of Jersild, "Adolescence is the period through which a growing person makes transition from childhood to maturity." Adolescence, in the opinion of most educational psychologists, begins between the age of 12 to 24 years. Compared to boys, girls enter the period of adolescence a couple of years earlier. According to Dr. Jones, adolescence is the recollection of infancy. It parallels the states of infancy and childhood in being patterned into the conditions, the first of growth and the second of maturation.

1. State of growth. In this state, the adolescent is seen to be very active and unstable as well as disturbed. He gives the impression of being somewhat lost, and is subject to rapidly varying moods of dejections and elation, enthusiasm and deep lethargy, etc. The main thing concerning this period in life is that the adolescent is no longer a child but an adult, though the society in which he lives continues to treat him as a child. Secondly, he climbs down from the dizzy heights of imagination that he reached in his infancy and childhood and steps firmly into the real world. Both these factors engender in him a constant fear of reproof and criticism at the hands of others. He often becomes helpless and pitiable, shy and repressed. This does not indicate that he runs away from the real world, but that he tries to modify it according to his own notions. In efforts of this kind, elation and dejection is often seen wearing a look of anxiety.

2. State of maturation. By the time he enters this stage, he has calmed down a bit and shown signs of stability. He carves a niche for himself in his society, and gradually, his tendencies, habits and activities become stable and regular.

MENTAL DEVELOPMENT IN ADOLESCENCE

In adolescence the individual is so transformed that he wears a new and unrecognised look. Mental changes in this period of life find their best expression in the work of poets as they depict the mental states of young men and women. Adolescence exhibits the following mental characteristics generally :

1. Development of mental abilities. In adolescence the individual's nervous system becomes more strong with the result that his mental activities show greater tenacity and system. Ability to think, to solve problems, to differentiate and evaluate.

2. Sexual development. From the psychological viewpoint, the most significant characteristic of the period of adolescence is sexual development. According to Dr. Jones, the repressed sexual force of infancy, that continued latent through the period of childhood, once again awakens as the individual passes through various stages of sexual development. The truth of the matter is, that even if it is not the only tendency, sexual tendency is undoubtedly the most prominent and stable tendency to be found in adolescence. Hence, to disregard it is to make a fatal mistake as it is the most harmful form of negligence conceivable. The development in this sphere is so rapid that his entire personality appears to be coloured by it. Sexual development in adolescence finds its expression in attraction towards strangers, rather than towards such small activities as the young boy's anxiety and nervousness, biting of fingernails, putting a pencil in one's mouth, tying knots in handkerchiefs, etc. Both physical and mental teaching in this age can use the sexual tendency as an important force. Normally, the development of the sexual passes through the following three stages :

(i) *Auto-eroticism* : In the beginning of adolescence, sexual tendency manifests itself in self-love but this self-love differs from the infant's self-love. In infancy, the child finds physical pleasure in exploring and touching various parts of his own body. But in the adolescent self-love, the individual dresses himself well and meticulously, observes his face continuously in the mirror, and does his very best to make himself as presentable as possible. Many young men and women passing through this stage can be seen humming as they look at themselves in the mirror. They are content to be with themselves and love only themselves. As yet they have no time to observe and appreciate others. Freud calls this the state of narcicism. The term has a long story behind it, from which the term originated. Narcissus was a Greek prince of almost unparalleled beauty, who could not find anyone more handsome than himself, he loved himself probably justifiably. A flower is called narcissus, and it grows by the side of lake in such a manner that its image is visible in the water. Young men and women in their teens behave in a similar manner as they love to look upon themselves and beautify themselves. One of the most prominent and common malpractices in which the adolescents indulge is masturbation. The American psychologist Kinsey, in his famous report, has mentioned the various ways in which young men and women derive pleasure from their sexual experiences.

Sometimes the feelings of guilt that arise as a result of indulgence in these activities lead to the formation of complexes that are very harmful to the mental development of individuals. The one and only means of escaping such consequences is proper sex education. In order to impart the right attitude towards the sexual tendency to young people, it is essential that teachers and parents tell them everything frankly so that they may adopt this healthy attitude.

(ii) *Homosexuality* : Progressing from the stage of self-love, young boys and girls are attracted to members of their own sex, either older or younger than themselves. Homosexual love of this age is accompanied by great anxiety and deep affection but latter on it turns into heterosexual love. Persons of this age can often be seen caressing each other, roaming together, preferring only each other's company, sleeping together, praising each other and finding other modes of expressing their mutual attraction. Some girls also develop the habit of exciting each other's sexual organs. Similar aberration is present in boys in the form of sodomy, which leads to feeling of guilt and crime if the person is reproved for these activities. Such bad habits can be got rid of only through the medium of sensible guidance and sex education of the children by the parents and teachers. It is always desirable that adolescence passing through this phase should be controlled sensibly but it is equally essential that all control exercised over them should be in the form of loving advice rather than punishment.

(iii) *Heterosexuality* : The state of homosexuality in adolescents is succeeded by sexual maturity, a state of moral hetero-sexual relations between men and women. Young men and women who have attained this age can often be seen being attracted to members of the other sex, meeting each other, talking inessentially for hours on end, putting their best feet forward to attract the other and hold such attraction adopting the latest fashions to appear the more attractive, going for walks together, visiting picture houses together, caressing each other and sometimes even going to the extent of actual sexual intercourse, though this often has disastrous results as the girls become mothers even before they are married. The strength of this sexual tendency can neither be curbed nor can any strict control upon it prove efficacious even if it is considered desirable. Excessive restrictions on meetings between boys and girls in colleges and universities only leads to greater indiscipline and misconduct. Hence, many educational psychologists have advised that instead of restricting communication between them, relations should be encouraged. On the other hand, the traditions that have continued our culture stress the complete segregation of the sexes during this period. In the modern context any effort at emulating these traditions can only prove foolhardy in the future, and in any case such efforts are not likely to prove efficacious. Uncontrolled and impassioned contacts can only lead to such ostensible and detestable consequences as suicides, unmarried mothers, social corruption, etc. Hence it is essential that the youth of today be provided with proper sex education and encouraged to develop a healthy attitude towards sex. This will have the desirable effect preparing them for responsible parenthood when they ultimately get married.

Another method of solving problems of the sexual impulse, besides sex education, is inspiring young men and women to develop interest in various kinds of games and sports, dances, singing, art, painting, etc. It is a matter of universal regret, particularly among the enlightened population of the nation, that nearly 99% of teachers and guardians find it embarrassing to discuss any sexual matter with their young charges. The consequences are undesirable as the young inexperienced adolescent learns the same things from bad and uncouth companions who convey to him all the aberrant forms of sexual information. Such a situation is true of many civilised societies, and all the more of India. When the adolescent observes that his teachers and guardians prefer to keep all sex information secret and concealed from him, he forms a guilt complex regarding sex. Due to the normal stage of development, he can do nothing to abate the force or strength of the urge, and he is helpless as no assistance from his teacher is forthcoming. Thus, he either indulges all his energies in trying to control the instinct, losing all interest in studies in which he cannot concentrate, or forms abnoxious and deforming habits, or as an alternative contracts serious mental disease through excessive repression. Hence teachers and parents should assist adolescent males and females to organise, control and sublimate the sexual impulse through adequate sex education.

3. Hero worship. Generally speaking, adolescents evince a strong tendency towards hero worship, though the criterion of heroism is not the same in all children. Possession of any quality that attracts an individual child the most is sufficient qualification for a man or woman to become his ideals. While one child may regard a wrestler as a hero, another may profess allegiance to a scientist, yet another may be devoted to a film personality or a political leader. In schools some teachers impress their students considerably with the result that they come to be tenderly and affectionately regarded by them, also being imitated by the tender children. Sometimes this hero worship turns in love. It is not till considerably later that the young man turns his thoughts to his own heroic qualities, when he begins praising them. The tendency to hero worship can be turned to good account by inculcating a proper character and personality in the child's mind. For this it is essential that the teacher himself should represent the highest ideals, as he is the best example that the child can facilely imitate.

4. Religious feeling. Many adolescents become positively and deeply religious in this period of their lives. One can often observe them loving God in some one image, talking to Him, sacrificing themselves to Him and prying to Him. India is particularly productive of such specimens since, for one, the religious tendency is deeply ingrained in the people's mind, and for another, in Indian society young boys and girls meet great leaders and famous personalities on very rare occasions. While religious tendency protects the young inexperienced child from many bad habits, it sometimes helps in making him somewhat impractical. Teachers can help to create a healthy attitude towards religion.

5. Gregariousness. Adolescents are always acutely desirous of being among their friends, of praising them and of improving their relation with them. Often, they form definite groups in which each adolescent has his specific status and a role to suit him. This status and role plays an important part in determining his status and role in adult life.

6. Extroversion. In this period, the child once again regains his extrovert flamboyancy, taking deep interests in his surroundings and other individuals, their activities and conflicts. In school, too, he likes to take part in all kinds of activities. And it is matter of joy with him if he can spend the larger part of his time in the company of his friends. Various individuals become engaged in programmes of social service and welfare. In this manner does the adolescent announce the interest that he takes in the real world. This interest can be usefully exploited to ingrain in him such useful qualities as self dependence, self determination, cooperation, discipline, honesty and the quality of maintaining good relations with others or develop the social instinct. This is the age in which the foundations of good citizenship can be deeply laid.

7. Lack of stability and adjustment. It has been pointed out earlier, too, that in his adolescence the growing individual is at the threshold of his life although he is rarely if ever considered an adult by his seniors. From the psychological point of view, he takes himself seriously enough not to consider himself a child, and likes to be treated as an adult. Evidently, he shows considerable instability and lack of adjustment. His adaptation to his environment is upset by such small considerations as the growth to pimples on his face or the presence of other small physical deformities. In fact, it is a stage in which he learns to lead adult life in every sphere and direction. Hence, the presence and continual development of problems is only natural. And these problems are susceptible to ready solutions if the seniors are prepared to extend their sympathetic cooperation and guidance.

8. Excessive sentimentality. The adolescent is very sentimental and emotionally unstable, although at this age his mind is fairly well developed. Of the many feelings that drive him, the strongest are the desire to win praise and self respect, any injury to or repression of them leading to serious malformations and even open rebellion. Sentimentality can be turned to good use in developing cultural traits in the adolescent. Participation in programmes of dancing, acting, music, painting, etc., makes the emotional life more stable.

9. Excessive imagination. Although the adolescent is as much in this world as any other living, yet he is prone to much imaginary fights into the world of fancy. The smallest thing can persuade him to temporarily abandon the world of reality the turn to the imaginary world. Such excessive imagination manifests itself in the strong tendency towards daydreaming, but some gifted children express their creative and aesthetic imagination through literature, music and painting, besides other arts.

10. Particular interests. In adolescence, as the individual develops both in mind and body, his interests vary. Progressively the boys and girls develop the interests of their adult counterparts. Girls show this development in such interests as the use of various cosmetics, efforts at appearing beautiful, reading or taking interest in romantic novels, love stories, dramas or poems, participating in music, art and acting programmes, etc. Boys manifest their approaching adulthood in the form of various active games, running around, doing acts of valour, developing a vocation that they are to pursue in their adult life. Both boys and girls take constant interest in developing friendship with members of the other sex and maturing it to fruition through conversation, intimacy, letters and romance.

11. Development of the mind. In adolescence, the mind develops rapidly. The cells of the nervous system increase rapidly, and the chemical composition of the nerves also undergoes a change. In this way, the mind and the nervous system rapidly matures. In this period along with physical and mental development, practice helps to develop mental abilities. Linguistic ability also registers improvement during this period. In his adolescence the child develops the vocabulary that he possesses. His vocabulary reveals general intelligence. Mental development, too, reaches its apex in adolescence. Despite the inevitable individual differences that are invariably present, mental maturity achieves its completion normally by the age of twenty. Practice or experience contributes considerably to this maturation. Normally, the individual's intelligence continues on the same level, or, in other words, even in different ages the intelligence quotient of an individual remains more or less the same. Many detailed studies have revealed that during the first five years of life, the mental development is greater than that achieved during the following five. In this manner, the mental development during the ages of 10 and 15 is greater than that during

15 and 20, in respect of rapidity. At the age of ten, the mental development of a child is at its fastest. Following this, as the child approaches the stage of adolescence, the speed of mental development slows down. In his infancy, the child only acknowledges and indicates the feeling of sensations, while at the age of three he is in a position to distinguish between objects, animals and human beings. At six, he is capable of describing a picture that he has seen, but in his adolescence he rises above description to the level to interpretation of the pictures that he sees. In this manner, one can see constant development and improvement in the mind's reactions to stimuli. Generally, an individual's memory is tested by the number of digits he can remember after they have once been announced to him. In adolescence, the ability to remember digits improves with age and reaches its highest peak at the age of twenty.

EDUCATION OF ADOLESCENTS

The sensible teacher can make his teaching psychological if he has knowledge of an adolescent's mental development. The intensity and proper use of imagination can help to make an individual a poet, painter, sculptor or a psychologist. Intelligence, observation, reasoning and thinking having reached the required state of development in adolescence, the school and college curriculum can be fairly diversified and made comprehensive. The truth of the matter is that actual education begins only in adolescence since at this stage the young boys and girls treat themselves as adults and they come to entertain a serious and responsible attitude to their education. What is needed is that the teacher should inspire them to work hard in their studies through self inspiration.

(1) Physical development is rapid during adolescence. The bodily structure develops at a rapid pace. This age is the time of revolutionary physical development as in this age young boys and girls attain to their maximum heights and specific bodily developments, conforming to their respective sexes, take place. Hence, they should be trained in games and beneficial exercises. In educational institutions, they should be specially trained in health and bodily development since, if they do not pay attention at this stage they are not likely to appear handsome later on in life.

(2) The extreme sentimentality of adolescence can be used to induce the girls and boys to learn literature, music, art and science. This age is propitious for the teaching of all subject. Transfer of learning during this period is considerable.

(3) Good conduct, proper interests and good habits of living can be developed in boys and girls by making adequate use of the strong sexual tendency that is a strong motivating force. In adolescence, the sexual organs of the boys and girls undergo rapid development. In girls, the menstrual cycle starts while the boys are subject to nightly

emissions. The sexual organs are covered by hair. Persistent development in the girl's breasts sometimes leads of pain. Lacking knowledge of the basis and cause of all these physiological changes, boys and girls are often subjected to much perplexity. Many of the girls are not even aware that the blood emitted during the menstrual cycle does not happen to them alone but to every other girls passing the same stage of development. This leads to much anxiety and sometimes even results in the creation of guilty feelings. Not knowing the manner in which they should dress hygienically during the menstrual cycle they are sometimes put in very embarrassing situations that are very painful to them. They are even rendered ridiculous. It is a matter of no little sorrow and pain that much changes are inevitable in the lives of every young men and women, but almost all of them have to get over them through trial and error. The parents, who have themselves been through these conditions, are content to leave the helpless children on their own resources and wit. This is not a desirable practice. In this connection it is for the parents to inform the children of all necessary details and methods, without making secret of anything. It is never a good practice to hate or scold or deliver moral lectures if one sees an adolescent developing bad habits. It is a matter of physiology and psychology, and it should be treated accordingly. It is for the teacher to inform to growing boy and girl of the complete facts about the male and female body, and to train them adequately in all forms of hygiene.

(4) Hero worship and idealisation are two very useful tendencies with which the adolescent is endowed. This stage in his development is particularly efficacious for laying the foundations for a good character. He should be given the lives of great men to read and to draw what lesson he can from them. High ideals stand revealed to him, and he can think in terms of greater characters as opposed to the imaginative pictures of heroes that he has been sketching to himself. The adolescent should be persuaded to read extensively. It is never desirable to prevent him from reading stories and novels. All that is needed is that he should be intelligently guided in forming his taste by being taught to read interesting works of great novelists and psychologists so that his knowledge of human nature increases and his sexual tendency reduces its hold upon him.

(5) The adolescent is by nature a rebel against the traditions and customs prevailing in his society. His rebellious instinct can be channelled to good use by the teacher who can help to develop a generation which hates all the bad traditions and rids society of them. Adolescents can easily be induced to think of social development and improvement. They can be taught to rise above their narrow interests and comprehend the spirit of nationality, internationality and universal love.

(6) It is no less important to impart ethical, moral and religious education to the child. Although all educational psychologists fail to

see eye to eye on this subject, moral and religious education can benefit the recipient only if it is psychological and simple.

(7) In adolescence the individual should be given vocational guidance after his mental capacities, inclinations and interests have been examined. His education should conform to the vocation that he is going to pursue in the future so that he may not be a misfit in any occupation but should rather be able to earn a comfortable living, establish a household and contribute actively to national development.

SOME COMMON DIFFICULTIES OF ADOLESCENTS AND SOLUTIONS

1. Lack of interest in school work. Sometimes the school is not appealing to the adolescents. The best way to help a student who lacks interest in school work is to find out his interests and then to tie these interests to school work by giving a disinterested student something he likes to do, the school accords him recognition and approval, and stimulates to increase his efforts and widen his interest.

Remedy. Undue emphasis should not be given to school marks or parents wishes. Remedy in the selection of the various school subjects. The interest of the child should be measured through various techniques mentioned earlier. If a pupils placed with the wrong teacher then a change of teacher may be advisable.

2. Lack of proper study schedule. The following principles may be kept in view while planning study schedules :

(i) The same subject may be studied at the same time of the day and at the same place.

(ii) Some time for review must be provided daily.

(iii) The same topic must be studied on the same day it is taught in the class.

3. Insufficient study habits. Following basic study principles should be followed by the adolescent :

(1) Studying the same subject at the same time and at the same place.

(2) Knowing and keeping in mind the purpose of the lesson assigned.

(3) Practising recall while reading.

(4) Taking notes as one proceeds.

(5) Raising questions while reading.

(6) Learning the material in a way in which it will be used later.

(7) Keeping attention focused on the job at hand.

4. Inability to read effectively. The causes of reading deficiency are : poor visual perception, poor auditory acuity, immature eye movement habits, low intelligence, left-handedness, emotional factors, lack of interest and the lack of reading experience. The school authorities should find out the causes of poor reading ability of the child and take steps accordingly.

5. Adjustment to emotional disturbances. The emotions of adolescents must be understood by them and by their elders. The weight, stature and sexual maturation are the chief sources of an adolescent's emotional maladjustment.

Remedy. Preaching and lecturing should be avoided by the counsellor. He will need a great deal of skill in the delicate business of establishing relations with the adolescent and of encouraging the adolescent to help himself.

6. Sex adjustment. Certain kinds of sexual behaviour can have many serious results both for girls and boys. To save from such results information about sex must be given to them in a scientific manner. Sympathetic counsellors should be chosen to be the confidants of confused or troubled young people.

7. Adjustment with the school discipline. Sometimes students must submit to tyrannical teachers. Schools should not implant habits of unquestioning obedience which inhibits the growth of young people towards true independence. The teachers should be considerate to the needs of the adolescents.

8. Vocational adjustment. The tragedies and the wastes that come from unaided or inadequately aided efforts to decide important question of vocational adjustment are evident to anyone, who looks about him. The school should assume this responsibility in this direction.

Hints for Adjustment of Adolescent's Needs

(1) Opportunities should be given to them to discuss their views.

(2) Their views should be considered sympathetically.

(3) All attempts be made to understand their views.

(4) Literature, history, science and other subjects should be taught in a way, that it illuminates the joy of work and the deep meaning of love of honour and courage and of independence.

(5) Every teacher should deal with the vocational usefulness of his subjects, the way to develop good study habits and the relationship between efforts and results.

(6) Special classes may be conducted to teach mental hygiene.

(7) School clubs, sports, and games hobbies, etc., can be made the instruments of more than immediate pleasure in making use of their creative abilities.

(8) The counsellor should make use of all helpful resources outside the school includes parents, various youth welfare agencies, employment bureaus, doctors, etc.

(9) Conducting individual interviews; the counsellor should collect and make use of all the available information concerning adolescent.

QUESTIONS FOR EXERCISE

1. Enumerate some problems of adolescent boys and girls that confront teachers. As an effective counsellor what can you do to solve these problems?
2. Write an explanatory note on 'Problems of Adolescence'.
3. What are the problems of boys and girls during the period of adolescence? What are their bearings on adjustment in schools.

34

GUIDANCE OF PROBLEM CHILDREN

What is a Problem Child?

Problem children as is evident from the term applied to them, are children whose behaviour is not normal and it results in some or the other problem of adjustment being caused. In the words of Valentine, "Problem children is generally used to describe children whose behaviour or personality in something is seriously abnormal." In this manner the class of problem children includes all those juveniles whose character or personality shows some signs of abnormality. Some behavioural abnormalities that seem to indicate this condition are — stealing, lying, annoying children weaker and younger than themselves, not doing home assignments, running away from school, or arriving late at school. They can also be called defects or abnormalities concerning character or personality because conduct of this nature indicates shortcomings in both personality as well as character.

For an understanding of the psychology of problem children it is necessary that a detailed analysis of the behaviour be made and the problematic form of behaviour distinguished from the normal forms. It must here be recalled that the problem child is not a member of a group distinct from the normal child groups. There is no distinct line that distinguishes him from his more normal counterparts as to some extent, and at varying stages in childhood the behaviour of every child becomes problematic. Almost every child, at some stage or the other and for one reason or another tells a lie or steals something. Hence, it is not quite desirable to declare one completely problematic and another more or less completely normal. It has been seen that very often the child is prone to much naughtiness between the ages of two and five, and his conduct appears somewhat problematic and strange. But as he continues to grow older this naughtiness disappears and he no longer appears a problem child. It is for this reason that specialists have made very detailed studies into problem behaviour. In his book on educational psychology, Cronbach made a mention of an experiment or study by Richard Henderson which had revealed the symbols of problematic behaviour that were considered the most sure signs of problematic trouble by the best trained and particularly intelligent research workers.

CAUSES OF PROBLEMATIC BEHAVIOUR

Problematic behaviour can have two kinds of causes — (1) hereditary and (2) environmental. Hereditary causes include physical, emotional or nervous defects but sometimes these may also be the result of weakness. The environmental factors are the following :

1. Atmosphere of home. One major cause of problematic behaviour is the contaminated behaviour that exists in many homes. A large majority of problem children come from broken families of divorced persons. In a study conducted by Bannister and Rooder it became known that 66 per cent of the children come from homes that have an improper atmosphere. Certain other studies traced abnormal behaviour to such diverse causes as poverty, lack of recreation, absence of care, almost complete absence of affection and love, cruel behaviour of step mothers or other relatives, too much cinema seeing, etc. Where the entire family is compelled to live in a small house with only two rooms the child may have occasion witnessing of which has the worst influence upon his undeveloped mind and leads him to forming bad sexual habits. Signs of problematic behaviour are also generated in children who come from homes the atmosphere in which is either strictly disciplinarian or completely lax and uninhibited. Much of what is said in the following chapter regarding juvenile delinquents is also true of the problematic children.

2. Bad company. Besides the family another agency that plays an important role in developing signs of abnormal behaviour in the child is his companionship. Falling into bad company the best of children learn stealing, smoking, physical outrage, cruelty or sex habits of a bad nature.

3. Atmosphere in college. Another important case of problematic behaviour is the defective and contaminated atmosphere of the college. It is only natural for children to show signs of abnormal behaviour when they are compelled to study in colleges or schools in which the teachers present improper and immoral ideals before them, the method of teaching is disgusting or uninteresting, and where there is absence of wholesome recreation, etc.

CURE OF PROBLEM CHILDREN

Hence, the cure of problematic children demands the removal of all objectionable elements from the atmosphere at home and in college as well as from the child's company. The main facts to be noted in this connection are the following :

1. Measures concerning the family. Valentine has made the following suggestions concerning the administration of discipline in the family :

(i) Discipline should not take the form of pressure or fear but should aim at ultimate self control in the child.

(ii) Level of conduct should not be too high.

(iii) The behaviour of parents should be benevolent, and there should be every possible cooperation between the home and school.

(iv) Discipline and rules should be relative.

(v) The child should never be allowed to feel that he is not loved by anyone.

Following these suggestions it will be possible to improve the atmosphere in the family. Residences of families should normally be as far as possible from prostitution houses, gambling dens and factories, etc. Children should not be allowed to view very inflammatory or highly sexually arousing films. Parents should be affectionate and understanding in their behaviour, as the child's behaviour, character and personality depends upon these corresponding elements in themselves. Thus, they must present the best ideals to the children, and should the child develop any undesirable symptoms it should be dealt with psychologically rather than having recourse to physical punishment.

2. Good company. The company that a student keeps outside the house, in the college or in the neighbourhood should be carefully studied and kept in mind. If he has had the misfortune of falling into bad company tactful methods should be employed to wean him of it and introduce him into better circle of friends. It is equally improper and unjustified to give the child too much pocket money or to give him none at all. There should be adequate arrangement for his recreation.

3. Methods adopted by schools. Schools can adopt the following measure for the prevention or cure of problematic behaviour in the students :

(i) *Presentation of high ideals by teachers* : In the school the teacher is no less than an ideal to the student or child, hence it is essential that the teacher's character, personality and conduct should be of the highest order and exemplary so that the best ideals become personified in him.

(ii) *Interesting method of education* : If the method of education or teaching be not interesting the children run away from school and fall into very bad habits. If they are taught by more interesting methods they will be interested and thereby prevented or protected from many ill usages.

(iii) *Proper use of educational apparatus* : In schools through the medium of libraries and reading rooms children and students should get healthy literature so that their thinking may take on a healthy hue and proper form.

(iv) *Balanced curriculum* : The curriculum in various classes for students should be so designed as not to strain the student too much, but at the same time provide him with a variety of knowledge.

(v) *Arrangement of extra-curricular programmes* : Where the question of preventing problematic behaviour in children is concerned, much more can be gained by extra-curricular activities such as picnics, touring, camps, scouting, community, singing, dancing and debate, etc., than can be achieved through the formal curriculum.

(vi) *Means of healthy recreation* : If the child is to be persuaded to avoid any unhealthy means of entertainment it is necessary that various kinds of games and means of recreation be available to him so that he can enjoy himself without injuring his development.

(vii) *Self discipline* : Discipline in the college should not be foisted upon the student but should take the form of autonomous or self discipline. This will help to increase a sense of responsibility without being a burden upon them.

(viii) *Synthesis between family and school* : In order to prevent or to cure problematic behaviour in the child it is essential that the teacher and parents should jointly endeavour to achieve it. Hence, family and school should be synthesized.

(ix) *Guidance* : Children are often faced with problems the solution of which is beyond their own ability, and this results in difficulty that manifests itself in the form of symptoms of problematic behaviour. Hence, the school should provide for individual, educational as well as vocational guidance.

CHILD'S DEFECTS AND ABNORMALITIES

Children can have both defects and abnormalities. The general system of education is devised for the average and normally healthy children, as a result of which it cannot incorporate the development of abnormal children since they need special arrangements. One has to speak louder than when one is speaking to a normal person if one wants to communicate with a deaf individual. A modern teacher is concerned not only with the development of a majority of average children, but also with the development of brilliant, backward, defective and abnormal children. Hence the system of education should also provide for such individuals. Unfortunately many circumstances conspire to make provision of such facilities impossible in all schools. Nevertheless, the teacher should definitely be aware of the defects and abnormalities that mar the development of a child, or arise during its progress. Here these defects will be divided into various categories concerning physical, mental, characters, etc.

PHYSICAL DEFECTS AND ABNORMALITIES

Almost any and every organ of the body can be deformed through defects, and it is not possible to list all such defects. Secondly, all of them do not have any effect on education. Thus, the physical defects and abnormalities that are to be treated of here, are specifically those that are particularly important for the point of view of educational process.

1. Defects of the head. Of all the parts of the body, the head is most important since it houses the brain. Hence, removing defects of the head is most important thing. Common defects of the head are the presence of leeches, skin eruptions, pus, etc., that are mainly caused through the head being left unclean. A child cannot himself keep his head clean. Parents should keep an eye on its cleanliness. One definite measure that must be taken very regularly is that it should be cleaned with soap or other cleaning ingredient, and another is its regular massage with oil, and proper hair combing. It is always advisable for young students to keep hair short and trimmed. This both avoids putting much weight on the head and also makes for easier cleaning and maintenance. Oils that are used for lubricating the head should be those that have a good effect on the head and brain. Application of the oil itself should not involve mere smearing of it on the head but be more of the nature of massage so that the oil penetrates into the roots. There are a variety of oils available for the purpose, but only the best should invariably be preferred. If the child develops some disease of the skin on the head or acquires leeches, his head should be shaved clean following which he should be submitted to expert medical advice and care. In the classroom, the teacher himself should see the extent to which his wards keep cleanliness. If they tend to be dirty, he should invite their parents to school, and point out the desirability of cleanliness and personal hygiene.

2. Defects of the eye. Another organ of the body that has considerable importance from the educational viewpoint is the eye. It, too, is another organ that is prone to many defects in the case of children. Some defects are innate, and even hereditary, but many others are the result of excessive strain on the eye.

Schools should provide facilities for regular periodical checks of the children's eyes so that it should be possible to know of a defect as soon as possible. Besides making arrangements for having any such defects cured the teacher should also advise the student as to the proper mode of eye care. Power of the eyes can be maintained and increased through such expedients as splashing cold water on the eyes, standing facing the sun early in the morning with closed eyes, planning, deep breathing, consuming almonds, white pepper, etc., and other things that increase the power of the brain. Students should never be careless on this score since it is on this that their entire future is based. Finally, as has been pointed out earlier, teachers should read books published by Dr. Bates and other nature cure specialists, so they can acquaint their students with various exercises of eye that keep them in good health. One very useful book on this subject is Harry Benjamin's *Better Sight Without Glasses.*

3. Defects of the ear. After defects of the eye, come the defects of the ear that are no less harmful. Some children are born deaf, with the result that they also remain dumb since language cannot be learned without hearing. Being deaf, they cannot profit by studying in the normal kinds of schools. Special schools have now been provided for the education of such handicapped children where the deaf can learn many things that the normal people know. Consequently, they are also in a position to achieve a good status in society. Another defect that afflicts the ear is a difficulty to hear slight sounds. Their problem resembles the problems of the deaf to some extent. But in their case this shortcoming can either be cured or made less abnoxious through the use of some mechanical devices. Social adjustment is a problem for deaf children and for those who are hard of hearing. Teachers and other well wishers must devote some of their attention to these problems. It usually happens that in large classes, teachers have no way of knowing the various physical ailments that are affecting their students. Hence, it is for them to examine their students from time to time through tests, and advise their guardians of their condition periodically. It is as necessary to cure defects of the ear as it is to provide for their general care. Living continuously in an area that is very noisy may lead to serious auditional consequences since such conditions can cause deafness. There have been definite cases of traffic policemen in big cities going deaf through being constantly in the centre of extreme noise. When the ear accumulates dirt, most people are in the habit of cleaning it with some sharp-edged instrument a practice that is most deprecable as it endangers the ear drum. If there is dirt within the ear, then it should be removed in such a manner that it does not endanger ear drum. Itching in the ear can be cured or at least relieved by putting lukewarm castor oil or oil of neem in it. And even otherwise if some oil is put in the ear from time to time, it prevents extreme dryness of the ear. Too much dirt or any disease of the ear is a condition that only expert physician or ear specialist can treat. Considerable damage can result in such cases even from the least evidence of place in the front of the class so that they may not miss too much of what the teacher says.

4. Defects of the teeth. Dental care is as important as the care of any other part of the body. Usually, parents pay little attention to the care of the children's teeth. Carelessness can lead to serious diseases such as pyorrhoea, that can lead to serious general complications apart from irreparably damaging the teeth. This happens as food reaches the stomach through the teeth. It is for the teachers to arrange for periodical checking of children's teeth, and for instructing them and their careless parents in the care of teeth. Cleanliness of teeth can be achieved through very regular brushing with some good dental cream or delicate branches of the neem tree. Whenever something is eaten, it should be followed by a careful gargling of the mouth so that all residue that is embedded in the teeth is eliminated. Decay of teeth often results from children drinking sweetened milk at night immediately before going to sleep since they do not then wash their mouths. Even if every meal is not succeeded by brushing of the teeth, they should be cursorily cleaned by carefully running a finger over them and removing any matter that sticks between the teeth.

5. Defects of the speech. Some children are afflicted by defects of speech, such as stumbling over words, mispronunciation, etc. Many of these defects can be got rid of through the simple expedient of regular practice. Demosthenes, a famous speaker of Greece, stuttered from birth. He made a habit of going to the seashore and speaking with pebbles in his mouth, a habit that finally cured him of the trouble after he had persisted with it for a long time. Children who falter and stutter are usually teased and laughed at by other children with the result that their social adjustment is considerably hindered. The child himself develops many undesirable attitudes. Presence of such defects makes it imperative that the advice of a good physician be sought in order to remove them. Sometimes a condition of stuttering is actually induced by parents who first imitate children because the child's faltering tongue is pleasant to listen to. And, they often try to remind out defects and faults in their posture, their manner of reading, the angle of light, etc. Girls who do not know the way of carrying themselves gracefully, unwittingly deprive themselves of much of their natural charm and poise. The truth of the matter is that the right sort of carriage hides many defects while it brings into prominence all the good qualities of the individual.

Mental defects and abnormalities

Besides the physical defects and abnormalities, one also finds mental shortcomings and abnormalities in children. For example, some children have a very low intelligence quotient while those with below 20 are regarded as mentally retarded. On the other hand, some children show abnormal intelligence quotients, while those with scores of 130 and above are considered abnormal and gifted. Besides these variations within wide limits, children can also possess many kinds of mental aberrations. Mental complexes, inferiority complexes and superiority complexes are among the more normally found conditions of the mind in children, although their being found commonly does not reduce the ill effects that they have upon the personality. Some children are also subject to epileptic and other kinds of fits. Fainting fits also are not quite unknown. Some children are over-sexed in that the sexual urge is very intense in them. Other children give evidence of neuroses and psychoses. Such mental diseases can only be cured under expert medical advice and care. Sometimes, manifestations of mental diseases are misinterpreted as extreme obstinacy in the child, for which he is severely castigated and punished by parents and even teachers. This not only does not cure the child, but rather further precipitates the conditions of illness. If the child is to be protected from emotional complexes, it is essential that he be treated with sympathy, love and understanding, with a little bit of common sense being thrown in for good measure. His problems should be understood and he should be assisted in his efforts to overcome them. Every school curriculum should make the proper provision for education of backward as well as exceptionally intelligent children. Extra-curricular programmes should also be adequately modified to suit the needs of children.

Defects and Abnormalities of Character

Children exhibit defects and abnormalities concerning character, in addition to defects and complications in the physical and mental aspects of their being Development of child's character is an essential part of the educative process. Character is evident in conduct, and conduct is formed of habits that are acquired in childhood. Hence, proper care and attention to the child can save him from forming harmful habits that become permanent in the form of character elements. Faults of character usually have their origin in sex motivated activity. And in this, much of the responsibility can be placed squarely upon the shoulders of teachers and parents. Actually speaking, it is the parents and not the children who are to be blamed for these bad habits since it is for them to satisfy the child's curiosity of all forms, to explain everything to him sympathetically rather than beating him to put children of the manner in which they used to speak. In fact, even when the child pronounces incorrectly, parents should encourage them patiently to speak correctly so that the wrong pronunciation should not become a habit. Defects of speech can be more easily corrected in childhood than at a later stage. Yet, it is not quite right to plunge the child into complexities very early, since such a method can affect his emotional development adversely. A child's pronunciation depends to a considerable extent upon the pronunciation of other family members. Hence, teachers and parents should take care to pronounce words correctly when speaking in the presence of children. If the child persists in stuttering and faltering, he should be sympathetically assisted rather than criticised or looked down upon. In this respect, family members are particularly responsible.

6. Defects of the nose. Concerning children, presents should also remember that cleaning of the nose is also important. Lack of proper care can lead to serious complications and consequences. A child himself cannot keep his nose properly clean, so that all responsibility for his hygiene is upon his parents. As soon as any disease of the nose or difficulty in breathing is discovered, the child should be submitted to the care of an expert.

7. Extreme delicacy of the body. Another defect of the body is its extreme delicacy or weakness. A weak child finds social adjustment difficult since other children take advantage of his incapacity and bother him. General weakness of the child's body can normally be alleviated through proper food and exercise. Hence, parents should see to it that other children do not worry their weak friends, and at the same time to do their best to improve the general health and debility of the children.

8. Crippled children. Some children become crippled either through some accident or even in pregnancy. Some children experience difficulty in social adjustment and adaptation since other children are prone to make fun of the cripple. Some parents develop a habit of mentioning the child's crippled condition in front of him, and showing their disgust at it. This has the worst possible effect upon the child's mind. In fact, children of this kind should be treated with more love and care than normal children, though it should be remembered that he should not be reduced to complete helplessness and dependence where he can do nothing on his own, but needs the assistance of his parents. Sensible parents can help in the adjustment of their children. Becoming crippled, the child's education should not be reduced in any measure as adequate and proper education can lead even cripples to considerable achievement and progress.

9. Other physical defects. In order to preserve the children from normal defects, teachers should train them to walk, sit, read, write, etc., in the correct manner. Many physical defects can result if the child forms a habit of walking crookedly, sitting in a doubled up position, or reading in a reclined position. Eyes can be adversely affected if the child develops a habit of reading with the book either too close or too far from the eyes. Furniture in the classroom should be comfortable and well-designed. Teachers should interrupt the students to point an end to the string of questions he puts forward, to create such a healthy and affectionate atmosphere in the home that healthy development of the child's character is almost ensured. Once the presence of some criminal streak in the child's character is discovered, it can be eliminated through some illuminated and sensible manoeuvring. Once the sense of self-regard is developed in a child, his character then usually progresses in the right and desired direction.

STEALING

Some children start on a career of crime by stealing when they are only 5 or 6 years of age. They begin with stealing things from the house, stealing food and other domestic things. Then, gaining in confidence, they extend the sphere of their activity of the neighbourhood. Such children are often apprehended stealing books from other children when they go to school, with the result that their well-wishers and parents have sometimes to stand for much disgrace and embarrassment in front of strangers. Knowing of the child's activity, they give him a sound beating, but once the habit of stealing has set in, there is no getting rid of it, at least not so easily. Hence, what is more important is that they should not be given an opportunity to acquire any such habit in the first place. Yet, if he does form any such habit, it is essential that efforts at destroying a habit should be very tactful and imaginative. In either condition, it is essential to divine the reason why any child steals. Modern educational psychologists have discovered why children steal, and in this connection have shed some light on the psychological factors involved. Knowledge of these elements will help teachers and parents to solve the problem of stealing by children.

Causes of Stealing

Main causes why children steal are the following :

1. Sense of insecurity. Children develop a sense of insecurity when the family is in turmoil, when children are indifferently treated by the parents or when they are frequently punished by them. If parents lie to their children and the children manage to find out that the parents have been misleading them, they feel insecure. And this sense of insecurity sometimes induces the child to steal. Hence, it is essential that the calm and peace of family life be maintained intact, children should be told the truth as far as is practicable and they should be treated with love.

2. Spoiling through excessive love. Love and affection are things for which the child rightly yearns, but too much of them can spoil him and make him very obstinate. A child who has his full of love and affection has far too many needs and while these needs can be satisfied in a family that is financially strong, in poor families this creates a problem. Descent from a strong financial position to an inferior level of income also creates a problem, and the child begins to steal. It is, of course, not inevitable that members of poor families steal. On the contrary, one finds habits of stealing in children who come from the richer families. Stealing or not is more positively concerned with the child being spoiled. Hence, it is essential that the child should be scolded if he does anything undesirable.

3. Strict discipline. Presence of extreme discipline in the family leads the child to complete repression of many of his tendencies. And repression leads to the formation of sentimental complexes that complicate his adjustment activity, for the fulfilment of which he turns to theft. Too much beating and punishing also instigates the child to stealing since this gives him a sense of independence. Hence, where discipline in the family is concerned, it is never desirable to wield the rod with a liberal hand.

4. Dissatisfaction of needs. The basic cause why a child steals is that his needs are not satisfied. If a child gets enough to eat, wear and play within the home he has no need for stealing. Generally, a child should also be given some pocket money when he goes to school. What actually happens is that when the child sees other children spending money on all kinds of things, it is natural for him to want the same things. When he finds no resources to do so, he steals things from school and money from his own home. It should also be remembered that if all the child's demands are promptly met with, instead of breaking off the habit of stealing, there is every possibility that it will be intensified. Lack of control spoils the child so that he has no compunctions in stealing.

5. Sex problems. Psychological studies have revealed that a child steals because of an unconscious desire to satisfy his repressed sexual desires. Scolding and punishing the child if he enquires after his curiosity on matters of sex leads to the formation of guilt complex in the child, and he learns, stealing, lying and other bad habits.

6. Sense of adventure. Some children find stealing an adventure, and the excitement involved is the main consideration. Plucking flowers where it is prohibited gives them a sense of thrill.

7. Imitation. Where children observe other members of the family stealing, it is comparatively more natural for them to adopt such activities. Some women surreptitiously remove money from their husband's pockets, some other children in the family are prone to stealing. And the child imitates them.

Eliminating the Habit of Stealing

On the basis of the above mentioned causes of stealing among children, the teacher can discover the cause of stealing in the case of an individual child with the parent's help. In fact, a child's stealing is less a crime but more a bad habit and defect of character. In order to kill this habit in the child, a teacher will advise the parents to maintain an atmosphere of peace and calm within the family, to love the child, to provide him with a reasonable amount of spending money, and to look after him carefully. Children who find stealing thrilling because of the adventure involved can be broken of the habit by being busied in games that involved adventure and require courage. Children who steal because of an unconscious desire arising out of the repression of sexual impulses can be guided into the right mode of behaviour by being told the healthy things about sex and by affectionate behaviour. Actually, within the family a system should be developed whereby the children should use only what is theirs and not to pickup anything belonging to any other family member. Such a step will develop his sense of possession over what is admittedly his, and will also develop in him a habit of keeping his hands off things that do not belong to him. Scolding or punishing a child after his stealing has come to one's notice is not a very constructive measure, neither is there anything to be gained by ignoring theft. If such a condition is precipitated, the teacher can coolly discuss things with the parents and discover the caused that lead the child to crime, and will remove them before trying to break him of the habit.

LYING

Meaning and Kind of Lying

Conscious and wilful saying of a thing that is known to be incorrect is called lying. If a child says something that is incorrect but is not aware of its invalidity, it is incorrect to call him a liar. He is a liar only when he has knowingly said something that is untenable. Habits of lying of this type must be removed. Lying can be of many kinds. The famous criminologist Cyril Burt has classified lying in the following manner :

1. **Playful lies.** In infancy and childhood, sometimes the child tells a lie just for the fun of it. It is no crime, it is just wantonness.

2. **Lie of confusion.** When something is in doubt, the child fails to distinguish between true and false, and says that which is false.

3. **Lie of vanity.** Some children lie for the sake of false vanity. They talk of things that they have never done. Such lying satisfies their false vanity.

4. **Lie of revenge.** Sometimes the child who has been defeated and has no means of wreaking revenge upon the winner, turns up spreading false gossip and creating all kinds of false information to manifest his superiority over his adversary.

5. **Selfish lie.** Telling a deliberate lie in order to conceal some fault of one's own doing is called a selfish lie. For example, when some children are caught being naughty, they invent all kinds of false reason to escape the natural reckoning.

6. **Lie of loyalty.** A child is very loyal to his group and tries to cover up its objectionable activities by telling lies.

7. **Pathological lie.** Some lying is the result of many abnormalities and mental complexes in the individual. Such lies resulting from mental diseases can arise due to the following causes :

(a) Overactive imagination,

(b) Facility in the use of words,

(c) To hide certain bad sex habits.

Cure of Lying

Once the child evinces the habit of telling lies, the teacher must endeavour to end it, since its persistence will adversely affect the development of his character and leave incomplete the function of education. Hence, teachers who catch their students telling lies, use many ways of curing them. Some of the main methods are the following :

1. Psychological treatment. In psychological treatment, the child is treated with love and affection in order to discover the causes of his lying. Having discovered them, the teacher tries to persuade the child and also causes such changes in his environments that the need for telling lies ceases to exist.

2. Indirect punishment. According to modern educational psychologists, direct punishment of the child leads to development of feelings of hatred and revolt against his teacher, hence this mode of retribution is not desirable. As an alternative some forms of indirect punishment can be used that often prove to be more effective even than direct punishment. Some such methods are — not talking with the child, ignoring him, being indifferent towards him.

3. Avoid provocative occasions. Generally speaking, the teacher should always try to avoid all occasions that may provoke the child into lying. Testing the child by deliberate creation of such situations is not very expedient since there is no bad habit that the child is incapable of picking up. Hence, as far as is practically possible and feasible, one should avoid all occasions that provoke lying in children.

4. Confession. When a lie is detected the first time, one must try to make the child confess that he is in the wrong. This inspires him to repent, and the embarrassment involves acts as a sufficient deterrent in case of future provocation. His self respect is injured, if he has to confess. Secondly, having confessed to his fault and having promised not to repeat it, the child himself does his best to avoid all such occasions.

5. Positive instruction. According to modern educational psychologists, a teacher should avoid negative instruction and direction as far as possible, and try to make his directive positive. It is more expedient to say always tell the truth than to order the student to avoid lying. Children have an almost natural tendency of contradicting all negative orders, being more prone to accepting positively worded requests and orders.

6. Rational attitude towards the child's imagination. A child is naturally imaginative. He imagines all sorts of things by imaginatively putting himself in different situations. Sometimes he fails to do these things in the concrete, he boasts that he has done this or that, and that he has seen this or that plane. Hence, realizing child's sensitivity with regard to imagination, one should take the child to see new places, give him the independence and freedom to play all kinds of games, give him new things. When this is done, he will not tell lies among his friends for the simple reason that there will be no need to do it.

Finally, it can be said that successful elimination of the child's lying habits depends upon the teacher's psychological insight, patience, and tactful behaviour. He can benefit in his efforts by the suggestions of educational psychologists.

Some children are prone to cause pain to other children junior to themselves. The teacher observes that one child is annoying a younger without any apparent reason. On the other hand, one student comes to him with the report that a class-fellow has beaten him up. Sometimes, reports of this kind are untrue and maliciously reported. But whether the report is a lie or a fact it is for the teacher to investigate and find out, as otherwise his wards are inclined to lose faith in him, and the discipline of the school is seriously jeopardized. The child making the complaint should be sympathetically treated and made to understand that this problem will be solved and in future he will not be molested. Now, the major problem that remains is how to prevent some children from annoying others without reason. Usually, teachers punish and thrash youngsters who do these wanton things with the result that the student is awed and under the influence he is not prone to repeat his exploits. Yet, though this helps to maintain the proper discipline in the class, it defeats the purpose of education. The teacher's object is not to prevent the children from being naughty but eliminating the causes that lead him to undesirable behaviour. Hence, if he is to completely cure the child of his habit of wantonly causing pain to his juniors, it is essential that he discovers the basic causes that originated the tendency.

Causes of Teasing other Children

The tendency of testing other children wantonly is one that reveals a streak of cruelty in the child. And in this the environment in the family plays a large part. Main causes in this connection can be the following :

1. Cruel behaviour on the part of family members. The child has an invariable tendency to imitate the conduct of family members. If members of the family quarrel with each other and the stronger and older beat the youngsters in the family the child will follow suit.

2. Absence of discipline in the family. Lack of discipline in the family permits the children to quarrel with each other, the seniors almost invariably triumphing over the juniors by beating them. And many parents have not the strength of will to prevent such insane behaviour. Hence it can only be expected that children from such families will injure smaller children in school. It is sometimes seen that the parents take a hand in the punishing to stop their children behaving in this manner. This may create a state of enforced peace and acquiescence in the home, but when in school, the child will imitate his parents and injure and beat children younger and weaker than himself.

3. Relations between parents and child. If the relations between parents and children are not loving and confident, the child becomes irritable, quarrelsome and selfish. He will manifest these qualities fighting children younger than himself. The tendency towards cruelty is further promoted by the prejudiced and base behaviour of parents towards their children.

4. Lack of discipline in school. In schools where senior students are seen beating and overpowering youngsters, there is little or no discipline. Teachers must adopt psychological means to create an atmosphere of discipline and rational obedience in the school.

There can be some other reasons, besides those mentioned above, why big children may injure and worry smaller children. For example, being oversexed, some children tease their juniors. Whatever the situation, the teacher must try to discover the causes involved in the situation and then try to eliminate them. Acting on two fronts, the teacher must use love and affection to persuade the student while he tries to eliminate the causes that have led to the formation of such a habit in him. Half of his battle is won if he can convince the child's parents of the need of improving the atmosphere at home. He must also try to make the student realise that it is indecent to tease smaller children. Secondly, it is for him to train the children to cooperate and work in an atmosphere of mutual confidence, love and sympathy. Once such an atmosphere has been successfully created in the school, incidents of big boys worrying small ones will be reduced. Teachers should keep an eye on such various tendencies as over sexuality, aggressiveness, false vanity, and criminal tendency that arise in children from time to time, and should also resort to tactful behaviour in trying to eliminate them.

AVOIDING TASKS ALLOCATED FOR HOME WORK

In most schools, teachers allot some work to the students to complete at home. Sometimes, due to various causes that create unpredictable circumstances, the child fails to do this, but he is not to blame. But, if a child makes it a habit to avoid doing the allotted work, the teacher must do his best to break the child of such a habit. This habit can be caused by any one of the following :

1. Improper atmosphere in the home. The atmosphere in some children's houses is not at all conducive to any sort of serious effort, as a consequence of too much noise and lack of any quiet corner.

2. Lack of interest and enthusiasm. Children who are not interested in academic pursuits and have no enthusiasm for it, usually do not complete the work allotted to them.

3. Little respect and awe of teacher. If a child does not respect a particular teacher and holds him in no awe whatsoever, then that teacher's commands have no particular value for him. In fact, he does the very contrary of what is required of him. His neglecting the work allotted for completion at home is all that can be expected from the child under the circumstances.

4. Other causes. In addition to these above causes, there can be many other reasons why a student may fail to complete the work required of him. For example, if the child has failed to understand a particular lesson taught in school, how can he be expected to do any problems pertaining to it?

Solution and Cure

Keeping in mind these various causes, the teacher should see to it that students do the work that he allots to them as their home work. In this effort he can, on the one hand, request the children's parents to improve the atmosphere at home, and, on the other, he can improve his own conduct in the classroom. He must be able to win the respect and admiration of his students. Having done this it will be easy for him to have his orders obeyed. Nevertheless, if some student persists in disobeying the instructions of the teacher, then it becomes necessary to administer some indirect punishment to persuade the student to abandon his lax ways. Among them is indifference to the particulars student, abstaining from holding conversations with him, and other means whereby the student himself should realise the teacher's displeasure. A teacher must invariably avoid any situation that may lead students to develop feelings of antipathy and hatred towards him, or to feel that the work allocated for home is an unnecessary burden forced upon him. Proper methods of education and desirable behaviour on the teacher's part coupled with adequate interest and inspiration in the work cause students to do their home work ethusiastically, and sometimes even go to the length of doing work on their own initiative if the teacher does not allot any, and showing it to him. Such children should be praised in front of the whole class. This will have the two-fold effect of adding to their already exuberant enthusiasm, as well as inspiring the other students to emulate them and win the teacher's admiration.

ABSCONDING FROM MATHEMATICS CLASS

Mathematics is one subject that has created aversion in more than one student and they all do their best to avoid it. Some of these children are enterprising enough to run away from the mathematics class. If this sort of truant behaviour is constantly noted, then the teacher is compelled to take note to solve it. He must first of all uncover the causes that induce the child to have such irresponsibility. Main causes could be from among the following :

1. Low level of maturity. Mathematics is one subject that essentially requires the presence of a certain level of maturity in its students. At different levels of maturity, the curriculum relating to mathematics should be different.

2. Defects of educational method. If the teacher takes it upon himself to teach mathematics by a method that makes the subject appear easy to the student, he will not play truant from the class. Hence, sometimes, one of the reasons why students avoid the mathematics class could be a defective and unimaginative method of teaching.

3. Student's personal difficulties. If the student has no interest in academic study, lacks enthusiasm and inspiration regarding it, a subject as notoriously dry as mathematics is the least likely to hold his attention. Repeated failure is another thing that may discourage him. There can be numerous other similar problems that may prompt the student to avoid the mathematics class. And for this, attitudes, mental abilities and qualities of the personality have a special significance.

Solution and Cure

The teacher should try to discover the causes of a student's running away from the mathematics class, and having done so, should try to remove it. The child should constantly practise in this difficult subject. Lessons should start with simple questions that are comparatively easy to solve. Success will increase his enthusiasm, and he will be eager to delve into more difficult problems. In teaching mathematics the teacher should adopt a method that makes it easy to grasp so that students achieve a kind of auto-inspiration in learning it. Besides this, if the children are found avoiding these classes through some personality defects, then the teacher should consult their parents, and through loving and affectionate behaviour, try to eliminate these shortcomings.

BEING LATE FOR SCHOOL

Causes

Being occasionally late for the class is nothing unusual. But if a student persists in being late for the school, the teacher has of necessity to investigate and find out the cause for it, since punctuality is an important asset and a part of personality development. There can be many causes why a child is consistently late for the class, main ones among them being the following :

1. Parent's carelessness. Children can be punctual in reaching school only if their parents prepare them for school well in time. If they are careless in this respect, it is only natural that their children should be late for school.

2. Aimless wandering. Another reason why children, who are prepared for school in time by their parents, reach the school late is that they fall into bad company and play on the wayside or roam around before reaching the school. Once a child falls into a company of vagrants it is only natural for him to develop a liking for wandering. It is a kind of wander lust.

3. Tendency to avoid classes. The fundamental reason why the child is always late for school is that there is nothing in the class to interest him, and he wants to avoid it, any way. Tendency to run away from classes can be inspired by many things, among them are uninteresting methods of teaching, strict discipline, level of education being higher than the child's level of mental development, bad atmosphere in the classroom, very strict administration in school, etc.

4. Other causes. There cannot be the same reason for children being late for school. Due to different reasons and under different circumstances, children do this. It is quite possible that a child may have a special passion for some particular form of exhibition and that this exhibition may be situated on his way to school so that he may be tempted to spend a few minutes there everyday.

Cure and solution

Whatever it may be, the teacher must begin his investigation to examining the reasons why a student is delayed on his way to school. And then, efforts can be made to eliminate these causes, a venture that requires the cooperation of the parents. Parents and teachers can cooperate to punish the child indirectly and thus break him of his habit. Parents must do their bit by preparing the child for school with a good bit of time to spare. If the atmosphere in school and the method of teaching is defective, it can be removed and education made more interesting. It is the duty of his seniors to save the youngster from bad company. A child naturally likes to live in the group, be it a group of good children, or one of bad children. The sole method of having the child avoid bad company is that he be put in good company. Then, he will not try to go to bad company. Parents should communicate with the teacher at regular intervals to find out whether their child is reaching the school in time. If this is not done, it is up to the teacher to immediately inform them if he thinks it fit. Such cooperation and sensible behaviour can help to rid the child of this bad habit. Secondly, this problem can also be solved by teaching the child all the virtues of punctuality. Some people fail to see the significance of doing things at the time allotted for their doing. Punctuality is a quality that is developed both in school and at home. Having become habituated to having meals, getting up, going to sleep at appointed hour and doing many things by the clock will develop into such a strong habit that he will be instinctively compelled to get to School in time. Otherwise, he is apt to reason out the little difference it makes by being late for school. But, before inculcating the wisdom of punctuality in children, it is essential that the parents and teachers themselves be very punctual. Teachers who themselves are usually late for their class can hardly expect to convince their students that punctuality is a virtue. Punctuality is a thing that is best learned by imitating one's seniors. If parents and teachers themselves are very punctual, the child will drop the habit of being late for school.

QUESTIONS FOR EXERCISE

1. What do you understand by a problem child. What are the factors which lead to the development of problem child?
2. "The problem child is in need of a psychologist in as much as the sick child is in need of a physician." Discuss this statement with special reference to any two types of abnormal behaviour usually met with in the class-room.
3. What are the common causes of truancy in school children? What can the teachers do to help the truant child?
4. How will you deal with the following types of children :
   (i) A child given to stealing.
   (ii) A child bullying and teasing other children.
   (iii) A child suffering from the defect of lying.
   (iv) A child given to smoking.

35

Guidance of Backward Children

What is a backward child?

Generally speaking, no mother or father is easily prepared to accept that their child is mentally backward. But modern intelligence test techniques have indubitably established that some children are mentally backward. A backward child is more in need of assistance than one with average or above average intelligence, hence in modern school teachers are expected to pay particular attention to the weak students in their classes. A backward child, evidently, is one who has an intelligence quotient lower than the average child. In the words of Cyril Burt, "A backward child is one who in the middle of the school career, is unable to do the work of the class below that which is normal for his age." In this way, the backward child falls fare behind other children of his age in matters of study. In school, such children remain in the same class for many years, and fail to progress upward. Educational psychologists have no single opinion of the intelligence quotient below which a child can definitely be called backward. Yet generally, psychologists classify those children as backward whose intelligence quotient falls below 85.

PROBLEMS OF BACKWARD CHILDREN

Children who are backward have certain problems that are peculiarly their own. Having a very low intelligence quotient, they require to be taught many things by others. A backward child cannot lead, he is more in a position to need the help and sympathy of friends and relatives. A child who is very feeble minded, having an intelligence quotient of 70 or less, cannot obtain education in the ordinary schools, and has to be sent to special institutions. Emotional adjustment of the child is completely integrated if he fails in the same class time after time. In a class, teaching approximates to the average level of students. Hence, it is only natural for the backward child to meet with failure. Failure in school leads to the assumption that he will also be a failure in life. His ambitions are destroyed and he becomes hopeless.

Backward child also faces difficulties in social adjustment. In the group he does not easily grasp even the smallest thing and rules of play have to be repeated for his benefit. His colleagues naturally heckle him. It is possible that a spark of leadership may be ignited in him if he communicates with those younger than himself but on the same intelligence level. But there he is unwelcome since other children steer clear him because of his physical superiority. Adults pay him little or no attention, instead he is scolded from time to time. In adolescence and adulthood, too, the position of the child does not improve. He is made the butt of every joke. Activities of the group are usually on a higher level, so that he does not fit in them either.

CAUSES OF BACKWARDNESS

It is not even possible to recount all the various causes of backwardness, but the main causes are the following :

1. Physical causes. Due to many physical defects and abnormalities, the child lags behind other average children. Such physical conditions would be weakness of eyes, deafness or being hard of hearing, stuttering, being weak or crippled, etc. This also has an adverse effect upon his social adjustment.

2. Mental defects. It has been indicated earlier that the backward child has a very low intelligence quotient, as compared with that of an average child. Having a low intelligence, his other mental characteristics and abilities also do not compare favourably with the average child.

3. Educational immaturity. Physical and mental shortcomings in the child result in educational immaturity. Putting it differently, he has not adequate maturity to grasp the teaching that is customary for his age level.

4. Emotional factors. The child's social adjustment is detected by his mental and physical abnormalities, and he meets with successive failures. He meets with criticism on every account. Hence it is natural for him to manifest anxiety, tension, depression and other emotional factors. Sometimes, though every other defect is absent the child is backward in his class for no better reason than these psychological or emotional factors.

5. Atmosphere in the home. One reason of backwardness can also be the atmosphere in the home. Proper development of the child cannot occur in a virulent family atmosphere. Hence, he falls behind children of his age group. And among the factors that contribute to the defective atmosphere in the home are constant quarreling and fighting between parents and children, unbalanced diet, strict discipline, absence of all peace and calm, poverty, etc.

6. Lack of interest. Sometimes, even though the child is free from all the defects and shortcomings mentioned above and even those that have not been mentioned, the child falls behind the rest of the class for the simple reason that he cannot stir any interest in the various subjects being taught. This causes repeated failure.

7. Factors concerning the schools. The school can be a veritable storehouse of factors that inhibit the child's development such as inadequate method of teaching, uneducated teachers, undesirable atmosphere, inadequate curriculum, defective time table, disgusting relations between students and teachers, etc. All these causes conspire to make even the average child look backward.

Cyril Burt's opinion

Different educational psychologists have stressed different factors present in the analysis of backward children and their causes. Different factors have been considered more or less important. Cyril Burt has allocated importance to the various factors in backwardness in the following proportions :

Cause	*Percentage*
Poverty	20%
Home atmosphere	16%
Educational causes	11%
Health	8%
Neighbourhood	3%

Even if this kind of guesses are not relied upon, one can still say that backwardness is considerably aggravated through the contribution of physical and mental defects, atmosphere in the home, emotional causes, lack of interest in subjects of education, neighbourhood and school, etc.

IDENTIFICATION OF BACKWARD CHILDREN

Modern schools are led to believe that the backward children in a class should be specially attended to. Hence the teacher must know how to distinguish and recognise a backward child. This can be done in four steps :

1. Discovering the child's A.Q. Tests in arithmetic, language and general knowledge can be used for discovering the child's A.Q.

2. Discovering I.Q. Selective children with an intelligence quotient of below 85 their exact I.Q. should then be calculated.

3. Individual intelligence tests. Now the result obtained from the group intelligence tests should be examined for their reliability by obtaining results through individual intelligence tests and coinciding the two conclusions.

4. Rating by teachers. Following this, rating by teachers should be sought concerning children who appear to be backward so that the results of tests are confirmed by educated insight.

5. Case history. After all the above tests have been completed, the child's detailed life history should be prepared.

SOLUTION OF EDUCATION OF BACKWARDNESS

Most of the so-called backward children can be improved. In the case of children with intelligence quotients below 70, no improvement is possible through education in the ordinary schools since they need to be sent to specialised schools and institutions. In children with intelligence quotients between 70 and 85, considerable improvement is possible even in regular educational institutions. Many of these children can be raised to the level of average normality through cures so that they can find success in school and later life. If they are given some encouragement and are shown some success, they learn many simple activities. But this requires modification of the curriculum, the teacher's method of teaching, and separate educational establishments are not essential as they require only special attention and periodical expert examination. But with children of intelligence quotients below 70 separate arrangements are unavoidable.

1. Curriculum. Often many children fail repeatedly in the same class for the simple reason that the curriculum does not suit them. Consequently, the teacher must modify his curriculum to meet the requirements of backward children so that it contains only those subjects. The entire curriculum should be so fashioned that when the backward child completes his course, he should be fitted to adopt some particular profession. Basic education should be emphasised in the curriculum. Children can also be trained for some specific professions and vocations.

2. Method of teaching. The sole quality of a teaching method is that student should grasp what it has to teach. Hence, there should be different methods of teaching for students on different levels. It is evident that backward children will not gain much if they are taught by a method that is found suitable for average children. For them, there should be a special method of teaching with the following characteristics :

(*a*) pace of teaching should be slow;

(*b*) lesson should be repeated more than once.

BACKWARDNESS AND RETARDATION

In categorising backwardness, Schonell introduced the Mental Age concept, and 'Subject' or 'Educational Age', as determined by standardised tests. According to Schonell Backwardness is measured in terms of the difference between the Educational Age and Chronological Age, Schonell goes on to introduce the concept of 'Retardation', which is measured in terms of the extent to which the Educational Age falls below the Mental Age. This approach is based on the hypothesis that a child cannot be expected to perform at a level above that of his innate ability as expressed in terms of Mental Age.

CASES ILLUSTRATING SCHONELL'S DEFINITION OF BACKWARDNESS AND RETARDATION

Case	I.Q.	C.A.	M.A.	E.A.	Classification	Comments
A	100	10	10	10	Neither backward nor Retarded	Satisfactory
B	100	10	10	8	Backward and Retarded	Both Remedial
C	80	10	8	8	Backward only	Irremedial
D	80	10	8	6	Backward and Retarded	Retardation only Remedial
E	120	10	12	10	Retarded only	Remedial
F	70	10	7	8	Backward only	Irremedial
G	120	10	12	8	Backward and Retarded	Both Remedial

SLOW LEARNERS

Meaning

Prof. T.N. Birkett states, "A slow-learning child is one whose capacity for learning the kind of material which is taught in the ordinary school is limited by some deficit in intellectual capacity. Limited intelligence, however, this may be defined, is the chief characteristic of the 'Slow learner'.

Classification

1. Children, whose capacity for education or training is limited by low intelligence, cover a fairly wide I.Q. range from approximately 40 to 80 or 90. However, students whose I.Q. ranges between 50/55 and 85/90 are capable of benefiting from the kind of education which is offered within the normal school system. These may be subdivided into two groups :

(i) The Educable Mentally Retarded (I.Q. range 50 to 70).

(ii) The Dull Normals (I.Q. range 70 to 85).

2. Trainable mentally retarded. Students whose I.Q. range is between 35/40 and 50 and are usually termed as the Trainable Mentally Retarded. Provision for education of such children may be made outside the normal school system.

Characteristics. Sullivan has summarised the characteristics of slow learners as follows :

1. Short attention and concentration span.
2. Slow reaction time.
3. Limited ability to evaluate materials for relevancy.
4. Limited powers of self-direction.
5. Limited ability to work with abstractions and to generalise.
6. Slowness to form association between words and phrases.

7. Failure to recognise familiar elements in new information.
8. Habits of learning very slowly and forgetting very quickly.
9. Very local point of view.
10. Inability to set up and realise standard of workmanship.
11. Lack of originality and creativeness.
12. Inability to analyse, to do problem solving, or think critically.
13. Lack of power to use the higher mental processes.

Guiding Principles for Slow Learner

1. Data collection. Maximum information about such children should be secured and their interests should be discovered.

2. Special classes. Special classes for slow-learning children.

3. Partial segregation. It has been stated, "The children should be included in the total school set-up, regularly participating in assembly programmes, organised play, and other activities enjoyed by all children." The problems should be clearly explained.

4. Short assignments. Assignments given to the students should be broken up into short and simple units.

5. Drill work. Sufficient drill work should be done.

6. Summaries. Frequent summaries of the important points of discussion should be used.

7. Praise. Pupils should be praised occasionally when they have done their assignments well.

8. Proper evaluation. Good set of tools should be provided for proper evaluation.

9. Close supervision. Supervision should be very close.

10. Audio-visual aids. Auditory and visual aids facilitate learning among slow learners.

11. Opportunities for creative expression. Opportunities should be provided to slow-learning children for expression of creativeness with their hands.

12. Diagnostic tests. Diagnostic tests should be used in working with slow-learning children.

13. Curricula according to interests. Courses and curricula should be selected by the students on the basis of aptitude, interest and need with the help of their counsellors.

14. Vocational programmes. Vocational programmes should not be forced upon slow-learners as such children do not always have the necessary aptitude to acquire vocational skill.

15. Equality of opportunity in recreational programmes. Recreational programme athletics, music, art, dramatics, etc., should be opened to all on an equal basis. To quote Mones, "When these people are accepted in secondary schools, the schools, clubs, the bands, the patrols, the clean-up squads, the down and ground squads, the cafeteria patrols, athletics teams are all possible instrumentalities of their education. If they can find educational outcome in the way of developing traits, attitudes, purposes, and satisfactions that will give them a sense of integrated personality."

16. Remedial teaching. Remedial teachers may be appointed who meet such students twice a week.

17. Cooperation of all agencies. All agencies engaged in the children's welfare work should co-operate to help and guide slow learners.

QUESTIONS FOR EXERCISE

1. Define slow-learning children. Suggest necessary steps for their education.
2. "Backwardness can be prevented." Comment.
3. How would you provide guidance to the slow-learning children?
4. Describe the guiding principles for the education of the slow-learners?
5. What is Backwardness? Explain its causes.
6. How will you identify backwardness? Suggest remedies to backwardness.

36

Guidance of Gifted Children

Definition of Gifted Children

1. Hillingworth. "By a gifted child we mean one who is far more educable than the generality of children are. The greater educability may lie along the lines of one of the arts, as in music or drawing, it may lie in the sphere of mechanical aptitude, or it may consist in surpassing power to achieve literacy and abstract knowledge."

2. Paul Witty, Ruthy Strang, Havighurst and many others. "The term 'gifted children' should include all those children who give promise of creativity of a high order in any worthwhile line of human endeavour."

Characteristics of gifted children. In 1916, Terman set the lower limit for the gifted person at 110 on the Revised Stanford Binet Simon Intelligence Scale In 1937, only children having I.Q. of at least 120 (1.25 sigmas above mean) were judged to be very superior. Some years later, children with I.Q. 125 or above in the major classes of Cleveland, Ohio, were classed as superior. Goddard used 120 as the lower limit in forming classes for gifted children including both those with special artistic and mechanical talents and those who excelled in creative thinking and abstract reasoning. Discarding the I.Q. standard Ralph W. Tyler defined the gifted child as one who is exceptional in the amount rate and the quality of his production or a combination of these; a child who may do much more school work than the average student does the work faster and performs with much higher quality.

Exceptionally gifted children. Psychologists do not agree about the level of intelligence required for a child to be considered gifted. While some psychologists believe that an intelligence quotient of 120 denotes exceptional gifts, others believe that the gifted child must have an I.Q. of 140. Children with an intelligence quotient higher than 140 can be accepted as exceptionally gifted. Only one out of 400 children belongs to this category. Such exceptionally gifted children have an intelligence quotient ranging between 140 and 190. But an I.Q. of 170 or more is rarely seen, while an I.Q. between 140 and 150 is more common.

Difference from Average

In addition to his greater intelligence, the gifted child differs from the average child in other respects also. Physiologically, the gifted child is frequently better built. He is emotionally better balanced than the average child. Leaving aside the exceptions, it is often seen that the child is gifted not only in terms of intelligence but also in terms of other individual qualities, in which he is more developed. Apparently, the gifted children enjoy the benefits of nature and environment. Most of such children are born into families with a fairly high social and economic level. They, therefore, belong to the more well-to-do group of families with the result that the care lavished on them, the food provided, the education, etc., are all considerably better than that enjoyed by the average child. Besides, they also get good training in controlling their habits and emotions, which helps in developing many exceptional qualities of character and personality.

Frequently, the gifted child is one to two inches taller and a few pounds heavier than the average child. At the time of joining school, such children are seen to be 4 or 5 pounds heavier than the others. At the age of 15, such children are 10 to 15 pounds heavier. In addition to this the gifted children do not normally suffer from headaches, they have clearer skins, they are less irritable, less inclined to exhaustion and less susceptible to such common maladies as cold. In one study a group of 220 successful and 170 unsuccessful candidates were compared, and it was found that the successful candidates suffered from fewer physical defects than the unsuccessful ones. In this case there was one exception, since the gifted competitors were found to suffer from a higher incidence of visual defects. One possible explanation of this may be their excessive use of the eyes in reading and study. But physiologically they were neither weak nor dwarfed. In fact, they were taller and heavier.

It should be remembered that all gifted children are not better than the average child in their physiological characteristics, emotional stability or social adjustment. In fact, quite a few of the gifted children are below the average in this respect. In actual fact, gifted children differ from each other very much in these respects. As a general rule, all that can be said is that defects lead to more defects while good qualities generate more good qualities, although this, too cannot be accepted as a universal rule. For this reason, it is desirable that each gifted child should be studied individually.

PROBLEMS OF THE GIFTED CHILD

As in the case of the backward child, the gifted child is also unlike the average child. As a result, certain problems arise in his case also. These problems should also be tackled with the same care and attention as is accorded to the backward child, although it is now certain that the teacher identifies a backward child much sooner than he can recognise the gifted one. It may also happen that the teacher may completely fail to observe the qualities of the gifted child, and may even consider him backward. Such a situation is extremely harmful because it hinders the gifted child's proper development, and at the same time creates administrative problems for the school and the class. The future of any nation depends upon the proper development of all the gifted children born in it. Hence, school should make special provisions for their training. But the parents also must accept responsibility for their training and education.

EDUCATION OF GIFTED CHILDREN

The following suggestions have been given for the education of gifted children :

1. Selection. The first step in their education is to find out which child is gifted. This selection can be made with the help of marks obtained at previous examinations the advice of the class teachers, the results of psychological tests and the reports given by parents.

2. No separate classes. Some psychologists have suggested that gifted children should be taught in separate classes set apart for them. But this is not a very good psychological suggestion for this may engender a feeling of vanity and superiority in them.

3. Curriculum. Many psychologists have suggested that the gifted child should be made to study some subjects in addition to the normal syllabi intended for the average class. This is a more practical suggestion because the gifted child's abilities can be better developed by the more comprehensive syllabus. It will also help to remove inactivity, social difficulties, and also create a better atmosphere in the class. But it must be remembered that the syllabus should never be so extensive as to become a burden on the child.

4. Faster promotions to higher classes. It has also been suggested by some psychologists that the gifted child should be promoted to higher classes more rapidly than the other children. This will give them a chance to develop their minds and also save time. But from the standpoint of the child's social development, this may not prove very beneficial. He will tend to be handicapped by the fact that all the other children in his class will be older than him. It is, therefore, better if the gifted child is given some additional work, but without promoting him to the higher class.

5. Individual education. Nowadays many psychologists are of the opinion that the gifted child should be educated individually with the teacher generally acting as a guide without undue interference. The child is given a particular task to perform within a fixed period. The teacher keeps an eye on his development and provides him with fresh programmes as he goes along. This method of education has proved the most useful in the case of gifted children.

6. Extra curricular activities. Another way of developing the qualities of the gifted child is to engage him in extra curricular activities such as games, music, dancing, other arts, practice for debates and sports competitions.

7. Facilities and apparatus. Gifted children can also be given certain kinds of special facilities such as fee concessions, opportunity to do work of exceptional responsibility or importance, etc. The school should also provide many kinds of means for learning the arts, games and other activities. Very often the gifted child finds a good library as a very good aid.

It is clear from the above exposition that the teacher can play an important role in nation building by helping in the proper development to the gifted children tendered in his care. In actual fact, the proper development of the gifted child depends considerably more upon the intelligence, wisdom and the sense of responsibility of the teacher. He should try to make arrangements for developing special qualities in his more gifted children. But in this connection, the responsibility of the parents in not less than that of the teacher, because different means can be adopted for the child's development as effectively at home as in the school. The parents should also take special care of such children. If this is not done, their balanced development is retarded. Besides, they may even become very difficult problems for their parents. If a child shows some extraordinary skill at some particular work, he should be sent to a school in which he can also facilitate the development of gifted children by providing fee concessions and other kinds of monetary aid. Thus an environment can be created in which the future leaders of the national may develop and grow.

CLASSIFICATION OF GIFTED CHILDREN

According to Terman gifted children may be divided into three categories :

1. Superior. Those having Intelligence Quotient between 100 and 120. Intelligence Quotient 120 may be regarded as the lower limit of the gifted.

2. Very superior. Those having Intelligence Quotient between 120 and 140.

3. Near genius. Those having Intelligence Quotient 140 or more.

L.X. Magnifico divided the gifted into two groups as follows :

(1) a child whose ability, as indicated by an intelligence test, is within the range of the upper 2 or 3 per cent of the population;

(2) a child having outstanding ability in a given field, for example, music or art.

Criteria for gifted. Paul Witty has enumerated the following criteria for defining gifted children :

1. A large vocabulary, accurately used.

2. The use of phrases and sentences at an early age, the ability to tell or reproduce a story.

3. Interests in books and later enjoyment of atlases, dictionaries and encyclopaedias.

4. Interests in calendar and clocks.

5. Ability to concentrate longer than most children.

6. Early discovery of cause and effect relationship.

7. Early development of mental faculties. Gifted children often learn to read before they enter school.

8. Proficiency in drawing, music or other art forms.

BEHAVIOUR PATTERNS OF GIFTED CHILDREN

1. Physical characteristics. They are physically better than the normal children. Their faces are usually bright. They possess vigour and vitality.

2. Intelligence. Their intelligence is high and 'g' factor of intelligence is very strong. Some have a very strong 's' factor.

3. Varied interests. Their interests are more varied than those of normal children. A gifted child of eight may read novels, write long essays, study such subjects as history, geography, astronomy, grammar, physics and music.

4. Inquisitive nature. They are extremely inquisitive and quick in understanding.

5. Superiority in academic work. Gifted children are characterised by general superiority in academic work. Even in the elementary school, they do their best on tests of reading and language. 45% of Terman's group of gifted children, learned to read before entering school. Regarding one child, Terman says, "As early as 21 months she read and apprehended simple sentences, by 26 months her reading vocabulary was more than 700 words."

6. Leadership. Terman states, "Even in leadership and social adaptability traits in which gifted children are thought to be especially deficient, most studies show gifted children to be somewhat superior to children of the general school population."

ADJUSTMENT PROBLEMS OF GIFTED CHILDREN

1. Revolt and mischief. He revolts against the parents and teachers when they do not recognise him, and sometimes creates mischief in order to catch their attention or to show his superiority.

2. Lack of stimulation. There is lack of stimulation for him in the subjects of his interests when he does not get opportunities of progressing according to his own pace.

3. Inferiority complex. Because of lack of opportunities and lack of recognition he sometimes develops inferiority complex.

4. Boastful conceit. Too much of recognition or applauses by the parents and teachers develop boastful conceit in him.

5. Nuisance. When he is not properly guided becomes a nuisance. He utilises his superior intelligence in mischief, indiscipline, gang-formation and revolts against his elders.

APPROACHES TO MEETING THE NEEDS OF THE GIFTED

1. Acceleration. It offers opportunity for a gifted pupil to move at a pace appropriate to his ability and maturity and to complete an educational programme in less than the ordinary amount of time. It involves advancing the gifted child rapidly from grade to grade in school so that he enters college earlier than others.

2. Segregation or ability grouping. The gifted pupils may be placed in special groups for all or part of the school day to provide for enrichment of their experiences in both depth and breadth, and to permit them to stimulate one another.

3. Enrichment. It consists in giving the gifted child the opportunity to go deeper or to range more widely than the average child in his intellectual, social and artistic experience. Enrichment programme may be characterised by : (i) emphasis upon the creative or the experimental; (ii) emphasis on the skill of investigation and learning; (iii) independent work, stressing initiative and originality; (iv) high standard of accomplishment; (v) co-operative planning and activity that provide opportunity for leadership training and experiences in social adjustment; (vi) individual attention given by teacher to student; (vii) First-hand experiences; (viii) flexibility of organisation and procedure; (ix) extensive reading and (x) concern with community responsibility.

SPECIAL TREATMENT TO THE GIFTED

1. Rapid promotion or double promotion. If a child shows an extraordinary achievement in one class, he may be given a double promotion to place him in a setting suiting him most. But at occasions such promotions prove to be very detrimental to the child because while the child may be a gifted one in comparison with the students of his previous class he may not show the same progress in the next class with the students of different mental and physical make-up resulting in his mental retardation in the new setting. Age, social maturity and health — all these factors should be given due weightage in rapid or double promotion.

2. Homogeneous grouping. It is a common practice in some of the schools to group students into various sections, according to their intellectual, physical and social interests. This is very useful in large schools where classes can be divided into different sections.

3. Enrichment of the curriculum. The gifted students may be encouraged to study a variety of books and reference material. Provision for a sufficient variety of activities should exist on the co-curricular side in a school so that the students may develop various social and moral qualities of a high order. Triple Track plan introducing elasticity in the classification of the students is very popular in American schools. According to this scheme the authorities prescribe a uniform syllabus for all. Average children cover it within the normal period, the dull in a large period and the gifted in a shorter period in comparison to average children.

4. Special schools. Separate schools have been provided for such students, in some of the advanced countries of the world. In this system a large number of students will be deprived of practice in leadership which they get in association with average children. Brown feels that keeping these children as an integral part of the school is most important in affecting their future personal happiness. Living in a world of mixed people — superior, normal, inferior, good, bad and indifferent. And they have every right and more need, to be prepared for that.

5. Summer schools. Planned during summer vacations these schools have very successfully tried in the U.S.A. Academically talented students are selected from different parts of the country on the basis of psychological tests, interview and previous school record and are brought together for a special educational programme very challenging and planned under the expert guidance of a band of talented teachers. The students are provided with the best available books to consult for writing their project reports and for holding discussion in the class. Usually science including mathematics, social studies and literature are covered.

The students return to their regular schools after the programme is over.

Conclusion of Researches Regarding Gifted Children in U.S.A.

1. Percentage. Children 40 to 50 per cent in advance of their age in school achievement tests are usually not more than 14% beyond their age grade status when no provision has been made for their special education.

2. Drill. "Drill" may be very much reduced or even eliminated in teaching the bright.

3. Artificial motivation. It is not required, provided that the subject matter be really suited to the intelligent interests of such children. Their native intellectual curiosity is keen and the scope of their interest broad.

4. Projects. As a method, projects are well suited to the bright children, "socialised recitations" and joint enterprises on the pupil's own or partial responsibility are well carried on.

5. Reasonable. Management, control and discipline may be conducted on a the basis of reasonableness and sound logic.

6. Highly qualified. Particularly, able teachers who are themselves of high intelligence, well informed, acquainted with the psychology of the bright, and free from prejudice, jealousy and superstition are required for gifted children.

EDUCATION OF THE GIFTED IN INDIA

Recommendations of the Education Commission 1964-66

1. Deprivatory home environment. In a large Majority of the homes, the environment is deprivatory on account of the illiteracy of the parents and poverty and does not allow the available native talent to develop itself fully.

2. A good deal of potential talent never enters school. At the primary stage, the proportion of children not enrolled varies from 10 to 60 per cent in different areas. Even among those who enter, about 40 per cent are eliminated in Class I itself and only about 25 per cent, belonging to about the top 20 per cent of families in the society, complete primary education. Secondary education is largely a privilege of the top 10 per cent of the families and higher education of the top 5 per cent.

3. Talent does not flower fully. Even the talent that enters school and succeeds in climbing the educational ladder does not flower fully because it is not discovered sufficiently early and is often studying in poor schools. For the best results in quality, talent has to be located early and allowed to grow in the best atmosphere and under the best teachers.

4. Multisided identification. The highly gifted students are far too creative to be confined within the perimeters of class-room instruction, textbooks and examinations. The genius in one field is generally poor in several others. In our examination system, a genius is more likely to fail or put up only a mediocre total of marks than to come out at the top. Ramanujam and Tagore could only pass the routine examinations where the mediocrities shone. One should, therefore, search separately for each special talent, whether in mathematics, science, literature, fine arts, sports or technology.

The Pool of Ability

Providing secondary and higher education to all the potentially able students is a very high target which even affluent societies find it difficult to achieve. This should, however, be the goal towards which India should continually move. In the transitional period, immediate effect should be given to ensure that all gifted students (at least the top 5—15 per cent of all students), who complete primary or secondary education, are enabled to study further in institutions of secondary (or higher) education. It will be necessary to provide a large number of scholarships for this purpose.

The universities and colleges could select talented students from the schools in different subjects at any appropriate stage, say, in the age-group 13-15, and help them to develop their knowledge in special fields through individual guidance with the provision of laboratory facilities.

Need for a Reliable Criterion

Steps should be taken to devise suitable techniques for identifying talent at this stage. Each State should organise a testing service at the end of the primary stage (Class VII or VIII) and also at the end of the lower secondary stage (Class X) and make its assistance available to all the schools. This service could be of considerable help to students and institutions. They would obtain useful information about their performance; in relation to the district, state or even the national average level of attainment. Apart from its utility to students and parents such information would also be of great assistance to the Education Departments in the award of scholarship.

Role of Every Institution

Every educational institution should be assisted to develop a programme for identifying the brighter children attending it and for providing them with special enrichment programmes to suit their needs and to help in their growth. These programmes, the nature of which would vary from stage to stage and from one type of institution to another, would have to be carefully designed and teachers would have to be trained in putting them across. 'Talent' should not be understood in the traditional sense only in all these programmes, but should cover a wide range of mathematical, verbal, artistic and experimental skills. Scholarships and encouragement should be available, on a basis of equality, to all talent at all stages of education.

Role of the Education Departments

The responsibility for the development of this comprehensive programme should be squarely placed on the Education Departments working in collaboration with the universities. The secondary stage is the most crucial for discovery and development of talent, and unfortunately, it is precisely at this stage that the scholarship programme is now weak. Its development will, therefore, have to be accorded high priority.

Recommendations

1. **Five years of effective primary education.** The provision of five years of good and effective primary education to every child will enable the country to cast its net for talent to the widest extent possible.

2. Scholarships. The large programme of scholarships proposed at all stages will ensure that all gifted students, or at least the top 5 to 15 per cent of the relevant age-group, will be enable to receive the highest education possible.

3. Placement. The placement programme will also make it possible for them to study in the best institutions available at each stage.

4. Enrichment programmes. It is also necessary to introduce enrichment programmes for the brighter students in as many schools as possible and ultimately in every school. The performance of talented students in the enrichment programmes should be recorded in special certificates indicating to the colleges or other institutions of higher education their special abilities and attainments. The enrichment programmes should not degenerate into coaching for passing examinations with higher marks.

5. Flexibility in the school curriculum. It would enable the schools to provide enriched or advanced courses for the talented and help them to progress at their own speed. This will also release time for teachers to help the average and backward students.

6. A variety of extra-mural programmes. These can also be organised for the talented students, either separately by each school or by schools acting in cooperation or by the Education Departments.

7. A five to six-week sumer vacation programme. It can be arranged for a group of academically talented children from different schools, brought together to an educational centre having special facilities of staff, library, laboratory and equipment. The programme may be renewed for the particular group from year to year, so that the students get an opportunity to develop their special talent over a number of years.

8. Well-planned visits. These may be arranged to laboratories, museums, and other places.

9. Contact with eminent persons. Talented students may be brought into contact with persons engaged in the types of work for which the students show special ability or interest. These persons may be able to provide occasional opportunities for the students to work in their special fields.

10. Hostels or day centres. These may be made available for those students whose home environment is not conducive to proper study.

The Role of the Counsellor

With his detailed knowledge of each talented students in a unique position to formulate a programme of enrichment for him and to suggest the necessary modifications in the curricular and extra-curricular requirements. Where special counsellors are not available, trained teachers will bear this responsibility. The class room atmosphere and the attitudes of teachers is of considerable importance. In a social and educational set-up like Indian where the relationship between the teacher and the taught is still largely authoritarian, the general tendency is to suppress urges and interests that deviate from the class norm. Therefore, the first requirement for the promotion of talent is for the teachers to create an atmosphere of free expression in the class-room and to provide opportunities for creative work.

QUESTIONS FOR EXERCISE

1. Who are gifted children? How can they be identified in a group of children? Outline a suitable programme for their education bearing in mind their psychological make-up and needs.
2. What are the problems of gifted children. Suggest remedies.

37

CAREERS EDUCATION AND GUIDANCE

IMPORTANCE OF CAREER EDUCATION AND GUIDANCE

Working Together for a Better Future, a publication of the Department of Education and Science and the Department of Employment, U.K. (1987) has explained the significance and the scope of careers education and guidance as follows :

1. Looking forward to a better future. Young people need to be better educated and trained for adult life. They must have a wide range of opportunities in education and training. And they must have information and guidance to allow them to make sound choices as they go through school and beyond.

2. Beginning at home. The process starts in the home. Families and friends have a crucial role to play in shaping people's expectations and aspirations. This should be properly recognised in schools. Parents should be involved to the fullest extent in what their children are doing and the choices they are making.

3. Continuation of schools. Schools play a vital part in developing expectations and capabilities from the earliest age. Good schools encourage self-awareness, the ability to work with others, and a sense of initiative and enterprise-qualities which are every bit as valuable in adult life as examination certificates. A broad and balanced curriculum makes the most of each pupil's potential in every area — regardless of sex, ethnic origin or disability.

4. Vocational success. From the primary years onwards much can be done to give children insights into the world of work and a preparation for the decisions ahead which will affect the future directions of their lives. Full and reliable information and sensitive guidance must be available at the right times for all if these decisions are to be properly informed.

5. Choice of subjects. When choice of options for further study first have to be made — around 13 + it is essential that the right decisions are taken in each case — the crucial stage for which pupils must be fully prepared.

6. Information for choice. At 16 + and 17 +, important choices have to be made between staying on at school or going on to college, vocational training or employment. These choices must be properly informed.

7. Choice among options. Those children on the point of leaving school or college need a realistic appreciation of all the choices open to them. At subsequent stages too, students must have access to relevant, reliable and complete information and skilled guidance about options.

CAREER MASTER

Role of the Career Master

1. He helps to ensure that each pupil's curriculum is broad and balanced and appropriate to his or her career intentions as they develop.

2. He provides a programme of careers education as part of the curriculum for each pupil.

3. He suggests ways in which relevance and practicality can be pursued.

4. He points to the dangers of sex or racial stereotyping or setting too low expectations.

5. He helps other teachers to relate their work to local industry and commerce.

6. He searches out opportunities for links with employees.

7. He ensures that work experience for pupils is properly matched to individuals needs.

8. He uses the available information technologies to the full.

9. He maintains readily available information on further and higher education, training and job opportunities; and seeing that it is well used.

10. Works with Careers Service to provide individual counselling and guidance to pupils and their parents.

11. He works closely with the Careers Service in monitoring the progress of each during their transition from school and, whenever possible subsequently.

Specific Duties and Responsibilities

1. To form and organise the school guidance committee.

2. To set up an educational and occupational information centre in the school.

3. To give orientation talks to students regarding guidance services available in the school.

4. To orient class X pupils and their parents with regard to the electives available in the senior secondary school.

5. To orient pupils of classes X and XII with regard to university and non-university courses, apprenticeship schemes, etc.

6. To collect and displaying educational and occupational information.

7. To disseminate occupational and educational information through talks, group discussions, film-shows, etc.

8. To prepare news albums.

9. To arrange career talks by experts from different fields.

10. To organise Career Days, Career Weeks, Career Conferences, etc.

11. To arrange visits to places of work like industries, business establishments, offices, higher educational institutions, etc.

12. To organise Parents Days.

13. To organise a "Guidance News" Section in the School Magazine.

14. To give orientation talks to students of class VIII in the feeder schools, prior to their joining the secondary or senior secondary school or orientation talks to new pupils as soon as they have joined class IX of the secondary school.

15. To acquaint students with and assisting them to adopt proper methods of study.

16. To arrange individual discussions with pupils and parents for giving them educational and occupational information.

17. To notify employment opportunities available to secondary and senior secondary school students.

CAREER INFORMATION SERVICE

Types of Information provided

1. Occupational opportunities after the completion of class X and class XII.

2. Courses available after the completion of class X and class XII.

3. Scholarships and stipends, etc.

4. Competitive examinations.

5. Occupations suitable for girls.

6. Occupations for the handicapped.

7. Occupations based on intelligence and interest.

8. Apprenticeship facilities available.

9. Training facilities.

Filing Information

To facilitate the use of information material it is essential that some types of filing system is used. Following are some of the important methods of filing :

1. Alphabetical system. It is a simple and an easy procedure in which files are arranged according to the names of the occupations in alphabetical order. All material on any one occupation is collected and filed together. Material on related occupations cannot be grouped together unless numerous cross reference cards are used.

2. National classification of occupations. Occupational information may be filed on the basis of the National Classification of Occupations (NCO). In the NCO occupations are classified under families, families are combined into groups and groups are assigned to divisions. There are eleven divisions consisting of 75 groups which are divided into 331 families under which occupations are classified. This system is useful when occupational information material is plentiful.

3. Filing on the basis of school subjects. Occupations related to each school subject may be filed separately, such as occupations related to literary subjects, scientific subjects, home science, fine arts, etc. There may be further sub-classifications under each, if necessary. This system is very helpful for students who often go by their subjects.

Developing a Job Folder

The following points should be considered for selected jobs to be included in the job folder :

1. Jobs in which the students are interested.
2. Jobs available in the community.
3. Jobs which may be taken up soon after they leave school.
4. Jobs in which large number of openings are available.

Collecting information for the job-folder. Follows methods may be used to collect information for the job folder :

(i) Occupational survey of the locality.
(ii) Contact with the employers.
(iii) Use of questionnaires of collecting information.

AN OUTLINE OF A CAREER TALK

1. Introduction

(i) A brief history of the occupation.
(ii) Scope and information of the occupation in modern India.

2. Nature of Work and Working Conditions

(i) The general nature of the work involved.
(ii) The work done mainly outdoor or indoors, or both.
(iii) The place of work noisy, crowded, humid, dusty, etc.
(iv) The work done mainly with others or alone.
(v) The work done on a shift system.
(vi) The employment steady or seasonal.
(vii) Employment in this occupation found mainly in urban areas, rural areas, or both.

(viii) The related occupations to which a worker may be transferred, jobs to which he may be promoted.

(ix) Rate of accident involved in the occupation.

(x) Diseases related to the occupation.

3. Recruitment for Entry into the Occupation

(i) The categories of personnel employed.

(ii) The entry jobs.

(iii) The level of education that is required for entry into this occupation.

(iv) School subjects or school activities useful for entry into this occupation.

(v) Institutions providing training facilities for entry into this occupation.

(vi) The entrance qualifications required for entry to the training course. The duration of the course, cost of training, etc.

(vii) The physical and personal qualifications required for entry into the occupation.

(viii) Any special abilities or interests required.

(ix) Any age limit.

(x) Any special licence or membership in any organisation required or any special examination required for entry into the job.

(xi) Apprenticeship or on-the-job training required in the occupation.

4. Method of Recruitment

(i) Job to be secured through an employment exchange.

(ii) Application for the job to be made in response to a "wanted advertisement" in the newspapers.

(iii) Direct application.

(iv) Application to be sent through the Public Service Commission.

(v) Recruitment made periodically or otherwise.

(vi) Vacancies reserved for scheduled castes/tribes, backward classes, etc.

5. Wages and Other Benefits

(i) The starting salary and allowances.

(ii) The avenues of promotion.

(iii) Promotion based on seniority only.

(iv) Scope of recognition for outstanding work.

(v) Bonus offered or not.

(vi) The leave or vacation to which the employee is entitled.

(vii) Provision for benefits like employment insurance, provident fund, gratuity, pension, free medical aid, free quarters, free education for children, etc.

(viii) Compensation paid for accidents.

(ix) Scope for further training while on the job and rise in the occupation.

6. Employment Outlook

(i) The immediate local and national employment outlook.

(ii) The employment opportunities in the next few years likely to increase or decrease.

7. Employer-Employee Relationship

(i) Nature of relationship between the employer and employee.

(ii) Frequency of strikes in recent years in the industry.

(iii) Whether the employees benefited or suffered as a result of the strike.

(iv) The trade unions to which employees in this industry are usually affiliated.

QUESTIONS FOR EXERCISE

1. Explain the importance of Career Planning. What are the questions involved in career planning?
2. Describe the role of the career master in the career planning of students.
3. What are the duties and responsibilities of career master?
4. Discuss the importance of the career information centre. How can it be organised effectively?
5. State the different ways of filing information.
6. Give an outline of Career Talk.

BIBLIOGRAPHY

Allport, G.W., Vernon, P.E. and Lindzey, G., *A Study of Values.* Boston : Houghton Mefflin.

Anastasi, Anne, *Psychological Testing.* London : Mecmillan Company.

Anne, Roe, *The Psychology of Occupations.* New York : John Wiley and Sons.

Arbuckle, Dugald, A., *Counselling : Philosophy, Theory and Practice.* Boston : Allyn and Bacon Inc.

Barrie, H., *et al., The Theory and Practice of Vocational Guidance.* London : Pergamon Press.

Beck, Carlton, E., *Philosophical Foundations of Guidance.* Englewood Cliffs, New Jersey : Prentice Hall.

Bennett, Margaret E., *Guidance and Counselling in Groups.* New York : The Ronald Press.

Bernard, H.W. and Fullmer, D.W., *Principles of Guidance : A Basic Text* (Indian ed.). New Delhi : Allied Publishers Private Ltd.

Bloom, A. Martin, *Successful Programmes and Practices for Counselling the College-Bound Student.* Englewood Cliffs, New Jersey : Prentice-Hall, Inc.

Borow, Henry and Lindsey, Robert V., *Vocational Planning for College Students.* Englewood Cliffs, New Jersey : Prentice-Hall, Inc.

Bulletins 1-12. *Educational Psychology Unit.* NCER, New Delhi.

Carrol, B.A., *Mental Hygiene : The Dynamics of Adjustment.* New York : Prentice-Hall.

Cattell, B.A., *Abilities : Their Structure, Growth and Action.* Boston : Houghton Miffein Co.

Cormack, M.L., *She who Rides a Peacock : Indian Students and Social Change.* Delhi : Asia Publishing House.

Cottle, William C. and Downie, H.M., *Procedures and Preparation for Counselling.* Englewood Cliffs, New Jersey : Prentice Hall.

Cronbach, L.I., *Essentials of Psychological Testing.* New York : Harper.

Crites, J.O., *Vocational Psychology.* New York : McGraw Hill.

Crow, Lester, D. and Crow, A., *An Introduction to Guidance Principles and Practices.* New York : American Book Company.

Dantwala, M.L., *Report of the Committee of Experts on Unemployment Estimates.* Delhi : Planning Commission.

Dictionary of Occupational Titles, Vol. I to IV; Washington : Government Printing Press.

Downing, Lester, N., *Guidance and Counselling Services.* New York : McGraw Hill.

Dunsmoor, C.C. and Miller, L.M., *Principles and Methods of Guidance for Teachers.* Scranton PG, International Textbook Co.

Education Commission Report. New Delhi : Ministry of Education, Government of India.

Effectiveness of Services Rendered by University Employment Information and Guidance Bureaux. New Delhi : CIRTES.

Effectiveness of Vocational Guidance Service at Employment Exchanges. New Delhi : CIRTES.

Ellis, A., *Humanistic Psycho-therapy : The Rational-Emotive Approach.* New York : Julian Press.

Erickson, E.N., *Identity : Youth in Crisis.* New York : Norton.

Feldman, Kenneth, A., *College and Student Education.* New York : Pergamon Press, Inc.

Feldman, K.A. and New Comb, T.A., *The Impact of College on Students.* San Francisco : Jossey-Bass Publishers.

Frank, H. Krouse, *Counselling Technique with Youth.* Ohio : Charles and Merril.

Freeman, Frank S., *Theory and Practice of Psychological Testing.* New Delhi : Oxford and IBH Publishing Company.

Froehlich, C.P. and Hoyt, K., *Guidance Testing.* Science Research Associates, Inc.

Frustrchi, Marian Alexander, *Issues in Occupational Education.* Orient Longmans, Reprinted in India by S.S. Patwardhan Sangham Press, Poona.

Fuster, J.M., *Psychological Counselling in India.* Macmillan, Bombay.

Gallaghen, Phillip, J. and Thomas, Charles C., *The Counselling Centre in Higher Education.* Illinois : Springfield.

Garret, A., *Interviewing : Its Principles and Methods.* New York : Family Service Association of America.

Gaur, J.S. and Saraswat, R.K., *Occupational Literature* : An Annotated Bibliography. New Delhi, NCERT.

Ginzberg, Eli, *Career Guidance.* New York : McGraw Hill.

Ginzberg, Eli, *Occupational Choice.* New York : Columbia University Press.

Goldman, L., *Using Tests in Counselling.* New York : Appleton Century Crofts.

Guilford, J.P., *Fundamental Statistics in Psychology and Education.* New York : McGraw Hill.

Gulati, J.S., *Occupational Selection and Educational Preparation*. New Delhi : NCERT.

Hahn, M.E. and Maclean, M.S., *Counselling Psychology*. New York : McGraw Hill.

Hamrin, S.A. and Paulson, B.P., *Counselling Adolescents*. Chicago : Science Research Associates.

Hamrin, S.A., *Initiating and Administering Guidance Services*. Bloomington : McKnight and McKnight Publishing Company.

Handbook for Orientation of New Students. New York : U.S. Educational Foundation in India.

Handbook for Student Advisors. New Delhi : U.S. Educational Foundation in India.

Handbook on Vocational Guidance. New Delhi : CIRTES, Ministry of Labour and Rehabilitation, Government of India.

Hansen, James C., *Counselling Process and Procedures*. New York : Macmillan.

Hatch, Ramend N. and Steffle, Buford, *Administration of Guidance Services*. Englewood Cliffs, New Jersey : Prentice Hall.

Heath, Douglas, H., *Growing up in College*. San Francisco : Hossey Pass Inc. 165, Montgomery Street.

Heckel, Robert V., *Leadership and Group Behaviour*. New Delhi : US Educational Foundation in India.

Hollis, Joseph William and Hollis, Lucila, *Organising for Effective Guidance*. Chicago : Science Research Associates.

Hoose, William N. Van (ed.), *Counselling and Guidance in the 20th Century*. Boston : Houghton Mifflin Co.

Hoppock, Robert, *Occupational Information*. New York : McGraw Hill.

Hoppock, Robert, *Occupational Information : Where to get and How to use it in Counselling and Teaching*. New York : McGraw Hill Book Co., Inc.

Howes, Harold, R. and Parker, Clyde, A., *A Survey of Student Services in Indian Higher Education*. New Delhi : US Educational Foundation in India.

Humphrey, Anthony J. and Traxler, Arthur E., *Guidance Services*. Chicago : Science Research Associates, Inc.

James, A.R., *Vocational Education and Guidance : A System for the Seventies*. Columbus, Ohio : Charles E. Marrill, Publishing Co.

Jones, A.J., *Principles of Guidance and Pupil Personnel Work*. New York : McGaw Hill.

Khorshed, A.W., *Guidance Movement in India*. Guidance Services Series, No. 4, NCERT, New Delhi.

Knapp, Robert H., *Practical Guidance Methods for Counsellors, Teachers and Administrators*. New York : McGraw Hill Book Company, Inc.

Knight, R., *Intelligence and Intelligence Tests* (2nd ed.), London : Methuen and Co. Ltd.

Krause, Frank H., *Counselling Techniques with Youth*. Ohio : Charles and Merril.

Kroth, J.A., *Counselling Psychology and Guidance*. Springfield, Illinois : Charles C. Thomas.

Krumboltz, J.D. and Thoresen, C.E., *Counselling Methods*. New York : Holt, Rinehart and Winston.

Kuder, F.D., *Kuder Preference Record, Occupational Form B*. Chicago : Science Research Association, 57, West Grand Avenue.

Long L. and Mehtra, P.H. (eds.), *First Mental Measurement Handbook for India*. New Delhi : NCERT.

Matarazzo, J.D., *Wechsler's Measurement and Appraisal of Adult Intelligence*. Baltimore : Williams and Wilkins.

Mathewson, Robert H., *Guidance Policy and Practice*. New York : Harper and Row.

McGowan, J.F. and Schmidt, L.D., *Counselling Readings in Theory and Practice*. New York : Holt, Rinehart and Winston.

McKinney, F., *Counselling for Personnel Adjustment*. Boston : Houghton Mifflin.

Mehdi, Bager, *Integrated Student Personnel Services in Higher Education*. New Delhi : NCERT.

Miller, Carrol, H., *Foundations of Guidance*. New York : Harper and Brothers.

Miller, Frank W., *Guidance : Principles and Services*. Ohio : Charles E. Merrill Books.

Miller, G.W., *Success, Failure and Wastage in Higher Education*. London : University of London, Institute of Education.

Milner, Patricia, *Counselling in Education*. London : J.M. Dent & Sons Ltd.

Moreno, J.L., *Psychodrama*. Vol. I, Beacon House, New York.

Morris, Charles, G., *Psychology : An Introduction*. Englewood Cliffs, New Jersey; Prentice Hall.

Mursell, J.L., *Psychological Testing*. Longmans.

NCERT Interest Inventory (Senion Form), Delhi : NCERT.

Ohlsen, M.M., *Group Counselling* (2nd ed.), New York : Holt Rinehart and Winston.

Parker, Clyde, A., *Selected Readings in Student Services for Indian Universities and Colleges*. New Delhi : US Educational Foundation in India.

Pasricha, Prem, *Counselling Services for the University Students in U.S.A.* Baroda, M.S. University.

Pasricha, Prem, *Guidance and Counselling in Indian Education*. New Delhi : NCERT.

Patterson, C.H., *Counselling and Psychotherapy*. New York : Harper and Row Publishers.

Pepinsky, Harold B. and Pepinsky, Pauline Nichols, *Counselling Theory and Practice*. New York : The Ronald Press Company.

Perez, J.F., *Counselling Theory and Practice*. Reading, Mass : Addison Welsley.

Peters, H.J. and Hansen, J.C. (ed.), *Vocational Guidance and Career Development*. New York : Macmillan.

Pinto, Diana V., *Counselling : Theory, Research and Practice*. Chicago : Rand McNally College Publishing Company.

Robinson, F.P., *Principles and Procedures in Student Counselling*. New York : Harper and Row.

Roeher, E.G., Smith, G.B. and Erickson, E.E., *Organisation and Administration of Guidance Services*, 2nd ed., New York : McGraw Hill.

Rothney, J.W.M., *Guidance Practices and Results*. New York : Harper Brothers.

Sanford, N., *Where Colleges Fail*. San Francisco : Jossey Bass Publishers.

Schwarz, P.A., Krug, R.E., *Ability Testing in Developing Countries : A Handbook of Principles and Techniques*. New York : Praeger.

Shartle, Carrol L., *Occupational Information*. N.J. Prentice-Hall.

Shertzer, B., *Career Planning*. Boston : Houghton Mifflin Co.

Shertzer, B. and Stone, S.C., *Fundamentals of Counselling*. Second ed., Boston : Houghton Mifflin.

Siegel, Max (ed.), *The Counselling of College Students Function, Practice and Technique*. New York : Free Press.

Slocum, Walter L., *Occupational Careers : Sociological Perspective*. Chicago : Aldine Publishing Company.

Smith, M.R. (ed.), *Guidance Personnel Work. Future Tense*. New York : Teachers College Press, Columbia University.

Spearman, C.E., *The Nature of Intelligence and Principles of Cognition*. London : Macmillan.

Strang, Ruth, *Counselling Techniques in College and Secondary School*. New York : Harper and Brothers.

Steward, N.R. and others, *Systematic Counselling*. Englewood Cliffs, No. 6, Prentice-Hall.

Super, D.E., *Psychology of Careers*. New York : Harper Row.

Thorndike, R.L. and Hagen E., *Measurement and Evaluation and Psychology and Education*, 3rd edition. New Delhi : Wiley Eastern Pvt. Ltd.

Tolbert, E.L., *Introduction of Counselling.* New York : McGraw Hill.

Tolbert, E.L., *Counselling for Career Development.* Boston : Houghton Mifflin.

Traxler, A.E. and Norla, R.D., *Techniques of Guidance.* New York : Harper and Row.

Tyler, L.E., *The Work of the Counsellor;* New York : Appleton Century Crofts.

——, *The Work of Counsellor,* third ed. New York : Appleton Century Crofts.

——, *The Collegiate Counsellor,* second ed. New York : Appleton Century Crofts.

UNESCO : *The Organisation of Educational and Vocational Guidance.* International Bureau of Education, Geneva.

Vaughan, T.D., *Educational and Vocational Guidance Today.* London : Routledge and Kegan Pal.

Vernon, P.E., *Intelligence and Cultural Environment,* London : Methuen.

Vernon, P.E., *Personality Assessment.* London : Methuen Co. Ltd.

Warnath, Charles F., *New Directions for College Counsellors.* London : Jossey Bass Publishers.

Warters, Jane, *Technique of Counselling* (3rd ed.), New York : McGraw Hill.

Wedge, B.M., *Psychological Problems of College Men.* Yale University Press.

Weitz, Henry, *Behaviour Changes Through Guidance.* New York : Wiley and Sons Inc.

Williamson, E.G., *Student Personnel Services in Colleges and Universities.* New York : McGraw Hill.

Wolpe, J., *The Practice of Behaviour Therapy.* New York : Pergamon Press.

Wren, Gilbert C., *The Counsellor in a Changing World.* Washington : American Personnel and Guidance Association.

Wren, Gilbert C., *Student Personnel Work in College.* New York : The Ronald Press Company.

Zeran-Franklin R. and Riccio, Anthony C., *Organisation and Administration of Guidance Services.* Chicago : Rand McNally and Co.